Java in Plain English

Second Edition

Java in Plain English

Second Edition

Brian Overland

a subsidiary of Henry Holt and Company, Inc.
115 West 18th Street
New York, NY 10011
http://www.mispress.com

Printed in the United States of America.

First Edition—1996

Second Edition—1997

Library of Congress Cataloging-in-Publication Data

Overland, Brian R.

Java in plain English/by Brian Overland.-- 2nd ed.

p. cm

ISBN 1-55828-563-6

1. Java (Computer program language) I. Title.

QA76.73.J38083 1997

005. 13'3--dc21 97-30978

CIP

10 9 8 7 6 5 4 3 2 1

MIS:Press books are available at special discounts for bulk purchases for sales promotions, premiums, and fundraising. Special editions or book excerpts can also be created to specification. For details contact the Special Sales Director at the address above

---

Associate Publisher: *Paul Farrell*

Managing Editor: *Shari Chappell* **Copy Edit Manager:** *Karen Tongish*

Editor: *Debra Williams Cauley* **Copy Editor:** *Betsy Hardinger*

Production Editor: *Danielle De Lucia* **Techincal Editor:** *Miles O'Neal*

Dedication

To Matthew, Aaron, and Katelyn, who are the light of the world and the promise of the future, and to Mom, who was right about the stock market.

Acknowledgments

The second edition involved modifying, refining, and then further modifying. I'm grateful to the staff at MIS:Press for being willing to take so many small batches of changes. Debra Williams Cauley and Danielle De Lucia were unfailingly patient, responsive, and capable, listening to my constant haranguing about the format and figures. They made major improvements, which, I think, should boost the usability of the book as much as any other factor.

The book was also helped by the good sense and the encouragement of Miles O'Neal, the technical editor, especially on the tricky subject of exception handling. Further encouragement was provided by Paul Farrell, the publisher, and Randy Sears, a Java programmer who used the first edition on a daily basis. Thanks also to Dave Makower and Edith Au, who contributed to the first edition. And a number of people contributed in important ways to the production of the book, including Karen Tongish, Matt Casper, and Gay Nichols. Special thanks to Mark Overland for his insights on new technologies and media.

And thanks go to Sun Microsystems, for providing a language that is fun to learn and well supported on the net.

CONTENTS

PART I: A Quick Introduction to Java Programming

PART II

Introduction to the Second Edition

There's a warm, familiar scent as you enter the kitchen in the morning. The sun is rising, the coffee is brewing, and you know Java is here to stay.

Since its release, Java has become not merely another language but a fundamental new architecture. And more than that, it's becoming an industry. By the hundreds of thousands (or even more), people are looking for ways to learn it, master it, or at least have a basic understanding of what it's about. To this extent, Java's success equals that of C, C++, and Microsoft's Visual Basic.

It is not hard to understand why. Beyond its networking capabilities, Java has a multiplatform design. This means that for the most part, a Java program doesn't care whether it's running on Windows, Macintosh, or UNIX. As we move into an era of more communication between computers, this flexibility is vital.

Java: The Good and the Not-So-Good

You can write Java to create applications for your own use, as well as commercial applications or applets for the Web. To this extent, it's fair to compare Java to other established tools such as Basic. A couple of points emerge from this comparison.

On the one hand, some things are easy to do in Java. Its application programming interface (API) makes handling graphics, threads, and network operations easier than with many other APIs. And if you are interested in object-oriented programming, you'll find that Java lives up to your best hopes.

On the other hand, some things that are easy to do in other languages are not at all obvious in Java. How to do these simple tasks was one of the areas of emphasis in the first edition of this book, and it gets even more emphasis in this edition. (See, for example, Chapter 6, "Common Programming Tasks.")

ORGANIZATION OF THE SECOND EDITION

I mentioned that Java training is almost an industry. Wandering through any bookstore, you can get the impression that there are almost as many people writing about Java as trying to learn it!

So a book must justify its right to exist. The goal of *Java in Plain English* has always been to summarize the language and its API so that, despite the book's small size, you can use it to get a simple, straightforward answer to almost all day-to-day programming questions—all without having to look to another source (in most cases). I understand that this aim is ambitious: one could easily devote a couple of thousand pages (larger pages!) to explaining the arcane use of each method and field in the API. What you hold in your hands, I hope, is a good compromise.

It's hard to cover everything, and in the first edition some areas got less coverage than was ideal. The enhancements in this edition address some of these areas:

- There is now a great deal more about Java database programming (JDBC). In particular, this edition covers many JDBC examples you can type in and run immediately.
- The "Quick API Reference" (Part V) includes more examples on everything, including difficult areas such as networking.
- The Glossary (Part VII) is substantially expanded to address some of the new concepts and new technologies that have emerged this past year.

Here is a blow-by-blow summary of what you can expect to find in the second edition:

Part I. A Quick Introduction to Java Programming. As before, this concise tutorial is aimed mainly at people who already understand C or C++. I don't spend 100 pages, as do many books, rehashing the **while** and **do** loops you already know about from C. The new material includes a chapter on common programming techniques and a JDBC tutorial.

Once you're familiar with the basics of Java, the tutorial (Chapter 7, "JDBC Quick Start") should help you start using JDBC in the shortest possible time.

Part II. Java Language Reference. This part contains syntax and discussion of each keyword as well as other basic parts of the language such as arrays, methods, classes, and objects. The enhancements in this edition include expanded focus on casting and exception handling.

Part III. A Plain English Guide to API Topics. This list of tasks serves as a cross-reference to the API Quick Reference.

Part IV. Class Summaries. In the first edition, this was combined with the "API Quick Reference" but has been placed in its own section here for ease of use. This section briefly describes all the classes, organized by package, so that you can scan it to get a quick overview of the entire API.

Part V. API Quick Reference. This is probably the most important part of book; it says something about almost every method and field in the API, omitting descriptions only when the use is obvious or explained elsewhere. The enhancement here is the inclusion of examples for most classes in the API, including previously neglected areas such as menus, networking, and JDBC. The format is also improved, so you should find this part of the book easier to use.

Part VI. Useful Tables. These tables summarize events, fonts, colors, key codes, and other information. I've added several important tables for database programming.

Part VII. Glossary of Java Terminology and Concepts. A few of the topics covered in Part II (such as classes, objects, and packages) are also covered here but the focus is on simplifying each concept and giving a broader context rather than explaining syntax. I added a number of entries here to update the book.

JAVA: THE VERSIONS MARCH ON...

Java 1.0 was the original version, of course. It did not yet include JDBC.

Java 1.01 fixed some bugs and, more significantly, added JDBC, the Java database API. *Java in Plain English* covers all these features.

Java 1.1 adds some new areas to the core API, including JavaBeans and more techniques for customized event handling. Java Beans—much like custom controls in Visual Basic—enables you to create graphical objects that work with integrated development systems. (Whew! That's a mouthful.) This means you create objects with "design-time" behavior.

There is some discussion of these features in the Glossary, but size considerations make it increasingly difficult to cover them in detail. Hopefully, they await a future book...

DOCUMENT CONVENTIONS

The document conventions are the same as in the first edition. Except when the material gives syntax for arrays, brackets mean optional items.

Table I.1 *Document conventions*

STYLE	DESCRIPTION
keyword	Anything in bold is intended to be typed as shown. This includes keywords and operators.
placeholder	Text in italics indicates something that you supply, such as an argument or variable name.
[*optional_item*]	Anything in brackets is an optional item: you can choose whether to include it. Exception: where brackets are intended literally, they are in bold: **[ ]**.
item, item, ...	Ellipses (...) indicate a repeated series or, in some cases, part of an example that has been omitted for brevity's sake.

HOW TO REACH THE AUTHOR

Comments on the book—including how to improve it—are more than welcome. I can be reached directly at Briano2u@aol.com. You can also send a note in care of MIS:Press at http://www.mispress.com.

PART I

A QUICK INTRODUCTION TO JAVA PROGRAMMING

CHAPTER ONE

Applets and Oranges

Before you can do anything with Java, you need to understand the basic procedures for developing programs. That's the purpose of this chapter—to show how Java is used to produce the two major kinds of programs: applets and applications.

(In spite of the chapter title, you can't really use Java to create oranges, although you can color things orange if you like. More about that in Part I's Chapter 3, "Fun with Graphics.")

An *applet* is a program embedded inside a Web page. It's downloaded across the Internet along with other contents of a page, including text and graphics. The applet is the interactive, intelligent part of a Web page, and users execute applets with the aid of a Java-compliant Web browser. Java's most popular use is to create applets.

An *application* is more or less the same kind of beast you're familiar with if you've been programming on a PC. It runs directly on a local machine. Unlike applets, Java applications have relatively few restrictions and can perform all the basic functions you can perform in most other languages. Java is a good general-purpose programming language. And Java's built-in API makes it easy to write applications that can establish network connections, write to the disk, or display information.

Ultimately you may find applets more interesting, but we'll start by examining applications, because they are closer to the traditional model of software development.

GETTING STARTED

If you haven't done so already, you'll probably want to install the Java Development Kit (JDK). The JDK contains all the executables you need to create applications and applets as well as all the Java standard classes and helpful utilities such as appletviewer, which enables you to view applets quickly and easily. You can download the JDK from Sun Microsystems' Java FTP site:

```
ftp://www.javasoft.com/
```

A number of books include a compact disc that installs the JDK. However, downloading from the Sun Microsystems site is more likely to provide a current version. In any case, you can use the JDK free of charge.

To write Java programs, you can use any text editor. Java does not require the use of an integrated development environment, although some are available (such as Microsoft's Visual J++).

APPLICATIONS: REMEMBER THE "MAIN"

A simple application uses **main( )** as a point of entry, just as C and C++ do. The following application prints the text "Hello Java!" followed by a blank line. As with all applications, you run it directly on your local computer.

```
class HelloJava {

     public static void main(String args[]) {

          System.out.println("Hello Java!");

     }

}
```

If you enter this program into a file yourself, give it the following name: **HelloJava.java**. You can give the file a different name, but it must have a **.java** extension. In building Java programs, it is usually easiest to give the source file the same base name as the class containing **main( )**.

Creating and Running the Application

After entering the source code in the file **HelloJava.java**, compile the application using the following command:

javac HelloJava.java

If this command is successful, the Java compiler (**javac.exe**) produces a class file, **HelloJava.class**. If the compile was unsuccessful, go back and make sure you entered the program exactly.

HelloJava.class represents the program in an intermediate binary form. You can now run the program, but only with the aid of the Java interpreter (**java.exe**):

java HelloJava

Any time you want to run the program, repeat the last step. Of course, if you change the program you must recompile it.

Figure 1.1 summarizes the Java development process for applications.

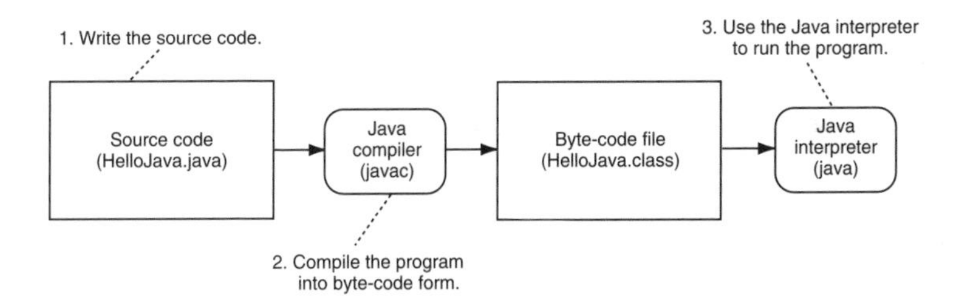

Figure 1.1 *Developing and running Java applications*

Understanding the Code

The first thing you should notice about the application is that all the code is contained inside a class declaration. Almost all statements in all Java programs must appear inside classes. The first line starts the declaration of the class, HelloJava, which gives its name to the program:

```
class HelloJava {
...
}
```

The class contains a declaration of a single method, **main( )**. A *method* is the same thing as a function, except that it's defined inside a class and in many cases operates on an object. We're not concerned with objects just yet, so think of a method as another kind of function. The three middle lines define the method, **main( )**:

```
public static void main(String args[]) {
    System.out.println("Hello Java!");
}
```

As in C and C++, the **main** keyword has a special meaning: it's the program entry point. When you execute the application, the Java interpreter looks for a method with the signature **public static void main( )**. The attributes may seem arbitrary (**static** and **void** are actually quite meaningful), but for now, you should just remember to use them.

The statement inside the method does all the work of the application. This statement calls the **println( )** method of the **System.out** object. This method call looks similar to a function call, but **println( )** cannot be called directly. Figure 1.2 shows a syntactical analysis of this statement.

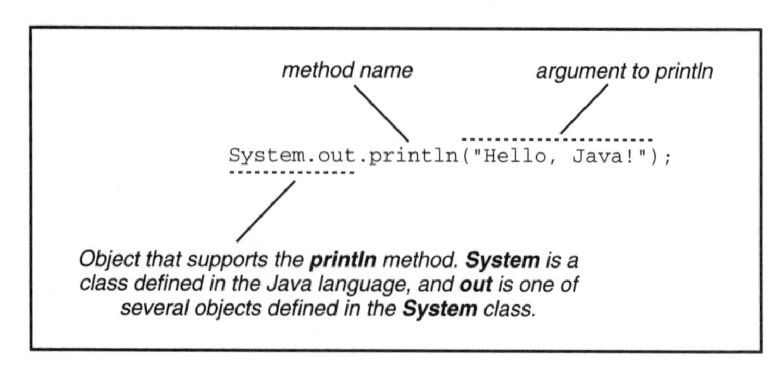

Figure 1.2 *Analysis of a call to println*

The rest of this section comments on Java/C++ differences within the example.

Notice the following differences in the sample between the Java and the C++ ways of doing things:

- **main( )** is a method and not a function, and it must be given exactly the attributes shown. As with all methods, **main( )** must be defined entirely inside the class. Java does not use prototypes.
- The arguments to **main( )** have type **String** and not **char***. As you might expect, arguments to **main( )** are command-line arguments. **String** is a special class defined in the Java language. **String**, rather than arrays of **char**, is used for most string handling.
- The call to **println( )** uses both a class and an object reference. Note that the context operator (::) is not used in Java. Instead, Java uses dot syntax (.) for class references as well as object references. In C++, the call would have been written as "System::out.println( )."
- The class declaration is not terminated with a semicolon (;) as in C++. Java's syntax is simpler in this respect. Semicolons are used only to terminate individual statements. You never use them after a closing brace (}).

Summary: Application Syntax

In general, the simplest applications have the following syntax:

class *program_name* **{**

  public static void main(String *args***[]) {**

    statements

  }

}

Here, substitute the name of your own program for *program_name*. You can use any name you want for *args*, although "args" works fine. (For the use of this argument, see "main Method" in Part II.)

You can define any number of other methods as long as you place them inside the class declaration. (Remember, methods are the Java version of functions.) A more complete syntax is as follows:

class *program_name* **{**

variable_declarations

public static void main(String *args*[]**) {**

statements

}

static *return_type method_name*(*argument_list*) **{**

statements

}

...

}

In Part I's Chapter 2, "Java Building Blocks," I'll discuss how and why you would use Java to create more than one class. Like a structure type in C/C++, classes can define data fields. They can also declare functions, called *methods*.

In the meantime, you can experiment by adding more statements to this simple application. For example, here is a variation on the sample application that uses several statements:

```
class HelloJava {
    public static void main(String args[]) {
        System.out.println("This is an example of");
        System.out.println("a program that prints");
        System.out.println("several lines.");
    }
}
```

APPLETS: GETTING INTO THE WEB

Applets are not necessarily harder to write than applications, but they require a different structure. Remember that applets are programs that run inside a Web page rather than directly on a local computer. Here is a simple applet:

```
public class HelloApplet extends java.applet.Applet {
     public void paint(java.awt.Graphics g) {
          g.drawString("Hello Java!", 5, 20);
     }
}
```

If you enter this program into a file, give it the following name: **HelloApplet.java**. Here, the base name of the file *must* match the name of the class (HelloApplet). If you use a file name other than **HelloApplet.java**, make sure that the file name changes as well. The reason the names must match is that HelloApplet is a public class.

Building and Running the Applet

After entering the applet source code, you run the Java compiler on the source file just as you would for an application:

javac HelloApplet.java

If this command is successful, the Java compiler (**javac.exe**) produces the applet's class file, **HelloApplet.class**. If the compile was unsuccessful, go back and make sure you entered the program exactly.

The file **HelloApplet.class** represents the applet in intermediate binary form. The next step is to place the applet into a Web page, although it can be a very simple page. Use an HTML file to create this page. The <APPLET> tag in the HTML file creates the link to the applet and sets the size of the applet's display area.

To create a Web page for the applet, enter the following code in a text file and name the file **HelloApplet.html**.

```
<HTML>
<HEAD>
</TITLE>Hello Applet</TITLE>
</HEAD>
```

```
<BODY>
Here is an applet.
<P>
<APPLET code="HelloApplet.class" width=400 height=400>
</APPLET>
</BODY>
</HTML>
```

Most of the commands in this file are fairly standard. In fact, you can reuse the same text for HTML files for other applets. The critical line, the only one that must change, is the <APPLET> tag. Here, you could substitute the name of another applet for "HelloApplet."

```
<APPLET code="HelloApplet.class" width=400 height=400>
```

To view the applet, execute the HTML file. A Web browser reads the HTML and responds as appropriate. When the browser reads the <APPLET> tag, it displays the applet in a window of specified size.

When you're developing applets, it's convenient to use the appletviewer utility provided by the JDK. This utility cannot be used to browse the Web, but it can read HTML files and display applets available on the local computer. The appletviewer takes a single argument—the HTML file:

appletviewer HelloApplet.html

When you first attempt to use the appletviewer utility, it displays a copyright message and requires your acceptance. Be advised: you must click the OK button to proceed, and, unless you have a large monitor, it may be difficult to see the OK button at first. Scroll the appletviewer window, if necessary, until you can see the button.

Figure 1.3 summarizes the applet development process.

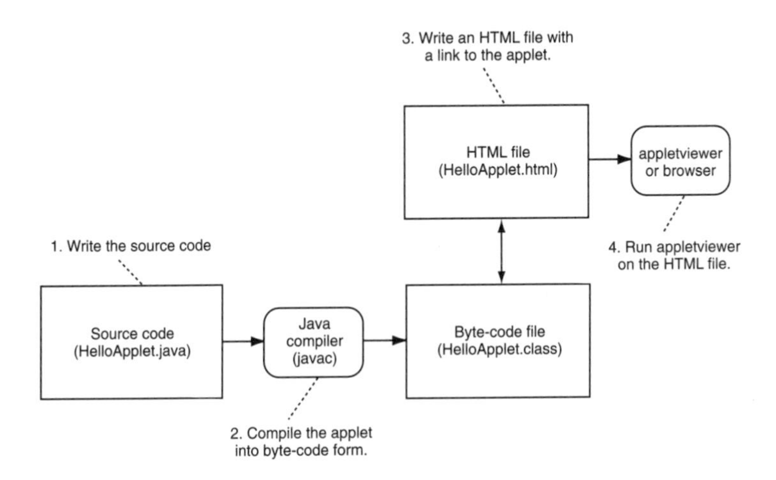

Figure 1.3 *Developing and running Java applets*

Understanding the Code

As with applications, all the code in an applet is contained inside a class declaration. This class declaration is a little more complex.

```
public class HelloApplet extends java.applet.Applet {
...
}
```

This class declaration uses the **extends** keyword to indicate that our class, HelloApplet, inherits from **java.applet.Applet**, a class defined in the Java API. This class provides a series of built-in capabilities.

One of the features of the **java.applet.Applet** class is that it provides a special method, **paint( )**, that tells Java how to repaint the screen. It doesn't repaint the whole screen, but only that portion assigned to the applet. The class HelloApplet *overrides* the **paint( )** method and provides its own, custom version of this method:

```
    public void paint(java.awt.Graphics g) {
        g.drawString("Hello Java!", 5, 20);
    }
```

When the Java interpreter needs to repaint the applet for any reason, it calls the applet's **paint( )** method and passes a graphics object (g). This object provides access to the display area. It's similar to a display context in Windows programming but is easier to use. You can use the graphics object to call graphics methods such as **drawString( )**. The arguments to **drawString( )** are the string to be printed ("Hello, Java!") followed by the x and y coordinates at which to place the top-left corner of the string. These coordinates are in pixels.

If you do not override the **paint( )** method, the applet uses the default implementation of **paint( )**, which does nothing. You can override a number of useful methods for the applet, including **init( )**, which performs initialization, and **start( )**, which is called to start the applet running. (You might override the latter if the applet involved multiple threads.) You can override as many or as few of these predefined applet methods as you need.

The rest of this section comments on Java/C++ differences within the example.

- The expressions **java.applet.Applet** and **java.awt.Graphics** are examples of classes referred to through their packages—**java.applet** and **java.awt**. There is nothing exactly like packages in C or C++, but their use here is somewhat like namespaces in ANSI C++. The next chapter explains how to get rid of the package qualifier in class names by using the **import** statement.
- The classes themselves are **Applet** and **Graphics**. By convention, only class names have initial capital letters. This makes it easier to determine parts of the language at a glance. Any name preceding a class name must necessarily be a package name.
- Both the class, HelloApplet, and the **paint( )** method must be declared **public**. Java supports **public**, **private**, and **protected** for methods and variables, but only **public** for classes. (Other modifiers are supported: see "Classes," "Methods," and "Variables" in Part II.)

- The **public** keyword is applied directly to individual methods. No colon (:) is used after **public**.
- There is no terminating semicolon (;) at the end of the class declaration.

SUMMARY: APPLET SYNTAX

Applets can be much more elaborate than the ones shown here, but the following syntax summary gives you some idea of what to expect in every applet, including the most simple ones:

```
public class applet_name extends java.applet.Applet {
    public void paint(java.awt.Graphics g) {
        statements
    }

    [ public void init( ) {
        statements
    }]

    [other_methods]
}
```

Here, the brackets indicate optional items. In addition to **paint( )** and **init( )**, you can define a number of methods that have special meaning inside an applet. For example, there are some methods that are called in response to an event such as a mouse click.

HOW JAVA WORKS ON MULTIPLE PLATFORMS

It may seem inconvenient that Java requires both a compiler and an interpreter. However, this fact is one of the things that make Java platform-independent. The compiled form of a program is a byte-code file; byte codes consists of binary instructions for a hypothetical processor. Each individual platform has its own Java interpreters (such as **java.exe**, net browsers, and appletviewer) that decode the instructions for the local system. An interpreter works by reading a byte-code instruction, carrying out an action immediately, and then reading the next instruction.

The same byte-code files can be executed on all Java-compatible platforms, because each platform has its own interpreter (see Figure 1.4). Each interpreter carries out instructions as appropriate for its platform. At the same time, the intent of Java's designers was to make behavior across all platforms as consistent as possible. This is one reason that many of Java's features are implemented at a fairly high level of abstraction.

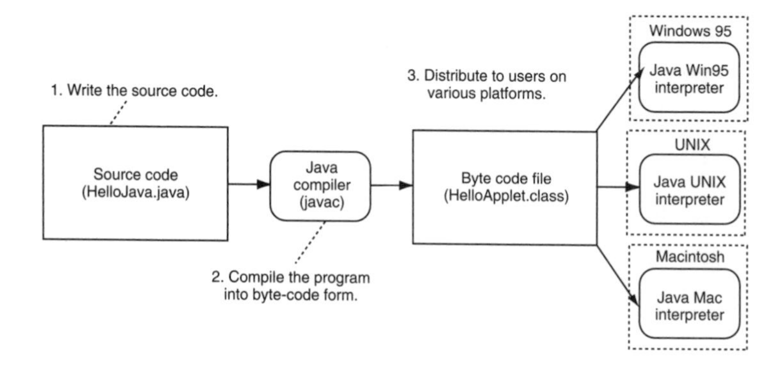

Figure 1.4 *Java program running on multiple platforms*

CHAPTER TWO

Java Building Blocks

In its program structure, Java is not quite like any programming language you've worked with before. Java has a unique scheme that organizes programs into *packages*, *classes*, and *objects*. These terms have specific technical meanings in Java. Java also has a special feature called *interfaces*, which we'll cover in a future chapter.

The general idea of a Java class is close to the C++ concept, so if you have a background in C++, you're definitely ahead of the game. But classes are, if anything, even more important in Java. All method definitions and variables must be placed inside classes. Nothing is global!

A Bigger, Better Class

Chapter 1, "Applets and Oranges," introduced a simple class used in an application. Interestingly enough, the entire program consisted of just this class declaration:

```
class HelloJava {
     public static void main(String args[]) {
          System.out.println("Hello Java!");
     }
}
```

Here, the class declaration consists of a single method, called **main( )**. However, classes can consist of any number of two basic kinds of class members, called *fields*:

- variables
- methods

Remember that methods are the Java equivalent of functions. The following program demonstrates the use of a variable and several methods. Note that **double** is the Java double-precision floating-point type.

```
class PrintTemps {
     static double fahr;

     public static void main(String args[]) {
          System.out.println("Here is a Fahr/Cent
          table.");
          printValues();
     }

     static void printValues() {
          for (fahr = 0.0; fahr <= 100.0; fahr +=
10.0) {
               System.out.print(fahr);
               System.out.print('\t');
               System.out.println(convert(fahr));
          }
     }

     static double convert(double f) {
          return (f - 32.0) / 1.8;
     }
}
```

Notably, each field is declared **static**. In this case, the **static** keyword is required in each of these places for the program to be compiled.

The **static** keyword has the same effect here as it would in a C++ program: static variables are not stored in individual objects, and static methods do not operate on objects. In effect,

static says that none of these fields has anything to do with individual objects of this class. But because this simple program does not use objects, the **static** keyword does not yet pose any real limitations.

There's another consequence of **static**: static methods can refer only to fields of the class that are also static. This is why the variable, fahr, and the other two methods—printValues( ) and convert( )—must be declared with the **static** keyword. The sequence of the program is as follows:

1. The program entry point, **main( )**, gets called first.
2. **main( )** calls the functions printValue( ) and convert( ). Because **main( )** is static, the other methods must also be static, or **main( )** cannot call them.

Given this Catch-22, how do nonstatic methods ever get called? Simple: the restriction against using nonstatic fields is lifted when **main( )** uses fields of *other* classes. For example, the **print( )** and **println( )** methods (discussed next) are nonstatic.

For the most part, the use of static in Java is identical to its use in C++. However, static can't be used with global functions, because Java does not support global functions.

The print statements in this example point out some useful features of Java. First, The **System.out** object supports both **print( )** and **println( )**; the difference between these two functions is that after **println( )**, Java prints a newline. Pascal programmers should feel right at home seeing these two old friends. The **System.out** object, incidentally, is an instance of the API **PrintStream** class, which is where you'll find these methods declared.

In C++ terms, **print( )** and **println( )** are *overloaded methods.* This means that they can take a variety of arguments. You can give **print( )** or **println( )** an argument having any of Java's primitive types:

```
System.out.print(fahr);
System.out.print('\t');
System.out.println(convert(fahr));
```

The expression '\t' is a special character representing a tab.

The rest of the example is straightforward if you know C or C++. If not, the **for** statement probably looks new to you. Look up the topic "for Statement" in Part II for more information. The addition-increment operator is also used here (fahr += 10.0). This is shorthand for the following:

```
fahr = fahr + 10.0
```

A Class with Nonstatic Methods

In all but the most trivial programs, you'll probably have a number of classes. A Java program, in fact, is essentially a collection of classes.

But what is a class, and why ever write more than one? The answer is a little complicated, because in Java, classes have more than one use. Moreover, you need to understand all the uses of classes to really understand Java.

So far, classes have been used to represent *the program*. In Java, it is the name of this class, and not the name of the source file, that determines the program name. To take the program in the previous section as an example, you could put the code in a file named **myfile.java**. Then you compile the code by using this file name:

javac myfile.java

But you do not *run* the program by using the file name. Instead, you feed to the Java interpreter the name of the class containing **main( )**. If you glance back at the example, you'll see that this class name is PrintTemps. Therefore, the following command runs the program, no matter what the name of the source file is:

java PrintTemps

As was suggested in Chapter 1, it simplifies things to give the file and the class the same name. In applets, giving the file and the class the same name is required, because the applet class is public.

So sometimes a class represents the main program. Another use for classes, probably the one most familiar to C++ programmers, is to create a new type. Classes are very much like structures in C, records in Pascal, and user-defined types in Visual Basic. The big difference—and what makes Java object-oriented—is that you can give classes built-in functions (methods).

The following example uses classes two ways. One class represents the main program (TestFractions), and the other class creates a composite data type (Fraction).

```
class TestFractions {
     public static void main(String args[]) {
          Fraction fract1 = new Fraction();
          Fraction fract2 = new Fraction();
          fract1.setValues(5, 8);
          fract2.setValues(7, 11);
          if (fract1.compare(fract2) > 0)
               System.out.println("5/8 is > 7/11");
          else
               System.out.println("5/8 is not >
               7/11");
     }
}

class Fraction {
     int numerator, denominator;

     void setValues(int n, int d) {
          numerator = n;
          denominator = d;
     }

     int compare(Fraction otherFract) {
          int us = numerator * otherFract.denominator;
          int them = denominator * otherFract.numerator;
```

```
            if (us > them)
                return 1;
            else if (us == them)
                return 0;
            return -1;
        }
}
```

This is the first example in the book to really deal with objects. There's a lot to digest here, so I've kept it simple.

The central feature of this example is that it introduces a new type, Fraction. The purpose of most classes is just that: to define a new type. The type can be made up of any combination of other types, including: **boolean**, **char**, **byte**, **short**, **int**, **long**, **float**, and **double**. In this case, Fraction is a type made up of two integers called numerator and denominator (see Figure 2.1). There are also two methods—setValues and compare—that help you manipulate the objects.

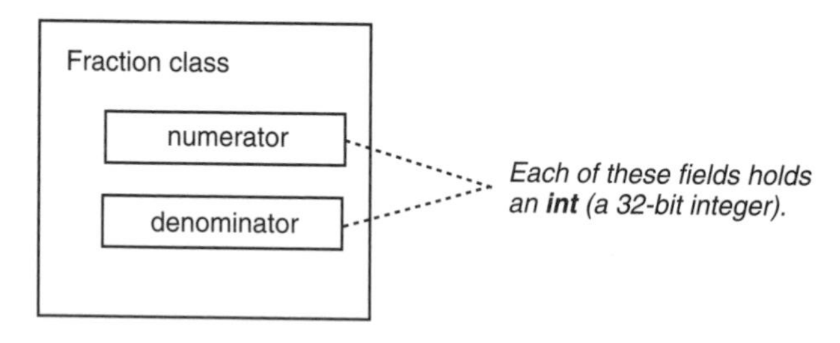

Figure 2.1 *Structure of the Fraction class*

The first thing that the **main( )** does is to create two objects of Fraction type:

```
Fraction fract1 = new Fraction();
Fraction fract2 = new Fraction();
```

In Java, creating an object is generally a two-step process. You define an object variable (in this case, fract1) and then use the **new** operator to allocate an object in memory. Note that this step is *not* required when you create a variable of primitive type, such as **int** or **double**.

The creation of fract1 and the Fraction object could have been done in two separate lines:

```
Fraction fract1;
fract1 = new Fraction();
```

However, Java is very liberal about initialization of variables. You can combine these two statements into one, creating both the variable (fract1) and the object it refers to:

```
Fraction fract1 = new Fraction();
```

The rest of the example calls methods through the two objects: fract1 and fract2. If you're not familiar with objects and methods, read the next section. Otherwise, you can skip it.

In C++, you never need to allocate object variables and objects separately. In other words, C++ lets you create objects the obvious way:

```
Fraction fract1, fract2;
```

In Java, an object variable such as fract1 or fract2 is only a reference; this means that before fract1 or fract2 can be used, it must first be associated with actual objects. The new operator creates the objects.

Another difference illustrated in this example is that the main function can freely refer to fields of the Fraction class. Unlike C++, fields of Java classes are not private by default.

If you're a C++ programmer, you may have noticed that there is no use of a **delete** operator, **free( )** function, or other memory cleanup mechanism in the source code. This is not a careless omission: Java does not have a **delete** operator. Instead, all unused memory is intelligently cleaned up by the Java garbage collector, which runs as a background thread. You can forget about freeing memory, knowing that the Java interpreter will take care of this programming issue for you. Life is easy!

BACKGROUND: OBJECT ORIENTATION

The previous section introduced objects and object-oriented programming. The basic idea of object orientation is simple: it means that programs are designed around data structures. The individual instances of user-defined data types (classes) are called *objects*.

Java, unlike C++, does not consider instances of primitive data—such as int or double—to be objects. The distinction is important, because only objects, and not primitive data, require the use of the new operator.

The first hurdle in understanding object orientation is to be clear on the difference between classes and objects. The relationship is roughly the same as that of a data type to specific values. For example, the Fraction class defines a type with two integer fields: numerator and denominator. Fraction is the class. The variables fract1 and fract2 refer to individual objects of this class. Fraction defines the data fields, but fract1 and fract2 hold specific values for those fields (see Figure 2.2).

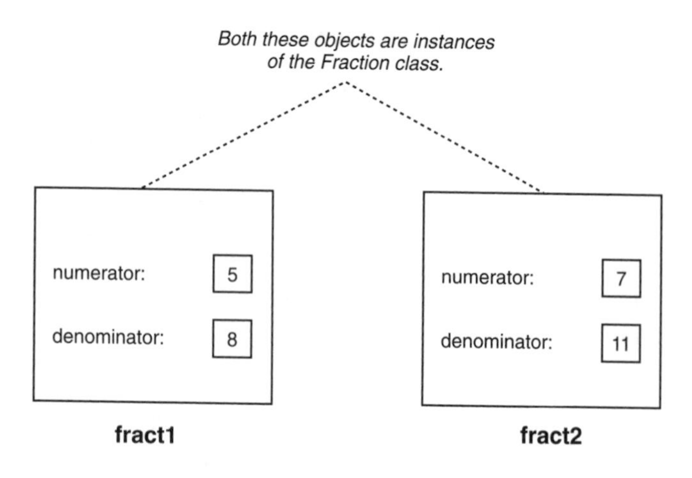

Figure 2.2 *Objects of the Fraction class*

This idea should not be difficult, because the relationship here is the same as that between a C structure type and an instance of that structure. In fact, you can use Java classes just as you would use structure types.

Here is where it gets interesting. In Java, even the function code is organized around classes and objects. The function code, of course, is made up of methods. Generally speaking, a method provides a way of communicating with or manipulating objects of a particular class. The Fraction methods, for example, let you manipulate Fraction objects.

Here's the definition for setValues( ), a simple method of the Fraction class:

```
void setValues(int n, int d) {
     numerator = n;
     denominator = d;
}
```

As a Fraction method, this method can be applied to instances of the Fraction class, such as fract1. You can call the method by using the syntax *object.method*:

```
fract1.setValues(5, 8);
```

Because setValues( ) is called through the object fract1, this statement has the effect of setting values in fract1. When the method adjusts the values of numerator and denominator, it is *fract1*'s fields, and not those of another object, that get set.

In contrast, the next statement sets the values of fract2's fields.

```
fract2.setValues(7, 11);
```

When you make the call fract1.setValues( ), Java assumes that the variable names in the setValues( ) definition—numerator and denominator—are fields of fract1. When you call the method through fract2, it's assumed they're fields of fract2.

This should be clear, but there is one point that's easy to miss: although the methods operate on objects, they are declared in the class. The objects fract1 and fract2 respond in similar ways to setValues( ), because they belong to the same class. Another class might implement setValues( ) in a different way.

The bottom line is that individual objects have their own data values, but they share the same code. Figure 2.3 illustrates this idea; fract1 and fract2 have their own data but share the methods defined for the Fraction class.

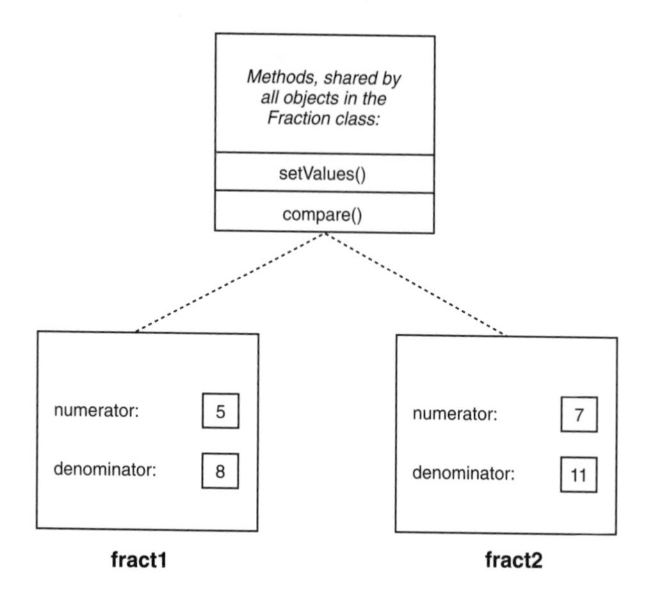

Figure 2.3 *Code and data in the Fraction class*

So a class is essentially a structure definition that, optionally, can have methods. The methods provide built-in functionality for objects of the class. You can use the methods to manipulate with and communicate with the objects.

But how is a method different from a C function? Here are the most essential differences:

- Method definition code can make unqualified references to variables in the same class. For example, you can use "numerator" rather than "object.numerator":

```
myFract.numerator      // Qualified reference
                       (valid //anywhere)
numerator              // Unqualified reference –
                       valid //only in Fraction
                       methods
```

- When you call a method, references to unqualified variables are considered fields of the current object (the object through which the call was made). This is significant, because the method can refer to *any* field of the current object, even fields declared **private**.
- Method definition code can make unqualified references to other methods of the same class, even those declared **private**.

NOTE

The previous discussion does not apply to static variables and methods. Static methods are limited to referring only to static variables of the class.

CONSTRUCTORS

The purpose of the setValues( ) method is to set initial values for the two variables numerator and denominator. It's more efficient to do this with a *constructor*, which is a method that is automatically called when a new object is created.

Java constructors follow almost exactly the same rules that C++ constructors follow. A constructor has the same name as the class itself, and it has no return type (not even **void**). You can, however, write any number of constructors as long as they have different argument lists. For example:

```
class Fraction {
     int numerator, denominator;

// Constructors
     Fraction()
          {numerator = denominator = 0;}

     Fraction(int n, int d) {
          numerator = n;
          denominator = d;
     }
...
```

This last example uses the line-comment symbol (//), which indicates that the rest of the line is a comment. This is the same comment symbol used in C++.

With the Fraction (int, int) constructor defined, the main method in the TestFractions class can declare, allocate, and initialize the two Fraction objects all at once:

```
class TestFractions {
     public static void main(String args[]) {
          Fraction fract1 = new Fraction(5, 8);
          Fraction fract2 = new Fraction(7, 11);
...
```

The arguments to the expression "new Fraction( )" determine which constructor gets called. In this case, the constructor called is the one that takes two integer arguments.

PROGRAM ORGANIZATION AND PACKAGES

A Java program is basically a collection of classes. Each class that is compiled gets placed in its own class file. But how do you organize these classes?

Any class that has a properly declared **main( )** method can serve as a program entry point. That class can then refer to any other class in the current directory (or in a directory searched by Java). This gives Java a freewheeling, open-ended structure compared with C and C++. Here are some of the differences:

- You don't have to do anything special to make classes in one file available to another file. The only consideration is that if one file is dependent on class declarations in another file, then at compile time, the other file must exist in either compiled or source-code form. (Thus, if you do things in the right order, even mutual cross-references between source files are not a problem.)
- Within any given source file, classes can be declared in any order. Methods can also be defined in any order, regardless of how they cross-reference each other.

- Consequently, Java has no concept of prototypes, **extern** declarations, or header files. Forward references to classes and methods are not a problem.
- All the fields of one class are accessible to other classes except for fields you specifically declare **private**. (This is automatically true only if the classes are in the same package, a fact I'll return to after introducing the concept of packages.)

The only problem with this system is that you can accumulate many classes, all of which automatically have access to one another. This arrangement is fine until you start to have so many classes that you run out of names. The obvious solution is to create a different directory for each software project.

But sometimes you may develop classes that you want to make available to all your projects. In fact, as an object-oriented language, Java encourages this kind of reuse. To help facilitate the development of class libraries, Java provides a feature called the *package*. Class names in a package do not conflict with those in another package, because each package creates its own namespace.

How Packages Work

Classes are always stored in individual files, regardless of packages, but all the members of a package are stored in the same subdirectory. The use of packages also changes the rules by which classes can refer to each other. In effect, packages provide an extra layer of encapsulation, because not all classes in a package are visible to code outside the package.

To place a source file in a package, put a **package** statement at the beginning of the file. This statement, if included, must be the first statement in the file.

package *package_name*;

The *package_name* must be the same as the name of the subdirectory in which the class file is to be placed. The name can contain embedded dots (.), as explained in the next section, to show that it is in a nested subdirectory.

Being placed in a package has the following effects on a class:

- Other classes in the same package can refer to the class, even if they're declared in another file. This, of course, is standard behavior.
- However, a class can be referred to from outside the package only if the class is declared **public**. Public classes have special restrictions: there can be no more than one public class in any given source file, and it must have the same name as the base name of the source file.

Most classes in the Java API are public, because otherwise you could not use them in your own code. Everything in the API is organized into packages.

Figure 2.4 illustrates the effect of the **package** statement on three source files. Note that the package name, cars, is the same as the name of the subdirectory containing the package. This is required. Figure 2.4 uses arrows to show how classes in this example are able to access other classes.

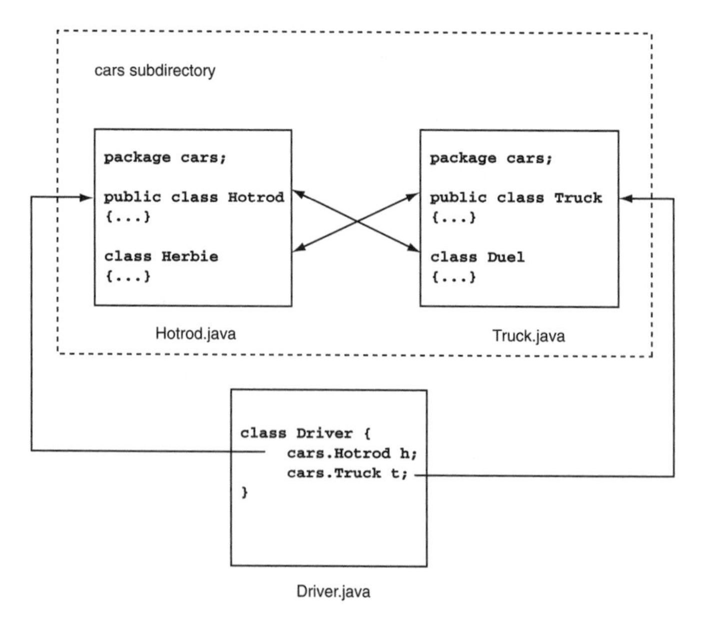

Figure 2.4 *Example of package use*

Two files—**Hotrod.java** and **Truck.java**—are placed in the cars package. Because they are in the same package, all the classes in these files (Hotrod, Herbie, Truck, Duel) can refer to one another.

The class Driver is defined in **Driver.java** and is not part of the cars package. Therefore, Driver can refer only to the package's public classes: Hotrod and Truck. These class names must match the names of their respective source files, because they are public classes.

There's one other consideration that will start to come up when you write your own packages. The fact that a class is public does not mean that its *fields* are accessible outside the package. The default access level for all fields (both variables and methods) is to be accessible within the current package but not from outside. If a class is public, then declaring a field **public** makes the field accessible outside the package as well. If the class is not public, declaring the field **public** has no effect. See the topic "public Keyword" in Part II for more information.

This is a lot of information to digest, so let's recap four vital points:

- The package name must be the same as the name of subdirectory containing the class.
- Only public classes are available to code outside the package.
- The name of a public class must be the same as the base name of the source file.
- A field is not visible outside its package unless both the class and that field are declared **public**.

Packages and Directory Structure

In Java, some package names have embedded dots (.) that separate parts of the name. Such a name indicates that the classes in the package are to be found several levels down in the directory hierarchy. For example, consider this package name:

```
package briano.util.tools;
```

Because this name has three parts (briano, util, tools), the package is to be found three levels down in the directory system.

Figure 2.5 illustrates the relationship of the name to the directory structure. The first subdirectory (in this case, briano) must be located under a directory that the Java interpreter would normally search: by default, this is the current directory, although you can use the CLASSPATH variable, as explained in the next section. The rest of the package name traces a path through the directories.

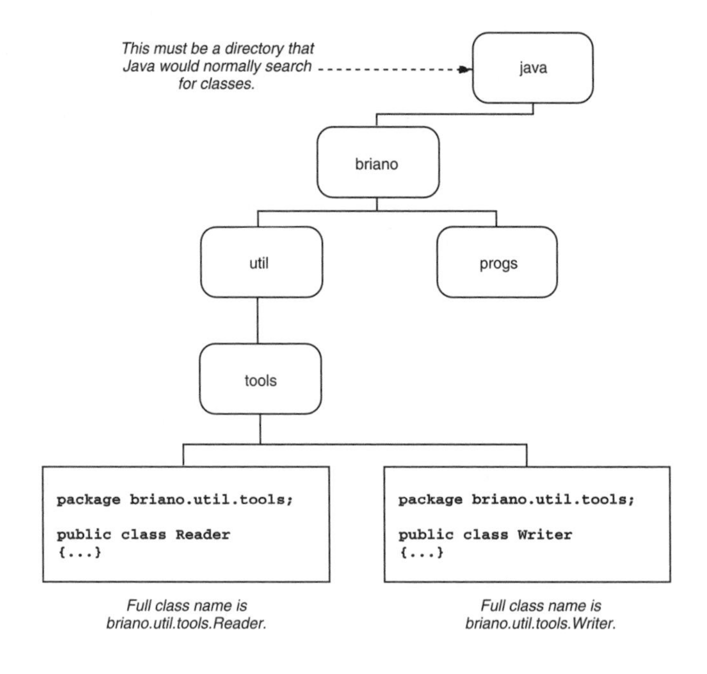

Figure 2.5 *Directory structure for package briano.util.tools*

Inside the source files for the classes themselves, the **package** statement must spell out the entire package name—in this case, briano.util.tools.

NOTE

In using the Java API, you'll notice that the packages have names such as java.awt.image and java.awt.peer, even though there is probably no java\awt\image or java\awt\peer

subdirectory on your computer. However, when the Java interpreter runs a program, it looks in the \java\lib directory (actually the \lib directory under the Java home directory) to find the file classes.zip. When unzipped, this file contains the complete directory structure for the API as well as all the API classes. You should not attempt to unzip this file yourself.

How Java Searches for Classes and Packages

There are a number of Java utilities that search for class files, including the Java compiler and the Java interpreters. In every case, Java searches for class files as follows:

- If the CLASSPATH environment variable is set, Java searches all directories listed in this environment variable, in the order listed.
- Otherwise, Java searches the current directory.

If the class is part of a package, Java uses the package name to look for a subdirectory under one of the directories it would normally search for classes. For example, assume that on a Windows 95 system, the CLASSPATH environment variable is set to this:

```
CLASSPATH=C:\mystuff;C:\java\packages
```

Then Java could resolve a reference to class mathpack.Trig by finding the file in either of these locations:

```
C:\mystuff\mathpack\Trig.class
C:\java\packages\mathpack\Trig.class
```

In setting CLASSPATH, it is a good idea to use the current-directory symbol (.) so that Java always searches the current directory first. Doing so preserves Java's default search behavior.

```
CLASSPATH=.;C:\mystuff;C:\java\packages
```

Regardless of how the CLASSPATH environment variable is set, Java also looks for API classes in the **classes.zip** file in the lib directory of the Java home directory. This file typically has the file path \java\lib\classes.zip.

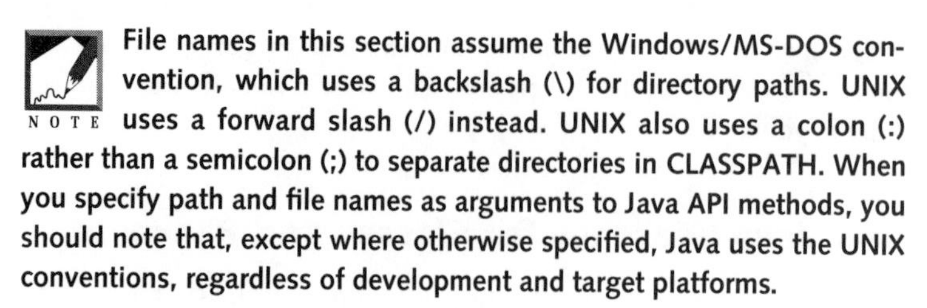

NOTE **File names in this section assume the Windows/MS-DOS convention, which uses a backslash (\) for directory paths. UNIX uses a forward slash (/) instead. UNIX also uses a colon (:) rather than a semicolon (;) to separate directories in CLASSPATH. When you specify path and file names as arguments to Java API methods, you should note that, except where otherwise specified, Java uses the UNIX conventions, regardless of development and target platforms.**

THE IMPORT STATEMENT

Most of the packages you'll want to use are in the Java API, especially when you begin programming in Java. Some of the API classes have long package names, such as **java.awt.image.ImageObserver**.

The **import** statement lets you refer directly to classes in a package. Note that the **import** statement does not change the way that Java searches for classes nor affect any of the rules that apply to accessing classes and fields in a package. When you first start using Java, the **import** statement looks a lot like the C **#include** statement. But its purpose is quite different: the only effect of the Java **import** statement is to let you refer to a class by a shorter name.

Look at the introductory applet example from the previous chapter:

```
public class HelloApplet extends java.applet.Applet {
     public void paint(java.awt.Graphics g) {
          g.drawString("Hello Java!", 5, 20);
     }
}
```

References to **java.applet.Applet** and **java.awt.Graphics** can be replaced by **Applet** and **Graphics**, respectively, as long as you first use **import** statements:

```
import java.applet.Applet;
import java.awt.Graphics;

public class HelloApplet extends Applet {
     public void paint(Graphics g) {
          g.drawString("Hello Java!", 5, 20);
     }
}
```

In this case, the use of **import** statements does not make the total size of the program smaller, although it does make some of it easier to read. However, in more serious applications, some of the class names may come up many times. In this case, use of **import** statements will definitely reduce the amount of typing you must do.

Another way to use an **import** statement is to use the following syntax:

import *package*.***;**

This statement has the effect of importing the names of all classes and interfaces in the indicated *package*. For instance, the previous example could be rewritten as follows:

```
import java.applet.*;
import java.awt.*;

public class HelloApplet extends Applet {
     public void paint(Graphics g) {
          g.drawString("Hello Java!", 5, 20);
     }
}
```

Classes and interfaces in the java.lang package can be referred to directly, without importing.

CHAPTER THREE

Fun with Graphics

If you've programmed with typical hard-core GUI systems such as Windows, a pleasant surprise awaits you: Java provides you with the same basic functionality, but in a simpler, cleaner programming model. At its heart is the **Graphics** object, which is easy to use once you understand the *object.method* syntax.

If you haven't programmed with a GUI system before, don't worry. You don't have any weird GUI programming stuff to unlearn.

So now, let's plunge into the colorful world of graphics. The examples in this chapter don't do anything terribly fancy—they basically just display information—but upcoming chapters will add the ability to get information and to animate the graphics.

Applets, Apps, and Graphics

First, a word about the role of graphics in Java programming generally. As Chapter 1 pointed out, there are two main kinds of Java programs: applications and applets. Yet in many books on Java, you'll notice that graphics seem to be the exclusive province of applets. Applications often seem to be relegated to simple utilities and console applications. This might well lead you to ask, are Java graphics reserved for applet use only?

In theory, not at all. If you can get a valid **Graphics** object, you can perform graphics operations. But, you can't just call the **Graphics** class constructor. You must get a **Graphics** object passed to you by something called a *component*. This is easy to do in an applet, because every applet has at least one built-in component: the applet itself. A component can respond to events, and it is notified when it is time to update the screen.

In an application, you can create components by using certain features of the Abstract Windowing ToolKit (AWT), which is explained in the next chapter. The first step is to create and show a **Frame** object. Until you learn how to create components, however, it's easiest to create graphics effects by programming simple applets. So this chapter focuses on applets.

THE GRAPHICS OBJECT

In Java, you perform most graphics operations by manipulating the **Graphics** object directly. Once you get the object, you call its methods to do everything: write text, draw figures, and specify fonts and colors. The most common way to get the **Graphics** object is to write a **paint( )** method, in which you are passed a **Graphics** object automatically:

```
public class HelloApplet extends java.applet.Applet {
     public void paint(java.awt.Graphics g) {
          // Paint the applet here.
     }
}
```

The applet itself, by the way, is also an object. There can be many instances of an applet, because the user can use the appletviewer to clone multiple versions of an applet.

The **Graphics** object, g, provides a handle to the applet's display area (see Figure 3.1). If passed in through **paint( )**, g provides a handle to the part of the display area that needs to be repainted, an area known as the *clipping rectangle*. You can write all over the applet's display area, but only the region in the clipping rectangle is updated.

Often, the entire display needs to be redrawn. This is the case, for example, when the applet is first displayed. But in some cases only a corner needs to be redrawn, such as when a window overlaps the applet but then is moved away.

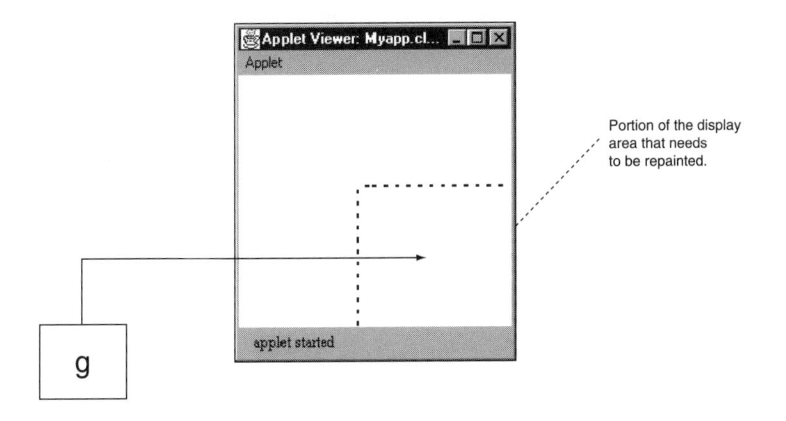

Figure 3.1 *The Graphics object, g, used in the paint method*

None of this has any effect on the way you write the **paint( )** method except in one respect: the purpose of **paint( )** is to restore an existing image. If the image needs to change, you must make sure that the entire area affected is repainted, either by calling **repaint( )** to refresh the screen or by grabbing the **Graphics** object directly. At the end of this chapter, you'll find an example of the latter technique.

In any case, once you have the **Graphics** object, you call its methods to perform any graphics action you want to execute. As elsewhere, these statements use the *object.method* syntax. Chapter 2, "Java Building Blocks," stated that methods are often used to manipulate objects of a particular class. In this case, calling a method through the **Graphics** object has the effect of changing some aspect of the display area.

```
public class Myapplet extends java.applet.Applet {
     public void paint(java.awt.Graphics g) {
          g.SetColor(Color.blue);
          g.SetFont(new Font("Arial", Font.BOLD, 12));
          g.drawString("Hello there Java!", 20, 20);
     }
}
```

DISPLAYING TEXT

The **drawString( )** method is Java's principal method for displaying text on the screen. The other two methods—**drawChar( )** and **drawBytes( )**—do exactly the same thing except that they accept string data in a different format.

The following example displays the string "How do you take your Java?", placing the baseline of the string 10 pixels from the left edge and 30 pixels from the top edge.

```
g.drawString("How do you take your Java?", 10, 30);
```

The **drawString( )** method and the other two drawing methods use the current settings for background color, foreground color, and font properties. The next section explains how to change color settings.

Setting Background and Foreground Colors

Background color is a property of the applet and should be set in the applet's **init( )** method using the **setBackground( )** method. Because both of these methods are fields of the applet class, you can refer to **setBackground( )** directly from within **init( )**. You don't need to qualify the reference as *object.method*.

```
import java.awt.*;
import java.applet.*;

public class Myapplet extends Applet {
     public void init() {
          setBackground(Color.blue);
     }

     public void paint(Graphics g) {
          g.drawString("The field is blue.", 20, 20);
     }
}
```

The reason that the background color should be set in the **init()** method is that the background color is used to fill the display area before **paint()** is ever called.

The expression **Color.blue** is a constant defined in the **Color** class. This constant is declared **static**, meaning it's a class variable. Consequently, you can refer to this constant directly through the class using the syntax *class.field*. You don't have to first create a **Color** object.

The **Color** class is a good example of a class with a dual purpose: it defines a set of useful constants, but it also defines **Color** as an object type. Many classes in the API work this way. They define useful constants but they can also be used to create objects. When a field is a class field, there is exactly one copy of it, and it does not depend on object creation. (Class variables are stored as if they were global variables.) In the API, you can see which fields are class fields, because they are declared with the **static** keyword.

All this means that the **Color** class provides a set of useful constants (**red**, **blue**, **cyan**, **white**, **black**, **gray**, and so on), but the class can also be used to create new objects of type **Color**. In Java, there's no conflict in a class being used in more than one way.

In C++, you would refer to the expression Color.blue as Color::blue. C++ also supports static class variables but uses the scope operator (::) to qualify references through a class.

Aside from background color, common attributes of the display area are set through the **Graphics** object. To set foreground color, call the **setColor( )** method from within **paint( )**. The following example applet sets both foreground and background colors:

```
import java.awt.*;
import java.applet.*;

public class Myapplet extends Applet {
     public void init() {
          setBackground(Color.blue);
     }
```

```
        public void paint(Graphics g) {
                g.setColor(Color.red);
                g.drawString("Red on blue.", 20, 20);
        }
}
```

Again, **setColor( )** and **drawString( )** are qualified references, because they are methods of class **Graphics**, whereas **setBackground( )** is a method of the applet and does not need to be qualified.

For a complete list of **Color** constants, see "Color Class" in Part V, "API Quick Reference."

Setting the Font

To specify a font, create a **Font** object and then pass that object to the **setFont( )** method. In Java, you can do all this neatly in a single statement:

```
g.setFont(new Font("Helvetica", Font.PLAIN, 12));
```

The arguments to the **Font** constructor are the font name, a number indicating font style, and the point size. The statement is interesting because it uses the **Font** in two ways. **Font.PLAIN** is a class field and can therefore be used before a font object is created. Then the method call **new Font( )** calls a **Font** class constructor to create the object.

The following example specifies a font that is both bold and italic:

```
g.setFont(new Font("Arial", Font.BOLD + Font.ITALIC, 14));
```

You can also set the font in the applet's **init( )** method. The **init( )** method is called just once: when the applet is loaded. Sometimes it's useful to set the font as a graphics method—if, for example, you need to change fonts during a repaint. But if you're going to stick to one font, it's most efficient to set it once in **init( )** by calling the applet's own **setFont( )** method. Remember that **setFont( )**, when applied to the applet, does not need to be qualified when called from within another applet method:

```
public void init() {
     setFont(new Font("Arial", Font.BOLD + Font.ITALIC, 14));
}
```

For a list of supported fonts, see Part VI, "Useful Tables."

Using Font Metrics

A number of text operations require measurement of font properties. In the most obvious and common case, you want to display more than one line of text in an applet. To print the second line, you would need to know how far to move down. This distance depends on the height of the current font.

The following example prints two lines of red text in 14-point Arial font against a white background:

```
import java.awt.*;
import java.applet.*;

public class Print2 extends Applet {
     FontMetrics fm;
     int y;

     public void init( ) {
          setBackground(Color.white);
          Font myFont = new Font("Arial", Font.PLAIN, 14);
          setFont(myFont);
          fm = getFontMetrics(myFont);
          y = fm.getHeight();
     }

     public void paint(Graphics g) {
          g.setColor(Color.red);
          g.drawString("First line of text.", 5, 20);
          g.drawString("Second line of text.", 5, 20 + y);
     }
}
```

This example introduces the use of the **FontMetrics** class. This class is declared in the **java.awt** package, so it is already covered by the **import** statements. Note that all the classes could have been imported individually, although that would have made the applet source code a couple of lines longer:

```
import java.awt.Graphics;

import java.awt.Font;

import java.awt.FontMetrics

import java.applet.Applet;
```

This applet must do a number of operations just once. For efficiency's sake, these operations are performed in the **init( )** method, which the appletviewer or browser calls once when the applet is loaded. After the font is created and the distance between lines is calculated, there is no need to do these operations again. As in a previous example, the background color must also be set in **init( )**.

```
public void init() {

    setBackground(Color.white);

    Font myFont = new Font("Arial", Font.PLAIN, 14);

    setFont(myFont);

    fm = getFontMetrics(myFont);

    y = fm.getHeight();

}
```

In this applet, information must be communicated between the **init( )** method and the **paint( )** method. Specifically, the height, y, is calculated in **init( )** and is later used in **paint( )**. This communication requires the use of instance variables rather than temporary or local variables. Remember that instance variables are variables declared at the class level but not declared **static**:

```
FontMetrics fm;

int y;
```

When run, the applet, Print2, produces the display shown in Figure 3.2.

Figure 3.2 *The Print2 applet displaying two lines of text*

This applet specifies a particular font, but you can always use the default font if you want to. You can get font metrics for the current font by calling the applet's **getFont( )** method:

```
fm = getFontMetrics(getFont());
```

You might think that you can create a FontMetrics object by using a constructor, but FontMetrics is an abstract class and cannot be directly instantiated. You must call the applet's getFontMetrics( ) method to get a FontMetrics object. The applet actually hands you an instance of a FontMetrics subclass. In the Java language, a subclass can be used anywhere its superclass could be used. This means that the object you get back from getFontMetrics( ) is fully usable.

Using Other Font Metrics: A Summary

The **FontMetrics** class supports a series of measurements for each font. Each of these measurements can be accessed through the appropriate "get" method of **FontMetrics**. For example, in the previous example, **fm.getHeight( )** returns the height of the font. See Part V for a complete list of methods.

Figure 3.3 shows the available font measurements in a graphical context. The characters shown are representative of all other characters in the font.

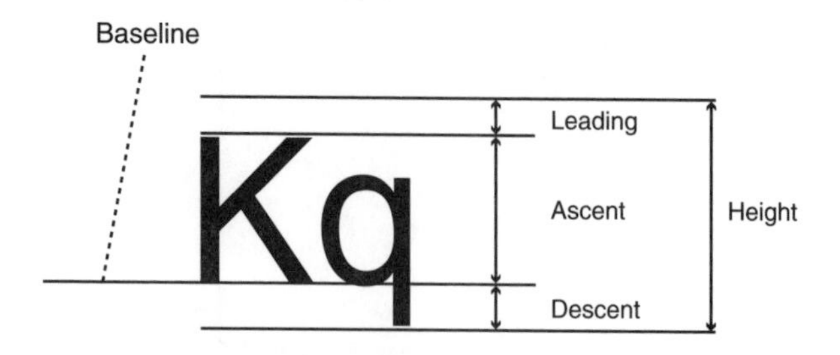

Figure 3.3 *Graphical summary of font metrics*

DRAWING FIGURES

The **Graphics** class supports a large set of methods for operations such as drawing lines, drawing circles and squares, and filling in regions. All of them can be called through the **Graphics** object, g. (Of course, g is an argument, and you can use any argument name you wish.)

```
    public void paint(Graphics g) {

// Draw a line from (0, 0) to (150, 100)
         g.drawLine(0, 0, 150, 100);

// Draw square at (170, 20), size 100 x 100
         g.drawRect(170, 20, 100, 100);

// Draw circle at (120, 100), in area size 80 x 80
         g.drawOval(120, 100, 80, 80);
    }
```

This example, when put into an applet and executed, gives the output shown in Figure 3.4. To see all the output, you may need to resize the appletviewer window after starting the applet.

An alternative is to change the parameters to the <APPLET> tag in the HTML file so that the size of the window is at least 300 by 200 units.

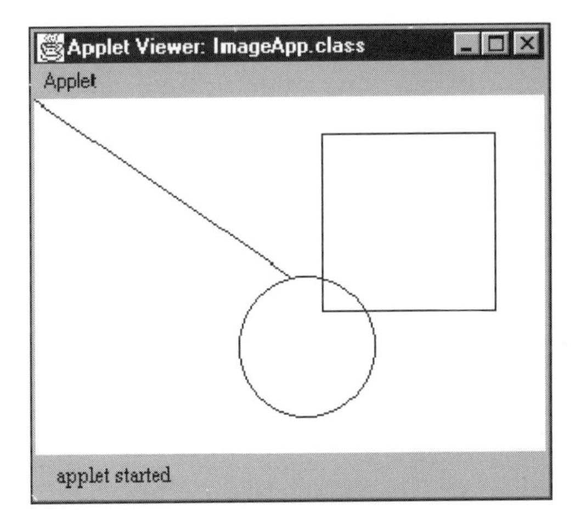

Figure 3.4 *Sample graphics output*

In the case of the **drawLine( )** method, the arguments specify two end points, using (x, y) coordinates. The call to **drawLine( )** in this example draws a line from the point (0, 0) to the point (150, 100).

In the case of **drawRect( )** and **drawOval( )**—and many other graphics methods as well—the first two arguments specify a corner, and the last two specify width and height. Thus, the call to **drawRect( )** specifies an upper left corner of (170, 20), width of 100, and height of 100. Calls to **drawOval( )** interpret arguments the same way, except that they draw an oval *inscribed* within the indicated rectangle. Figure 3.5 shows an example of another oval.

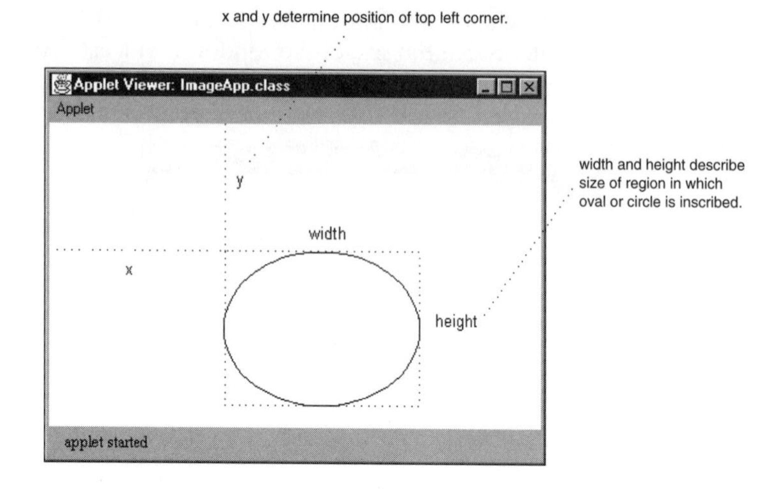

Figure 3.5 *Arguments to the drawOval( ) method*

One of the more versatile Java graphics methods is **drawPolygon( )**, which takes as its argument a set of any number of points. At run time, Java connects the dots to produce a polygon as elaborate as you want. (Its cousin, **fillPolygon( )**, uses similar mechanics.) This method is relatively simple to use. Most of the work lies in determining which points to connect.

To use **drawPolygon( )**, you may first need to draw a diagram of the figure you want to create. Then determine the coordinates. Figure 3.6 shows a figure to be drawn and the coordinates of each of the six points.

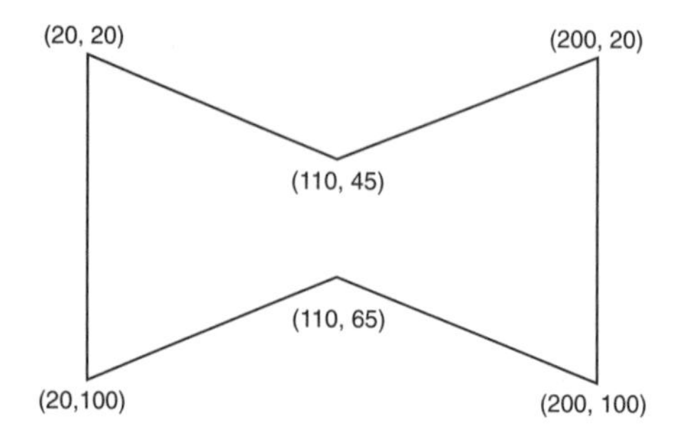

Figure 3.6 *A polygon with six points*

The next step is to write down the point values, placing the x and y coordinates in two columns (see Table 3.1).

Table 3.1 *Coordinates for a polygon with six points*

X VALUE	Y VALUE
20	20
110	45
200	20
200	100
110	65
20	100
20	20

Although there are only six points, this table has seven rows. This is because the **drawPolygon( )** function does not connect the dots back to the first point unless that point is listed at the end.

From this table, we create two integer arrays: an x array and a y array. These arrays, along with the number of points (seven), are given as arguments to the **drawPolygon( )** method. In Java, you can create arrays either by using the **new** operator or by initializing with an aggregate as done here. For more information, see the topics "Aggregates" and "Arrays" in Part II.

```
public void paint(Graphics g) {
    int xArray[] = {20, 110, 200, 200, 110, 20, 20};
    int yArray[] = {20, 45, 20, 100, 65, 100, 20};
    g.drawPolygon(xArray, yArray, 7);
}
```

The use of the **drawPolygon( )** method may not seem novel, because you could have created the same effect by repeatedly calling the **drawLine( )** method. The real power of polygons comes when you use the **fillPolygon( )** method to color in the region you construct. For example:

```
    public void paint(Graphics g) {
        int xArray[] = {20, 110, 200, 200, 110, 20, 20};
        int yArray[] = {20, 45, 20, 100, 65, 100, 20};
        g.fillPolygon(xArray, yArray, 7);
    }
```

Another way to create this same applet is to use the API **Polygon** class, which defines a data type that is essentially an ordered collection of points. After creating a **Polygon** object, you can use the **addPoint( )** method repeatedly to add all the points you want.

This next example creates the same polygon in the context of a complete applet. Note that the polygon is allocated and initialized in the **init( )** method. As mentioned before, it's always more efficient to do things in the **init( )** method if they need to be done only once. Similarly, in the preceding examples, it would have been more efficient to initialize the arrays in the **init( )** method.

Remember that any information communicated between different methods must be represented by class or instance variables and not by local variables. That is the case with the variable poly in this example. As an instance variable, it is declared outside of methods but must be allocated, as well as initialized, in **init( )**.

The **Polygon** class is part of the **java.awt** package, so it is automatically imported by the first **import** statement.

```
import java.awt.*;
import java.applet.*;

public class PolyApp extends Applet {
    Polygon poly;   // Object variable referring to poly
                    // is declared at class level.

    // init() method.
    // All the actions here need to be performed just
    once.
    public void init() {
        poly = new Polygon();
```

```
        poly.addPoint(20, 20);
        poly.addPoint(110, 45);
        poly.addPoint(200, 20);
        poly.addPoint(200, 100);
        poly.addPoint(110, 65);
        poly.addPoint(20, 100);
        poly.addPoint(20, 20);
    }

    // paint() method.
    // The polygon already exists, just needs to be
    redrawn.
    public void paint(Graphics g) {
        g.fillPolygon(poly);
    }
}
```

When the applet is compiled and then loaded by an HTML file, it produces the output shown in Figure 3.7.

Figure 3.7 *Effect of the fillPolygon( ) method*

BLASTING PICTURES TO THE SCREEN

One of the important techniques in graphics programming is to display a stored image from a file or Web site. In Java, displaying images centers on use of the **Image** class. This class defines a data type that represents any kind of stored graphical image. Whereas a **Graphics** object is a temporary handle for a drawing area, an object of type **Image** is persistent. As you'll see here and in later chapters, the **Graphics** and **Image** classes are often used together, but they have distinctly different uses.

The following application loads an image file and displays the image on screen. This application assumes that you have a file named **joe.surf.yellow.small.gif** (this is all one file name) on your disk and that it's located in the directory \java\demo\ImageTest\graphics. If you installed the JDK with \java as your home directory, the file should be in that location.

```
import java.awt.*;
import java.applet.*;

public class ImageApp extends Applet {
     Image joe;

     public void init() {
     String file = "/java/demo/ImageTest/graphics/"
     + "joe.surf.yellow.small.gif";
     joe = getImage(getDocumentBase(), file);
     if (joe == null) {
          System.out.println("joe not found.");
          System.exit(0);
          }
     }

     public void paint(Graphics g) {
          g.drawImage(joe, 0, 0, this);
     }
}
```

The first field in the class is an object variable named joe, of type **Image**. As with all object variables, joe is only a reference; you must assign joe an actual object before it can be useful.

```
Image joe;
```

The statements in the **init( )** method create an image and assign it to joe. First, the code creates a string that specifies the file location and name. Here, the **String** class's concatenation operator (+) helps split the statement into two physical lines for convenience. Following the UNIX convention, Java API methods always use the forward slash (/), rather than backward slashes (\), to separate directory names. The Java interpreter running on the target computer translates file path names as appropriate for the local system.

```
String file = "/java/demo/ImageTest/graphics/"
  + "joe.surf.yellow.small.gif";
```

The next statement calls the applet's **getImage( )** method to load the image file into memory. It also constructs an **Image** object for—and assigns the object to—the variable joe. The first argument must have type **URL**, a class in the **java.net** package. A URL is a uniform resource locator, and it can specify any available Web page. Thus, the **getImage( )** method can easily load image files from remote locations. In this case, all we want is a URL for the local machine. It turns out the applet's **getDocumentBase( )** method returns this URL. The second argument to **getImage( )** specifies the file name.

```
joe = getImage(getDocumentBase(), file);
```

The **getImage( )** method does not need to be called more than once, no matter how many times the image is drawn. Therefore, the call to **getImage( )**, along with the string assignment, is placed in the **init( )** method.

The **paint( )** method is the logical place to do the drawing of the image. The **drawImage( )** method puts up the image in the display area. The first three arguments specify the **Image** object and the x, y coordinates at which to place the image. The coordinates specify the top-left corner of the image relative to the applet's display area.

```
public void paint(Graphics g) {
     g.drawImage(joe, 0, 0, this);
}
```

The fourth argument uses the **this** keyword, which refers to the current object—that is, the object for which the code is being executed. In applet code, **this** simply refers to the applet itself. (Remember that an applet is an object.)

In C++, the this keyword is a pointer to the current object. Java has no pointers, and it treats this as a reference. The C++ equivalent to Java's use of this would be *this.

In any case, the **drawImage( )** method expects an object of type **ImageObserver** as its fourth argument. An image observer is an object that plays a role in the loading of the image. If not all of the image data is available when needed, the image observer says, in effect, "Inform me when more data becomes available." The image observer then updates the image using the new data as it becomes available.

It might be time-consuming to write your own image observer. Fortunately, all applets—as well as all classes derived from **Component**—function as image observers. The easy solution is therefore to give **this** (a reference to the applet) as the fourth argument.

When the applet is first loaded, you'll probably notice that painting joe takes a little time. This is because the file is being loaded into memory while painting happens. However, subsequent painting of joe (try iconizing and then restoring the applet) is very fast.

If you want to, you can cause the application to display the image in one fell swoop. This involves using a media tracker to monitor the loading of the image. To use this approach, make the following changes:

- Add an **implements Runnable** clause to the applet declaration and declare a **MediaTracker** object as an instance variable:

```
public class ImageApp implements Runnable {
MediaTracker tracker;
// Rest of class...
```

- Insert the following lines of code at the very end of the **init( )** method. These statements initialize the media tracker and start a new thread:

```
tracker = new MediaTracker(this);
tracker.addImage(joe, 0);
Thread runner = new Thread(this);
runner.start();
```

- Add the following **run( )** method to your applet class. You *must* use the name "run." This code causes a repaint as soon as loading is complete:

```
// run() method. Defines thread behavior.
    public void run() {
        try {tracker.waitForID(0);}
        catch(InterruptedException e){;}
        repaint();
    }
```

- Rewrite the **paint( )** method so that it doesn't draw the image unless it is completely loaded:

```
public void paint(Graphics g) {
    if (tracker.checkID(0, true))
        g.drawImage(joe, 0, 0, this);
}
```

Many of the concepts used in this code may be new. For now, just go ahead and use the code. The concept of threads, as well as the **try** and **catch** keywords, is introduced in Chapter 5,

"Animation and Threads." You might also look at "MediaTracker Class" in Part V, "API Quick Reference."

The new code uses a two-prong strategy. First, it spins off a separate process, or *thread*, which waits for loading to finish. This waiting happens by calling the **waitForID()** method. As soon as loading is complete, the thread causes an immediate repaint and dies—this is all it does.

Second, the code for **paint( )** is altered so that image drawing is prevented during loading. This is necessary because it's possible for repaints to occur at any time. The call to **checkID** returns a Boolean: before loading is complete, this method returns **false**. After that, it always returns **true**.

GRABBING A GRAPHICS CONTEXT (SCRIBBLE)

This section features the Java version of the now-famous Scribble app (harking back to my Visual Basic days).

In most applets and applications, you use a graphics object within **paint( )** and then forget it. For certain kinds of applications, however, you need to grab the graphics object and do a quick operation directly to the display. The Scribble applet does just that: every time the mouse moves, Scribble grabs the graphics object and draws a line.

The Scribble applet has several key features:

- It uses **mouseMove( )** and **mouseEnter( )** to handle mouse actions. The next chapter, "Components and Events," has more to say about event handlers and the flow of events.
- It grabs the graphics object directly by calling the applet's **getGraphics( )** method. Scribble would be too slow if you had to wait for a repaint after each mouse move.
- It releases the graphics object quickly by calling the graphics object's **dispose( )** method. This forces the release of the graphics context associated with the object.

The use of **dispose( )** is key to the smooth working of the applet. If you attempt to write Scribble without calling this method, you may find (as I did) that after a large number of mouse moves, the applet locks up. The **dispose( )** method ensures that the graphics context is immediately released back to the system. Be advised, though: once **dispose( )** is called, the graphics object cannot be used again until the next call to **getGraphics( )**.

Here is the complete code for Scribble:

```
import java.awt.*;
import java.applet.*;

public class Scribble extends Applet {
     int oldX, oldY;

     public boolean mouseMove(Event evt, int x, int y) {
          Graphics g = getGraphics();
          g.drawLine(oldX, oldY, x, y);
          g.dispose();
          oldX = x;
          oldY = y;
          return true;
     }

     public boolean mouseEnter(Event evt, int x, int y) {
          oldX = x;
          oldY = y;
          return true;
     }
}
```

After you read Chapter 5, you should be able to figure out how to restore the display by replenishing from an offscreen buffer. This technique involves drawing simultaneously to the screen and the buffer after each mouse move and then overriding **paint( )** so that it copies the buffer to the screen. This approach enables Java to correctly restore the display after resizing or iconizing, something it cannot do now.

Figure 3.8 shows a sample Scribble display.

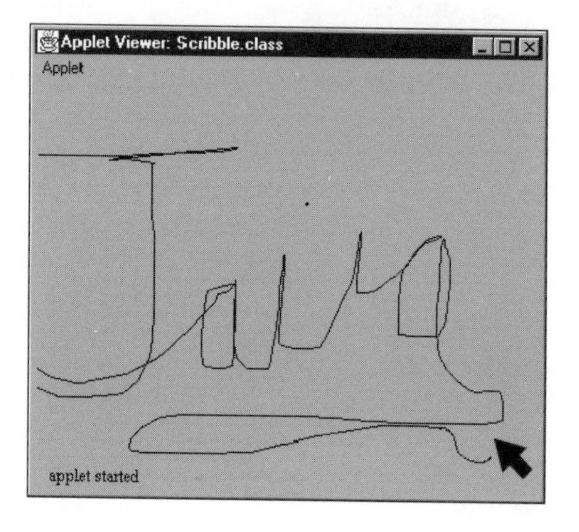

Figure 3.8 *The famous Scribble applet*

CHAPTER FOUR

Components and Events

Drawing everything from scratch is usually the hard way to do things. For most programs, you'll want to take advantage of Java's built-in graphical objects. These objects are provided in Java's Abstract Windowing ToolKit (AWT), a set of classes provided in the **java.awt** package. In fact, you've already used the AWT, because graphics are also a part of this package.

The AWT provides easy ways to create dialog boxes, text boxes, buttons, scroll bars, and many other kinds of graphical objects, called *components*. As in other GUI systems, these objects interact with the user and respond to events. But there's more. Java's layout managers, which you'll learn about in this chapter, actually place the components on the screen for you.

THE JAVA AWT HIERARCHY

Before we dive into the world of components and events, it's useful to understand how components relate to the elements presented in the last few chapters. Figure 4.1 shows the part of the Java API class hierarchy that includes components and applets.

The relationships in Figure 4.1 are not physical ones; this hierarchy relates to inheritance. (See the next section for an explanation of inheritance.) The **Applet** class has the characteristics of all the classes it inherits from.

The **Applet** class inherits many of its most important methods, including **paint( )**, from the **Component** class. When you look up **Applet** in Part V, "API Quick Reference," you may often need to consult **Component** to find a method.

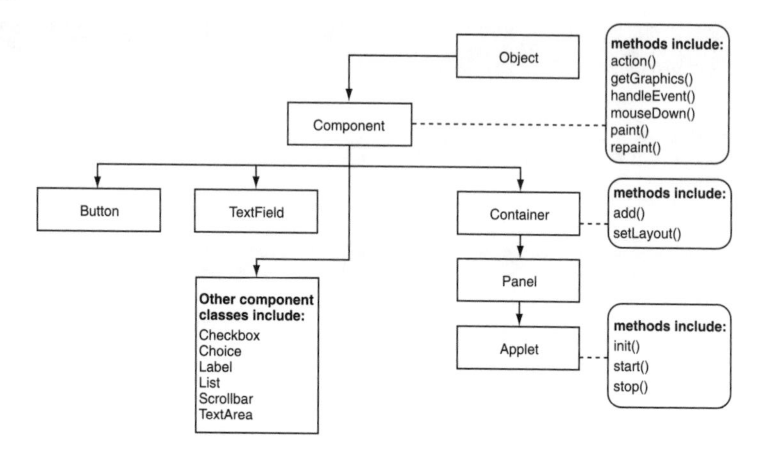

Figure 4.1 *Components and applets in the class hierarchy*

The **Applet** class also inherits from the **Container** class, which provides the ability to physically contain other components. Any class that inherits from **Container** can create objects that function as containers: a container can hold other objects within its borders. Thus, an applet can contain other components.

Finally, the **Applet** class inherits from **Panel**. A *panel* is a window subsection not marked by a physical border. If you look at an applet closely, you'll see that it does not completely occupy all the space inside the browser or appletviewer. An applet has characteristics of a component, a container, *and* a panel.

NOTE

Java does not support multiple inheritance, so each class has only one direct superclass. However, a class may have many indirect superclasses (ancestors), as is the case here.

Figure 4.1 suggests how important the **Component** class is. In theory, you can write a **paint( )** method for any component and perform graphics operations. Of course, many components have built-in displays, such as a label on a button, so you won't want to override **paint( )** in those cases. You might, however, want to override **paint( )** for a panel, which by default is blank.

BACKGROUND: INHERITANCE

If you've been programming in C++ or another object-oriented language, feel free to skip this section. If you are a C person or a Basic person or just want a quick review, stick around.

Inheritance is one of the most popular features of object orientation. It is a simple idea, although much theory has been written about it. The first thing you need to know is that inheritance applies to classes; objects are involved only as far as their classes are affected. The rest is easy.

Basically, if class B inherits from class A, B automatically gets all of A's fields. B gets all of A's built-in behavior, because B inherits all of A's methods. The only exception is constructors—B must define its own. The Java interpreter will, by default, call A's default constructor to help create an object of type B. But generally, you should write the appropriate constructors for each individual class.

In Java, the **extends** keyword creates inheritance relationships. Consider three simple classes: A, B, and C. Each class is the *subclass* (or *child* class) of the one before it, and each successive subclass adds additional fields. A subclass need not add new fields, but most of them do. Any declarations in a class either add to or override the fields of its *superclass* (or *parent* class).

```
class A {
     int a, b;
     void setFields(int newA, int newB) {
          a = newA; b = newB;
     }
}

class B extends A {
     double x, y;
}

class C extends B {
     int c;
```

```
        int getC() {return c}
        setFields (int newA, int newB) {
            a = newA;
            c = b = newB;
        }
}
```

Figure 4.2 shows how these inheritance relationships work. Each successive generation adds new fields. Note that by inheriting from B, C gets all of A's fields as well.

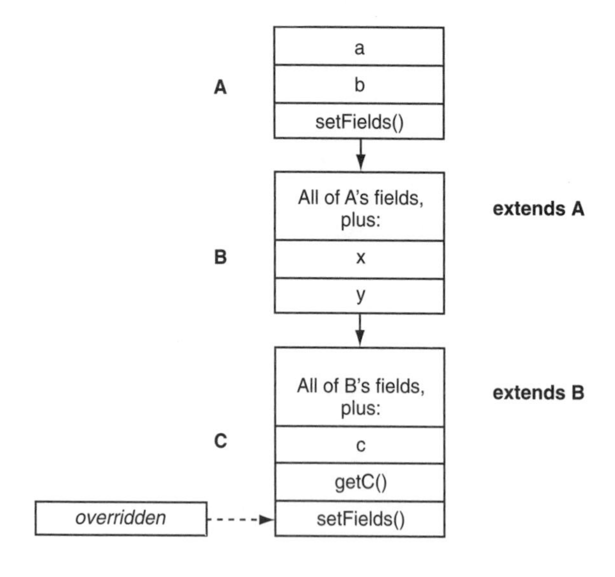

Figure 4.2 *A sample inheritance hierarchy*

There is one other twist in this example. Class C defines the setFields( ) method, even though it was already defined in Class A. (If the argument list differed in type information, they would be separate, overloaded methods, but here they have the same signature.) So in this case, C overrides the definition of setFields( ). This is an important phenomenon in Java. Often, you will customize the behavior of an API class by subclassing that class and then overriding one or more methods. In fact, this is exactly what happens when you write an applet; you subclass the **Applet** class and then override applet methods such as **paint( )** and **init( )**.

Furthermore, this sort of subclassing works because Java observes an important rule (as does C++): anywhere an instance of a class is expected, an instance of a subclass is accepted as well. Thus, the browser or appletviewer expects to create an instance of **Applet**, but you cause it to create an instance of your applet instead—although your applet is actually just a subclass of **Applet**.

For now, the most important thing to remember is that often, some of the most important fields of a class are inherited from ancestor classes. In the case of **Applet**, both **Component** and **Container** contribute important methods. Admittedly, this argument sometimes makes it more difficult to look up a method in the API, because not all the methods are in one place. However, if you clearly understand the purpose and scope of each class in the hierarchy, it's usually clear where to look for a method.

OVERVIEW OF JAVA UIs

Java uses a different model for generating user interfaces (UIs) than you are probably used to. Instead of positioning components on a container by specifying exact size and position, Java uses a *layout manager*. A layout manager sizes and positions all the components according to a general scheme.

"But wait!" you say. "How can Java presume to position my components for me? I know best where they should go!"

If you were creating a user interface for a specific platform, this might be true. But Java is designed to create programs for multiple platforms. When you're developing a program on a Macintosh, you can lay out a user interface so that it looks good on... well, a Macintosh. But other platforms may have different sizes and resolutions. What's more, when you write an applet you may not have any control of the size of the applet window.

Java's solution is to assign a layout manager to each container. (The applet is a container, but Java also supports other kinds of containers, such as windows, panels, and dialog boxes.) The layout manager is an object that determines the size and position of the immediate children. If the size of the container changes, the layout manager repositions everything in the container according to a general scheme.

The basic procedure for creating and displaying a component is simple:

1. Define a variable to refer to the component. (Actually, this step is required only if you need a way to refer to the component later.)
2. Create the component by using the **new** operator.
3. Add the component to a container by calling the container's **add( )** method.

For example, the following statements create a button and add it to a container. The text "Click me!" is displayed on the button. The **Button** constructor sets this text.

```
Button theButton;
// ...
theButton = new Button("Click me!");
theContainer.add(theButton);
```

The order in which you add components affects how the layout manager positions them. For example, if the layout manager is an instance of the **FlowLayout** class, it positions the components from left to right in the order they were created.

Although every container has a default layout manager, you can assign a new layout manager by calling the container's **setLayout( )** method. For example:

```
theContainer.setLayout(new BorderLayout());
```

The Java API provides a series of standard layout-manager classes—**FlowLayout**, **BorderLayout**, **GridLayout**, and **GridBagLayout**—but it is possible to write your own. The topic "Using Alternative Layouts," at the end of this chapter, provides more information.

AN APPLET WITH COMPONENTS

Applets aren't the only kind of graphical programs Java can produce. But let's first look at how an applet with components works. Later, we'll examine an application with the same components.

The following applet, simple as it is, demonstrates issues common to much more complex applets. This one features two text boxes, labels for the text boxes, and a command button.

```
import java.awt.*;
import java.applet.*;

public class ConvApplet extends Applet {
// Instance variables for components.
// These must be declared here; if local, then other
methods
//  (to be added later) wouldn't be able to use them.
     Label     labF, labC;
     TextField textF, textC;
     Button    convButton;

     public void init() {
          labF = new Label("Fahr:");
          add(labF);

          textF = new TextField(15);
          add(textF);
```

```
            labC = new Label("Cent:");
            add(labC);

            textC = new TextField(15);
            add(textC);

            convButton = new Button("Convert");
            add(convButton);
        }
}
```

The only method overridden here is **init( )**. It's not necessary to write anything for **paint( )**, because once the five components are added to the applet, they are automatically redrawn as needed.

The code that creates and adds the components is straightforward. Here, I've spaced the statements so that it is easy to see pairs of related statements: the first statement creates a component; the second statement adds it to the applet. The use of the **add( )** method does not need to be qualified here, because it is being applied to the applet itself. Here is the first pair of statements:

```
            labF = new Label("Fahr:");
            add(labF);
```

The argument to the **Label** constructor specifies the label text. In the next pair of statements, the argument to the **TextField** constructor specifies the size in characters.

```
            textF = new TextField(15);
            add(textF);
```

As elsewhere in Java, we must use the **new** operator to allocate an object in memory unless the type is primitive data. (In addition to **new**, you can allocate strings and arrays through the use of string literals and set aggregates.) There is no **delete** operator, because Java cleans up unused memory itself.

To test this applet, I used an HTML file with the following <APPLET> tag:

```
<APPLET code="ConvApplet.class" width=300 height=200>
```

After compiling the applet and running the HTML file, I got the results shown in Figure 4.3. The results on your computer may differ.

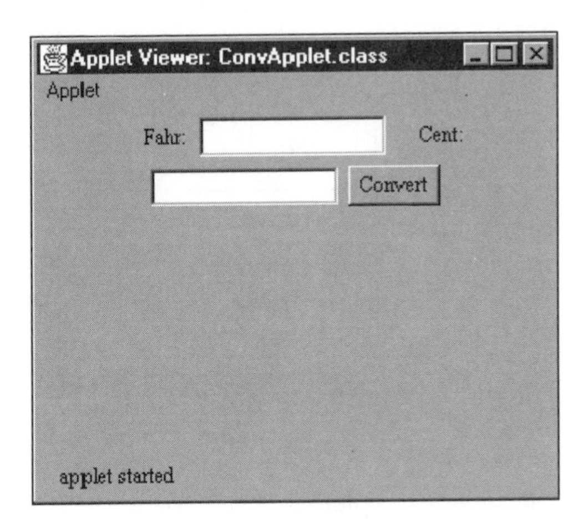

Figure 4.3 *The ConvApplet program, first cut*

This arrangement is clearly unsatisfactory. In fact, it's awful! One of the things that went wrong here is that because no layout manager was specified, Java used the **FlowLayout** manager by default. That style would work fine for some applets, but it doesn't work here.

Another problem is that the labels don't stay with their associated text boxes. This is easy to fix by introducing panels. The applet itself is a panel, and you can create any number of other panels yourself. Essentially, a panel is a container that it is part of another container. There are no visible borders around a panel, but it acts as a grouping mechanism.

The revised strategy for this application creates a panel around the first two components and a panel around the second. Figure 4.4 shows the resulting container/component relationships.

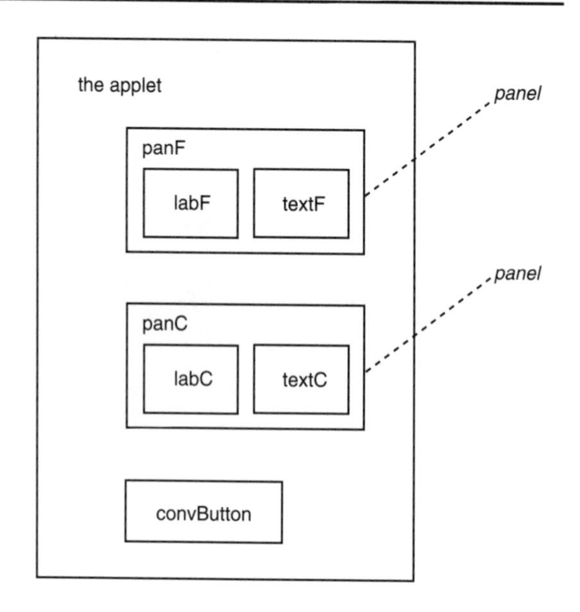

Figure 4.4 *Container relationships involving panels*

The following revised applet code uses panels and the **BorderLayout** class. Because an object of this class is in use, components are added to the applet in specific zones, or anchors. The zones determine what part of the applet a component is attached to: "North," "South," "East," "West," or "Center."

The labels and the text boxes are not added directly to the applet but rather are added to panels. Remember that panels are containers as well as components of the applet. Each panel retains its own layout manager, so *within* the panels, the zones are not used. When a component is added to a panel, the **add( )** method must be qualified, as in "panF.add(textF)."

```
import java.awt.*;

import java.applet.*;
```

```
public class ConvApplet extends Applet {
     Panel      panF, panC;
     Label      labF, labC;
     TextField textF, textC;
     Button     convButton;

     public void init() {
          setLayout(new BorderLayout());

          panF = new Panel();
          panC = new Panel();

          labF = new Label("Fahr:");
          panF.add(labF);           // Add to panel.
          textF = new TextField(15);
          panF.add(textF);          // Add to panel.
          add("North", panF);       // Add panel to applet.

          labC = new Label("Cent:");
          panC.add(labC);           // Add to panel.
          textC = new TextField(15);
          panC.add(textC);          // Add to panel.
          add("Center", panC);      // Add panel to applet.

          convButton = new Button("Convert");p
          add("South", convButton);
     }
}
```

Figure 4.5 shows the final look of the applet.

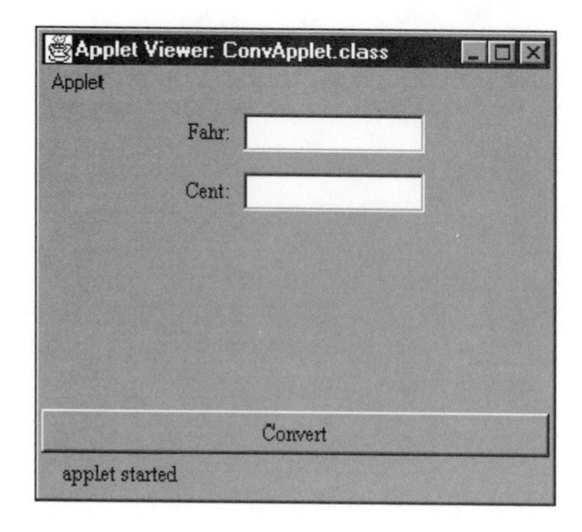

Figure 4.5 *Applet using panels and BorderLayout*

RESPONDING TO EVENTS

Interactive Web pages and applications can react to user actions. This is what *events* are all about. An event is an occurrence—typically a user action of some kind—that a component can respond to in one of its methods. In Java, events flow from one component to another until a component handles the event and returns **true**.

Mouse clicks and keystrokes are among the more interesting events. Button actions are among the simplest, and that's what we'll focus on in this chapter.

Responding to an Action

A container of a button can handle a button click as an **action( )** event. In the example introduced earlier, the applet is the container of the button convButton. To handle the event, we write an **action( )** method for the applet:

```
public boolean action(Event e, Object arg) {
     if (e.target == convButton) {
          Double temp = new Double(textF.getText());
          double d = temp.doubleValue();
```

```
            d = (d - 32.0 ) / 1.8;
            textC.setText(String.valueOf(d));
            return true;
      }
return false;
}
```

The structure of this method is fairly simple. First, it checks the target of the event to see whether the event happened in the button (convButton). If it did, the method handles the event by doing the following: convert text to a number, d; perform a calculation on d; and display the results.

In Java, there are wrapper classes corresponding to each kind of primitive data. The wrapper class for **double** (double-precision floating point) is the class **Double**. Although a wrapper class represents primitive data, it represents it in the form of an object, so instances of a wrapper must be created with **new** just as any other object is. One of the principal uses of the wrapper classes is to convert between string and numeric data. Figure 4.6 shows how data conversion works in this program.

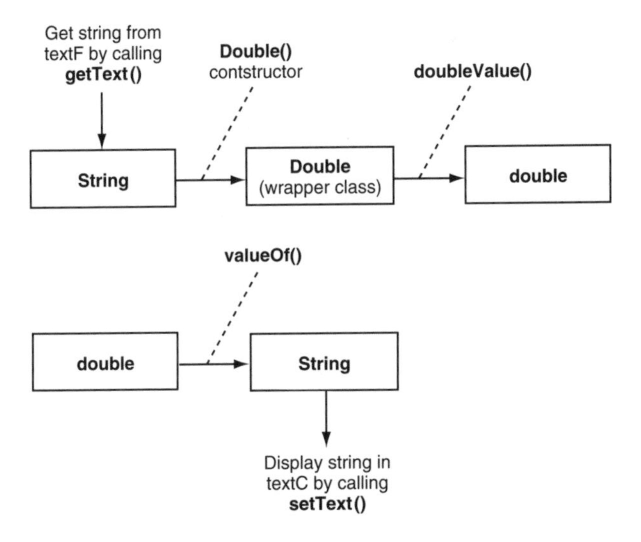

Figure 4.6 *Converting between string and numeric data*

In this example, the methods **setText( )** and **getText( )** transfer data in and out of text fields. These methods are fields of the **TextField** class. Other methods include **doubleValue( )**—of the **Double** class (but inherited from **Number**)—and **valueOf( )**, which is a class method of the **String** class. All except the last one are instance methods, meaning that they work on individual objects.

If the code decides to handle the event, it returns **true**. Otherwise, it returns **false**, which causes the Java interpreter to look for another event handler. All event handlers have type **boolean** so that they can indicate whether or not they handled the event.

A shortcut for using String.valueOf(d) is to use the following expression:

```
""+d
```

This expression forces a conversion of d's value to String type.

The Flow of Events

When a user clicks on a blank part of an applet, a **mouseDown** event is generated. So it may strike you as strange that to respond to a button click, you write an **action( )** method and not **mouseDown( )**.

But each type of component generates only certain kinds of events. Applets and panels, for example, generate low-level events such as **mouseDown**, **mouseUp**, **keyDown**, and **keyUp**. Buttons generate **action** events.

As Figure 4.7 illustrates, an applet does not get an **action** event directly. However, after the button generates an **action** event, its default behavior is to pass the event to its container. The container may pass the event to its container, and so on. The process stops only when the top level is reached or when an event handler responds to the event and returns **true**.

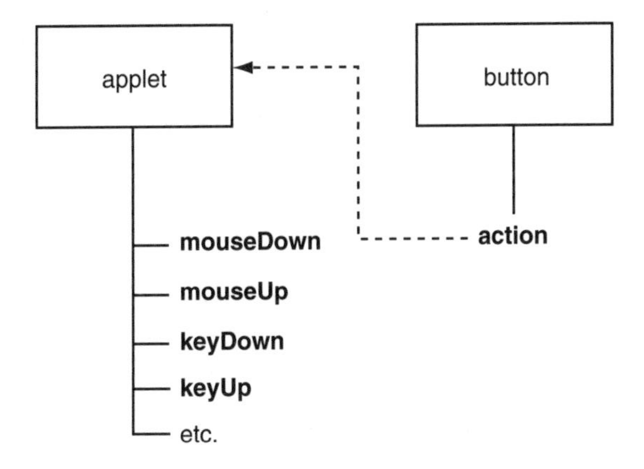

Figure 4.7 *Applet and button events*

For this reason, an applet can respond to any action generated by any of its components. An event eventually flows up to the applet if it isn't handled by the component. This arrangement is convenient, because it helps you centralize all your event-handling code in one class.

You could have written an event handler inside the button class. This technique requires more coding and is usually unnecessary, because the **action** event flows up to the applet. If you handled the event inside the button, you would need to follow these steps:

1. Write your own button class by subclassing **Button**.
2. Write a constructor for your class. Use the **super** keyword to invoke the superclass constructor:

   ```
   MyButton(String text) { super(text); }
   ```

3. In the applet code, use your button class to create the object:

   ```
   MyButton convButton;
   ...
   convButton = new MyButton("Convert");
   ```

4. In your subclass, write the **action( )** method. You might need to call **getParent( )** to get a reference to the applet, which in turn would give you access to other components.

Within each component, there is another kind of event flow. When an event occurs, control first passes to the **handleEvent( )** method for the component. This method takes as its argument an **Event** object that contains complete information about the event, including the event ID. The default behavior for **handleEvent( )** is to test the event ID and then call the appropriate method for the specific event: for example, it calls **action( )** if the ID is **ACTION_EVENT**, **mouseDown( )** if the ID is **MOUSE_DOWN**, and so on.

The **Event** class defines many useful constants, including the event IDs and keystroke codes. See "Event Class" in Part V, "API Quick Reference."

You can override **handleEvent( )** and use it as a generic event handler if you choose. Remember that **handleEvent( )** must return **true** or **false** to indicate whether it handled the event. For events not handled directly, you should call the default handler (which is defined in the superclass) by returning **super.handleEvent( ).**

```
// This version of handleEvent() prints a diagnostic if an
// action event was received, but otherwise behaves normally.

public boolean handleEvent(Event e) {
     if (e.id == Event.ACTION_EVENT) {
          System.out.println("Action event received.");
          return action(e, e.arg);
     }
     return super.handleEvent(e); // Call default handler.
}
```

When testing for event IDs, remember that the ID constants are class fields of the **Event** class. These constants must be qualified as **Event.***constant*, as with **Event.ACTION_EVENT** in the example.

In summary, here is how an event is handled:

1. The user performs an action, such as clicking the mouse.
2. The affected component determines what kind of event is generated, if any. This happens automatically and is a built-in feature of components. For example, a button recognizes a mouse click as an **action** event.
3. Java calls the component's **handleEvent( )** method, passing an **Event** object that contains information describing the event (including the event ID).
4. Unless overridden, the **handleEvent( )** method calls the specific event handler for the component, such as **action( )** or **mouseDown( )**, depending on the event ID.
5. If the event is handled, **handleEvent( )** returns **true**. Otherwise, it returns **false**, causing the event to be sent to the container, with steps 3, 4, and 5 then repeated. The type of the event remains the same. Thus, a button's **action** event is still an **action** event even when it reaches the applet.

More About the Action Event

Every type of component responds to user actions in different ways. **Button** objects, for example, respond to mouse clicks by generating an **action** event. **TextField** objects generate an **action** event when the user presses the **Enter** key. A **TextField** object also generates **KeyDown** and **KeyUp** events as the user types individual keys, letting you filter input if you choose. Note that with text components, it is not necessary to override event handlers just to enable the standard editing capabilities.

Table 4.1 summarizes the meaning of the **action** events for the five types of components that generate them. Generally speaking, the **action** event indicates that the user has made a choice or selection of some kind. In some programs, just handling the **action** event gives you sufficient interaction with the user.

Table 4.1 How the action event works with various components

COMPONENT TYPE	ACTION CAUSED BY	TYPE AND CONTENT OF THE SECOND ARGUMENT
Button	Clicking the button	**String**, containing name of the button
Checkbox	Clicking check box on or off	**boolean**, containing on/off state (true = selected)
Choice	Selecting a new item	**String**, containing the name of the item
List	Double-clicking an item	**String**, containing the name of the item
TextField	Pressing the **Return** key	**String**, containing the text box contents

AN APPLICATION WITH COMPONENTS

It's easy to write an application that does everything that an applet can do, including graphics operations and adding components. Here's one way to write the application:

1. Instead of subclassing **Applet**, write your applet code as a subclass of **Frame**.
2. Add an event handler that exits the application when the **WINDOW_DESTROY** event occurs. The user causes this event by attempting to close the frame window.
3. Write a class containing **main( )**. In the definition for **main( )**, do the following: create an object of your **Frame** subclass and then call the **init( )**, **resize( )**, and **show( )** methods for that object.

Note that **init( )** is not a method you inherit from **Frame**, but you can always write an **init( )** method anyway. In this case, it's convenient to use an **init( )** method; if you're adapting code from an applet, you probably already have an **init( )** method definition. However, if you write an application from scratch, it's more efficient to place this same code in a constructor.

Here is a version of ConvApplet written as an application:

```
import java.awt.*;
import java.applet.*;

class ConvPrg {
     public static void main(String args[]) {
          ConvFrame frm = new ConvFrame();
               frm.setTitle("ConvFrame program");
               frm.resize(300, 200);
               frm.init();
               frm.show();
     }
}

class ConvFrame extends Frame {
     public boolean handleEvent(Event e) {
          if (e.id == Event.WINDOW_DESTROY) {
               System.exit(0);
               return true;
          }
          return super.handleEvent(e);
     }

     // Place the rest of the class declarations here.
     // Include all the methods and variables you'd normally
     // put in an applet...
}
```

The **Frame** class inherits from the **Component**, **Container**, and **Window** classes. You can use **Frame**, as is done here, to generate a new window. One of the major differences between user interfaces of applets and those of applications is that in applications, you must generate the initial window yourself. In addition, the application has responsibility for responding to user requests to close the window.

In the **handleEvent( )** method, it's important to call the default handler. Otherwise, events get swallowed rather than routed as normal. The default handler is invoked as a superclass method:

```
return super.handleEvent(e);
```

When you're writing applications, you cannot call API methods that are defined only in the **Applet** class. For example, you cannot call **Applet.getImage( )**. Usually, however, there is an alternative mechanism that you can use in applications. For example, to load an image, first get the frame's toolkit object and then call **getImage( )** through this object. The following method illustrates this technique:

```
// You can add this method to your frame classes to enable
//  frame code to load images.
Image getImage(String filename) {
     Toolkit tk = getToolkit();
     return tk.getImage(filename);
}
```

For more information on the **Toolkit** class, see Part V, "API Quick Reference."

USING ALTERNATIVE LAYOUTS

The default layout manager for each container is an instance of the **FlowLayout** class. You can, however, specify a different layout manager for any given container by calling the container's **setLayout( )** method. The argument to the method is an instance of one of the layout classes: the instance must first be instantiated (by using **new**) before being passed to **setLayout( )**. For example, the following statement sets the layout manager for the current applet:

```
setLayout(new GridLayout(3,3));
```

Each individual container has its own layout manager. This arrangement provides maximum flexibility. In the ConvApplet3 example presented earlier in the chapter, the applet uses the **BorderLayout** class while the panels within the applet continue to use the default, **FlowLayout**.

It is possible to write your own layout class. Every layout class must implement the **LayoutManager** interface. To implement an interface, you provide definitions for all the functions declared in the interface. Basically, an interface is a set of services, which are represented by its methods. Every class can implement the services in different ways. For more information, see the topic "Interface Keyword" in Part II and "LayoutManager Interface" in Part V, "API Quick Reference."

NOTE

Programs should never call any of the methods defined in the LayoutManager interface. These methods are for internal use only.

The next few sections describe the layout-manager classes provided in the API.

FlowLayout

A **FlowLayout** object (which is the default) arranges components from left to right in the order they were added to the container. This layout manager treats components almost like text. After the right edge of the container is reached, the layout manager positions the next component at the left edge, starting in a new row.

One of the **FlowLayout** constructors lets you specify alignment using constants defined in the **FlowLayout** class: **CENTER**, **LEFT**, and **RIGHT**. Another constructor lets you specify alignment as well as horizontal and vertical gaps between components.

BorderLayout

A **BorderLayout** object places components in several different zones that relate to the container's borders: "North," "South," "East," "West," and "Center." These zones are also called *anchors*. Adding a component in the "South" zone, for example, guarantees that it will be attached to the bottom part of the container, no matter how the container is resized.

Use of a **BorderLayout** object is ideal for containers that need to have certain components placed specifically on the top, bottom, or side. For example, in a paint program you might want to position a toolbox or palette on the right side of the display area. Another use of **BorderLayout** might be to position a set of button commands along the top or the bottom. Although only one component should be placed in each zone, that component can itself be a container holding several components.

Zones are not equal. The layout manager allocates the top and bottom first and then the sides. The "Center" zone gets everything that remains. Figure 4.8 shows a general picture of this layout.

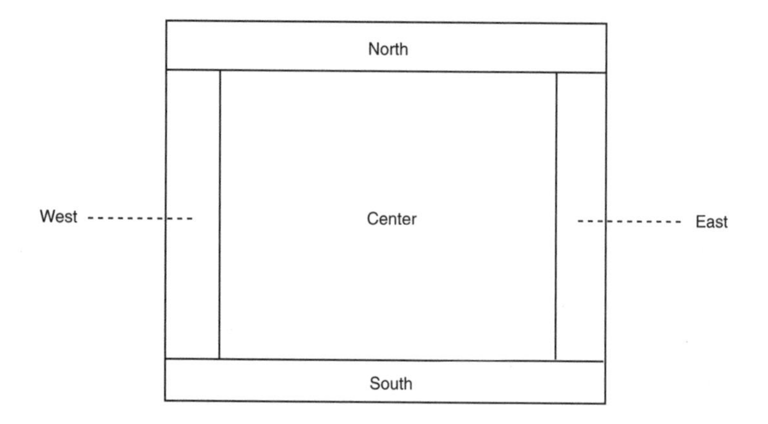

Figure 4.8 *The BorderLayout scheme*

CardLayout

A **CardLayout** object simulates a HyperCard user interface, which looks like a stack of objects in which no more than one component is fully visible at a time. You call methods of the **CardLayout** class to show the next component (or "card"), the previous one, the first one, or the last one. Use of this layout class is particularly appropriate for programs such as a card file or Rolodex. Usually, this layout works best when you have a collection of components that have the same type, such as a set of frames, panels, or text areas.

GridLayout

A **GridLayout** object positions components in a two-dimensional grid. The rows and columns are specified in the **GridLayout** constructor. The grid is not divided by visible lines. However, as much as possible, components align into rows and columns.

As with **FlowLayout**, a **GridLayout** object arranges components in the order they were added to the container, starting at the left and moving to a new row when the current row is filled. The principal difference is that a **GridLayout** object maintains a set number of components per row.

GridBagLayout

The **GridBagLayout** class is roughly similar to the **GridLayout** class, but it is much more sophisticated. Using this class requires more coding, but it allows maximum flexibility in positioning and sizing your components. Like the **GridLayout** class, **GridBagLayout** uses a series of rows and columns that determine sizes and alignment but are not delineated by visible lines.

You adjust sizes by attaching a constraint to each component. A *constraint* is an object of the **GridBadConstraint** class, and each constraint specifies a number of attributes, including the position, the size of the component in terms of grid cells, the margins, whether or not the component grows in size when the container does, and other information. See "GridBagConstraint Class" and "GridBagLayout Class" in Part V, "API Quick Reference."

CHAPTER FIVE

Animation and Threads

Animation is a word that shares a root with *animal* and *animate*. And no wonder—animated objects, like animals, have the power to move of their own accord. When you use Java's animation capabilities, you can create objects that move around the screen without prompting by the user. Although this book doesn't go into the fine points of advanced animation, you can apply similar animation techniques to animate an object in place. The animation in this chapter moves an object around the screen.

In Java, animation requires the use of *threads*, a concept explained in this chapter. The thread capability is one of the features of the Java API that harness the powers of modern computers. Although threads are called *processes* on some systems, the basic idea is the same: a thread is a background task that runs independently of the main program. Like a second-unit director in a movie company, a thread goes off and works on its own schedule.

THE JAVA THREAD/ANIMATION MODEL

In Java, animation is handled by a second thread (see Figure 5.1). (If you need more background, skip ahead to the next section, "Background: Threads.") You create this second thread by using the **Thread** class. You can have as many extra threads as you have thread objects. First, create an object of the **Thread** class and then call its **start( )** method. In response to **start( )**, the Java interpreter calls your **run( )** method, which you can define in the same class that starts the thread. The **run( )** method is the starting point for all threads other than the program's main thread.

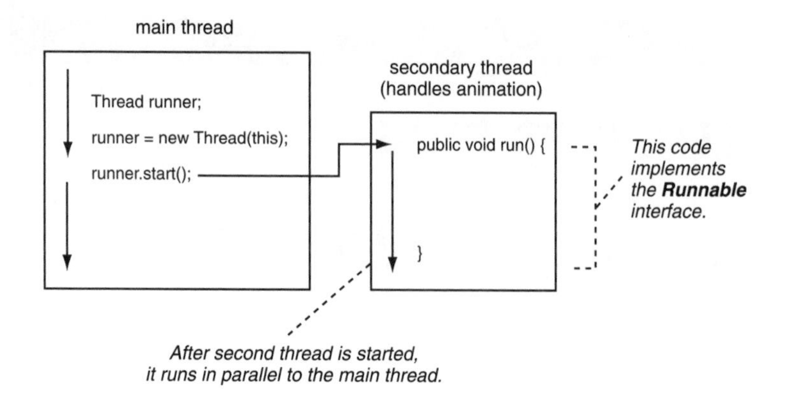

Figure 5.1 *The Java thread programming model*

Creating a Thread

Figure 5.1 includes what may at first look like a strange line of code:

```
runner = new Thread(this);
```

In plain English, what this statement means is this:

When runner starts, use the **run( )** *method defined in this class.*

The argument to the **Thread** constructor is significant because of the object's class. Java looks at the object's class to find a **run( )** method there. The **run( )** method gets associated with this particular thread.

The **this** keyword refers to the applet itself. (In general, **this** refers to the current object.) Therefore, in this example, Java uses the **run( )** method defined in the applet class.

Suppose you specified a different object in the constructor:

```
runner2 = new Thread(threadDirector);
```

In this case, Java would look at threadDirector and determine its class. Then, when runner2 was started, it would call the **run( )** method defined in threadDirector's class.

Java is flexible when it comes to creating multiple threads with different behavior. For each thread, you can specify a different object and therefore a different **run( )** method (unless, of course, the objects are of the same class).

Implementing the Runnable Interface

There's one more piece to the puzzle of thread behavior. The previous section described how a class defines thread behavior by defining a **run( )** method:

public void run( ) {

Put_your_thread_behavior_here

}

Only one other thing is required: the class that includes this method must declare that it implements the **Runnable** interface. This is easily done with the **implements** keyword.

Java uses the term *interface* in a special way. (Actually, it is nearly identical to the concept as used in Microsoft's Component Object Model.) An interface is a set of services that a class agrees to implement. These "services" are actually abstract methods. A class implements these methods by providing definitions for them.

In the case of the **Runnable** interface, a class must implement just one method: **run( )**. In effect, implementing **Runnable** is a way of saying, "I agree to provide a definition for **run( )**." Requiring that a class implement **Runnable** is Java's way of making sure that a **run( )** method can be called when a thread is started.

Interfaces have many other uses in Java. For more information, see the topic "Interfaces" in Part II.

BACKGROUND: THREADS

Java threads are no different from multithread programming concepts on other systems. If you're familiar with the concept, you can safely skip this section.

What Is a Thread?

Modern computer systems have multitasking capability that enables several programs to run at once. In actuality, the programs aren't running at the same time (unless the computer has parallel processors), but the processor switches so quickly between programs that they appear to run simultaneously. What's more, each program can proceed, usually at acceptable speed, without waiting for the other programs to terminate.

Threads are a special form of multitasking. They introduce the following twist: when a program is multithreaded, two or more tasks can be running that originate in the same program. The upshot of this is that a single program can cause multiple activities to occur simultaneously. This capability is useful if a program needs to print a document or do intense computation in the background, for example, while still managing to interact with the user in a timely manner.

All programs automatically have at least one thread. This thread, which we might call the main thread, is the one that starts when the program is loaded into memory. To add a second, third, or fourth thread, a program uses the **Thread** class and the **Runnable** interface.

Why Are Threads Needed for Animation?

In the old world of MS-DOS programming—if you ever programmed in MS-DOS—you could act as if you were the only game in town. If you wanted to show an animation demo, for example, you probably just went ahead and did it. But GUI systems require everyone to be a good citizen, and Java is no exception.

Even after your applet starts an animation effect, it should continue being fully responsive to the user. Maybe the user will want to pull down the Applet menu, for example, or perform an action to close the applet window. But if your applet or application were single-threaded and went into an infinite loop to do animation, it would no longer be able to respond to methods such as **paint( )**, **action( )**, or **handleEvent( )**. From the user's point of view, the UI would suddenly become inoperable.

Multithreading is the solution. After the animator thread is started, it can go off and do its own thing. The main thread continues, running in parallel, all the time responding to user actions. The secondary thread goes off and does the fun stuff, while the main thread sticks around to interact with the user. If the user resizes the applet window, for example, the main thread is the one that calls **paint( )** in response to that event. The animator thread doesn't know anything about it.

THE BASIC ANIMATION APPLET

Once you understand the use of threads in Java, it's easy to start writing applets that use animation techniques. Most animated applets use the same template.

NOTE

You can write animated applications as well as animated applets. You can adapt the applet code here to work in an application, as described in Chapter 4, "Components and Events." However, applications generally do not have start( ) and stop( ) methods.

The following applet contains the basic code for animation. In a real example, you would substitute a value for time_delay, which specifies a delay in milliseconds. But otherwise you can use this same code.

```
import java.awt.*;
import java.applet.*;

public class Animator extends Applet implements Runnable {
     Thread runner;

     public void start() {
          runner = new Thread(this);
          runner.start();
     }

     public void stop() {
          runner.stop();
     }
```

```
    public void run() {
        while(true) {
            // Advance animation and cause repaint.
            try {Thread.sleep(time_delay);}
            catch (InterruptedException e){;}
        }
    }

    public void paint(Graphics g) {
        // Paint current animation
    }
}
```

Much of what you see here is standard code for creating, starting, stopping, and pausing the animation thread. You can use this standard code in one applet after another. Here, I've named this thread "runner," although you can give it any name you like.

Much of this code is necessary because the browser or appletviewer program calls the applet in response to user actions. Table 5.1 summarizes applet methods that get called and describes how an animated applet should respond.

Table 5.1 *Applet methods that the animation thread should respond to*

APPLET METHOD	SITUATION AND RECOMMENDED RESPONSE
init( )	The applet has just been loaded into memory. This is the logical place to allocate objects owned by the applet.
start( )	Either the applet has just started or else the user is resuming operation after making the applet pause. Although you can check the thread's state and choose to suspend the thread when it is paused, it is usually sufficient (and simpler) to create a new thread.
stop( )	The user has caused the applet to suspend operation, possibly by pulling down a menu or clicking the title bar. Calling the thread's **stop()** method ends thread execution.

The real animation work takes place in the **run( )** and **paint( )** methods. The **run( )** method includes some interesting code you may not have seen before:

```
while(true) {
        // Advance animation and cause repaint.
        try {Thread.sleep(time_delay);}
        catch (InterruptedException e){;}
}
```

This method employs the **try** and **catch** keywords, which are part of the Java exception-handling syntax. If this seems complex or alien right now, don't worry. Just include the **try** and **catch** statements as they appear here, substituting a time_delay value of your choice. This value is in milliseconds (thousandths of a second). For example, if you wanted the applet to pause half a second between each drawing, you would use the value 500.

In case you're curious, here's what's going on: the **sleep( )** method causes the current thread to go to sleep for the specified number of milliseconds. When the interval elapses, the system wakes up the thread. In the meantime, however, it's possible that something might interrupt the thread before it is scheduled to wake. Such a situation generates an exception of type **InterruptedException**. The code must respond to this exception, which it does by using the **catch** keyword. In this case, the exception handler doesn't do anything, although it could (such as printing an error message).

Java does not require all exceptions to be handled, by the way. Exception handling is optional for exceptions derived from the **RuntimeException** class. But the **InterruptedException** type is not derived from **RuntimeException**, so it must be handled or the Java compiler complains.

For more information on exception handling, see the topic "Exception Handling" in Part II. See also Appendix A, which lists mandatory and optional exceptions.

Java's rules for exception handling are nearly the same as those for ANSI C++. The principal difference is that Java requires that exception classes be derived, directly or indirectly, from the Throwable class.

A CONCRETE EXAMPLE

The following example creates a simple animation: a big black dot that moves down and across the screen. Most of this example is the same as the code template in the previous section. The additions are the definition of two coordinate variables, x and y; statements in the **run( )** method that increment these values and force a repaint; and a call to the **fillOval( )** method to draw the dot.

Be forewarned that you will almost certainly see a noticeable flickering when you run the applet. Don't worry. We'll take care of that problem in the next section, "Smoothing Out the Animation."

```
import java.awt.*;
import java.applet.*;

public class Animator extends Applet implements Runnable {
     Thread runner;
     int x, y;    // Current coordinates of the dot

     public void init() {
          x = y = 0;   // Start in top left corner.
     }

     public void start() {
          runner = new Thread(this);
          runner.start();
     }

     public void stop() {
          runner.stop();
     }

     public void run() {
          while(true) {
               x += 4;     // Move x to new location.
               y += 4;     // Move y to new location.
```

```
            repaint(); // Force a repaint now.
            try {Thread.sleep(250);}  // Pause .25 secs.
            catch (InterruptedException e){;}
        }
    }

    public void paint(Graphics g) {
        g.fillOval(x, y, 50, 50);   // Paint the dot.
    }
}
```

In this example, I have commented all statements that involve some change or addition to the basic animation code template. Uncommented lines, in this case, are part of the template.

SMOOTHING OUT THE ANIMATION

You may feel that the annoying flickering of the dot in the last example spoiled the fun. In a nutshell, this flickering is caused by inefficient drawing and redrawing of the dot and its surrounding background. The techniques for smooth animation presented in the next sections have the effect of updating the screen much more efficiently.

Not all animation presents the complex challenges of a moving image. For example, if a figure stays in place but displays changing pictures, you need only do the following: clip the picture's area before redrawing (this will be the same rectangle every time) and then override **update( )** so that it all it does is call **paint( )**.

The techniques presented in the next two sections—clipping and double buffering—are not dependent on each other. Sometimes using just one or the other is enough. Double buffering is the more powerful technique, and you can often get good results using it alone. On my system, I found that the animation ran 10 percent faster using both techniques rather than using double buffering only. A slightly more optimal performance, therefore, was achieved by using both of them.

Technique 1: Clipping

The technique of *clipping* restricts repainting to as small an area as possible. In the example presented earlier, the applet redraws the entire display just to repaint the dot. A much better approach is to determine exactly what needs to be redrawn and then call the **clipRect( )** graphics method to limit the repainting.

This technique is straightforward. Obviously, the old dot needs to be erased and a new one drawn at the new location. If you merge the two affected areas, you get the total area that requires repainting. Figure 5.2 shows how this clipping area is determined. Note that the resulting area must be in the shape of a rectangle, so the corners are filled out.

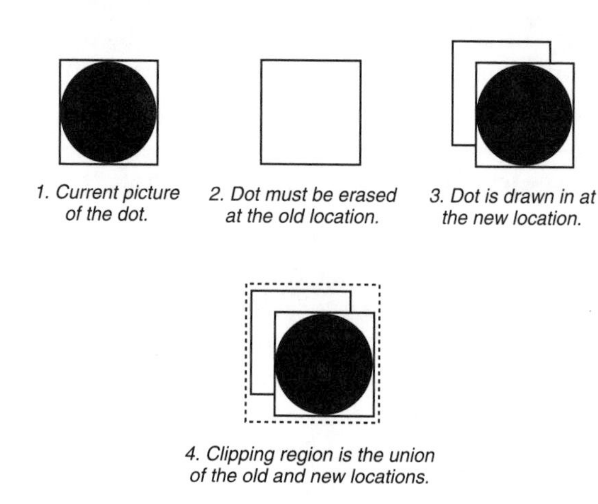
1. Current picture of the dot.
2. Dot must be erased at the old location.
3. Dot is drawn in at the new location.
4. Clipping region is the union of the old and new locations.

Figure 5.2 *Determining the clipping rectangle*

Technique 2: Double Buffering

The default behavior for updating the screen does the following:

1. Fill the display area with the background color.
2. Call the **paint( )** method to draw foreground lines, text, figures, and so on.

This approach is fine for static displays, where the graphics are repainted once in a while. But for animation programs, which may replenish images several times a second, it involves too much redrawing.

Animation should be as smooth as possible. Ideally, the image and its surrounding background should be painted together in a single drawing operation. The solution is *double buffering*, a technique that uses an offscreen image stored in memory.

With double buffering, the program paints into this offscreen image, drawing and redrawing as necessary. Then, when the image is complete, the code blasts it to the screen in a single smooth operation. Figure 5.3 summarizes double buffering as a two-step process.

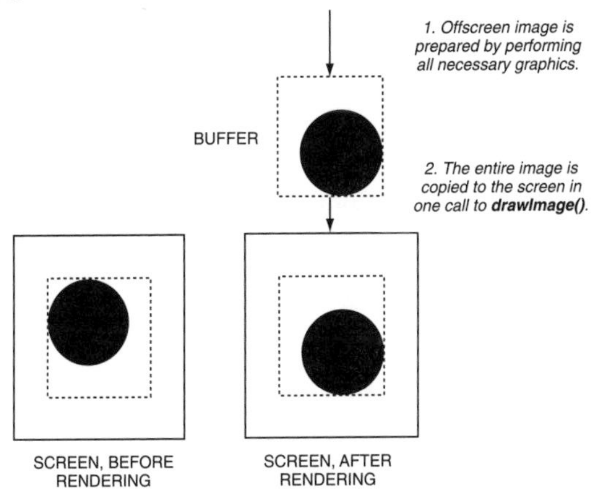

Figure 5.3 *Animating movement through double buffering*

Remember that screen operations are costly both in time and in the effect on the eye. Buffering is a way of achieving screen-access economy.

The Revised Animation Code

The following code shows the clipping and double-buffering techniques in use together. Combining these techniques makes for the fastest, smoothest animation possible with Java.

First, some new instance variables are added to the applet:

```
Image buffer;
int curw, curh;
```

The **Image** object, named buffer, is the offscreen drawing area. Its dimensions are made to match the applet's width and height, stored in curw and curh, respectively. If these dimensions change for any reason (the user might resize the applet, for example), buffer must be resized immediately.

Aside from the variable definitions, all the new code is in the **run( )** method, shown next. This code introduces a couple of important techniques. After determining the clipping region, it writes to the buffer by getting the buffer's graphics object and calling **update( )**, passing the object as an argument. This approach tricks the applet into updating the buffer instead of the screen. Then the code blasts the image to the screen by getting the applet's graphics object and calling **drawImage( )**. It does not wait for a repaint, which would be too slow.

Both operations use the **getGraphics( )** method. As I mentioned in Chapter 3, you cannot get a valid graphics object by calling the **Graphics** constructor directly. But any component or image will gladly pass you its **Graphics** object if you call **getGraphics( )**.

```
public void run() {
          while(true) {
// Create new buffer if none exists OR if applet is resized.
               if ( (buffer == null) ||
                    (curw != size().width) ||
                    (curh != size().height) )
               {
                    buffer = createImage(size().width,
                              size().height);
                    curw = size().width;
                    curh = size().height;
               }

// Determine clipping region.
          Rectangle oldRect = new Rectangle(x, y, 51, 51);
               x += 4;
               y += 4;
```

```
                Rectangle newRect = new Rectangle(x, y, 51, 51);
                Rectangle r = newRect.union(oldRect);

// Update offscreen buffer instead of the screen.
                Graphics g = buffer.getGraphics();
                g.clipRect(r.x, r.y, r.width, r.height);
                update(g);

// Copy buffer directly to display in a single drawing operation.
                g = getGraphics();
                g.clipRect(r.x, r.y, r.width, r.height);
                g.drawImage(buffer, 0, 0, this);

                try {Thread.sleep(250);}  // Pause .25 secs.
                catch (InterruptedException e){;}
            }
        }
```

Final Touches: Follow the Bouncing Ball

If you take the example from earlier in this chapter and add the variables and the new version of **run( )** as shown in the previous section, you should get smooth movement. (It actually is slightly jerky because it is moving four pixels at a time, but you can experiment with that.) In any event, the flicker should be gone.

This last section adds a finishing touch to make the applet more interesting to watch. Right now, the dot moves down and to the right until it vanishes off the screen, never to return unless the user selects the **Reload** command from the Applet menu. (Boring.) It's much more fun to bounce the ball off the walls of the application. And it's easy—here's how:

- If the left edge of the dot is at coordinate zero or less, start moving right.
- If the right edge of the dot is equal to or greater than the right edge of the applet (indicated by the applet's width), start moving left.
- Otherwise, continue in the current direction.
- Make similar adjustments along the y axis.

To make these adjustments, horizontal and vertical movement are controlled by the instance variables deltaX and deltaY, respectively. The values are adjusted, if needed, after each movement.

Here's the completed applet, in its entirety, using deltaX and deltaY to control movement:

```
import java.awt.*;
import java.applet.*;

public class Animator extends Applet implements Runnable {
     Thread runner;
     int x, y;    // Current coordinates of the dot
     Image buffer;
     int curw, curh;
     int deltaX, deltaY;  // Current direction of move

     public void init() {
          x = y = 0;   // Start in top left corner.
          deltaX = deltaY = 4; // Move down and right to start.
     }

     public void start() {
          runner = new Thread(this);
          runner.start();
     }

     public void stop() {
          runner.stop();
```

```
    }

    public void run() {
        while(true) {
// Create new buffer if none exists OR if applet is resized.
            if ( (buffer == null) ||
                    (curw != size().width) ||
                    (curh != size().height) )
            {
                    buffer = createImage(size().width,
                                size().height);
                    curw = size().width;
                    curh = size().height;
            }

// Determine clipping region.
            Rectangle oldRect = new Rectangle(x, y, 51, 51);
            x += deltaX;
            y += deltaY;
            Rectangle newRect = new Rectangle(x, y, 51, 51);
            Rectangle r = newRect.union(oldRect);

// Update offscreen buffer instead of the screen.
            Graphics g = buffer.getGraphics();
            g.clipRect(r.x, r.y, r.width, r.height);
            update(g);

// Copy buffer directly to display in a single drawing operation.
            g = getGraphics();
            g.clipRect(r.x, r.y, r.width, r.height);
            g.drawImage(buffer, 0, 0, this);

// Make directional adjustments if we hit a wall.
```

```
                if (x <= 0)
                    deltaX = 4;
                else if (x + 50 >= size().width)
                    deltaX = -4;
                if (y <= 0)
                    deltaY = 4;
                else if (y + 50 >= size( ).height)
                    deltaY = -4;

                try {Thread.sleep(250);} // Pause .25 secs.
                catch (InterruptedException e){;}
            }
        }

        public void paint(Graphics g) {
            g.fillOval(x, y, 50, 50);  // Paint the dot.
        }
    }
```

CHAPTER SIX

Common Programming Tasks

Compared with C, C++, and Basic, Java does things a little differently. Although many aspects of Java programming are simpler than C++ and Windows, Java's approach to some common tasks is not always obvious. This chapter helps you use Java quickly by summarizing how to accomplish tasks in the following areas:

- Converting between numbers and strings
- Console input and output
- Graphical interface input and output
- Basic file operations

Converting between Numbers and Strings

Typically, data is displayed as a string but crunched as a number. Converting between these formats is therefore a common part of most Java programs. The next three sections survey this topic, which was introduced in Chapter 4, "Components and Events."

String to Integer

Converting a digit string to an integer is easy, because the Java API provides the **Integer.parseInt( )** method to do it in one step. The following example reads the digits in **aString** and stores the value in **i**:

```
int i = Integer.parseInt(aString);
```

The **Long.parseLong( )** method does the same thing except that the result is stored in a long integer:

```
long lng = Long.parseLong(aString);
```

These two methods, **parseInt( )** and **parseLong( )**—are *class* methods and can be used almost like global functions. No object creation is required.

String to Floating Point

Reading a floating-point string requires two-steps:

1. Create a **Double** object initialized from the string
2. Use the **doubleValue( )** method to convert from object to primitive data.

Figure 6.1 illustrates this process.

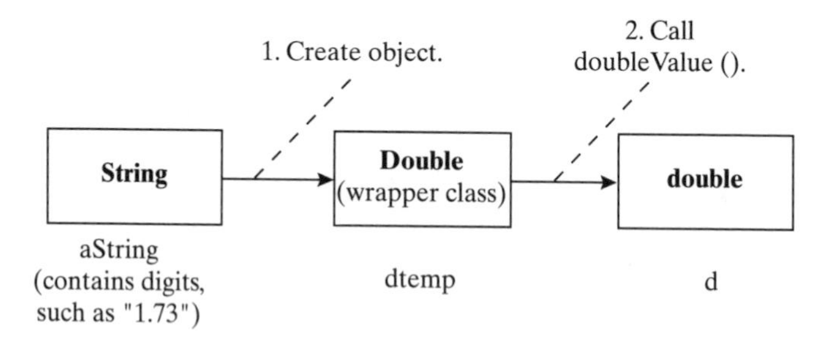

Figure 6.1 *Converting string to type double*

The following example illustrates the two steps, reading from the digits in **aString**:

```
Double dtemp = Double(aString); // 1. Create object
double d = dtemp.doubleValue();   // 2. Call doubleValue()
```

If you want more-compact code, you can combine the two steps, creating a temporary object on-the-fly and then calling the method. For example:

```
double d = (new Double(aString)).doubleValue();
```

The process is approximately the same for storing results as a float (single-precision) value. The main difference is that you call **floatValue( )** rather than **doubleValue( )**:

```
float f = (new Float(aString)).floatValue();
```

Numeric to String

Converting numeric values to strings is easy. One approach is to use **String.valueOf( )**. Although this is a class method, it returns a string object—namely, the string representation of a number.

```
int i = 101;
String aString = String.valueOf(i);
System.out.println("The value of i is " +
     String.valueOf(i));
```

String.valueOf( ) is overloaded so that you can give it any type of numeric input.

Another approach is to combine a numeric value with another string by using the string concatenation operator (+). In such an expression, Java automatically converts the number to a string representation.

```
System.out.println("The value of i is " + i);
```

Java performs this conversion even if the string is empty. For example, the following code initializes a string as a representation of the integer **i**:

```
String aString = "" + i;
```

CONSOLE INPUT AND OUTPUT

You've already seen many examples of console output. The **System.out** object provides two overloaded methods—**print( )** and **println( )**—that can be used to print to the screen in a Java application:

```
System.out.print("Print text, continue line... ");
System.out.println("Print text, then add a newline.");
```

NOTE

The only quirk with using print( ) is that if you want to force an immediate printing without a newline, you must call the flush( ) method. This is not necessary with println( ), because a newline flushes the buffer.

The technique for getting input from the console is more complicated. The **System.in** object is an instance of the **InputStream** class, which does not provide an easy way to read a whole line of input. The solution is to convert **System.in** to an instance of another class—**DataInputStream**—which provides the **readLine( )** method:

```
import java.io.*;
// ...
String s = "";
DataInputStream ds = new DataInputStream(System.in);
try {
     s = ds.readLine();
}catch(IOException e){;}
```

Because the **readLine( )** method has the possibility of throwing an exception, **IOException**, the code must place each call to **readLine( )** inside a **try-catch** block. (This requirement is annoying here, because it's unlikely that standard input would throw an exception.)

The following example shows repeated use of console input and output in a small program. To make the programming easier, almost all the input/output handling is moved to a utility function, **promptForInt( )**, which takes care of prompting, exception handling, and conversion to integer.

```
import java.io.*;
// main program - reads three integers and prints total
//
class ConsoleTest {
        public static void main(String args[]) {
                int a, b, c, total;

                a = promptForInt("Enter 1st integer: ");
                b = promptForInt("Enter 2nd integer: ");
                c = promptForInt("Enter 3rd integer: ");
                total = a + b + c;
                System.out.println("The total is: " + total);
        }

// promptForInt() - reads a string from the console and
//  returns first integer read.
//
        static int promptForInt(String prompt) {
                System.out.print(prompt);
                System.out.flush();
                String s = "";
                DataInputStream ds = new
                   DataInputStream(System.in);
                try {
                        s = ds.readLine();
                }catch (IOException e) {System.out.println(e);}
                return Integer.parseInt(s);
        }
}
```

A limitation of this program is that it permits entry of only one integer per line. If you want to, you can enter and read multiple items in a line by building a **StringTokenizer** object around the line read and then using **StringTokenizer** methods:

```
import java.util.*;
//...
StringTokenizer st = new StringTokenizer(s);
i = Integer.parseInt(st.nextToken()); // read a number
```

For more information, see **StringTokenizer** class in Part V, "API Quick Reference."

GRAPHICAL INTERFACE INPUT AND OUTPUT

Chapter 4 introduced the **action( )** event handler, which has a different meaning for each component. Often, you'll want to respond directly to mouse and keyboard events. This is easy to do in Java.

Panels, canvas, and window controls (including **Frame** components) recognize mouse events. The **Component** class provides a number of mouse handlers, including the **mouseDown( )** method:

```
class myFrame extends Frame {
//...
     public boolean mouseDown(Event e, int x, int y) {
          // Respond to mouse click at pos x,y.
     }
}
```

All components respond to keystroke events, which you can respond to by writing a **keyDown( )** or **keyUp( )** handler.

```
class myFrame extends Frame {
//...
     public boolean keyDown(Event e, int key) {
```

```
            // Respond to keypress "key."
      }
}
```

The **key** argument contains a simple Java character (such as *a*) if the user typed a printable character; otherwise, it contains one of the keycodes defined in the **Event** class, such as **Event.F2**.

The following example illustrates several of the most common input/output operations in an applet. The example responds to a mouse click by displaying coordinates.

```
import java.awt.*;
import java.applet.*;

public class MouseTest extends Applet {
        Panel pan;
        TextField txt;

        public void init() {
                setLayout(new BorderLayout());
                txt = new TextField(10);
                add("North", txt);
                pan = new Panel();
                add("Center", pan);
        }

        public boolean mouseDown(Event e, int x, int y) {
                txt.setText("x:" + x + ", y:" + y);
                return true;
        }
}
```

The applet has just two methods: **init( )** and **mouseDown( )**. The **init( )** method creates a simple user interface, using techniques described in Chapter 4. The **mouseDown( )** event constructs a string showing mouse position. As explained in the section "Numeric to String," Java automatically converts numeric values when they are combined with strings:

```
"x:" + x + ", y:" + y
```

This code builds a string such as "x:115, y:240", showing the x, y mouse position passed to the mouse handler. It's then a simple matter to pass the resulting string to the **setText( )** method, which displays the string in the text field:

```
txt.setText("x:" + x + ", y:" + y);
```

Figure 6.2 shows a sample view of the applet in operation.

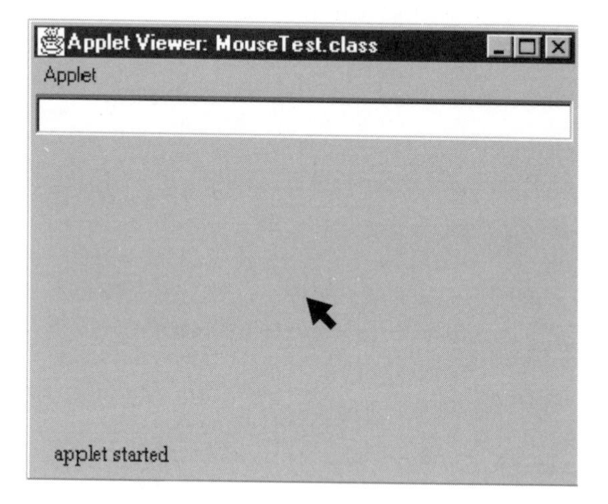

Figure 6.2 *The MouseTest applet*

The **setText( )** method is an example of a method that is specific to certain types of components. Along with **getText( ),** this method handles most input/output for text fields. Both methods are inherited from **TextComponent**. Sometimes looking up a method in Part V requires an extended search:

- Look up the topic for the component itself—in this case, **TextField**.
- Look up the superclass—in this case, **TextComponent**.

- Check the **Component** class if the method you need isn't found elsewhere. This class provides general capabilities, such as moving, hiding, resizing, and painting; it also contains all event-handling methods.

BASIC FILE OPERATIONS

Only applications can read or write to disk files or even read a directory. As a rule, net browsers prevent file operations, for the obvious reason that permitting file operations would enable an applet to destroy everything on your disk, or otherwise breach security.

This section gives a brief introduction to file operations. For more complete information, see the summary of the **java.io** package in Part IV, "Class Summaries"

Reading the Directory

The **File** class provides access to the directory system. This class is part of the **java.io** package, as are all Java API classes that support file operations. A **File** object represents one node in the file/directory system—either a single file or a single directory:

- If the **File** object represents a file, you can use the object to get file attributes but not contents. (See the next section for information about getting file contents.)
- If the **File** object represents a directory, you can use the object to get a list of directory items as well as other directory attributes. You can also use this object to create new subdirectories.

The following program prints the contents of the current directory:

```
import java.io.*;

class Dir {
        public static void main(String args[]) {
                File myDir = new File(".");
```

```
                String theList[] = myDir.list();
                int n = theList.length;
                for (int i = 0; i < n; i++)
                        System.out.println(theList[i]);
        }
}
```

The first statement in the program creates a **File** object that represents the current directory, specified by a single dot (".") in DOS/UNIX notation:

```
File myDir = new File(".");
```

The program calls **File.list( )** to get a list of children for this node (i.e., the current directory). This list is returned as an array of strings, which we assign to the array variable **theList**. Although Java arrays are similar to C/C++ arrays, each Java array contains its own **length** attribute. The program uses this attribute to determine how many items to print:

```
String theList[] = myDir.list();
int n = theList.length;
for (int i = 0; i < n; i++)
        System.out.println(theList[i]);
```

For more information on Java array syntax, see the topic "Arrays" in Part II. See **File** class in Part V, "API Quick Reference," for more uses of **File**.

Reading File Contents

If you come from the C, C++, or Basic world, you probably use a three-step process to read a file: open, read, and close the file. Java automates some of this process and uses exception handling to report conditions such as "File not found."

To open a file for reading, create a **FileInputStream** object, initializing with a string or other object. Java implicitly opens the file for reading. For example, you can use a **File** object to initialize a **FileInputStream** object:

```
File f = new File("STUFF.TXT");
FileInputStream fis = new FileInputStream(f);
```

You can also initialize a **FileInputStream** object directly from a string name:

```
FileInputStream fis = new FileInputStream("STUFF.TXT");
```

The example in this section reads a file by creating both types of objects—**File** and **FileInputStream**—and reading the name of a file from the command line. Figure 6.3 illustrates the general strategy.

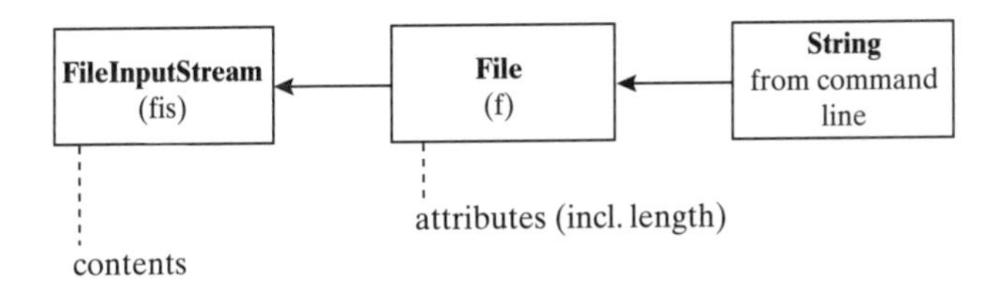

Figure 6.3 *Use of command line, File, and FileInputStream*

The program first reads the file name. Then it creates a **File** object and uses this object to determine length. Finally, it creates a **FileInputStream** object to read contents. The length is stored in the variable **n**, so the program reads **n** bytes. Here is the complete application:

```
import java.io.*;

class FileRead {
    public static void main(String args[]) {
        if (args.length < 1) {
```

```
                System.out.println("Specify file.");
                System.exit(0);
            }
            File f = new File(args[0]);
            int len = (int) f.length();
            byte ascii[] = new byte[len];
            try {
                FileInputStream fis = new FileInputStream(f);
                fis.read(ascii, 0, len);
                String theText = new String(ascii, 0);
                System.out.println(theText);
            }
            catch(IOException e) {System.out.println(e);}
        }
    }
```

This program first checks the command line and exits immediately if there is no argument. For more information about reading command lines, see the topic "main Method" in Part II.

```
            if (args.length < 1) {
                System.out.println("Specify file.");
                System.exit(0);
            }
```

Next, the program creates a **File** object and determines file length. An array named **ascii** is created to hold ASCII data from a text file. The program takes advantage of Java's dynamic sizing of arrays (much like Basic's) to allocate an array just big enough to hold the data.

```
            File f = new File(args[0]);
            int len = (int) f.length();
            byte ascii[] = new byte[len];
```

Finally, the program creates a **FileInputStream** object and reads data into the array. There are two statements that can raise an exception here: the **FileInputStream** constructor may report that the file cannot be found, and the **read( )** method may report that data is not available to be read. Both statements are placed inside a **try** block to catch I/O exceptions.

```
try {
    FileInputStream fis = new FileInputStream(f);
    fis.read(ascii, 0, len);
    String theText = new String(ascii, 0);
    System.out.println(theText);
}
catch(IOException e) {System.out.println(e);}
```

One of the subtleties of this program is that text-file data is assumed to be stored in ASCII format, whereas Java strings use Unicode. These formats are compatible except for the important detail that Unicode characters are 16 bits wide rather than 8. Fortunately, the **String** class provides a constructor that converts an array of ASCII bytes to a bona fide Java string, and it is used to initialize **theText**.

Other File-Handling Techniques

The Java API provides a **FileOutputStream** class, which does for output what **FileInputStream** does for input. You may also want to take advantage of the many specialized file I/O streams in the Java API (all part of the **java.io** package). In almost all cases, the procedure for using a specialized I/O stream is as follows:

1. Create a **FileInputStream** or **FileOutputStream** object. Remember to catch exceptions, which can be raised by constructors for these classes.
2. Use this object to initialize another stream object.

For example, **DataInputStream** provides methods for reading many kinds of data in a structured way rather than reading raw bytes; for this reason, it is frequently more easy to use than **FileInputStream**, especially when you are working with data files created by Java applications. The following code creates a **DataInputStream** object from a **FileInputStream** object:

```
FileInputStream fis = new FileInputStream("STUFF.DAT");
DataInputStream dataFile = new DataInputStream(fis);
```

The exception to this general procedure is the **RandomAccessFile** class, which constructs an object directly from a file name. See Part V, "API Quick Reference," for more information.

CHAPTER SEVEN

JDBC Quick Start

Entire libraries could be written about database theory—and no doubt have been. But you probably just want to see how JDBC *works*, so this chapter helps you get started using JDBC quickly. JDBC is Java Database Connectivity, one of the hot new topics in Java.

JDBC does not enable you to create entire database systems from scratch. It assumes that there is an existing database file created by a product such as Paradox, FoxPro, or Microsoft Access. JDBC enables your Java programs to communicate with the database, performing SQL queries and updates. The word *connectivity* means that you connect to a database and not that you create an independent application. But you'll be able to do a lot. It's easy to add entire new tables.

How JDBC Connects: A Brief Overview

Database engines know nothing at all about Java, so you need a driver to translate Java commands into actions. Some databases need JDBC-specific drivers, but if your database system is ODBC-compliant, Java can take advantage of an ODBC driver on your computer. I recommend this approach, because ODBC drivers support JDBC very well.

Figure 7.1 shows how Java works with an ODBC-compliant database. The JDBC-ODBC bridge is a driver that you should already have if you've recently installed JDK 1.02 or 1.1. Usually, the crucial step is to make sure you have an ODBC driver for your particular database file.

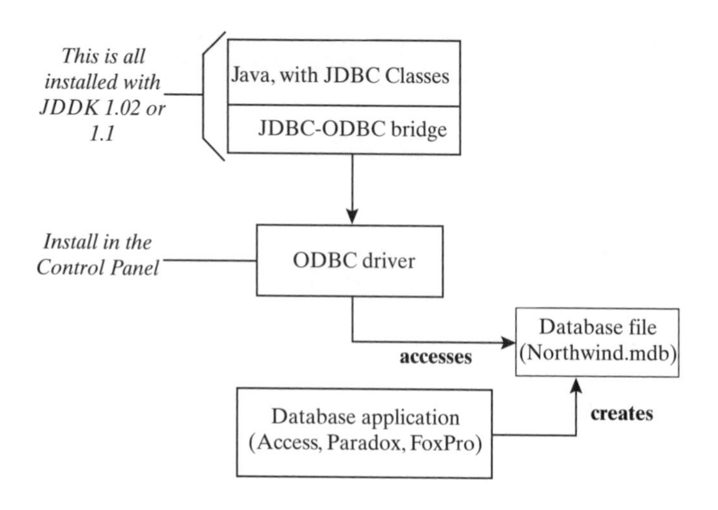

Figure 7.1 *JDBC accesses an ODBC database*

If you are not using an ODBC-compliant database, your database must have its own JDBC-specific driver. In that case, your JDBC driver replaces the JDBC-ODBC bridge, and the driver communicates directly with the database file.

Nearly all JDBC database operations involve the use of SQL (Structured Query Language). Why SQL? Remember that JDBC is designed to communicate with many different databases. The virtue of SQL is that it is a universal standard, and it is powerful enough to formulate almost any reasonable database command.

PREPARING TO USE JDBC

Don't skip this section—unless you want to spend a few hours wondering why JDBC doesn't work. For the most part, I'll assume that you have a database product that has an ODBC driver. This category includes nearly all the popular commercial database products on the market. There are smaller shareware products that are not ODBC-compliant. One that is recommended is the mSQL database application, which can be downloaded along with a JDBC driver. It is available at **http://www.imaginary.com/~borg/Java/java.html**.

Install a Database Application

Yes, in case it isn't clear by now, you need to have an independent database application that will create a file that JDBC will operate on. When you install a commercial product such as Microsoft Access, make sure that you ask for ODBC drivers to be installed if you're given a setup option.

Create a Database File

Create a database file for JDBC to operate on, as shown in Figure 7.1. It's helpful to place the file where your JDBC programs can easily access it. To start working with JDBC, I suggest moving the database to the same directory where you're developing the JDBC code. In my case, I was using Microsoft Access, which provides a sample database named **Northwind.mdb**. I simply copied this file to my JDBC sample code directory.

Install the Database/ODBC Driver

This step is crucial (unless you're not using an ODBC-compliant database). You must install an ODBC driver *specifically for your database file*. If you're using Windows, do the following:

1. Open the Control Panel.
2. Double-click the **32bit ODBC** icon.
3. In the Data Sources dialog box that appears, click the **Add** button.
4. A list of database applications appears. In my case, I selected the following:

   ```
   Microsoft Access Driver (*.mdb)
   ```

5. Fill out the dialog box form that appears. In my case, the dialog box asked for both a Data Source Name and a database location. I entered **Northwind.mdb** for both, but in the latter case I gave a complete path specification.

If you are using a platform other than Windows, follow the vendor's instructions for installing an ODBC driver for your database file.

Install the JDBC/ODBC Bridge

This step is already taken care of for you if you've installed a recent version of JDK 1.02 or JDK 1.1. To double-check, look at your **java** directory. In the **lib** subdirectory, you should find a **jdbc** directory. Under that directory, you should find a directory named **odbc**, which contains plenty of files.

If Your Database Is Not ODBC-Compliant

If you're using a smaller, shareware database application that is not ODBC-compliant, make sure you install a JDBC-specific driver if one is provided. Place it somewhere (such as your path) where your Java programs will have access to it.

NOTE

Nothing in this chapter should be seen as a strong endorsement of Microsoft Access, Windows, ODBC, or the Microsoft Corporation in general. I am not trying to sound like a Microsoft bigot or encourage world domination. However, all these pieces of software are in extremely wide use, and it is likely you use some of them. The code and procedures in this chapter should work well if you use an ODBC-compliant database application other than Access; just substitute your own database name for Northwind.mdb.

MAKING THE CONNECTION

Now we're off to the races. Your first goal is to get a **Statement** object that you can use to execute SQL commands on your database files. Getting this object is a fairly simple, three-step process:

1. Call **Class.forName( )** to load the database driver. (This is always the JDBC-ODBC bridge if you're working with any ODBC-compliant database.)

2. Get a connection to the database file, producing a **Connection** object.
3. Use that object to create a **Statement** object.

For example, to access my **Northwind.mdb** file, I use the following three statements:

```
Class.forName("jdbc.odbc.JdbcOdbcDriver");
Connection con = DriverManager.getConnection(
     "jdbc:odbc:Northwind.mdb");
Statement stm = con.createStatement();
```

If you're connecting to a different database, such as a Paradox database file, give a different argument to **getConnection( )**. For example:

```
Class.forName("jdbc.odbc.JdbcOdbcDriver");
Connection con = DriverManager.getConnection(
     "jdbc:odbc:MyDbase.db");
Statement stm = con.createStatement();
```

More about getConnection( )

You'll notice that the argument to **getConnection( )** is not a simple database name. Instead, it is a URL with a special format:

jdbc:*subprotocol:subname*

The *subprotocol* in this case is **odbc**, but it will be different if you're not using ODBC. The *subname* is driver-specific. With ODBC, *subname* is the Data Source Name you entered when installing an ODBC driver. (See the section "Install the Database/ODBC Driver" earlier in this chapter.)

Connecting to an mSQL Server

An mSQL connection requires a more complicated syntax than that of ODBC. After the protocol, **msql**, you need to supply a host name, a port number, and finally the file name. For example:

```
Class.forName("imaginary.sql.iMsqlDriver");  // mSQL driver
Connection con = DriverManager.getConnection(
     "jdbc:msql://hostname:1112/my_dbase");
Statement stm = con.createStatement();
```

ADDING A NEW TABLE

Now let's actually do something. To add a new table to a database, we need to execute the **SQL CREATE TABLE** statement, which has the following syntax:

CREATE TABLE *tablename (column_descriptions)*

Here, each *column_description* consists of a name and a type. For example:

```
CREATE TABLE silly (name char(20), job char(20), age int)
```

This is exactly the table we're going to create: a table with two columns holding strings up to 20 characters each and a third column holding an integer value. Here is the program:

```
import java.sql.*;

class AddSilly {
    public static void main(String args[]) {
        try {
            Class.forName("jdbc.odbc.JdbcOdbcDriver");
```

```
            Connection con = DriverManager.getConnection(
              "jdbc:odbc:Northwind.mdb");
            Statement stm = con.createStatement();
            stm.executeUpdate("CREATE TABLE silly " +
              "(name char(20), job char(20), age int)");
        } catch (Exception e) {
            System.out.println(e);
            System.exit(1);
        }
        System.out.println("Table silly created"
          + "successfully.");
    }
}
```

The first time you run this program, it should tell you that the table was successfully created. You can then open your database application and see that there is indeed a new table named **silly**. The second time you run the program, you should get an error message saying that the table already exists.

The key to this example is the call to the **executeUpdate( )** method of the **Statement** object. As mentioned earlier, you use this object to execute SQL commands. Call the **executeUpdate( )** method of this object to carry out any change to the database.

```
stm.executeUpdate("CREATE TABLE silly " +
  "(name char(20), job char(20), age int)");
```

INSERTING TABLE ENTRIES

A table is not much use without rows (table entries). To generate some rows, you can use the **INSERT INTO** statement:

INSERT INTO *tablename (column_names) VALUES (expressions)*

For example, the following SQL statements insert two rows into the **silly** table:

```
INSERT INTO silly (name, job, age)
     VALUES ('Brian', 'writer', 35)

INSERT INTO silly (name, job, age)
     VALUES ('Bobo', 'clown', 29)
```

We could, as in the previous example, simply execute these exact commands. It is more interesting and useful, however, to first prompt the user for data, then build SQL command strings to use this data, and finally execute the strings. Such a program demonstrates the power of SQL and JDBC: by building up command strings, you can do almost anything. Here is the program:

```
import java.sql.*;
import java.io.*;

class EditSilly {
   static String sql = "", name = "", job ="", age = "";

   public static void main(String args[]) {
       try {
           Class.forName("jdbc.odbc.JdbcOdbcDriver");
           Connection con = DriverManager.getConnection(
             "jdbc:odbc:Northwind.mdb");
           Statement stm = con.createStatement();
           while (true) {
               name = promptString("Enter name "+
                 "(<CR> to exit): ");
               if (name.length() == 0)
                   break;
```

```
                job = promptString("Enter job: ");
                age = promptString("Enter age: ");
                sql = "INSERT INTO silly(name, job, age)" +
                  " VALUES('" + name + "', '" + job +
                  "'", " + age + ")";
                System.out.println(sql); // diagnostic
                stm.executeUpdate(sql);
            }
        } catch(Exception e) {System.out.println(e);}
    }

    static String promptString(String prompt) {
        System.out.print(prompt);
        System.out.flush();
        String s = "";
        DataInputStream ds = new DataInputStream(System.in);
        try {
            s = ds.readLine();
        } catch (IOException e) {System.out.println(e);}
        return s;
    }
}
```

The strategy of this program is simple. After making the connection to the database file, it sets up a loop in which the user is prompted for name, job, and age values:

```
                name = promptString("Enter name "+
                  "(<CR> to exit): ");
                // ...
                job = promptString("Enter job: ");
                age = promptString("Enter age: ");
```

Here the program is using the **promptString( )** method—our old friend from Chapter 6—to prompt the user for input. If the user just presses **Enter** in response to the first prompt, the length of the name will be zero, and the program responds by breaking the loop and ending.

```
if (name.length() == 0)
    break;
```

The statements at the bottom of the loop build a command string and execute it. For example, suppose the three values entered were

```
Bill
ceo
42
```

The program builds the following command string:

```
INSERT INTO silly (name, job, age)
     VALUES ('Bill', 'ceo', 42)
```

Finally, the command string (which in this case is named **sql**) is fed to the **executeUpdate( )** method:

```
stm.executeUpdate(sql);
```

PRINTING TABLE CONTENTS (QUERYING)

The next example is smaller, but it manages to introduce a couple of new tricks. To get the contents of a table, you use the SQL **SELECT** statement. Here, the asterisk (*) means "select all columns."

SELECT * FROM *tablename*

Because this is a query and not an update, you call the **executeQuery( )** method, which returns the results in something called a *result set*:

```
String sql = "SELECT * FROM silly";
ResultSet rs = stm.executeQuery(sql);
```

Even though this query gets the entire contents of the table, there is a difference between a result set and a table: the result set can be read by JDBC. As with a table, the result set has a series of rows. You can read all the rows with code that looks like this:

```
while (rs.next()) {
     // Read a row of the result set
}
```

The **next( )** method of the **ResultSet** class gets the next row and returns **false** if there are no more rows. Significantly, the first call to **next( )** reads the first row.

Here is the program, PrintSilly:

```
import java.sql.*;

class PrintSilly {
    public static void main(String args[]) {
        try {
            Class.forName("jdbc.odbc.JdbcOdbcDriver");
            Connection con = DriverManager.getConnection(
              "jdbc:odbc:Northwind.mdb");
            Statement stm = con.createStatement();
            String sql = "SELECT * FROM silly";
            ResultSet rs = stm.executeQuery(sql);
            while(rs.next()) {
                String s = rs.getString(1) + "\t" +
                  rs.getString(2) + "\t" +
                  rs.getInt(3);
```

```
                System.out.println(s);
            }
        } catch(Exception e) {System.out.println(e);}
    }
}
```

In addition to **next( )**, which gets a row, this example uses two **ResultSet** methods to get values from the current row. The **getString( )** and **getInt( )** methods do roughly the same thing: they take a column number and then return the data in that column (within the current row). JDBC column numbers are one-based, meaning that the first column is position 1, the second is position 2, and so on.

In the case of the **silly** table, the first two columns are strings and the last one is an integer. Note that there is a different result-set method for getting each kind of data. Table 7.1 summarizes the methods used in this example.

Table 7.1 Common ResultSet methods

RESULTSET METHOD	DESCRIPTION
rs.**next( )**	Get next row of data.
rs.**getString(*n*)**	Within current row, get string data from column *n*.
rs.**getInt(*n*)**	Within current row, get integer data from column *n*.

The **while** loop is the heart of this example. Here, I've put in comments to help explain how it works:

```
while(rs.next()) {  // For each row:
    String s = rs.getString(1) + "\t" +  // Get name value.
      rs.getString(2) + "\t" +           // Get job value.
      rs.getInt(3);                      // Get age value.
    System.out.println(s);
}
```

BROWSING A DATABASE'S STRUCTURE

Another way to use a **Connection** is to create an object for browsing the structure of a database. This browser object belongs to the class **DatabaseMetaData**, admittedly a difficult name to pronounce.

```
DatabaseMetaData dmd = con.getMetaData();
```

The tongue-twister "metadata" also appears in another useful class: **ResultSetMetaData**. What is metadata? Normal data contains information about the world around us. *Metadata* contains information about the way other data is stored. Not surprisingly, one of the main uses of **DatabaseMetaData** is to get a list of all the tables in a database:

```
String tableTypes[] = {"TABLE", "VIEW"};
ResultSet rs = dmd.getTables(
    null, null, "%", tableTypes);
```

The call to **getTables( )** has four arguments: the first two are catalog and schema, which can be null. The third argument is the important one: it specifies a pattern to match. Here, "%" means "match any string." Therefore, it matches any table name. The last argument is an array of strings, each element specifying a table type. (For a list of possible values, see Table I in Part VI, "Useful Tables.")

Here is a complete program. You'll notice that because **getTables( )** returns its information in a result set, the code uses techniques similar to those in the previous section, "Printing Table Contents (Queries)."

```
import java.sql.*;

class ListTables {
    public static void main(String args[]) {
        try {
            Class.forName("jdbc.odbc.JdbcOdbcDriver");
```

```
                Connection con = DriverManager.getConnection(
                   "jdbc:odbc:Northwind.mdb");
                DatabaseMetaData dmd = con.getMetaData();
                String tableTypes[] = {"TABLE", "VIEW"};
                ResultSet rs = dmd.getTables(
                  null, null, "%", tableTypes);
                while (rs.next()) {
                   String name = rs.getString("TABLE_NAME");
                   String tt = rs.getString("TABLE_TYPE");
                    System.out.println(name + "\t" + tt);
                }
            } catch (Exception e) {System.out.println(e);}
        }
    }
```

To understand this example, you need to know that the **getTables( )** method returns a result set with a specific structure. Each row of the result set describes one of the tables found by **getTables( ).** Table 7.2 describes the fields of each row.

Table 7.2 *Result set for DatabaseDataMeta.getTables( )*

POSITION/NAME	TYPE	DESCRIPTION
1. TABLE_CAT	**String**	Table catalog (may be null).
2. TABLE_SCHEM	**String**	Table schema (may be null).
3. TABLE_NAME	**String**	Name of table.
4. TABLE_TYPE	**String**	Type of table: possible values are "TABLE" and "VIEW", among others.
5. REMARKS	**String**	Description.

In this program, I retrieve values in the result set by using a version of **getString( )** that takes string arguments:

```
while (rs.next()) {
    String name = rs.getString("TABLE_NAME");
    String tt = rs.getString("TABLE_TYPE");
    System.out.println(name + "\t" + tt);
}
```

The **getString( )** method can take either a column number or a column name. In this case, I found it more convenient to use column names. Remember that the columns referred to here are result-set columns and not table columns. And the columns of this result set contain information such as table name and description.

ONWARD AND UPWARD

As with Java in general, JDBC contains vast capabilities. I've only skimmed the surface here, but this chapter should give you a good idea of what JDBC can do.

Remember that once you get a **Statement** object, you can use it to do almost anything. But after you've used JDBC for a while, you may want to turn to Part V, "API Quick Reference", to check out the **PreparedStatement** and **CallableStatement** interfaces, which, in a sense, are advanced versions of **Statement**. You should also consult Appendix B "Common SQL Statements" to get a bigger picture of what SQL can do.

Real-world database applications can grow without limit, as a calculus student might say. But hopefully I've shown that even small JDBC programs can do significant work. If you enjoy database programming, I trust you'll have a lot of fun with Java.

PART II

Language Reference

ABSTRACT KEYWORD

Java vs. C++

The **abstract** keyword can be used to create abstract methods in Java; abstract methods are the equivalent of pure virtual functions in C++.

Syntax

To create an abstract method, place the **abstract** keyword at the beginning of a method declaration. Terminate the declaration immediately with a semicolon. Optionally, the method can have other modifiers, such as **public**.

abstract [*other_modifiers*] *type method_name***(***args***);**

An abstract method has no definition—that is, no executable code.

Any class that has at least one abstract method is an abstract class and must be declared with **abstract**. (See the example.) An abstract class cannot be used to create objects, but it can be used as a base class for other classes. A derived class can provide definitions for an inherited method so that the method is no longer abstract.

Abstract methods and classes have an important connection to interfaces. See the topic "interface Keyword" for more information.

Example

The following code declares a generic **Shape** class, with two abstract methods:

```
import java.awt.Graphics;

abstract public class Shape {
    abstract public void moveTo(int newx, int newy);
    abstract public void reDraw(Graphics g);
}
```

The next class, MyRectClass, is an example of a class that can be derived from Shape. Although Shape cannot be used to create objects, MyRectClass can. Note that in the MyRectClass class, the methods are not declared with **abstract**.

```
import java.awt.Graphics;

public class MyRectClass extends Shape {
     public void moveTo(int newx, int newy) {
          x = newx;
          y = newy;
     }

     public void reDraw(Graphics g) {
          g.drawRect(x, y, 20, 20);
     }
}
```

AGGREGATES

Java vs. C++

Aggregate syntax is roughly the same in Java as in C and C++, but Java treats strings differently (considering them **String** objects) and uses aggregates only to create array objects.

Syntax

An aggregate is a literal constant for a string or an array. An aggregate has one of the following forms:

"*string_of_characters*"

{*item*, *item*, ...**}**

Here, the ellipses are not intended literally but are used to indicate that there may be any number of *items*. Each *item* is a constant, variable, or other object. In any case, an item must be either an object or an instance of a primitive data type.

Java allocates memory for a string or array object whenever it encounters an aggregate. In the case of string literals, Java allocates an object of the **String** class. Such an object is not equivalent to an array of **char** as it would be in C or C++. See the topic "Strings" for more information.

When the set aggregate form is used, Java creates an array object of the appropriate size. (The set form uses the **{***item***,** *item***, ...}** syntax.) This is the only way to create arrays other than using the **new** operator. For example, the following array declaration creates an array variable, manyInts, but it allocates no integers in memory:

```
int manyInts[];
```

But the following declaration allocates an array of five integers, in which the variable manyInts refers to the array:

```
int manyInts[] = {1, 2, 3, 4, 5} ;
```

Usage 1: Character Strings

As in C and C++, string literals can be used to initialize string variables or can be passed as arguments. However, string literals are used to initialize variables of the **String** class, and not arrays of **char**, as in C and C++. For example:

```
String s = "Here is a string";
String Name = "John Doe";
System.out.println("My name is " + Name);
```

The last example uses the concatenation operator (+), which creates a **String** result from two **String** operands.

Characters in a string can include any Unicode character, including a number of characters specified by an escape sequence (such as to indicate a newline). For a table of escape sequences and other details of string behavior, see the topic "Strings."

Usage 2: Set Aggregates (Arrays)

In Java, set aggregates are only used to initialize arrays. In the simple case of initializing an array of numbers, Java accepts the same code as C and C++. For example:

```
int countdown[] = {10, 9, 8, 7, 6, 5, 4, 3, 2, 1} ;
```

You can initialize other kinds of arrays, but each item inside the brackets must be one of the following:

- An object.
- An instance of primitive data type, such as a number.
- A nested aggregate—which itself is actually an object, either of **String** type or an array.

The third category is not really a separate category. A set aggregate is itself an array object. In Java, multidimensional arrays are arrays of arrays, so you can initialize them as follows:

```
int matrix[][] = {{1, 2} , {4, 5} , {9, 10} } ;
```

This declaration creates matrix as a 3 x 2 array. In Java, there is no requirement that nested arrays have the same size. You can therefore create arrays like this:

```
int matrix[][] = {{1, 2, 3, 4} , {4} , {9, 10} } ;
```

This declaration creates matrix as an array of three array objects. The first object is an array of four integers, the second is an array of one integer, and the third is an array of two integers.

Except for strings, initializing an object (an instance of a user-defined class) always requires the use of the **new** operator. You can initialize arrays of objects, but each instance of a class must involve **new** and a constructor. For example:

```
class Pnt {
        int x, y;
        Pnt(int x, int y) {
                this.x = x;
                this.y = y;
        }
}
//...
Pnt pts[] = {new Pnt(10, 20), new Pnt(3, 4)} ;
```

But as long as each object has been allocated somewhere, you can use any combination of variables and other objects. Each object, of course, must have the appropriate type. For example:

```
Pnt p1 = new Pnt(3, 4);
Pnt pts[] = {p1, new Pnt(10, 20), new Pnt(3, 4)} ;
```

Strings, of course, are the one kind of object that can be created without using **new**. The following example creates a valid array of strings:

```
String words[] = {"Welcome", "to", "Java"} ;
```

ARRAYS

Java vs. C++

Java treats arrays as objects and not as compound types. This means that an array cannot hold elements until you use **new** or aggregate initialization to allocate space for the array. In other respects, Java arrays behave like arrays in C and C++, with indexes running from 0 to *size*-1.

In Java, arrays do not equate to pointers or addresses. You must use the index notation to access array elements.

Syntax

Typically, arrays are allocated with the **new** operator and are associated with an array variable in the same declaration:

type array_name[] = **new** *type*[*size*];
type array_name[][]... = **new** *type*[*size1*][*size2*]... ;

Arrays can also be declared and initialized through the use of aggregates:

```
int iarray[] = {1, 2, 3, 4, 5} ;
```

Once an array is declared and allocated, its legal indexes (or each dimension, if it's multidimensional) run from 0 to *size*-1. Thus, an array of size 100 runs from array[0] to array[99]. At run time, the Java interpreter catches illegal indexes and raises them as exceptions of class **ArrayIndexOutOfBoundsException**.

Array variables can be declared without immediately allocating an array in memory. An array can be allocated later using **new**. In multidimensional arrays, each element can be individually associated with a row of different length. (See "Examples.") When the **new** operator is applied to multidimensional arrays, any number of dimensions can be left blank as long as all the blank sizes are to the right of the fixed sizes. Such expressions create arrays of arrays, in which not all dimensions are yet allocated.

new *type*[*size1*][*size2*]...[ ][ ]...

Syntax: Variation

In declaring an array variable, you can choose to place brackets (instead of the variable name) after the type. For example:

```
int[] iarray = {1, 2, 3, 4, 5};
```

The choice of syntax is a matter of personal style.

Examples

This example declares a simple array of 100 integers and initializes each element to 5:

```
int iarray[] = new int[100];
for (int i = 0; i < 100; i++)
     iarray[i] = 5;
```

The next example declares a two-dimensional array and initializes each element to 0:

```
int matrix[][] = new int[ROWS][COLS];
for (int i = 0; i < ROWS; i++)
     for (int j = 0; j < COLS; j++)
          matrix[i][j] = 0;
```

The third example creates an uneven two-dimensional array: a matrix with rows of different length. This is uncommon but legal.

```
// Create weirdMatrix as array of two elements, each
//  element being a one-dimensional array of int not
//  yet allocated.

int weirdMatrix[][] = new int[2][];
weirdMatrix[0] = new int[3];       // First row: size 3
weirdMatrix[1] = new int[7];       // Second row: size 7
```

Array Arguments and Array Length

Although you should generally know the length of your own arrays, it is sometimes useful to determine their length dynamically. This is especially true of methods that take arrays as arguments. In Java, arrays are objects and have a built-in **length** field.

```
array_name.length
```

The preceding expression produces the length of the first-order dimension. In a two-dimensional array, the size of the second dimension could be produced by an expression such as this:

```
array_name[0].length
```

A simple example uses a method that takes an array of **long**, of any size, as an argument:

```
void zeroLongArray(long array[]) {
     for(int i = 0; i < array.length; i++)
          array[i] = 0;
}
```

Array parameter declarations never include sizes. The size of an array is an attribute (available in the **length** field) and not a determinant of type.

ASSIGNMENTS

Java vs. C++

Java's assignment syntax is similar to that of C and C++. However, assignment to an object changes the reference instead of performing a copy operation.

Syntax

The Java assignment operator creates an expression from two operands:

variable = *value*

The *variable* can be either a variable, a data member, or an element of an array. The notion of "l-value" is less important in Java than in C and C++, because Java does not support pointers. In general, expressions are legal on the left side as long as they are neither constants nor complex expressions.

As in C and C++, assignment expressions are expressions just like any other, so they can be reused in larger expressions. After assigning the *value* to *variable*, the expression evaluates to the value of *variable* after assignment. (See "Examples.")

Because object variables are references in Java, assignment to one of these variables does not result in copying of data between objects, as it would in C++. Instead, assignment to an object variable associates that variable with a new object in memory. You can also assign the special value **null** to an object variable, which causes the variable to have no current association with any actual object.

Examples

As in C and C++, you can take advantage of the fact that assignment is an expression and not a statement. The following statement uses nested assignment expressions. The effect is to assign the value 0 to all four variables. Associativity of assignment is right-to-left, so after 0 is assigned to d, it is assigned to c, and so on:

```
a = b = c = d = 0;
```

The next example demonstrates assignment to an object variable. The effect of this code is to make obj2 an alias for the same object that obj1 refers to. In other words, only one object is allocated, but it has two names.

```
MyClass obj1, obj2;

obj1 = new MyClass(); // Allocate an object.
obj2 = obj1;     // Make obj2 an alias for this same object.
```

If you want to get an actual copy of an object, use the **clone()** method. This method is defined in the **Object** class, which all other classes inherit from directly or indirectly. Note that all API classes that have a useable **clone()** method also implement the **Cloneable** interface.

```
MyClass obj1, obj2;

obj1 = new MyClass(); // Allocate an object.
obj2 = obj1.clone();  // Create a copy and assign to obj2.
```

AUTO (C++)

Java vs. C++

Not supported in Java.

The **auto** keyword has an obscure use in C and C++ as a way to declare that a variable is local and has automatic storage class. It is generally unnecessary even in these languages. Java does not support **auto**, because all variables are either class variables, instance variables, or local to a method (a member function). This arrangement tends to make scope and storage class simpler and better defined in Java.

BIT FIELDS (C++)

Java vs. C++

Not supported in Java.

See "BitSet Class" in the API Quick Reference for a capability similar to bit fields.

BITWISE OPERATORS

Java vs. C++

Java supports the same bitwise operators that C and C++ support. However, these operators work differently with Boolean expressions and integer expressions.

Syntax

Java supports the bitwise operators: AND (&), OR (|), and exclusive OR (^). When both the operands are integers, the operation compares bits in the two operands to determine the corresponding bit in the result.

integer **&** *integer*

integer **|** *integer*

integer **^** *integer*

~ *integer*

However, when the two operands have type **boolean**, the operations are actually logical operations. These operators always evaluate both sides of the expression fully. This is different from the operators && and ||, which use "short-circuit" logic to evaluate just one side when appropriate. (For example, if the first operand connected by && is false, the second operand is not evaluated.)

boolean **&** *boolean*

boolean **|** *boolean*

boolean **^** *boolean*

! *boolean*

The symbols ~ and ! perform bitwise and logical negation, respectively. In the other expressions, both expressions must be integer or both must be Boolean.

See also "Shift Operators."

Examples

The following example masks out all bits except the two least significant bits:

```
int test_value, result;
//...
result = test_value & 0x03;
```

Figure B.1 illustrates bitwise AND, OR, and exclusive OR between two sample integer operands.

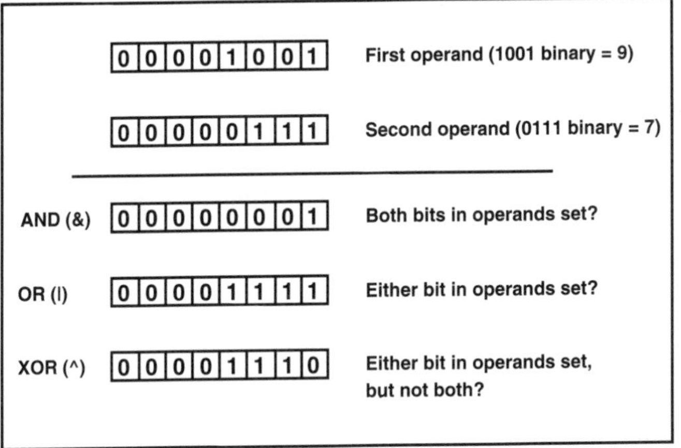

Figure B.1 *Bitwise operators*

BOOLEAN EXPRESSIONS

Java vs. C++

In Java, **boolean** is a distinct type rather than just another way of using integers. What's more, Java does not accept an integer expression where syntax calls for a Boolean expression. Thus, Sum > 0 is accepted as a conditional expression for an **if**, **for**, or **while** statement, but Sum is not. (See the example.)

Syntax

A Boolean expression consists of one of the following:

- The result of a comparison, such as Sum == 0 or N > 5.
- A Boolean variable.
- The constant **true** or **false**.
- Boolean expressions combined with one or more of the Boolean operators: and (&&), or (||), not (!).

Java supports the **boolean** keyword for the declaration of Boolean variables. Such variables might be useful in storing part of the result of a complex logical expression.

boolean *variable* [= *Boolean_expression*]**;**

Example

Assume that n is declared as an integer. The following **while** statement is legal, because it uses a Boolean expression (n > 0) for the conditional.

```
while (n > 0)
     amount = amount * n–;
```

But this **while** statement is illegal:

```
while (n)                        // ERROR! while(n) not valid
     amount = amount * n–;
```

BREAK STATEMENT

Java vs. C++

The **break** statement does the same thing in Java as in C and C++; it terminates a branch of a **switch statement** or breaks out of a loop. Java extends **break** syntax by adding an optional label target.

Syntax

The **break** statement has two forms:

break;

break *label***;**

The statement transfers execution to the first statement past the end of the innermost loop or **switch** statement. If *label* is specified, execution is transferred to the first statement past the end of the statement block (loop or **switch** statement) identified by the label.

Examples

This example uses **break** to terminate two branches of a **switch** statement. Without **break**, execution would fall through from one case to the next.

```
int n;
String NumberString;
// ...
switch(n) {
case 1:
          NumberString = "One";
          break;
case 2:
          NumberString = "Two";
          break;
```

This next example breaks directly out of two loops as soon as a zero element is found.

```
major_loop: for(int i = 0; i < 20; i++) {
                for(int j = 0; j < 20; j++) {
                     if (matrix[i][j] == 0) {
                          zero_found = true;
                          break major_loop;
                     }
                }
}
```

BYTE DATA TYPE

Java vs. C++

The **byte** data type is a primitive data type in Java, equivalent to **signed char** in most C/C++ implementations. Note that **byte** is an eight-bit signed number, whereas the Java **char** type is actually 16 bits and not eight bits.

Syntax

The **byte** keyword can be used to create eight-bit (one-byte) integer variables:

byte *declarations*;

The range is –128 to 127.

Example

The **byte** data type is most frequently used to create compact arrays of small numbers.

```
byte lottery_numbers[] = {2, 9, 13, 27, 55, 57};
```

CASE KEYWORD

Java vs. C++

The **case** keyword does the same thing in Java as in C and C++; it labels a branch inside a **switch** statement.

Syntax

This keyword turns a statement into a labeled statement:

case *constant_integer_expression***:**
    statement

Within a **switch** statement, if the test value matches *constant_integer_expression*, execution transfers to *statement* (unless another branch was taken first).

Example

The **case** keyword is only a label and not a control structure. This is why execution falls through unless you use **break**. In the following example, **break** prevents falling through to the default case.

```
switch(c) {
case 'a':
case 'e':
case 'i':
case 'o':
case 'u':
     is_a_vowel = true;
     break;
default:
     is_a_vowel = false;
}
```

CASTS

Java vs. C++

Casting is critical with certain parts of the Java API. A number of methods return type **Object**, which usually must be cast. Rules for casting in Java are similar to those for C and C++ except that you can only cast up and down through the class hierarchy.

Casting converts the type of an expression. Some casting is automatic, but Java will not automatically convert a data type if there is the possibility of loss of information; this situation requires an explicit cast. It's Java's way of making sure you know what you're doing.

Syntax: Explicit Cast

You can recast an expression to a different type by using the following syntax. The resulting expression, assuming it is valid, has the specified *type*.

(*type***)** *expression*

There are two common situations in which you need a cast:

- Assigning primitive data when it would resultin loss of precision or range. The most common example is assigning a floating-point constant(which by default has type **double**) to a **float** variable:

```
float f = (float) 3.97;   // Convert from double.
double d = 3.97;          // No cast needed.
```

- Assigning an object to a subclass type. A number of API methods return an expression of type **Object** which needs to be cast to a subclass:

```
Long theLong = (Long) theStack.pop();
```

Here's why Java requires the cast: **Stack.pop()** always returns a result of type **Object**. We can assume from this example that **theStack** is being used to hold **Long** objects, but there is no way for Java to know this. It would be too risky for Java to automatically cast an **Object** to **Long**, because an **Object** does not necessarily support all the fields that a **Long** supports.

You can assign to a superclass for free. For example, **Stack.push()** takes an **Object** argument—**Object** being the ultimate superclass—and no cast is required:

```
theStack.push(theLong);     // Automatic cast to Object
```

A **Long** object supports all the fields of the **Object** class, so there is no danger in passing a **Long** (or an instance of any class) when type **Object** is expected. It is only assigning to a *subclass* that requires a cast.

The principle behind all casting is consistent; it is the potential loss of information that requires a cast. You can easily get yourself into trouble by using casts that don't make sense, but the assumption is that you're an adult and have good reasons for whatever you do.

You also need a cast when you assign a long to an int:

```
long theLong = 100;     // 100 cast to long.
int i = (int) theLong;  // Cast required to go back to int!
```

Restrictions on Casting

You cannot cast outside the class hierarchy when dealing with objects. For example, the following code is illegal if neither A nor B is a subclass of the other. (In this context, "subclass" means a direct or indirect subclass, so that, for example, all classes are subclasses of **Object**.)

```
A a;
B b = (A) a; // Legal only if A is superclass or subclass.
```

With a little thought, you can see how to cast between any two classes if you do it in two steps (because all classes are related through **Object**). However, there is never a reason to do something like that. If you want to create different classes that support the same methods, you should relate them through inheritance. If classes do not support the same methods, casting between them is dangerous.

Another restriction that should be clear by now is that you can't cast between primitive data types and classes. However, the wrapper classes (such as **Long**, used in previous examples) are valid parts of the class hierarchy.

Implicit Casting and Promotion

Most of the time, you can combine numeric data into expressions without having to use explicit casts. Numeric expressions are cast according to a well-defined hierarchy. In the following list of types, whenever two types of expression are combined, the type lower in the list is cast to the type higher on the list:

double

float

long

int

short

char

byte

Casts between **boolean** and other types are never permitted. The easiest way to effect a conversion between **boolean** and an integer is to use the conditional operator (?:):

```
boolean b;
//...
int i = b? 1 : 0;
```

CATCH KEYWORD

The **catch** keyword is used to define an exception handler. See the topic "Exception Handling" for description, syntax, and an example.

The **catch** keyword has the following syntax. A **try** block must precede any **catch** block.

catch (*exceptionClass e***)** **{***statements***}**

Here, *e* is an argument name of your choice. You can use it within *statement* to refer to the exception that was caught.

CHAR DATA TYPE

Java vs. C++

In Java, the **char** data type is a 16-bit-wide integer that stores a single Unicode character value. Strings are not arrays of **char** as they are in C/C++, although you can convert string data to the **char** format.

Syntax

The **char** keyword can be used to declare variables that hold individual characters:

char *declarations***;**

The range is the entire set of Unicode characters. Although these are 16-bit values, the lowest 128 values are equal to their counterparts in standard ASCII. Note that individual character constants use single quotation marks. (See "Examples.")

In Java, strings are instances of the **String** class and are not arrays of **char**. However, you can convert **String** objects to arrays of **char** by using the **toCharArray( )** method of the **String** class. The **String** class also has a number of class (static) methods for dealing with arrays of **char**. See the topic "String Class" in the API Quick Reference for more information.

For a list of escape codes that can be used for special character constants, see the topic "Strings."

Examples

This example declares a variable holding a single character initialized to a newline:

```
char end = '\n';
```

This next example declares an array of **char** and initializes it by calling the **toCharArray( )** method:

```
String str = "data";
char charray[] = str.toCharArray();
```

Note that this code does *not* copy over a null-terminated string. In the example just shown, the variable charray is associated with a **char** array in memory containing exactly four characters: d, a, t, and a. There is no fifth byte for a null.

Another way to fill a character array is to use the **StringBuffer** class. This approach is most likely to appeal to die-hard C fans:

```
char carr[] = new char[MAXSIZE];
StringBuffer buffer = new StringBuffer("data");
buffer.getChars(0, 3, carr, 0);
```

For more information, see the topic "StringBuffer Class" in Part V, "API Quick Reference".

CLASS KEYWORD

Java vs. C++

In Java, classes are the most basic part of program organization, even more so than in C++. Java classes can be defined only with the **class** keyword; **struct** and **union** are not supported.

NOTE

Unlike C and C++, Java has no problem with forward references to classes and methods. Consequently, you can declare classes in any order.

Syntax

A class declaration has the following syntax. Unlike C++, Java does not terminate class declarations with a semicolon.

[public] [final] [abstract] class *class_name* **[extends** *super_class*] **[implements** *interfaces*] **{**

declarations

}

Here, brackets indicate optional items. The declarations consist of any number of method and variable definitions. Note that unlike C++, the default access level is not **private**; in this respect, Java classes are more like C structures. See the topics "Methods" and "Variables" for more information.

Syntax: Modifiers

The modifiers include any of the following, in any order: **abstract**, **final**, and **public**. Table C.1 summarizes the meaning of each modifier.

Table C.1 *Modifiers of the* ***class*** *Keyword*

MODIFIER	DESCRIPTION
abstract	The class contains one or more abstract methods (methods without definitions). If any method is declared **abstract**, then its class must also be declared **abstract**.
final	The class may not be subclassed.
public	The class is accessible both inside and outside the package. Methods and variables of the class are accessible outside the package if they are also declared **public**.

For more information, see individual topics for the keywords.

In each source file, there can be at most one class declared **public**. This class must also have a name that precisely matches the base name of the source file. Public classes and methods are significant not only because they are accessible outside the package but also because they serve as entry points into the application or applet.

Syntax: extends Clause

The optional **extends** clause specifies a single superclass (also called a *base class*). You can only specify one superclass, because Java does not support multiple inheritance.

extends *super_class*

All the fields (members) of the superclass are automatically fields of the current class. See the topics "Inheritance" and "extends Keyword" for more information.

Syntax: implements Clause

The optional **implements** keyword is followed by one or more interfaces. If there are more than one, they are separated by commas.

implements *interface1* [,*interface2*]...

An interface is similar to an abstract class, but interfaces are declared with a different keyword and have special restrictions placed on them. When a class implements an interface, it must provide a definition for each method declared in the interface. See "interface Keyword" for more information.

Examples

The following simple example declares a Pnt class with two members and a constructor, which is a method with the same name as the class. (See the topic "Constructors" for more information.)

```
class Pnt {
     int x, y;

     Pnt(int x, int y) {  // Constructor
          this.x = x;
          this.y = y;
     }
}
```

The next class declaration creates a subclass of Pnt by using the

extends keyword. The class inherits x and y and adds a variable and some methods, one of which is a constructor.

```
class PointTemp extends Pnt {
     private double degreesC;

     PointTemp(int x, int y, double d) {  // Constructor
          super(x, y);
          degreesC = d;
     }
     void Set_Fahrenheit(double degreesF) {
          degreesC = (degreesF - 32) / 1.8;
     }
}
```

The previous two examples use the keywords **this** and **super**. See the topics "this Keyword" and "super Keyword" for more information.

The final example shows the declaration of a class creating an applet. The class must be declared **public** and must be placed in a source file with the same name (Life). It implements **Runnable** because the applet involves more than one thread.

```
public class Life extends java.applet.Applet imple-
ments Runnable {
     boolean Grid[][] = new boolean[20][20];
     int Totals[][] = new int[20][20];
     int cellx, celly;
     Thread runner;

     // Method declarations follow
     //...
}
```

COMMENTS

Java vs. C++

Java supports the same comment symbols that C and C++ support.

Syntax

Both the line comment (C++) and the multiline comment (traditional C) are supported:

// comment_to_end_of_line

/ comment_text*

...

*more_comment_text */*

All text that appears inside a comment is simply ignored by the Java compiler. Comments may contain any information, preferably in human-readable form, that you find helpful when reviewing the source code.

Java also supports comments beginning with /**. This syntax creates a documentation comment which is the same as a standard comment, except that the **javadoc** compiler can be used to extract the comment text into a documentation file:

*/** doc_comment_text*

...

*more_comment_text */*

Example

This example uses comments to describe the purpose of each of its variables:

```
/* Declare a 2D array and two indexes. */

double matrix[][];   // 2D array; allocate space later
int r;               // Index to rows
int c;               // Index to columns
```

Example: Viewing Comments

You can view documentation comments by using the javadoc compiler provided in the JDK. (As explained earlier, a documentation comment begins with /**.) Simply specify the name of one or more source files as the argument to **javadoc**:

```
javadoc myclass.java
```

The javadoc compiler produces a file with an HTML extension; in this example, it produces a file called **myclass.html**. This HTML file displays information summarizing classes and fields in a **.class** file. It also includes any documentation comments that were placed in the source code.

COMPOUND STATEMENTS

Java vs. C++

Java uses the same compound-statement syntax that C and C++ use.

Syntax

A compound statement consists of one or more statements enclosed in braces:

{ *statements* }

A compound statement can appear anywhere a single statement can appear. Variables and objects declared inside the compound statement are local to the statement block. Unlike C, Java has no requirement that all variables and object declarations precede all executable statements.

Example

The following example executes two statements if the variable x is out of range. The two statements are grouped in a compound statement and therefore are *both* executed if the condition is true.

```
if (x < 0 || x > 100) {
     x_in_range = false;
     return -1;
}
```

CONDITIONAL OPERATOR (?:)

Java vs. C++

Java provides the same support for the conditional operator (:?) that C and C++ provide. However, note that the conditional expression must be a genuine Boolean expression, such as the result of a comparison.

Syntax

The conditional operator forms an expression from three subexpressions:

conditional_expr **?** *expr1* **:** *expr2*

The conditional expression, which must be Boolean, is evaluated first. If the result is true, *expr1* is evaluated; if it is false, *expr2* is evaluated. The result of the entire expression is *expr1* or *expr2*, whichever was evaluated.

Example

The following statement sets MaxNum to a if it is greater than b; otherwise, MaxNum is set to b:

```
MaxNum = (a > b ? a : b);
```

CONST KEYWORD (C++)

Java vs. C++

Not supported in Java. However, **const** is a reserved word and may be supported in future versions of Java.

You can use the **final** keyword to create variables with constant values in Java. When a variable is declared **static final** and is initialized with a constant, it creates a compile-time constant rather than an actual variable.

See the topic "final Keyword."

CONSTRUCTORS

Java vs. C++

In Java, as in C++, a constructor is a method that is automatically called when an object is created. Constructors are useful for initialization.

Because all Java objects are references, Java does not make the extensive use of copy constructors that C++ does. See the example for the Java equivalent of a copy constructor.

Syntax

A constructor has the same name as its class:

class(*args*)

For any given class, you can provide any number of different constructors, each with a different argument list. Note that constructors have no return type, not even **void**.

Example

This example declares a class with three constructors. Each constructor, like the class, is named Point.

```
class Point {
     int x, y;

     Point() {x = 0; y = 0; }    // default constructor
     Point(int newx, int newy)
          { x = newx; y = newy;}
     Point(Point p)              // copy constructor
          { x = p.x; y = p.y;}
// ...
```

CONTEXT OPERATOR (C++)

Java vs. C++

Not supported in Java.

Although Java supports classes and objects, elimination of the context operator (:) is one of the ways Java is smaller than C++. The context operator performs several important roles in C++ programming that are handled differently in Java:

- Clarification of scope: Java uses the dot (.) notation rather than the context operator. For example, **Color.red** is a valid expression, even though **Color** is a class and not an object.
- Referring to a member defined in a base class: In Java, you can use the **this** and **super** keywords to clarify scope. For example: this.x or super.x. The expression super.x refers to a member of the base class. This usage is unambiguous, because Java does not support multiple inheritance. See the topic "super Keyword."
- Defining a member function (method) outside the class declaration: In Java, all methods must be defined within the class declaration, so this is not an issue.
- Referring to symbols in namespaces: Java does not support namespaces, although packages can be used in a way similar to the way namespaces are used.

CONTINUE STATEMENT

Java vs. C++

The **continue** statement does the same thing in Java as in C and C++, advancing to the next iteration of a loop. Java also permits specification of a label to identify the loop. This arrangement helps make up for the lack of a **goto** statement.

Syntax

The **continue** statement has two forms:

continue;

continue *label*;

If *label* is specified, execution transfers to the top of the loop identified; the label must be attached to the first line of the loop. Otherwise, execution transfers to the top of the innermost loop. In either case, if the affected loop is a **for** loop, the increment portion of that loop is executed before the next iteration.

Example

In this example, if end_of_row returns the value **true**, the **continue** statement advances execution to the next iteration of the outer **for** loop. Note that **continue** does not cause skipping of the increment (in this case, i++).

```
major_loop: for(int i = 0; i < 20; i++) {
                for(int j = 0; j < 20; j++) {
                    amount += matrix[i][j];
                    if (end_of_row())
                        continue major_loop;
                }
}
```

DATA MEMBERS

Java vs. C++

Java classes have data members just as C++ classes do, but in Java they are usually called class variables and instance variables. In Java, all variables are either class, instance, or local, a policy that simplifies scope issues.

See the topic "Variables."

DATA TYPES

Java vs. C++

Java supports no unsigned integers, and it introduces the **byte** and **boolean** types. The sizes of some integers are different from those in typical C and C++ implementations.

Primitive Types

In Table D.1, all integer values (**byte**, **short**, **int**, and **long**) are signed, and all of them use two's complement format to represent negative numbers. In contrast to C and C++, the use of two's complement and data types of the size shown is not implementation-dependent.

Table D.1 *Primitive data types*

TYPE	DESCRIPTION	RANGE AND PRECISION
boolean	Boolean value (stored in one bit)	Two possible values: **true** or **false**
char	Unicode character (two bytes)	\u0000 to \uFFFF
byte	One-byte integer	–128 to 127
short	Two-byte integer	–32,768 to 32,767
int	Four-byte integer	Approx. –2.147 billion to 2.147 billion
long	Eight-byte integer	Approx. plus or minus 9 times 10^{18}.

float	Four-byte floating point	Approx. plus or minus 3.4 times 10^{38}. Seven digits of precision.
double	Eight-byte floating point	Approx. plus or minus 1.7 times 10^{308}. 15 digits of precision.

Note that although the **char** type holds a single character, the **String** type is not equivalent to an array of **char**. See the topic "Strings" for more information.

DEFAULT ARGUMENT VALUES (C++)

Java vs. C++

Not supported in Java.

Although the ability to declare argument lists with default values is sometimes a useful feature of C++, Java drops support for this feature in the name of simplifying the language. The same functionality, it should be noted, can be achieved by using method overloading.

Java has a related feature found in neither C nor C++: guaranteed variable values for primitive data variables. In Java, uninitialized variables have the value 0, 0.0, or **false**, as appropriate for the data type. This arrangement works for all kinds of variables that have a primitive data type. It does not work for objects, which must be explicitly initialized.

DEFAULT KEYWORD

Java vs. C++

The **default** keyword does the same thing in Java as in C and C++: it labels a default branch inside a **switch** statement.

Syntax

This keyword turns a statement into a labeled statement:

default:

  statement

Within a **switch** statement, if none of the case labels matches the test expression, execution transfers to the *statement.* Only one use of **default** can occur inside each **switch** statement.

Example

See the topic "switch Statement" for an example.

#DEFINE DIRECTIVE (C++)

Java vs. C++

Not supported in Java.

One of the main purposes of the **#define** directive in C and C++ is to create symbolic constants. You can do this in Java by modifying a variable declaration with the **final** keyword. Moreover, if you declare a variable as **static final**, you create a constant that can be used in calculations at compile time. The effect is to achieve the same optimization benefits that a **#define** constant has in C.

The other purpose of **#define** is to create macro functions. The Java alternative is to rely on writing methods, which can be overloaded to accommodate different types as needed. A sufficiently powerful Java compiler can in-line functions in an optimal fashion, producing the same benefit as macro functions.

See the topic "final Keyword."

DELETE OPERATOR (C++)

Java vs. C++

Not supported in Java.

Java eliminates the need for this operator. C++ expects you to release any memory allocated with the **new** operator. Java, in contrast, keeps track of memory associated with each object; after memory is no longer being used by any object, Java automatically releases that memory. This process, called *garbage collection*, runs in the background as a low-priority thread.

When an object variable goes out of scope, Java recognizes this and notes that the variable no longer refers to memory or other objects. When there are no references left to an area of memory, it can be freed by the garbage collector. There is, in effect, an internal "reference count" for objects and memory.

The longer the existence of an object variable, the longer it will hold onto memory. You can therefore influence memory management by making objects local wherever appropriate. Aside from this fact, however, you can program in Java without worrying about deleting objects or memory.

DESTRUCTORS (C++)

Java vs. C++

Not supported in Java. However, Java supports a similar concept in the form of **finalizer( )** methods inherited from the **object** class.

The Java garbage collector takes care of all the details of releasing objects and memory. See the topic "delete Operator (C++)" for more information. Because most destructors in C++ are concerned with releasing memory and because this is automated in Java, destructors are seldom necessary in Java.

When a class owns resources other than memory, you may need to write a **finalizer( )** method to perform cleanup.

DO KEYWORD

Java vs. C++

The **do** statement does the same thing in Java as in C and C++; it executes one or more statements as long as a condition is true. But note that the condition must be a genuine Boolean expression, such as a comparison.

Syntax

The **do** statement is one of the Java loop structures.

do
    statement
while (*condition***);**

The *statement* is executed at least once. After each execution of *statement*, if *condition* is true, the *statement* is executed again. The **do** statement differs from the **while** statement in that at least one execution of *statement* is guaranteed. See "while Statement" for the alternative syntax.

The condition must be a Boolean expression, such as Sum > 1.

Example

This example multiples amount by n as long as n is greater than zero.

```
do {
     amount = amount * n;
     n--;
}  while (n > 0);
```

DOUBLE DATA TYPE

Java vs. C++

The **double** data type has essentially the same characteristics as it has in C and C++, but its size is fixed for all time at 64 bits (eight bytes).

Syntax

The **double** keyword can be used to create 64-bit (eight-byte) floating-point variables:

double *declarations***;**

The range is approximately plus or minus 1.8 times 10 to the 308th power, with 14 places of precision after the decimal point. Tiny, nonzero values can get as close to zero as approximately plus or minus 4.9 times 10 to the –324th power. The type can also hold the value zero precisely.

The **java.lang.Double** class includes a number of class constants of type **double**, including **NEGATIVE_INFINITY**, **POSITIVE_INFINITY**, and **NaN** ("not a number."). Floating-point arithmetic never raises exceptions but may result in one of these values.

Example

The example creates temperature as an eight-byte floating-point variable with an initial value of 98.6. The second example declares two floating-point variables.

```
double temperature = 98.6;

double x, y = 2.0;
```

ELSE KEYWORD

Java vs. C++

The **else** keyword does the same thing in Java as in C and C++; it provides an alternative to an **if** statement.

Syntax

The **else** keyword appears in the following syntax:

if *condition*

    statement1

[**else**

    statement2]

Here, the brackets indicate that the **else** clause is optional. If included, both **else** and *statement2* must appear. See the topic "if Keyword" for more details and for an example.

EMPTY STATEMENTS

Java vs. C++

Empty statements are legal in Java as in C and C.

Syntax

An empty statement consists of a lone semicolon:

;

Java has relatively little use for empty statements. However, they are legal anywhere a complete Java statement would be legal. This means that Java is relatively forgiving (as are C and C++) if you type extra semicolons at the end of a statement. On the other hand, a semicolon is not legal anywhere a complete statement would not be legal.

EXCEPTION HANDLING

Java vs. C++

Java's exception-handling syntax is close to that of C++. The main differences are that all exception classes are derived from the **Throwable** class, and any method you write that might generate an exception without handling it must declare the exception with a **throws** clause.

Syntax

An *exception* is an unusual run-time event that must be handled immediately. Errors are the most typical cases of exceptions but are not the only ones. See the Glossary for a fuller description.

Java uses the following exception-handling syntax. Brackets indicate optional items.

try {

statements

}

[**catch(***ExceptionClass1 e1***){**

statements

}]

[**catch(***ExceptionClass2 e2***){**

statements

}]

...

[**finally {**

statements

}]

The statements inside the **try** block are executed unconditionally as part of the normal flow of execution. During execution of **try**-block statements an exception may be raised (by one of these statements or during a method call). If the exception is not handled by a more tightly nested block or method, the Java interpreter checks to see if one of the **catch** blocks can handle the exception.

Each exception is thrown in the form of an object, enabling exceptions to contain status information or error strings. Every exception class must be derived from the **Throwable** class. When the Java interpreter responds to an exception, it checks *ExceptionClass1*, *ExceptionClass2*, and so on until it finds a class that matches the type of the exception: there is a match if the exception's type is *ExceptionClass* or is derived from *ExceptionClass*. The statements inside the **catch** block are then executed. A **catch** block is not part of the normal flow of execution.

NOTE

Some early versions of Java supported the use of simple statements: that is, omission of the braces ({}) if try and catch blocks had only one statement each. However, not all versions of Java support this syntax, and many people discourage it as bad style anyway. To be safe, always use braces with try, catch, and finally keywords.

Inside the **catch** block, the code may decline to handle the exception by executing a **throw** statement:

throw;

In this case, the exception is passed along and the Java interpreter must search for another handler. Exceptions not handled by any code eventually reach the Java default exception handler, which prints a message and terminates execution.

Code in the **finally** block is executed unconditionally after execution leaves the **try** block. The **finally** block is guaranteed to be executed, whether the **try** block terminated normally or exited early due to an exception or **break** statement. The **finally** block is a logical place to put code that cleans up resources such as open file handle.

Example

This example shows a skeletal outline of exception-handling code.

```
try {
      // Open data file.
      // Attempt to read.
}
catch(EOFException e1) {
```

```
        // EOF reached; stop reading file.
}
catch(FileNotFoundException e2) {
        // File not found; print error msg.
}
catch(IOException e3) {
        // Misc. IO exception; print error msg.
}
finally {
        // If file still open, close it.
}
```

Declaring Exceptions (throws)

As you can see in Appendix A, "Java Exceptions and Errors," there are two kinds of exceptions: those that you must handle and those whose handling is optional. The optional exceptions are those derived from the **Error** and **RuntimeException** classes: each of these exceptions involves a common run-time error occurring in programs generally. Such exceptions are difficult to foresee when programming.

An exception such as **FileNotFoundException** happens only in response to certain method calls. Not surprisingly, Java requires you to handle these exceptions, because you have a good idea when they may or may not occur. For example, you watch for i/o exceptions (of which **FileNotFoundException** is a subclass) when you are doing file i/o work.

When you call a method that throws one of these mandatory exceptions, you have two choices. You can handle it in the code using a **try-catch** block, as explained in the previous section. Or you can declare your method with a **throws** clause: this tells the compiler, "I may throw this exception without handling it. Whoever calls me must handle it." For example:

```
void readFile(String s) throws IOException {
```

```
// ...
}
```

Every caller of this method must include a **try-catch** block for type **IOException,** or else include **throws IOException** in its own declaration. This is the Java equivalent of passing the buck.

Simplified Exception Handling

The paradox of exception handling is that it's bothersome in simple programs but necessary in professional-quality software. For your first programs, you probably should include a few lines that handle exceptions in a concise way.

You must place a statement after a **catch** clause, but it is legal to use an empty statement (;):

```
try {Thread.sleep(250);}
catch (InterruptedException e) {;}
```

I don't recommend this technique unless you never expect to see the exception. In this case, **InterruptedException** is unlikely to be thrown in a simple thread program, so it's fairly safe to ignore this exception.

However, it's usually a good idea to at least print a simple diagnostic. You can print an exception by passing it to the **println()** method. This method can take any object as argument. It responds by calling the object's **toString()** method, which in this case identifies the particular type of exception.

```
try {Thread.sleep(250);}
catch (InterruptedException e)
{System.out.println(e);}
```

For more diagnostic information, you can use a *stack trace*, which prints a list of all Java methods currently executing at the time of the exception. The exact place where the exception was thrown is listed first. All exception classes inherit the stack-trace capability from **Throwable**.

```
try {Thread.sleep(250);}
```

```
catch (InterruptedException e) {e.printStackTrace();}
```

Still another strategy is to place a **throws** clause in the current method's declaration, removing the need for a **try-catch** block. This means that the *caller* of the method must deal with the possibility of the exception. You can, if you choose, propagate the exception all the way up the line, even placing a **throws** clause in **main()**, thereby kicking back all responsibility to Java. Then you never need deal with the exception; but doing this tends to defeat the purpose of having exception handling in the first place.

EXTENDS KEYWORD

Java vs. C++

In Java, **extends** designates a superclass. In C++, a colon (:) is used for this purpose.

Syntax

When you declare a class, place **extends** and a superclass name immediately after the class name. (The superclass is sometimes called *base class* or *parent class*.)

[**public**] [**abstract**] [**final**] **class** *class_name* [**extends** *super_class_name*] **{**
    declarations
}

Use of **extends** *super_class_name* is optional. If omitted, the superclass is **Object** by default. Only single inheritance is supported for classes. The effect of inheritance is to implicitly include all the declarations of the superclass (except for constructors) in the current class declaration. See the topic "Inheritance" for more information. Also, see the topic "class Keyword" for additional **class** syntax.

The **extends** keyword can also be used in interface declarations. An interface can inherit only from other interfaces.

[**public**] [**abstract**] **interface** *interface_name* [**extends** *interface1*

[,*interface2*]...] **{**

declarations

}

After **extends**, there may be any number of *interfaces*. If there are more than one, separate them by commas.

Examples

This class declaration indicates that Pubs is the superclass for Newspaper. The effect is to create Newspaper as identical to Pubs except for the addition of two new members.

```
class Newspaper extends Pubs {
     public String  editor;
     public long    circulation;
}
```

In an interface declaration, the interface may inherit from any number of other interfaces:

```
interface Lang_Translator extends English, French, German {
     // declarations...
}
```

EXTERN DECLARATIONS (C++)

Java vs. C++

Not supported in Java.

Java does not have global variables in the sense that C and C++ have them, so there is no external storage. However, within the definition of a method, you have access to members of the same class. You also have access to members of another class as long as the following things are true:

- The compiled class information (**.class** file) is available in the appropriate directory. By default, this is the current directory. For information on how Java searches directories, see Chapter 2, "Java Building Blocks."

- The class is in the same package, or the class is declared **public**—in which case, the class can be in any package. If the class is in another package, both the class and individual members to be accessed must be declared **public**.

If you refer to a class in another package, you need to qualify the name of the class by using the syntax *package.Class*, unless you use the **import** statement to abbreviate the name as *Class*.

See the topics "class Keyword," "package Keyword," and "import Statement" for more information. See also Chapter 2, "Java Building Blocks."

FALSE KEYWORD

Java vs. C++

Because Boolean expressions are not the same as integers, Java provides the Boolean constants **true** and **false**. In C and C++, the values 1 and 0 would suffice.

Syntax

The **false** keyword is a predefined constant in the Java language. It represents one of two possible values for expressions of type **boolean**:

false

Example

Comparing a condition to **false** reverses its logical meaning:

```
boolean outa_range = false;

outa_range = (X < 0 || X > 100);

if (outa_range == false)

     // X is in range...
```

Note that using the logical negation operator (!) has the same effect:

```
if (!outa_range)
     // X is in range...
```

FINAL KEYWORD

Java vs. C++

In addition to providing some other uses, the **final** keyword provides the only way to declare symbolic constants in Java.

Syntax

When applied to a variable definition, **final** specifies that the value cannot change. The variable *must* be initialized in the definition. If the variable is also declared **static** and is initialized to a constant value, the variable becomes a compile-time constant (equivalent to a **#define** constant in C/C++), meaning that it can be folded into calculations at compile time.

final [*other_modifiers*] *type variable* = *value***;**

When applied to a class declaration, **final** specifies that the class can never be subclassed (made a superclass for any other class).

final [*other_modifiers*] **class** *class_name* [*extend, implement clauses*] **{**

declarations

}

When applied to a method definition, **final** specifies that the method can never be overridden by a subclass. If the method is also declared **static**, the compiler can potentially inline the method to optimize the program.

final [*other_modifiers*] *return_type method_name***(***args***) {**

statements

}

Example

This class declaration shows examples of each use of **final**:

```
final class MyClass {
     final float pi = 3.141592;
     final int freeze = 0, boil = 100;

     final float pi_quot(float x) {
          return pi/x;
     }
}
```

FLOAT DATA TYPE

Java vs. C++

The **float** data type has essentially the same characteristics as it does in C and C++, but its size is fixed for all time at 32 bits (four bytes).

Syntax

The **float** keyword can be used to create 32-bit (four-byte) floating-point variables:

float *declarations*;

The range is approximately plus or minus 3.4 times 10 to the 38th power, with six places of precision after the decimal point. Tiny, nonzero values can get as close to zero as approximately plus or minus 1.4 times 10 to the –45th power. The type can also hold the value zero precisely.

The **java.lang.Float** class includes a number of class constants of type **float**, including **NEGATIVE_INFINITY**, **POSITIVE_INFINITY**, and **NaN** ("not a number."). Floating-point arithmetic never raises exceptions, but may result in one of these values.

Example

The example creates temperature as an four-byte floating-point variable with an initial value of 98.6. The second example declares two floating-point variables.

```
float temperature = (float) 98.6;

float x, y = (float) 2.0;
```

Note that floating-point constants must be cast to type **float** before being assigned.

FOR STATEMENT

Java vs. C++

The **for** statement does essentially the same thing in Java as in C and C++; it executes statements repeatedly. However, in Java, the **for** statement enables special use of the comma (,) as an expression separator, and it also enables declaration of variables local to the **for** statement itself.

Syntax

The basic syntax of the **for** statement is the same as that in C and C++:

for (*initializer***;** *condition***;** *increment***)**
    statement

As in C and C++, the **for** statement syntax is essentially equivalent to the following **while** loop:

*initializer***;**
while(*condition***) {**
    statement
    *increment***;**
}

Each of the expressions has some special features not present in the C/C++ **for** statement, so you should probably examine the next few sections if you are new to its use in Java.

The initializer Expression

The *initializer* expression is executed just once, before the rest of the loop begins. Typically, it initializes a loop variable:

```
i = 0
```

You can use the comma to insert multiple expressions. This (along with the *increment* portion of the **for** statement) is the only place that Java enables this use of the comma:

```
i = 0, j = 0
```

A feature unique to Java lets you declare variables "on the fly" in the initialization expression. When you do this, the comma can be used only to separate variables in the list. You cannot combine this technique with the multiple-expression technique just shown.

```
int i = 0, j = 0
```

Variables have the same scope as the **for** loop when they are declared this way.

The condition Expression

The **for** loop executes as long as the *condition* is true. As elsewhere in Java, *condition* must be a genuine Boolean expression. Booleans include comparisons but not simple integer expressions. The *condition* in a **for** loop is typically a test to see whether a loop variable has reached a limit of some kind. For example:

```
i < array.length
```

The increment Expression

The *increment* expression is executed at the end of each iteration of the loop. Typically, this involves updating a loop variable:

```
i++
```

As with the *initializer* expression, Java permits the use of multiple expressions here, separated by commas:

```
i++, j++, k++
```

Examples

This simple example initializes all the members of an array:

```
int(i = 0; i < array.length; i++)
     array[i] = 0;
```

The second example uses a **for** statement to copy all the elements of arrayA to arrayB but in reverse order. The *initializer* declares the variables i and j and initializes them. These variables are local to the **for** statement. The *increment* expression uses the comma to separate two independent expressions, i++ and j--.

```
int arrayA[] = new int[50];
int arrayB[] = new int[50];
// ...

for (int i = 0, j = 49; i < 50; i++, j--)
     arrayA[i] = arrayB[j];
```

FRIEND KEYWORD (C++)

Java vs. C++

Not supported in Java.

Elimination of the C++ **friend** keyword is another way Java reduces the size of the language. The **friend** keyword in C++ is used principally as an aid for writing binary operator functions (operator overloading). The only other use for **friend** is to break encapsulation, which runs counter to the goals of object-oriented programming and design. Because Java does not support operator overloading, there is little reason to support **friend**.

FUNCTIONS (C++)

Java vs. C++

Technically speaking, Java does not have functions; it only has methods (member functions). In practical terms, this means that you must place all function code inside class declarations.

To use C++ terminology, we should say that Java has no global functions. However, Java supports and encourages the use of class methods, as opposed to instance methods. Class methods are declared with the **static** keyword and correspond closely to static member functions in C++.

A class method works very much like a global function. Class methods are not tied to individual objects (instances) and can be used without regard to whether you have instantiated a particular object. If you call a class method from within its own class, you can use the method directly as though it were a global function. You can also call class methods from other classes as long as the names are properly qualified. Using the **import** statement enables you to use the method name without worrying about the package name.

See the topics "Methods," "static Keyword," and "import Statement."

GOTO STATEMENT (C++)

Java vs. C++

Not supported in Java.

Structured programming generally discourages the use of the direct-jump statements such as **goto**. In C and C++, **goto** is still useful for breaking out of several loops directly and for responding to error conditions. Java provides labeled **break** and **continue** statements to break out of nested loops, eliminating the major use for **goto**. In addition, exception handling provides a way to respond to errors from anywhere in the program.

See the topics "break Statement," "continue Statement," and "Exception Handling."

HEXADECIMAL NOTATION

Java uses the same notation for hexadecimal notation used by C and C++. The syntax is **0x***num*; for example, 0x1A. See the topic "int Data Type." You can also use hexadecimal to specify a character code, as shown in Table G, "Java escape sequences," in Part VI.

IDENTIFIERS

Java vs. C++

Java uses the same rules for forming identifiers that C and C++ use.

Syntax

An identifier is a name that you create, as opposed to a keyword or operator. Identifiers serve as names for variables, classes, packages, and methods. As in C and C++, identifiers in Java observe these rules:

- An identifier must not be a reserved word (this includes all keywords).
- Identifiers consist of any of the following: the letters A–Z (uppercase and lowercase), the digits 0–9, and the underscore.
- The first character cannot be a digit.

Example

The following are all valid identifiers:

```
a
x04
count
this_is_Java
cuppaCoffee
MyClass
```

NOTE The Java API uses a naming convention that I have adopted in this book. The names of classes have the first letter capitalized. The names of all other symbols—including variables, methods, and packages—have the first letter in lowercase. Although the language itself does not require this approach, it is a useful convention for making programs easier to read.

IF STATEMENT

Java vs. C++

The **if** statement does the same thing in Java as in C and C++; it executes one or more statements if a condition is true. But note that the condition must be a true Boolean expression, such as a comparison.

Syntax

The **if** statement constitutes a single complex statement.

if (*condition***)**
    statement1
[**else**
    statement2]

The brackets indicate that the **else** clause is optional. You can, in effect, create **else if** clauses by making *statement2* an **if** statement. (See the examples.)

The condition must be a Boolean expression, such as Sum > 0. An integer expression, such as Sum, is not a valid condition.

Examples

The first example prints a message if n is not equal to zero. Note that using n itself as a condition would not be valid.

```
if (n != 0) {
    System.out.println("n not equal to zero.");
```

```
        return true;
}
```

The next example performs a series of comparisons.

```
if (a > b)
     System.out.println("a is greater than b");
else if (a == b)
     System.out.println("a is equal to b");
else
     System.out.println("a is less than b");
```

#IF DIRECTIVE (C++)

Java vs. C++

Not supported in Java.

The **#if** directive is supported in C and C++ primarily to support conditional compilation. This technique enables you to maintain one set of source code files, from which you generate different versions of the software. Conditional compilation is far less necessary or useful in Java, because a Java binary file executes equally well on all platforms that support a Java interpreter. Contrast this with C and C++, where you might well need to maintain different source files for 16-bit Intel systems, 32-bit Intel systems, Macintosh, and so on. Because **#if** is not really necessary in Java, eliminating it is another way of reducing the size of the language.

Java does not support any of the C/C++ preprocessor commands, including **#ifdef**, **#else**, **#endif**, and so on, for the same reasons it does not support **#if**. Eliminating the preprocessor step also helps make the Java interpreter much more efficient.

IMPLEMENTS KEYWORD

Java vs. C++

In Java, **implements** is used to indicate a special kind of inheritance, in which a class inherits declarations from an interface and provides implementations (definitions) for all its methods. In C++, this can be done by simply inheriting from abstract classes. Java uses the **implements** keyword because it treats interfaces in a privileged way. Only with interfaces can you get around Java's restriction against multiple inheritance.

Syntax

The *implements* keyword can be used within a class declaration. (This syntax does not include the use of **throws**. See the topic "class Keyword" for more information.)

[*modifiers*] **class** *class_name* [**extends** *super_class_name*]

[**implements** *interface1* [,*interface2*...]]

{

declarations

}

Here, the brackets indicate optional items. After **implements** appears, one or more *interfaces* appear. If there are more than one, they must be separated by commas.

For each interface that the class implements, it must provide method-definition code for all the methods declared in that interface. See the topic "interface Keyword" for more information on interfaces.

Example

The following code declares an interface called Shape, which declares two methods. Because Shape is an interface, the methods are implicitly declared abstract and are not given definitions.

```
import java.awt.Graphics;

interface Shape {
     public void moveTo(int newx, int newy);
     public void reDraw(Graphics g);
}
```

The class MyRectClass inherits declarations from the Shape interface. MyRectClass not only inherits from Shape but also *implements* it by providing definitions for each of the two Shape methods (moveTo and reDraw).

```
import java.awt.Graphics;


class MyRectClass implements Shape {
     int x, y;

     public void moveTo(int newx, int newy) {
          x = newx;
          y = newy;
     }

     public void reDraw(Graphics g) {
          g.drawRect(x, y, 20, 20);
     }
}
```

IMPORT STATEMENT

Java vs. C++

At first glance, the Java **import** statement seems to work much like the C/C++ **#include** directive: it makes classes declared in other files available. But any compiled, public class in the current directory (or a CLASSPATH directory, if CLASSPATH is used) is available without special declarations. The purpose of **import** is to let you refer to classes and interfaces without spelling out their package names.

Syntax

The **import** statement has two forms. In each case, *package* must be a complete package name such as **java.awt** or **java.applet**. You may include any number of **import** statements, but they must appear after the **package** statement, if any, and before the first **class** or **interface** declaration.

The first version of **import** lets you subsequently refer to the specified class without qualifying the name with the package. (See the example for clarification.)

import *package.class*;

The other version of **import** is similar except that it lets you refer to *all* the classes and interfaces in the package without qualifying the names with the package.

import *package.**;

Example

Without an **import** statement, references to the **Graphics** class must be qualified by its package, **java.awt**:

```
paint(java.awt.Graphics g) {
}
```

However, after using the **import** statement shown, you can refer directly to the **Graphics** class:

```
import java.awt.Graphics;
//...

paint(Graphics g) {
}
```

NOTE

The package java.lang is implicitly imported into all Java code, so you do not need to import it yourself. In other words, all classes in java.lang are directly available without the need to use the package name.

#INCLUDE DIRECTIVE (C++)

Java vs. C++

Not supported in Java.

The purpose of the **#include** directive in C and C++ is to support the inclusion of header files, which (among other things) include external declarations of variables and functions. But in Java, all public classes and interfaces are available as long as they have been compiled and the appropriate class information is present in the current directory (or a directory listed in the CLASSPATH environment variable, if CLASSPATH is used). In short, class information previously compiled is automatically available to your Java applications and applets.

Java's **import** statement is an aid to the use of other classes, because it enables you to refer to classes and methods more directly. The effect is vaguely similar to that of the **#include** directive in C and C++, although it does not actually do the same thing. None of the C/C++ preprocessor directives is supported in Java.

See the topic "import Statement" for more information.

INHERITANCE

Java vs. C++

Java and C++ support a similar inheritance mechanism. Inheritance is based on classes, which are object types (although interfaces can also inherit from one another). In Java, the **extends** keyword specifies a superclass. See "extends Keyword" for more information.

There are two key differences between the inheritance mechanism in Java and that in C++:

- By design Java classes cannot directly inherit from multiple classes. Eliminating multiple inheritance keeps the language simpler. It also enables the Java **super** keyword to be used unambiguously. At the same time, Java helps get around the limitations of single inheritance by letting a class implement any number of interfaces; in Java, an interface is a special kind of abstract class. See the topic "interface Keyword" for more information.

- All classes, with the exception of one, have a superclass. If you do not explicitly declare a superclass, the special class **Object** is the superclass by default. This class is part of the Java API and is defined in **java.lang**. All classes inherit, either directly or indirectly, from **Object**. A number of universal methods are defined in this class, including **equals()**, **wait()**, **finalize()**, **toString()**, and **clone()**. Some of these methods can be overridden. See the topic "Object Class" in the API Quick Reference for more information.

Limitations

In Java, a derived class automatically inherits all the members of the base class except for constructors. However, superclass constructors may be called from the derived class through the use of the **super** keyword. Note that private members of the superclass are inherited but are invisible, so they may appear not to have been inherited.

INSTANCEOF OPERATOR

Java vs. C++

The Java **instanceof** operator has the same general purpose of the run-time type information (RTTI) operators in ANSI C++.

Syntax

The **instanceof** operator is a Boolean operator that returns information on an arbitrary object at run time. It is particularly useful for determining whether a random object supports a particular method.

When used with a class, the **instanceof** operator returns **true** if the object is an instance of *class* or a subclass derived, directly or indirectly, from *class*.

object **instanceof** *class*

When used with an interface, the **instanceof** operator returns **true** if the object's class implements *interface* or is derived from a class that implements *interface.*

object **instanceof** *interface*

Example

In this example, the Test method is passed a random object, obj, which may be of type **Object** or a class derived from **Object** (in other words, any class). The example tests to see whether obj is an instance of the **String** class. If it is, then it is safe to call the **toLowerCase** method, which is a method of this class.

```
void Test(Object obj) {
     if (obj instanceof String)
          System.out.println(obj.toLowerCase());
//...
```

INT DATA TYPE

Java vs. C++

The Java **int** data type is similar to **int** in C and C++ except that its size is fixed at 32 bits (four bytes) for all implementations.

Syntax

The **int** keyword can be used to create 32-bit (four-byte) integer variables:

int *declarations***;**

The range is approximately plus or minus two billion: –2,147,483,648 to 2,147,483,647.

You can use hexadecimal and octal notation in Java just as you can in C (using **0x***num* and **0***num*). For example, 255 can also be written as 0xFF or 0377.

Examples

This example creates score as a four-byte integer variable with an initial value of 100. The second example declares two integer variables.

```
int score = 100;
int i, j;
```

Unlike C and C++, Java automatically sets uninitialized variables of primitive type to 0, although explicitly initializing them is good programming practice:

```
int i = 0, j = 0;
```

INTERFACE KEYWORD

Java vs. C++

In Java, an interface is like an abstract class—a class with methods that are not implemented. However, Java recognizes interfaces as distinct from classes and imposes a different syntax. The distinction is important in Java, because although interfaces have some limitations, they offer the only way around the restriction against multiple inheritance. In C++, an interface would be coded as just another class.

Classes inherit methods from an interface by the use of the **implements** keyword. See the topic "implements Keyword" for more information.

Syntax

An interface is declared with the following syntax:

[**public**] [**abstract**] **interface** *interface_name* [**extends** *interfaces*] **{**

declarations

}

Here, brackets indicate optional items. Interfaces are automatically abstract, so the **abstract** keyword is unnecessary, although legal. The optional **extends** clause may specify any number of other *interfaces* to inherit from. If there are more than one, they must be separated by commas (,).

The declarations can contain variables. The variables are automatically **static** and **final**, whether or not you use these keywords, and must be initialized to a constant expression. Interface variables are automatically public if the interface is public.

[**static**] [**final**] [**public**] *type variable* = *value*;

The declarations can also contain methods (usually the most important part of an interface). The methods are automatically abstract and do not contain a method definition; they are immediately terminated by semi-colons. Interface methods are automatically public if the interface is public. The methods cannot include constructors, and the only legal modifiers are those shown:

[**public**] [**abstract**] *return_type method_name*(*args*);

Example

An interface declares a list of services that each class implements in its own way. The class implements the interface by using the **implements** keyword and providing a definition (implementation) for each method declared in the interface. A class can have only one superclass, but it can implement any number of interfaces.

The following interface declares services for reporting status. Any class that implements this interface must provide a definition for each of the four methods listed.

```
public interface Status {
     boolean is_multithreaded();
     boolean is_active();
     int number_of_threads();
     void set_priority(int priority_num);
}
```

KEYWORDS

Java vs. C++

The Java, C, and C++ keywords include many of the same words. All but a few C++ keywords are also Java keywords. Java has some additional keywords, such as **package**, that support Java's unique features.

Summary

Table K.1 summarizes Java reserved words; most of these are keywords. However, there are some, marked by an asterisk (*), that currently have no use but are reserved for use in future versions of Java.

Table K.1 *Java reserved words and keywords*

abstract	boolean	break	byte	byValue*
case	cast*	catch	char	class
const*	continue	default	do	double
else	extends	false	final	finally
float	for	future*	generic*	goto*
if	implements	import	inner*	instanceof
int	interface	long	native	new
null	operator*	outer*	package	private
protected	public	rest*	return	short
static	super	switch	synchronized	this
throw	throws	transient	true	try
var*	void	volatile	while	

LABELS

Java vs. C++

In Java, statement labels are used in switch statements (as in C and C++) and as targets for break and continue statements. Java does not support a goto statement. The label syntax is the same as for C/C++.

Syntax

A labeled statement has one of three forms:

identifier: *statement*

case *constant_expression*: *statement*

default: *statement*

The first form is used to create a target of a **break** or **continue** statement. The other two forms are used only inside a **switch** statement block.

Example

This example labels the top of a **for** statement, giving it the name top_of_loop:

```
top_of_loop:
     for(int i = 0; i < 100; i++)
//...
```

For more information, see the topics "break Statement," "continue Statement," and "switch Statement."

LONG DATA TYPE

Java vs. C++

The **long** data type has a size fixed at 64 bits for all implementations.

Syntax

The **long** keyword can be used to create 64-bit (eight-byte) integer variables:

long *declarations*;

The range is –9,223,372,036,854,775,808 to 9,223,372,036,854,775,807 (approximately plus or minus 9 times 10 to the 18th power).

You can use hexadecimal and octal notation in Java just as you can in C (using **0x***num* and **0***num*). For example, 255 can also be written as 0xFF or 0377. You can also use the L suffix, as in 10L, to force a small constant to be stored as a **long**.

Examples

This example creates score as a 64-bit integer variable with an initial value of 100. The second example declares two integer variables.

```
long score = 100;
```

```
long i, j;
```

Unlike C and C++, Java automatically sets uninitialized variables of primitive type to 0, although explicitly initializing them is good programming practice:

```
long i = 0, j = 0;
```

MAIN METHOD

Java vs. C++

The **main()** method in Java has roughly the same purpose as the **main()** function in C and C++; however, it is an entry point only for applications and not for applets. Furthermore, in Java, **main()** is a method like any other and must be declared inside a public class.

Syntax

The **main( )** method is the entry point for an application and must be declared inside a public class. It should be given the attributes shown:

public static void main(String *args*[]) **{**

statements

}

The **main( )** method can instead be given an integer return type, in which case it must return a value. This value is received by the operating system.

public static int main(String *args*[]**) {**

statements

}

Here, *statements* must include at least one **return** statement.

In either case, *args* is an array of strings, each string containing a command-line argument. The first string in the array is the first argument on the command line after the class name itself. You can determine the number of command-line strings by referring to the **length** field of *args*.

Getting the Command Line

When using *args*, you may find it useful to review the unique features of Java arrays. (See the topic "Arrays.") **args[0]** and **args[1]** refer to the first and second command-line arguments, respectively, and **args.length** is equal to the total number of arguments. Figure M.1 shows how Java would parse the sample command line **java Printarg aa bb cc.**

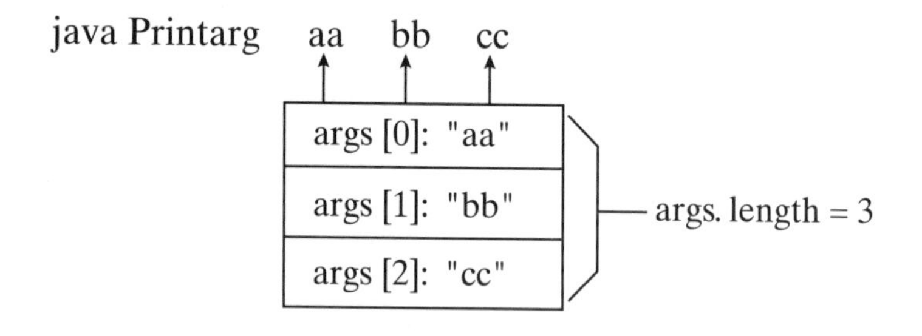

Figure M.1 *Getting arguments from a command line*

Example

The following example prints command-line arguments to the display, printing one to a line:

```
public class Printarg {
     public static void main(String args[]) {
          for (int n=0; n < args.length; n++)
               System.out.println(args[n]);
     }
}
```

This application must be contained in a source file named **Printarg.java**. When compiled and run, the application will be named Printarg. Consider the following command line:

```
java Printarg this is a test
```

This command line will result in the following output:

```
this
is
a
test
```

METHODS

Java vs. C++

Methods in Java are similar to function members in C++, but there are many differences. In particular, Java has no global functions and requires methods to be defined entirely within class declarations.

NOTE **Unlike C and C++, Java has no problem with forward references to classes and methods. Consequently, you can declare methods in any order without the need for prototypes.**

Syntax

Every method definition must occur inside a class declaration:

[*modifiers*] **class** *class_name* [*extends, implements clauses*] **{**

    ...

    method_declaration **{**

        statements

    }

    ...

}

This book assumes that all method definitions are inside a class declaration. The full syntax for a method declaration is as follows:

[*modifiers*] *return_type method_name***(***args***)** [**throws** *exceptions*] **{**

    statements

}

Here, brackets indicate optional items. Return type is not optional, although it may be **void**. (Exception: constructors have no return type.) This syntax is complete except for the case of **abstract** and **native** methods, which are terminated by a semicolon (;) in place of **{***statements***}** . See "abstract Keyword" and "native Keyword" for more information.

Syntax: Modifiers

The modifiers include any of the following, in any order: **abstract**, **final**, **native**, **static**, **synchronized**, **public**, **private**, and **protected**. The modifiers **private protected** can be used together, but neither one can be used with **public**. Table M.1 summarizes the meaning of each modifier.

Table M.1 *Modifiers for Java methods*

MODIFIER	DESCRIPTION
abstract	No definition is provided for the method. Definitions must be provided in subclasses.
final	Method may not be overridden in subclasses.
native	No definition is provided for the method. Definition is provided in another language, such as C.

private	Method can be accessed only within the class. This is not the default behavior; see discussion after end of table.
private protected	Method can be accessed only within the class and subclasses.
protected	Method can be accessed anywhere in the package and also by subclasses in other packages (if the class is public)
public	Method has same access level as the class.
static	Method is a class method; may refer only to static (class) variables
synchronized	Two threads cannot execute this method simultaneously.

For more information, see individual topics for the keywords. Note that if none of the access-level keywords is used (**public**, **private**, and **protected**), the method is visible to all other methods in the package but not outside the package. In contrast to C++ rules, in Java a method must be specifically declared **private** to be hidden to code outside the class.

Syntax: args

The Java argument-list syntax is almost identical to C++ but may not include default arguments. Also, if there are no arguments, leave the argument list blank; do not use **void**. In Java, unlike C, an empty argument list is unambiguous and means that the method takes no arguments.

type arg_name [**,** *type arg_name*]...

This syntax indicates that there may be any number of arguments. If there are more than one, separate them with commas.

Syntax: throws Clause

A method declaration may include an optional **throws** clause, which lists exceptions that a method may throw:

throws *exception1* [,*exception2*]...

This syntax indicates that the **throws** keyword is followed by one or more exceptions and that if there is more than one, commas are used to separate them.

The **throws** clause informs the compiler of exceptions that the method may throw without handling. Code that calls the method, therefore, should expect the possibility of being thrown these exceptions. Each such exception thrown must be declared in the **throws** clause, except for the classes **Error** and **RuntimeException** and their subclasses.

Examples

This example shows a simple method, Set_Pnt. This method is an instance method (it is not declared **static**) and is accessible throughout the package in which it appears.

```
class Pnt {
     int x, y;

     void Set_Pnt(int newx, int newy) {
          x = newx;
          y = newy;
     }
     //...
```

This next example shows a method, resetVars, that is private to the class and is a class method (because it is declared **static**).

```
class Myclass {
     private static int x, y;
     private static double ratio;
```

```
    private static displayString;

    private static int resetVars() {
        x = 0;
        y = 0;
        ratio = 0.0;
        displayString = "";
        return 0;
    }
    //...
```

This last example shows a method that uses a **throws** clause. Because the method is public, it is accessible to code in other packages if the class is also public.

```
public long scanFile(File theFile) throws
FileNotFoundException {
    long size;
//...
    throw new FileNotFoundException();
//...
    return size;
}
```

METHOD OVERLOADING

Java vs. C++

Method overloading is supported in Java just as in C++. (In C++, it is usually called *function overloading*.)

Example

Method overloading is a technique for creating different versions of the same method within the same class; each version has the same name but a different argument list. The different versions are actually separate methods, and each version has its own definition. During a method call, the Java compiler determines which version to call by examining the argument list.

As in C++, the argument lists must differ in the number of arguments, the types, or both. You cannot have two different methods with the same name and argument list, but with different return values. However, as long as the argument lists differ, the return types do not necessarily have to be the same.

This example overloads the method name SetPnts:

```
class Pnt {
     private float x, y;

void setPnts(Pnt pt) {
     x = pt.x;
     y = pt.y;
}

void setPnts(float newx; float newy) {
     x = newx;
     y = newy;
}
// ...
```

MODULUS OPERATOR (%)

Java vs. C++

The modulus operator does exactly the same thing in Java as in C and C++: it returns the remainder of the division of two integers. (It is also called the *remainder* operator.)

Syntax

The modulus operator (%) forms an expression from two integer subexpressions:

quantity % *divisor*

The syntax is the same as division (/), but the remainder is the result. For example, 7 divided by 2 is 3 with a remainder of 1, so the expression 7 % 2 evaluates to 1.

Example

A common use is to determine when an integer is exactly divisible by another integer. For example, the following function determines whether a number is odd or even. It returns **true** if the number is even, and **false** otherwise.

```
boolean is_even(int n) {
    return (n % 2 == 0);
}
```

In general, if a number n is exactly divisible by a divisor d, then n % d evaluates to 0.

NAMESPACES (C++)

Java vs. C++

Not supported in Java.

You can use classes and packages in a way that's similar to using namespaces. Declaring class methods and class variables (as opposed to instance methods and classes) has an effect similar to that of declaring global functions and variables, as you would in C and C++. References to class methods and variables must be qualified, although you can use Java's **import** statement to abbreviate the reference to the class. You can therefore manage access to symbols defined in another class or package just as you can manage access to symbols in a C++ namespace.

See the topics "package Statement" and "import Statement" for more information.

NATIVE KEYWORD

Java vs. C++

The **native** keyword is an extended feature of Java not supported by C or C++.

Syntax

The **native** keyword can be applied to method declarations to indicate that the method is implemented with native code. The declaration must be terminated by a semicolon (;).

native [*other_modifiers*] *return_type method_name***(***args***);**

Native code consists of code that runs directly on a particular platform. A native-code method would therefore consist of machine instructions instead of Java byte codes. A method declared as **native** is generated by another language (such as assembler or a C compiler) and linked to a Java program at run time.

Example

This example declares a single native method.

```
native void set_protection_level(int level);
```

NEW OPERATOR

Java vs. C++

The **new** operator returns a reference and not a pointer. This means that you assign the result to an object variable and not to an address expression. (See “Examples.”)

In Java, it is usually necessary to use **new** to allocate actual space for an object. This makes **new** more important than it is in C++, which provides other ways to create an object. When you define an object variable in Java, it is merely a *reference* to an object. The variable must be associated with an actual object in memory (allocated with **new**) before it can be used.

In contrast to C++, there is no matching **delete** operator and no need to explicitly release memory in the source code. The Java interpreter handles object destruction and memory management for you through its garbage collection process.

Syntax

The **new** operator can be used to create one or more objects:

new *type*()	*// Calls default constructor*
new *type*(*args*)	*// Calls constructor that takes args*
new *type*[*size*]	*// Creates array object*
new *type*[*size1*][*size2*]...	*// Creates multidimensional array object*

In each case, the **new** operator returns a reference to the appropriate type of object. In the last two cases, the operator returns a reference to an array. (Arrays are also types of objects in Java.)

Some of the sizes in the multidimensional case can be left blank. See the topic "Arrays" for more information.

Examples

The first declaration shows the **new** operator used to allocate a single object. The second example shows the **new** operator used to allocate an array of objects.

```
MyClass obj = new MyClass();
MyClass arrayObj[] = new MyClass[10];
```

Note that you do not need to use **new** when defining variables of primitive type (**int**, **short**, **long**, **float**, **double**, **boolean**, **char**) or of **String** type. Primitive data allocates actual space in data storage, and **String** objects can be initialized with quoted strings.

```
int  a, b, c = 200;
String  Name = "John Q. Public";
```

NULL CONSTANT

Java vs. C++

Although Java does not support pointers, the Java predefined **null** constant is similar to the **null** pointer value in C and C++, usually defined as **((void *) 0)**.

Syntax

In Java, **null** is a literal constant:

null

This value can be assigned to or compared to object variables. (An object is an instance of a class and not a primitive data type.) An object variable with the value **null** is not associated with any actual object in memory but instead is only an empty reference. In other words, an object with the value **null** currently holds the value "no object."

Assigning the value **null** to a thread causes the thread to stop running.

Example

One of the uses of **null** is to test an object variable to see whether it really holds an object. Only if the variable holds an object is it safe to refer to instance variables or methods:

```
if (myObject != null)
     System.out.println(myObject.toString());
```

OCTAL NOTATION

Java uses the same notation for octal notation used by C and C++. The syntax is **0***num*; for example, 057. See the topic "int Data Type." You can also use octal to specify a character code, as shown in Table G, "Java escape sequences," in Part VI.

OBJECTS

Java vs. C++

The concept of objects is roughly the same in Java and C++: an object is a packet of data with associated functions. Objects are distinct from classes in that an object is an instance of a class and therefore has a specific value; a class is an object's type.

There are some significant differences in the class-object model in Java when compared with C++:

- Unlike C++, Java considers objects and primitive data to be two different categories, and different rules apply. Most important, variables of a primitive data type contain actual data, but object variables are only references to objects—you must allocate objects in memory and then associate them with the object variables. Usually, this means that the use of the **new** operator (or calling a method that uses **new**) is required to allocate a new object in memory:

  class object_name **= new** *class***();**

- **String** is a special type. It is the only class that supports an extended operator (+, for concatenation). In contrast to objects of other classes, you can allocate a **String** object simply by using a quoted literal string. See the topics "Aggregates" and "Strings."
- Because object variables are references, assignment has the effect of simply associating one variable with the same location in memory as another variable; testing for equality (==) tests references to see whether they are associated with the same memory. To get around this behavior, which is counterintuitive for most people, Java provides the **equals()** and **clone()** methods, inherited from the **Object** class. See the topic "References" for additional discussion.

- All Java classes inherit, directly or indirectly, from the **Object** class. Therefore, all objects have the built-in functionality defined in **Object**. This is not true of primitive types, although primitive types have corresponding "wrapper" classes. These classes include **Boolean**, **Character**, **Integer**, **Long**, **Float**, and **Double**. For more information on the **Object** class, see the topic "Object Class" in the API Quick Reference.

For information on classes, see the topic "Classes." For examples of object allocation, see the topic "new Operator."

OPERATORS

Java vs. C++

Nearly all Java operators are also found in C and C++, but the Java operator set is somewhat smaller because it does not support pointers.

Summary of Precedence

Table O.1 shows precedence and associativity of Java operators.

Table O.1 *Precedence of Java operators*

OPERATOR(S)	TYPE OF OPERATION (IF NOT BINARY)	ASSOCIATION
++, −−, +, -, ~, !, (*type*)	Unary	Right-to-left
*, /, %		Left-to-right
+, -, + (string concatenation)		Left-to-right
<<, >>, >>>		Left-to-right
<, >, <=, >=, **instanceof**		Left-to-right
==, !=		Left-to-right
&		Left-to-right
^		Left-to-right

<table>
<tr><td>|</td><td></td><td>Left-to-right</td></tr>
<tr><td>&&</td><td></td><td>Left-to-right</td></tr>
<tr><td>||</td><td></td><td>Left-to-right</td></tr>
<tr><td>?:</td><td>Ternary</td><td>Right-to-left</td></tr>
<tr><td>=, +=, -=, *=, /=, %=, +=, -=,
<<=, >>=, >>>=, &=, ^=, |=</td><td></td><td>Right-to-left</td></tr>
</table>

Description of Operators (by Group)

The use of some operators is obvious (at least if you've programmed in another high-level language). Table O.2 provides an overview of some of the less obvious operators and suggests where to go for further information.

Table O.2 *Groups of operators*

<table>
<tr><th>OPERATORS</th><th>DESCRIPTION</th></tr>
<tr><td>==, !=</td><td>Test for equality and non-equality, respectively, as in C/C++.</td></tr>
<tr><td>~, !</td><td>Bitwise and logical negation. See the topic "Bitwise Operators."</td></tr>
<tr><td>%</td><td>Remainder (modulus) division. See the topic "Modulus Operator."</td></tr>
<tr><td><<, >>, >>></td><td>Left shift, right shift, and unsigned right shift. Valid only on integer operands. See the topic "Shift Operators."</td></tr>
<tr><td>&, ^, |</td><td>AND, exclusive OR, and OR, respectively; can be used on two integer or two Boolean operands. See the topic "Bitwise Operators."</td></tr>
<tr><td>&&, ||</td><td>Logical AND and OR.</td></tr>
<tr><td>?:</td><td>See the topic "Conditional Operator."</td></tr>
<tr><td>++, – –</td><td>Incremented and decremented operators, equivalent to n = n + 1 and n = n – 1</td></tr>
</table>

As in C and C++, Java supports a set of assignment operators, which have the following form:

operand1 op= operand2

Such expressions are equivalent to the following expression:

operand1 = operand1 op operand2

For example, a += b is equivalent to:

```
a = a + b
```

The target, *operand1*, must be an expression that can legally appear on the left of a regular assignment (=). Such an expression could be a simple variable or array element. In any case, *operand1* is evaluated only once.

The Java language set also supports characters for field access (.) and for array indexing ([ ]). Technically, these are not considered operators; they have the effect of qualifying a name, as in Basic and FORTRAN. This arrangement is appropriate in Java, because it does not translate field and element access into pointer arithmetic. Use of these symbols is resolved before operators are applied.

OPERATOR OVERLOADING (C++)

Java vs. C++

Not supported in Java.

Although operator overloading is a useful technique in C++, it was not adopted by Java. This omission serves the purpose of keeping Java a smaller, leaner language. All the operator functions you might write in C++ can be realized in Java by simply writing ordinary methods.

Java supports operator overloading in a very limited sense. For example, the addition operator (+) is reused by the **String** class to indicate string concatenation. However, Java does not extend the ability to define operators to user-defined classes, so, in that sense, there is no operator overloading.

PACKAGE STATEMENT

Java vs. C++

Packages have no close parallel in C or C++, although there are similarities to the concepts of module and namespace. But a single Java package can extend over multiple source files. All the classes in the same package have access to one another.

Syntax

The **package** statement, if it occurs, must be the first statement in a Java source file.

package *package_name***;**

The *package_name* can contain embedded dots (.) to separate different parts of the package name. The name must represent a subtree in the directory structure. For example, if the package name is **briano.util.tools**, all the classes in this package must reside in the directory briano\util\tools, in which briano is a subdirectory of a directory that Java normally searches. For more information on the intricacies of package naming and locations, see Chapter 2, "Java Building Blocks."

The statement places all the classes defined in the source file into the specified package. Other source files may contribute to this same package. Classes declared in the same package, even if declared in different source files, have access to one another. From outside the package, only public classes are accessible.

If a source file specifies no package, it is placed in the default package. Consequently, until you start placing code in packages, all the classes you write have access to one another, and name conflicts are possible.

Example

This example specifies that the classes defined in the source file are to be placed in the package **briano.util.tools**, which must reflect the directory structure.

```
package briano.util.tools;
```

POINTERS (C++)

Java vs. C++

Java does not support pointers at all. This is the most dramatic difference between Java, on the one hand, and C and C++, on the other. Java provides alternative mechanisms for things that involve pointers in C and C++:

- Arrays. In Java, you must use array indexing, just as you would in most languages, such as Basic or FORTRAN. This is a small concession, because array indexing is only slightly less efficient than pointer access. Java has better security and error checking, because it enforces array bounds instead of translating indexes into pointer expressions.
- Memory allocation. Java supports dynamic use of the **new** operator, just as in C++ (and in C with the **malloc( )** function). But in Java, the **new** operator returns a reference; this means that it associates the appropriate address with a target object variable but avoids pointer syntax.
- Pointers to callback functions. Because Java methods are polymorphic—meaning late bound—they work like virtual functions in C++. Consequently, it is easy to create a callback by building an interface or abstract class around it. Such an interface or class declares at least one method, which, in effect, is a callback function. Again, Java avoids the pointer syntax that C would require.
- Passing by reference. In this area, Java is least flexible, although workarounds are possible. In Java, object variables are references, so they can be associated with different addresses just as pointers are. All objects, therefore, are automatically passed by reference. If you want to simulate passing by value (perhaps to make sure you preserve the value of the original argument), you can use a copy constructor or **clone()** function, if available. For example:

```
// Copy the value, then modify ONLY the copy,
//  not the original.
```

```
public void doCalc(MyClass object) {
        MyClass objectCopy = new MyClass(object);
        // ...
```

Passing a primitive data type (such as **int**) by reference is more problematic. Primitive data is always passed by value. However, you can pass numeric data by reference by declaring an argument of class **Boolean**, **Character**, **Integer**, **Long**, **Float**, or **Double**. These types correspond to the primitive data types, but because these types are classes, the data is passed by reference. For example:

```
Float x = new Float(0.0);
Float y = new Float(1.5);
Translate_Points(x, y);  // Changes values of x
and y.
```

This example assumes that Translate_Points takes two objects of type **Float** (rather than **float**).

PRIVATE KEYWORD

Java vs. C++

The **private** keyword has a general meaning in Java similar to that in C++. However, the keyword must be applied to methods and variables individually. In Java, a method or variable can be declared **public**, **protected**, **private**, or **private protected** (using both keywords).

Syntax: private

Unlike C++, Java requires that **private** be declared for each individual member to which it applies. The declaration for a data member (variable) is as follows:

private [*other_modifiers*] *type items***;**

The declaration for a method is as follows:

private [*other_modifiers*] *return_type method_name***(***args***)** [*throws_* *clause*] **{**

statements

}

In each case, brackets indicate optional items.

A member that is declared **private**, but not **protected**, has no visibility outside the class. Even derived classes cannot access the member. A member that is declared **private** and **protected** is similar, but it can be accessed in classes derived from the current class.

Example

In this example, the instance variables x and y have private access. They cannot be accessed except within code for the Point class:

```
class Point {
    private float x, y;
//...
}
```

PROTECTED KEYWORD

Java vs. C++

The **protected** keyword has a general meaning in Java similar to that in C++. However, the keyword must be applied to a method or variable individually. In Java, a method or variable can be declared **public**, **protected**, **private**, or **private protected** (using both keywords).

Syntax: protected

Unlike C++, Java requires that **protected** be declared for each individual member to which it applies. The declaration for a data member (variable) is as follows:

protected [*other_modifiers*] *type items***;**

The declaration for a method is:

protected [*other_modifiers*] *return_type method_name*(*args*)
[*throws_clause*] **{**

statements

}

In each case, brackets indicate optional items.

A member that is declared **protected**, but not **private**, has general visibility within the package. The member can also be accessed within the method definitions of subclasses declared in other packages. This assumes that the class itself is declared **public**; otherwise, **protected** declarations have no effect.

A member that is declared **protected** and **private** does not have visibility outside the class except within subclasses. This state is closest to the C++ meaning of **protected**.

Example

In this example, the instance variables x and y have **private protected** access: they cannot be accessed except within code for the Point class and classes derived from Point:

```
class Point {
     private protected float x, y;
//...
}
```

PUBLIC KEYWORD

Java vs. C++

Although the **public** keyword has a general meaning in Java similar to that in C++, there are many differences. Java has public classes, which can be accessed from anywhere, including other packages. Within public classes, the **public** keyword can be used to extend this access to individual methods and variables.

Syntax: Class Declarations

The **public** keyword is one of the modifiers of a class declaration. (But note that **private** and **protected** cannot be used this way.)

[**public**] [**abstract**] [**final**] **class** *class_name* [**extends** *super_class_name*] **{**

declarations

}

Here, brackets indicate optional items. When **public** is applied to the class declaration, it makes the class available to all other classes, assuming that the class is placed in the appropriate directory. The default behavior is for a class to be available only to classes in the same package. (See "package Keyword.") Note that even though a class is available outside its package, members are not available outside the package unless they are individually declared **public** as well.

NOTE

In each source file, there can be at most one class declared public. This class must have the same name as the file. In addition, a class must be public to serve as the entry point of an applet or application.

Syntax: Members

Unlike C++, Java requires that **public** be declared for each individual field to which it applies. Here is the declaration for a public variable:

public [*other_modifiers*] *type variable_declarations*;

The declaration for a public method is as follows:

public [*other_modifiers*] *return_type method_name*(*args*) [*throws_clause*] **{**

statements

}

In each case, brackets indicate optional items. A member that is declared **public** cannot be declared **private** or **protected**.

If the member declaration occurs in a public class, then the effect of **public** is to let the member be accessed by classes outside the package as well as inside the package. Otherwise, **public** has no effect. The default behavior is for a member to be accessible by classes in the same package. To prevent this access, a member must be specifically declared **private**.

Example

In the following example, both the class Hello and the method, **main( )**, must be declared **public**.

```
public class Hello {
     public static void main(String[] args) {
          System.out.println("Hello, Java!");
     }
}
```

REFERENCES

Java vs. C++

In Java, all object variables, arguments, and return types are references. There is no need for a reference operator as there is in C++.

If you have programmed in C, you can think of references as pointer variables without the pointer syntax. If you have not programmed in C or C++, you can think of references as variables that first must be *associated* with actual objects in memory before being used.

In Java, assigning one object to another does not invoke a copy or assignment operator function. (You can copy between objects by using the **clone()** function, inherited from the **Object** class, but only if the class implements the **Cloneable** interface.) Instead, assigning to an object has the effect of associating the variable with another location in memory, much like pointer assignment.

Example

In the following example, the variables one_obj and arr_obj are associated with actual objects in memory; some_obj is not.

```
MyClass one_obj = new MyClass();
MyClass arr_obj[] = new MyClass[100];
MyClass some_obj;

some_obj = one_obj;      // some_obj is an alias for one_obj.
some_obj.update();     // Updates one_obj.
some_obj = arr_obj[10]; // some_obj an alias for arr_obj[10].
some_obj.update();       // Updates arr_obj[10].

some_obj = new MyClass(); // Create a new object.
```

The object variable some_obj is at first not associated with any object. However, it is used as an alias, first for one_obj and then for arr_obj[10]. The call to the update() function applies to a different object in each case. Finally, in the last line, a new object is allocated in memory and then associated with some_obj.

RETURN KEYWORD

Java vs. C++

Java supports the same syntax for **return** that C and C++ support.

Syntax

There are two versions of the **return** statement:

return *expression***;**

return;

The first version returns a value to the caller of a method. It should be used in any function that does not have a **void** return type. The second version does not return a value. Both versions have the effect of immediately exiting the current method.

Example

This example uses **return** to report the results of a calculation:

```
long factorial(int n) {
     long result = 1;
     while (n > 1) {
          result = result * n--;
     }
     return result;
}
```

SHIFT OPERATORS

Java vs. C++

Java supports left and right shift operators, as in C and C++. Java also supports an additional right-shift operator (>>>) that treats integer data as unsigned.

Syntax

Java supports three shift operators, as explained in Table S.1.

Table S.1 *Shift operators in Java*

OPERATOR AND SYNTAX	DESCRIPTION
integer << *num_bits*	*integer* shifted left by *num_bits*.
integer >> *num_bits*	*integer* shifted right by *num_bits*. Data is considered signed, so result is sign-extended into the leftmost bit.
integer >>> *num_bits*	*integer* shifted right by *num_bits*. Data is considered unsigned, so 0 is always placed into the leftmost bit.

In each case, *integer* is the data to be operated on. The operand *num_bits* is also an integer, but it should be a relatively small positive number. Shifts greater than 31, in the case of **int**, or 63, in the case of **long**, have the effect of losing all the original data.

None of these operations changes the original data operated on, *integer*; they simply evaluate to the indicated result. The assignment-operator versions (<<=, >>=, and >>>=) perform the same operations but change the original data.

Example

The following statements return different results. In the first case, the digit 1 is shifted into the leftmost position, preserving the negative sign of the number. In the second example, a 0 is shifted into this position.

```
int test = 0xFFFE;
int result1, result2;

result1 = test >> 1;     // Result is 0xFFFF;
result2 = test >>> 1;    // Result is 0x7FFF;
```

SHORT DATA TYPE (C++)

Java vs. C++

The **short** data type has the same characteristics in Java as it does in C and C++, but its size is fixed at exactly 16 bits (two bytes) for all time and is not in any way implementation-dependent.

Syntax

The **short** keyword can be used to create 16-bit (two-byte) integer variables:

short *declarations*;

The range is –32,768 to 32,767.

Example

This example creates score as a two-byte integer variable with an initial value of 100. The second example declares two integer variables.

```
short score = (short) 100;
```

```
short i, j;
```

Unlike C and C++, Java automatically sets uninitialized variables of primitive type to 0, although explicitly initializing them is good programming practice:

```
short i = 0, j = 0;
```

STATIC KEYWORD

Java vs. C++

Java supports the use of **static** with class fields, just as in C++. However, Java does not support the use of **static** with local variables. You refer to a static field as *class.field* and not *class::field*.

Java introduces a new syntax for **static**. Called the *static initializer*, it is occasionally useful for initializing class variables.

Syntax: Declarations

In Java, the **static** keyword is valid in three contexts: variable declarations, method declarations, and special blocks of code preceded by **static** (static initializers). In all three cases, these structures must appear at the class level and not inside method definition code.

When applied to variable declarations, **static** creates class variables. A class variable is created only once, and it is shared by all instances of a class:

static [*other_modifiers*] *type variable_declarations;*

When applied to a method declaration, **static** creates a class method. A class method cannot refer to other fields of the class unless they are also declared **static**. (This limitation applies both to variables and to other methods.)

static [*other_modifiers*] *return_type method_name*(*args*)

[*throws_clause*] {

statements

}

You can also place **static** in front of a block of code to create a static initializer. Such a block is executed just once, when Java loads the class:

static { *statements* }

Syntax: Access to Static Fields

One of the distinctive features of static fields, also called *class fields*, is that they can be referred to by their class name:

class.*staticfield*

Nonstatic fields, also called *instance fields*, can be referred to only by means of an instance. This means that you must create an object before you can refer to an instance field. Note that objects can be used to refer to *both* kinds of fields:

object.*nonstaticfield*

object.*staticfield*

For example, **NaN** is a variable in the **Float** class declared **static** and is therefore a class field. You can use the class name **Float** to refer to this field, or you can use a **Float** object:

```
Float.NaN
myfloat.NaN
```

Within a class's own methods, you can refer to other fields of the class without qualification (i.e., without a class or object name as a prefix). However, the use of **static** modifies this access:

1. Within a static method, statements can refer only to other static fields of the class.
2. Within a nonstatic method, statements can refer to any fields whether they are static or not.

Example: Static Fields

In the following example, the static method **ZeroStatic()** can refer to other fields of the same class only if they are static:

```
class MyClass {
        static int i, j;
        static double x;
        double y;

        static void ZeroStatic () {
                i = j = 0;    // Legal: i and j are static.
                x = 0.0;      // Legal: x is static.
        }
// ...
}
```

But a reference to y, a nonstatic field, would be illegal inside **ZeroStatic()**:

```
                y = 0.0;      // ERROR! y is not static.
```

Example: Static Initializer

You can use a static initializer to assign initial values to static fields. Usually, this assignment isn't necessary, but it might be useful if you need to set initial values before a constructor is ever called (or if the class is never instantiated). In this simple example, the block of code performs only simple assignments:

```
class MyClass {
        static int i, j;
```

```
        static double x;
        double y;

        static {
                i = j = 0;    // Legal: i and j are static.
                x = 0.0;      // Legal: x is static.
        }
// ...
}
```

Unlike the function **ZeroStatic()**, the static initializer will never be executed more than once. As with static methods, the statements can refer only to static fields of the class.

STRINGS

Java vs. C++

Java does not treat strings as arrays of **char** but instead as objects of the class **String**. Strings are not null-terminated; determine size by using the **length()** method of the **String** class.

Syntax: String Variables

Character strings, including all string literals, are objects of the class **String**. As part of the **java.lang** package, the **String** class is directly available without an **import** statement.

Although string objects are not primitive data types, you can create string variables by using the type name, **String**. You can use string literals rather than the **new** operator to allocate string objects.

String *declarations*;

Java strings are similar to Basic strings in some respects. You can declare Java strings without worrying about how much space is needed to hold individual characters. At the same time, Java string variables are object references and follow the general rules for Java objects. For example:

```
// Create three string variables, associate s3 with an actual
//  string.

String s1, s2, s3 = "the end";

s1 = "the ";     // Allocate string and associate with s1.
s2 = "the " + "end ";  // Create string thru concatenation,
                       // and associate with s2.

// If s2 and s3 refer to the same object, return true.

if (s2 == s3)
     String displayString = "s2 equal to s3";
```

In the preceding example, the conditional does not test the *contents* of s2 and s3 for equality but instead tests s2 and s3 themselves to see whether they refer to the same object in memory. In this case, the test would turn out to be false, because s2 and s3 refer to two different objects, each of which happens to contain "the end." To test object contents for equality, use the **equals( )** method inherited from the **Object** class:

```
if (s2.equals(s3))
     String displayString = "s2 equal to s3";
```

This approach to string comparisons, which may seem counterintuitive at first, follows from the way Java handles all objects (as opposed to primitive data).

NOTE

Although string variables can be associated freely with different string data, the actual contents of a **String** object cannot be changed. To do complex and efficient string manipulation, you should transfer string data to a **StringBuffer** object, which can be manipulated. You can also transfer string data to an actual array of **char** by using the **String** class **toCharArray** method.

For more information on the capabilities of the **String** class, see the topic "String Class" in the API Quick Reference.

Syntax: String Literals

As described in the topic "Aggregates," Java allocates an actual string object in memory whenever it encounters a quoted string. The object becomes an instance of the **String** class.

"*string_of_characters*"

Java represents string data as a series of Unicode character codes. Unicode characters are 16 bits wide and can represent a much larger character set than ASCII can. Because of the potential need to represent international character sets and because of the need for Java programs to work consistently on all platforms, Java uses Unicode as a universal standard.

In addition to alphanumeric characters (see the previous section, "Syntax: String Variables"), Java accepts escape sequences to represent special characters, as shown in Table S.2.

Table S.2 *Java escape sequences in strings*

ESCAPE SEQUENCE	DESCRIPTION OF CHARACTER
\b	Backspace
\f	Form feed
\n	Newline
\r	Carriage return
\t	Tab
\"	Double quotation mark
\'	Single quotation mark
\\	Backslash
xxx	Character corresponding to Unicode octal value; range is 000 to 0377
\\u*xxxx*	Character corresponding to Unicode hexadecimal value; sequence may include one to four hexadecimal digits

Individual characters, which are primitive data of type **char**, can also be represented with escape sequences. The representation of an individual character, as in C and C++, is as follows:

'*c*'

String Operations

The **String** type is unique among all classes in that it is the only class to support an operator:

string1 + *string2*

This expression forms a new string from two existing string objects. By assigning to a string variable (as shown earlier in this topic), you associate that variable with the new string.

As with all classes, the **String** class inherits methods from the **Object** class. Among the most useful of them is the **equals()** method introduced earlier in this topic. The **String** class does not support a usable **clone()** method, but you can create an independent copy of a string by using the **String** copy constructor:

```
String s1 = "A string."
String s2 = new String(s1);   // Make a copy from s1

if (s1 == s2)
     System.out.println("s1 == s2");   // This won't be
                                       //printed.
if (s1.equals(s2))
     System.out.println("s1 eq. s2"); // This will.
```

The **String** class defines a number of useful methods of its own, including **charAt()**, **compareTo()**, **length() substring()**, **toLower()**, **toUpper()**, and **toCharArray()**.

STRUCT DECLARATIONS (C++)

Java vs. C++

Not supported in Java.

All the uses for **struct** can easily be realized with the use of the

class keyword, which in Java (unlike C++) is the only keyword used to declare classes. Note that classes do not necessarily need to define new methods but can be used strictly as data types. The main reason **struct** is supported in C++ is for backward compatibility with C. In Java, compatibility with C takes a back seat to the goal of creating a smaller, simpler, leaner language. The **struct** keyword was therefore not included.

See "Classes" for information about declaring user-defined types.

SUPER KEYWORD

Java vs. C++

Java's **super** keyword is equivalent to a superclass (base class) reference in C++. It is also used to call a superclass constructor.

Syntax

Within a method, the **super** keyword refers to a member of the superclass. This arrangement is useful when you want to use the superclass version of a method, for example, rather than the overridden version.

super.*member*

You can also use **super** from within a class constructor to call a base-class constructor. In some cases, this may be the only way to initialize data declared **private** in the superclass. If used, the call to **super** must be the first statement in the constructor.

super(*args***);**

Example

In this example, assume that members x and y are inherited from the superclass, Point, and that they are declared **private** there. The use of **super** in this example invokes the Point constructor, Point(int, int).

```
class PointTemp extends Point {
     float temp;
     PointTemp(int x, int y, float temp) {
          super(x, y);
          this.temp = temp;
     }
// ...
}
```

SWITCH STATEMENT

Java vs. C++

The **switch** statement does the same thing in Java as it does in C and C++: jump to a different branch depending on the value of a test expression, which must be an integer.

Syntax

A **switch** statement contains a statement block, which contains statements labeled with **case**, and no more than one statement labeled as **default**.

switch (*expression*) {

case *constant_expression_1***:**

  [*statements*]

case *constant_expression_2***:**

  [*statements*]

...

case *constant_expression_n***:**

  [*statements*]

[**default:**

  statements]

}

Here, brackets indicate optional items. The action of the **switch** statement is to evaluate the *expression* and then jump to the **case** label with the value that matches the result (or **default**, if none of the case labels has a matching value).

In each block of statements, the last statement executed should usually be a **break** statement; otherwise, execution falls through to the next case. The reason **break** is needed is that the **case** keyword is just a label and not a statement, and it does not alter the flow of control. The **switch** statement jumps to one of the labeled statements, but from there execution continues normally unless interrupted with **break**.

Example

A **switch** statement is generally a more compact, more efficient version of a series of **if-else** statements. Consider this series:

```
if (n == 1)
     System.out.print("one\n");
else if (n == 2)
     System.out.print("two\n");
else if (n == 3)
     System.out.print("three\n");
else
     System.out.print("greater than three\n");
```

You can get the same functionality from a **switch** statement:

```
switch (n) {
case 1:
     System.out.print("one\n"); break;
case 2:
     System.out.print("two\n"); break;
case 3:
```

```
    System.out.print("three\n"); break;
default:
    System.out.print("greater than three\n");
}
```

SYNCHRONIZED KEYWORD

Java vs. C++

The **synchronized** keyword is an extended feature of Java not supported by C or C++. Both uses of **synchronized** create critical sections of code.

Syntax

The **synchronized** keyword can be applied to method declarations to specify that only one thread can execute the method at any given time. This requires all threads to obtain a lock before executing the method. If a thread attempts to gain the lock but another thread owns it, the first thread must wait.

synchronized [*other_modifiers*] *return_type method_name***(***args***){**

statements

}

The **synchronized** keyword can also be used to create a critical section of code within a method, causing a thread to wait for ownership of a particular resource:

synchronized (*object***)**

statement

When a thread reaches this code, it attempts to gain ownership of the lock for the specified *object*. If another thread owns the lock for this same *object*, the first thread must wait until the lock becomes available. After executing *statement* (which is usually a compound statement), the lock is relinquished.

NOTE

Java's handling of locks is deliberately kept at a fairly high level of abstraction. Individual operating systems may include many specific kinds of threads and locks (semaphores, read-write locks, and so on), but Java's thread model is sufficiently general that correctly written code should behave reliably and predictably on all platforms. With rare exceptions, Java programmers need not concern themselves with how locks are obtained or what form they take: the Java interpreter handles it.

Example

In the following example, no two threads are allowed to sort the same array at the same time. However, because of the way the code is written in this case, two different threads can enter the critical section of code simultaneously as long as they are sorting different arrays.

```
// Synchronize on array of double (darr), which can
//  be passed different values each time. Thread is
//  locked out only if another thread calls the method
//  with the same argument for darr.

void sortMe(double[] darr) {
     synchronized (darr) {
          // Insert code to sort the array.
     }
}
```

TEMPLATES (C++)

Java vs. C++

Not supported in Java.

Templates are a feature of ANSI-compliant C++ (supported by most recent C++ compilers) that enable you to specify types as parameters. Probably the most useful practical application of templates is the ability to write generalized collection classes. However, because all Java objects inherit from the root class

Object, it is not difficult to write generalized collection classes building upon the **Object** class as the base type. Any type of object may be passed as a parameter where **Object** is the type expected.

THIS KEYWORD

Java vs. C++

The **this** keyword has roughly the same purpose in Java as it does in C++, but it has two important differences. First, **this** is a reference and not a pointer. Second, **this** can be used within one constructor to call another constructor.

Syntax

Within a method, the **this** keyword refers to the current object being operated on: the object to which the method is attached. There are several ways to use **this**.

When combined with dot notation (.), **this** helps specify a member of the current object. This use is usually unnecessary unless there is a conflict in scope. (See the example.)

this.*member*

You can also use **this** to specify the current object as an argument to a method. This usage assumes that the class itself is the argument type expected:

*method***(this);** // Note: there may be other arguments.

Finally, Java enables use of **this** to call a constructor from within another constructor. When used this way, it must be the first statement in the constructor. This use is a coding convenience.

this(*args***);**

Example

This example illustrates two ways of using the **this** keyword:

```
class Size {
     public double width, height;
     public Size(width, height) {
          this.width = width; this.height = height; }
     public Size() {
          this(0.0, 0.0); // Call Size(width, height)
     }                    //  and set to 0,0.
}
```

THROW KEYWORD

This keyword raises or passes an exception and should not be confused with the **throws** keyword. (See the topic "Exception Handling" for information on exceptions.) The **throw** keyword supports two versions of syntax:

throw *exceptionObject;*

throw;

The first version raises a new exception of type *exceptionObject*, which must be a class derived from **Throwable**. The second version is valid only inside a **catch** block; it passes the buck to another exception handler.

The following example shows how you can use the **throw** keyword to throw an exception of type **IOException**. Remember that it is an *instance* the class that is thrown, and **new** is required to create it.

```
if (! file_readable)
     throw new IOException("Goofy i/o error.");
```

THROWS KEYWORD

The **throws** keyword is an optional part of a method declaration, which indicates that the method may generate a specified exception. See the topic "Methods" for description, syntax, and an example. See also "Exception Handling."

TRUE KEYWORD

Java vs. C++

Because Boolean expressions are not the same as integers, Java provides the Boolean constants **true** and **false**. In C and C++, the values 1 and 0 would suffice.

Syntax

The **true** keyword is a predefined constant in the Java language, representing one of two possible values for expressions of type **boolean**.

true

Example

One possible use of **true** is to create an endless loop. Such a loop needs an alternative mechanism to exit:

```
while (true) {
     // Do something.
     if (exit_condition)
          break;
     // Do some more.
}
```

TRY KEYWORD

The **try** keyword is used to create a block of code that is protected by an exception handler. See the topic "Exception Handling" for description, syntax, and an example.

The **try** keyword has the following syntax, in which:

try {*statements*}

// Exception handlers ("catch" blocks) should follow.

TYPEDEF DECLARATIONS (C++)

Java vs. C++

Not supported in Java.

The **typedef** keyword is not needed as much in Java as in C++, because Java eliminates pointer syntax and therefore tends to have simpler type declarations. The **typedef** keyword is also provided in C to create type names from structure declarations. Otherwise, you must precede the structure name with **struct**:

```
struct PointTag {
     int x, y;
} ;

struct PointTag a, b, c;   // One way of declaring
points.

typedef PointTag Point;    // This is another way.
Point d, e, f;
```

In Java, this use of **typedef** is unnecessary, because **class** declarations create type names directly.

UNSIGNED TYPES (C++)

Java vs. C++

Not supported in Java.

A C/C++ unsigned type has the same storage size as its counterpart (for example, **unsigned int** is the counterpart to **int**), but it does not represent any negative numbers. Instead, the negative half of the range is interpreted as representing large positive numbers. Thus, the range of **unsigned short** is 0 to 65,535 instead of –32,768 to 32,767. Unsigned types are useful when you need a variable that will never need to hold a negative value but can benefit from having the higher range available.

But eliminating unsigned types from Java makes the language smaller (one of the key design goals) and is unlikely to seriously hinder programming. If you need to represent larger positive numbers, simply switch to a larger type. Integer data types in the following series have progressively larger ranges: **byte**, **short**, **int**, **long**.

See the topic "Data Types" for more information.

VARIABLES

Java vs. C++

Java does not support global variables. In addition to local variables, Java supports class variables and instance variables, which are the same as C++ static and nonstatic data members, respectively.

Syntax

All Java variables that are not local must be declared within a class. Variables may be either class variables (declared with **static**) or instance variables (not declared with **static**). Class variables are created once for the class and have the same lifetime as the program. Instance variables are associated with objects.

Java supports the following general form of variable declaration:

[*modifiers*] *type items*;

A variable declaration has one or more items. If there are more than one, they are separated by commas. Each item has the following form:

name [= *initial_value*]

In these syntax displays, the brackets indicate optional pieces of syntax. The *initial_value* may be any valid expression. If *type* is a class, then it is common for the *initial_value* to be an expression using the **new** operator.

In any case, *type* creates actual data if the type is a primitive data type (such as **int** or **long**). Otherwise, the variable declaration creates only a variable that serves as a reference to a potential object.

NOTE

Unlike C and C++, Java provides reasonable default values for all variables of primitive type, regardless of scope. These values are 0 for integers, 0.0 for floating point, false for Booleans, and null for object variables. However, it is always a good idea to explicitly initialize variables yourself.

Syntax: Modifiers

The modifiers include any of the following, in any order: **final**, **static**, **volatile**, **public**, **private**, and **protected**.

The three access-level modifiers (**public**, **private**, **protected**) apply only to class and instance variables and not to local variables. The modifiers **private protected** may be used together, but neither may be used with **public**. Table V.1 summarizes the meaning of each modifier.

Table V.1 Modifiers for Java variables

MODIFIER	DESCRIPTION
final	Value cannot change. The variable must be initialized. If declared **static** and initialized to a constant, the variable is a compile-time constant rather than a true variable.
private	Variable can be accessed only within the class. This is not the default behavior; see discussion after end of table.
private protected	Variable can be accessed only within the class and subclasses.
protected	Variable can be accessed anywhere in the package, and also by subclasses in other packages (if the class is **public**).
public	Variable has same access level as the class.
static	Variable is a class variable. This means the variable is shared by all instances of the class and can be referred to through the class name rather than an instance.
volatile	Value of variable is subject to external change; compiler will not optimize by placing in temporary locations.

For more information, see the individual topics for the keywords. Note that if none of the access-level keywords is used (**public**, **private**, and **protected**), the variable is visible to all other methods in the package but is not visible outside the package. In contrast to C++ rules, in Java a variable must be specifically declared **private** to be hidden to code outside the class.

Examples

The following declarations show examples of class and instance variables. The variable secret may be accessed only by the class's own methods. The other variables may be accessed from anywhere, assuming that the code has access to an instance of the class. The variable number_of_uses requires access to the class but not necessarily to an instance.

```
class Point {
     static int number_of_uses;   // class variable
     double x, y;                 // instance variables
     private long secret;         // instance variable,
                                 // private
//...
}
```

VIRTUAL KEYWORD (C++)

Java vs. C++

Java does not use the **virtual** keyword from C++, but Java methods (except for those declared **final**) are similar to virtual functions. To facilitate Java's dynamic loading of classes, Java methods are late bound. This means that each object maintains its own pointer to the method table for its class. A method's address is not finally determined until run time.

The practical significance is that you can safely override methods you inherit from a base class. The appropriate method gets called at run time. For example, suppose that RoundedRect inherits from the class Rect, and that both define the method DrawMe:

```
// Declare object of a base type (Rect),
//  then allocate an object of the derived type
//  (RoundedRect).

Rect theRect;
theRect = new RoundedRect(10, 10, 50, 50);

theRect.DrawMe(); // Which version of DrawMe is called?
```

The question is, what implementation of the method does this code call? Does it call Rect.DrawMe (from the base class) or RoundedRect.DrawMe (from the object's actual class)? Because of late binding, the correct implementation will be called: RoundedRect.DrawMe. This is exactly how virtual functions work in C++.

Java does not support virtual base classes. They are unnecessary, because Java does not have multiple inheritance.

VOID KEYWORD

Java vs. C++

As in C and C++, Java uses **void** as a return type for methods that do not return any value. However, Java does not use **void** as a pointer type (because there are no pointers in Java) or for empty argument lists.

Syntax

A method that does not return a value is declared with **void** return type:

[*modifiers*] **void** *method_name***(***args***) {**

statements

}

As in C++, you must use **void** in declaring methods that do not return a value.

Example

This example features a **void** method, draw_me. Note that **void** is not used in the argument list, which is empty.

```
class Box {
     int top, left, height, width;
     public void draw_me() {
     //...
     }
}
```

VOLATILE KEYWORD

Java vs. C++

The **volatile** keyword does the same thing in Java as it does in C and C++: it identifies a variable whose value is subject to change from a source external to the program.

Syntax

The **volatile** keyword is one of the modifiers that may be applied to a variable definition:

volatile [*other_modifiers*] *type variable_list***;**

Declaring a variable as **volatile** informs the compiler that the variable's value is subject to change without warning; it therefore cannot be optimized by being placed in a temporary location or a register. Every time the value is read, the compiler must access the variable's own memory address.

Example

This example declares system_clock as **volatile**:

```
volatile long system_clock;
```

WHILE STATEMENT

Java vs. C++

The **while** statement does the same thing in Java as in C and C++; it executes one or more statements repeatedly as long as a condition is true. But note that the condition must be a genuine Boolean expression, such as a comparison.

Syntax

The **while** statement is one of the Java loop structures.

while (*condition***)**
    statement

The *condition* is first evaluated; if it is true, *statement* is executed, control returns to the top of the loop, and the cycle is repeated. If *condition* is false, the loop exits. The condition must be a Boolean expression, such as Sum > 1.

Example

This example multiples amount by n as long as n is greater than zero.

```
while (n > 0) {
      amount = amount * n;
      n--;
}
```

PART III

A Plain English Guide to API Topics

This section is designed to help you look up information that you need for completing various tasks in Java programming. The alphabetical list of keywords and phrases in the left-hand column describes the topic or task you want to do. The associated language element or keyword on the right will send you to the appropriate place in the API.

TASK OR SUBJECT	API REFERENCE
3-D drawing methods	Graphics.draw3DRect(), Graphics.fill3DRect()
Absolute value, getting	Math.abs()
Adding a component	Container.add()
Adding a menu	MenuBar.add()
Adding a menu bar	Frame.setMenuBar()
Adding a menu item	Menu.add()
Adding a menu separator	Menu.addSeparator()
Adding a table	Appendix B (CREATE TABLE)
Adding items to a list	List.addItem()
Adding points to a polygon	Polygon.addPoint()
Address on the net, specifying	InetAddress, URL
Appending string text	String.concat(), StringBuffer.append()
Applet parameters	Applet.getParameter()
Applet, starting another	AppletContext.showDocument()
Application, loading images for	Toolkit.getImage()
Arc, drawing	Graphics.drawArc()
Arrays, using flexible	Vector
Arrow keys, codes for	Event
Attributes, file	File
Audio clip, loading	Applet.getAudioClip()
Audio clip, playing	AudioClip, Applet.play()
AutoCommit mode, getting	Connection.getAutoCommit ()
AutoCommit mode, setting	Connection.setAutoCommit ()
Background color, setting	Component.setBackground()
Bell-curve distribution	Random.nextGaussian()
Black	Color.black
Blue	Color.blue
Bold, getting and setting	Font
Boolean, reading from a file	DataInputStream.readBoolean()

TASK OR SUBJECT	API REFERENCE
Boolean, writing to a file	DataOutputStream.writeBoolean(), PrintStream.print()
Brightening a color	Color.brighter()
Browsing table strucuture	DatabaseDataMeta.getColumns ()
Browsing the file structure	File
Buffer, flushing a	DataOutputStream.flush()
Buffering data input	BufferedInputStream
Buffering data output	BufferedOutputStream
Bytes, reading from a file	DataInputStream.readBytes()
Bytes, writing to a file	DataOutputStream.writeBytes()
Card stack layout	CardLayout
Case-insensitive string test	String.equalsIgnoreCase()
Case, testing and converting	Character
Catalog, getting	Connection.getCatalog ()
Catalog, setting	Connection.setCatalog ()
Changes to a table, commiting	Connection.commit ()
Character dimensions, getting	FontMetrics
Character processing	String, StringBuffer
Character, testing type of	Character
Characters, reading from a file	DataInputStream.Chars()
Characters, writing to a file	DataOutputStream.writeChars(), PrintStream.print()
Checking a menu item	CheckboxMenuItem
Checking image status	MediaTracker.checkForID()
Circle, drawing a	Graphics.drawOval()
Class, getting information on	Class
Clearing SQL warnings	Connection.clearWarnings ()
Client, acting as a	Socket
Client, creating	Socket
Clipping a rectangle	Graphics.clipRect()
Cloning an object	Cloneable, Object.clone()

TASK OR SUBJECT	API REFERENCE
Closing a file	InputStream.close(), OutputStream.close()
Closing a port	Socket.close()
Closing a SQL statement	Statement.close ()
Color filtering	RGBImageFilter
Color model, getting	Component.getColorModel()
Color model, getting	Toolkit.getColorModel()
Color Model, setting	ColorModel
Color number, translating from	IndexColorModel, Color.getHSBColor()
Column value, reading	ResultSet
Columns, getting a list of	DatabaseDataMeta.getColumns ()
Command button	Button
Committing data changes	Connection.comit ()
Communicating across a network	Socket, ServerSocket
Component, adding	Container.add()
Component, removing	Container.remove()
Concatenating text	String, StringBuffer.append()
Connecting an image filter	FilteredImageSource
Connecting to a database	DriverManager.getConnection ()
Connecting to a Web page	URL, URLConnection, AppletContext.showDocument()
Console metrics	Toolkit
Console, reading from	DataInputStream
Console, writing to	PrintStream, System.in, System.out
Constants, color	Color
Constants, event	Event
Constraints, setting layout	GridBagLayout
Container, getting reference to	Component.getParent()
Controlling image loading	MediaTracker
Controls	Component

TASK OR SUBJECT	API REFERENCE
Converting a character case	Character.toUpper(), Character.toLower()
Converting a string to bytes	String.getBytes()
Converting to a double	Double, Number.doubleValue()
Converting to a float	Float, Number.floatValue()
Converting to a long	Long, Number.longValue()
Converting to an integer	Integer, Number.intValue()
Coordinates, translating	Event.translate()
Copying an object	Cloneable, Object.clone()
Counting menu items	Menu.countItems()
Creating a checkbox	Checkbox
Creating a color	Color
Creating a command button	Button
Creating a custom component	Canvas
Creating a custom layout	GridBagLayout
Creating a dialog box	Dialog, FileDialog
Creating a frame	Frame
Creating a label	Label
Creating a list box	List
Creating a menu	Menu
Creating a menu bar	MenuBar
Creating a menu item	MenuItem
Creating a network client	Socket
Creating a network server	ServerSocket
Creating a new directory	File.mkdir()
Creating a new thread	Thread, Runnable
Creating a panel	Panel
Creating a polygon	Polygon
Creating a push button	Button
Creating a radio button	Checkbox, CheckboxGroup
Creating a rectangle	Rectangle

TASK OR SUBJECT	API REFERENCE
Creating a scroll bar	Scrollbar
Creating a separate process	Runtime.exec()
Creating a SQL statement	Statement.close ()
Creating a table	Appendix B (CREATE TABLE)
Creating a window	Frame
Creating an image from a source	Component.createImage()
Creating an Image object	Component.createImage()
Creating an option button	Checkbox
Cropping an image	CropImageFilter
Current date, getting	Date
Current time, getting	Date
Cursor type, setting	Frame.setCursor()
Custom components	Canvas
Customizing a layout	GridBagLayout
Cyan	Color.cyan
Cycling through an enumeration	Enumeration
Darkening a color	Color.darker()
Dark Gray	Color.darkGray
Database driver, loading	Class.forName ()
Database drivers, getting list	DriveManager
Database structure, browsing	DatabaseDataMet
Database types, getting	Types
Database, connecting to	DriverManager.getConnection()
Data types, and stream i/o	DataInputStream, DataOutputStream
Date of last file modification	File.lastModified()
Date, getting today's	Date
Day of the week, getting	Date.getDay()
Defining thread behavior	Runnable
Deleting a table	Appendix B (DROP TABLE)
Deleting rows from a table	Appendix B (DELETE FROM)

TASK OR SUBJECT	API REFERENCE
Descriptor, getting a file	FileDescriptor
Dialog box, creating	Dialog, FileDialog
Digits, converting radix of	Character.forDigit()
Dimensions, getting component	Component.size()
Dimensions, getting image	Image
Directory, access to a	File
Directory, creating a new	File.mkdir()
Directory, looking at contents	File.list()
Disabling a component	Component.disable()
Disabling a menu item	MenuItem.disable()
Dispatching events	Component.handleEvent()
Display device metrics	Toolkit
Display, writing output to the	PrintStream
Displaying a window	Frame, Component.show()
Displaying a window or component	Component.show()
Displaying an image quickly	Chapter 3, "Fun with Graphics"
Displaying an option menu	Choice
Displaying status-bar message	Applet.showStatus()
Double type, converting	Double
Double type, reading from a file	DataInputStream.readDouble()
Double type, writing to a file	DataOutputStream.writeDouble(), PrintStream.print()
Downloading from a Web page	URL
Drawing a pie-shaped wedge	Graphics.fillArc()
Drawing an arc	Graphics.drawArc()
Drawing Lines	Graphics.drawLine()
Drawing methods	Graphics
Drawing shapes	Graphics
Drawing to in-memory image	Image.getGraphics()
Driver, loading a database	Class.forName()

TASK OR SUBJECT	API REFERENCE
Drivers, getting list of	DriverManager
Dropping a table	Appendix B (DROP TABLE)
e, getting value of	Math.E
Editing text (components)	TextArea, TextField
Editing text (string manipulation)	String, StringBuffer
Enabling a component	Component.enable()
Enabling a menu item	MenuItem.enable()
Enumerating database drivers	DriverManager.getDrivers()
Enumeration, using	Enumeration
Equality, testing objects for	Object.equals()
Error, getting standard	System.err
Event constants	Event
Events, basic concepts	Chapter 4, "Components and Events"
Events, generating	Component.postEvent()
Events, keystroke	Component.keyDown(), Component.keyUp()
Events, mouse	Component
Examining table structure	DatabaseDataMeta
Exceptions, basic methods of	Throwable
Executing a separate process	Runtime.exec()
Executing SQL statements	Statement
Executing SQL stored procedures	CallableStatement
Exponential functions	Math
File attributes, getting	File
File dialog box	FileDialog
File, getting separator character	File.separator
File, random access to	RandomAccessFile
File, reading from a	FileInputStream, *often converted to* DataInputStream

TASK OR SUBJECT	API REFERENCE
File, writing to	FileOutputStream, *often converted to* DataOutputStream *or* PrintStream
File name, specifying	File
Filtering an image	FilteredImageSource, ImageFilter
Filtering color settings	RGBImageFilter
Filtering image by cropping	CropImageFilter
Finding a substring	String.substring()
Finding length of an array	Part II, "Arrays"
Finding string length	String.length()
Float type, converting	Float
Floating-point, reading from a file	DataInputStream.Float()
Floating-point, writing to a file	DataOutputStream.writeFloat(), PrintStream.print()
Flushing a data i/o buffer	DataOutputStream.flush()
Focus, moving	Component.moveFocus(), Component.requestFocus()
Focus, responding to change in	Component.gotFocus(), Component.lostFocus()
Font metrics, getting	Component.getFontMetrics()
Font properties, getting	FontMetrics
Font, setting	Graphics.setFont(), Component.setFont()
Forcing a repaint	Component.repaint()
Foreground color, setting	Component.setColor(), Graphics.setColor()
Formatting text output	PrintStream
Gaussian distribution, creating	Random.nextGaussian()
Generating an event	Component.postEvent()
Generic event handling	Component.handleEvent()
Getting a class from its name	Class.forName()
Getting a component's container	Component.getParent()

TASK OR SUBJECT	API REFERENCE
Getting a file descriptor	FileDescriptor
Getting a property setting	Properties.getProperty
Getting a reference to an applet	AppletContext.getApplet()
Getting a SQL statement	Connection.createStatement()
Getting a toolkit	Component.getToolkit()
Getting an Image object	Component.createImage()
Getting an image source	Image.getSource(), ImageProducer
Getting class information	Class
Getting component size	Component.size()
Getting current date and time	Date
Getting current font	Component.getFont(), Graphics.getFont()
Getting dimensions of an image	Image
Getting file attributes	File
Getting file input	FileInputStream, *often converted to* DataInputStream
Getting file length	File.length()
Getting file output	FileOutputStream, *often converted to* DataOutputStream *or* PrintStream
Getting file position	RandomAccessFile.getFilePointer()
Getting file separator character	File.separator
Getting font metrics	Component.getFontMetrics()
Getting font properties	Font, FontMetrics
Getting image property	Image.getProperty()
Getting list-box selection	List.getSelectedItem()
Getting list of a container's components	Container.getComponents()
Getting local URL	Applet.getCodeBase(), Applet.getDocumentBase()
Getting RGB values	Color
Getting rows of a table	ResultSet.next()

TASK OR SUBJECT	API REFERENCE
Getting scroll-bar position	Scrollbar.getValue()
Getting screen metrics	Toolkit
Getting SQL warnings	Connection.getWarnings()
Getting text	TextComponent
Grabbing the graphics context	Applet.Component.getGraphics()
Graphics context, grabbing	Applet.Component.getGraphics()
Graphics operations	Graphics
Graphics, getting in sync	Toolkit.sync()
Gray	Color.gray
Green	Color.green
Grouping components	CheckboxGroup, Panel
Grouping table entries	Appendix B (SELECT, GROUP BY)
Growing arrays	Vector
Handling events (generic)	Component.handleEvent()
Handling keystrokes	Component.keyDown()
Handling mouse events	Component
Height of font, setting	FontMetrics.getHeight()
Height of screen	Toolkit.getScreenSize()
Height, getting component	Component.size()
Height, getting image	Image.getHeight()
Hiding a component	Component.hide()
Hue, getting from color	Color.RGBtoHSB
Hue, setting	Color.HSBtoRGB
Hypercard-like interface	CardLayout
Icon, setting	Frame.setIcon()
Ignore-case string test	String.equalsIgnoreCase()
Image filter, connecting an	FilteredImageSource
Image loading, tracking	MediaTracker
Image source, getting	Image.getSource(), ImageProducer

Task or Subject	API Reference
Image, cropping an	CropImageFilter
Image, getting instance of	Component.createImage()
Image, getting raw data from	PixelGrabber
Image, loading an	Applet.getImage(), Toolkit.getImage(), Graphics.drawImage()
Image, providing raw data for	MemoryImageSource
Implementing thread behavior	Runnable
In-memory files	ByteArrayInputStream, ByteArrayOutputStream
In-memory image data, using	MemoryImageSource
In-memory image, drawing to	Image.getGraphics()
Indexing a string	String.charAt()
Infinity, testing for	Double.isInfinite(), Float.isInfinite()
Initializing an applet	Applet.init()
Input from a file	FileInputStream, *often converted to* DataInputStream
Input, getting standard	System.in
Input, keyboard	DataInputStream, System.in
Inserting entries in a table	Appendix B (INSERT INTO)
Inserting string text	StringBuffer.insert()
int type, converting	Integer
Integers, reading from a file	DataInputStream.readInt()
Integers, writing to a file	DataOutputStream.writeInt(), PrintStream.print()
Internet address, specifying	InetAddress, URL
Interpreting special key codes	Event
Intersection of rectangles	Rectangle.intersection()
IP address, using	InetAddress
Italic, getting and setting	Font
Iterating through a list	Enumeration
Joining tables	Appendix B (SELECT)

TASK OR SUBJECT	API REFERENCE
Keyboard input, reading	DataInputStream, System.in
Keystroke codes	Event
Keystrokes, responding to	Component.keyDown()
Label, creating	Label
Laying out a UI	Chapter 4, "Components and Events"
Layout manager, setting	Container.setLayoutManager()
Layout, creating a custom	GridBagLayout
Layout, forcing update of	Component.layout()
Layout, updating	Component.layout()
Layouts, introduction to	Chapter 4, "Components and Events"
Length of an array	array.length; *see* Part II, "Arrays"
Length of file, getting	File.length()
Light Gray	Color.lightGray
Line, drawing a	Graphics.drawLine()
List box, creating	List
List of database drivers, getting	DriverManager.getDrivers()
Listing options, component for	Choice, List
Loading a database driver	Class.forName()
Loading an image	Applet.getImage(), Toolkit.getImage(), Graphics.drawImage()
Loading an image, tracking	MediaTracker
Loading image in an application	Toolkit.getImage()
Loading pixel data for image	MemoryImageSource
Logarithmic functions	Math
Long integer, reading from a file	DataInputStream.Long()
Long integer, writing to a file	DataOutputStream.writeLong(), PrintStream.print()
Long type, converting	Long

TASK OR SUBJECT	API REFERENCE
Low-level network i/o	DatagramPacket
Lowercase, converting to	Character.toLowerCase()
Magenta	Color.magenta
Making a new directory	File.mkdir()
Mathematical functions	Math
Memory, used as a stream	ByteArrayInputStream, ByteArrayOutputStream
Menu bar, adding to frame	Frame.setMenuBar()
Menu bar, creating a	MenuBar
Menu command, responding to	MenuItem
Menu item, creating a	MenuItem
Menu items, with check mark	CheckboxMenuItem
Menu, adding to menu bar	MenuBar.add()
Menu, creating a	Menu
Menu, removing from bar	MenuBar.remove()
Message, status-bar	Applet.showStatus()
Metrics for a font	FontMetrics
Modal, setting condition	Dialog
Modification date, for a file	File.lastModified()
Monitoring image loading	MediaTracker
Mouse events, responding to	Component
Moving scroll-bar indicator	Scrollbar.setValue()
Moving the file pointer	RandomAccessFile.seek()
Moving the focus	Component.moveFocus(), Component.requestFocus()
Multiline text editing	TextArea
Multiple list-box selection	List.setMultipleSelections()
Music, playing	AudioClip, Applet.play()
Network operations, performing	Socket, ServerSocket
Normal distribution, creating	Random.nextGaussian()
Not a Number, testing for	Double.isNaN(), Float.isNaN()

TASK OR SUBJECT	API REFERENCE
Notifying other objects	Observable, Observer
Numbered line input	LineNumberInputStream
Observing another object	Observable, Observer
ODBC, using	Chapter 7, "JDBC Quick Start"
On/off conditions	Checkbox
Opening a file	FileDialog, FileInputStream, FileOutputStream
Opening a server socket (to listen for connections)	ServerSocket
Opening a socket (to transmit	Socket and receive data)
Option	Checkbox
Option menu	Choice
Orange	Color.orange
Output to a file	FileOutputStream, *often converted to* DataOutputStream *or* PrintStream
Output, getting standard	System.out
Paint mode, setting	Graphics.setXORMode()
Painting a component	Component.paint(), Component.repaint()
Painting a pie-shaped wedge	Graphics.fillArc()
Painting an image	Applet.drawImage()
Painting child components	Component.paintAll()
Painting methods	Graphics
Painting shapes	Graphics
Parameters, getting applet	Applet.getParameter()
Parameters, setting SQL	PreparedStatement
Parent, getting reference to	Component.getParent()
Password, using database	DriverManager.getConnection()
Path name, getting	File.getPath()
Pausing for a specified time	Thread.sleep(), Object.wait()

TASK OR SUBJECT	API REFERENCE
Performing security checks	SecurityManager
pi, getting value of	Math.PI
Pie-shaped wedge, painting a	Graphics.fillArc()
Pink	Color.pink
Pipe, data	PipedInputStream, java.io.PipedOutputStream
Pixel data, getting	PixelGrabber
Pixel data, producing image from	MemoryImageSource
Pixel data, saving	PixelGrabber
Placing a check mark on a menu	CheckboxMenuItem
Playing an audio clip	AudioClip, Applet.play()
Point, finding inside a shape	Polygon.inside()
Polygon methods	Graphics
Port, using for net i/o	Socket
Position on scroll bar, getting	Scrollbar.getValue()
Positioning a component	GridBagLayout
Precompiled SQL statements, using	CallableStatement
Primitive data, and stream i/o	DataInputStream, DataOutputStream
Printing child components	Component.printAll()
Printing component contents	Component.print()
Printing rows of a table	Chapter 7, "JDBC Quick Start"
Priority, setting thread	Thread.setPriority()
Process, starting a	Runtime.exec()
Producing image from pixel data	MemoryImageSource
Properties, system	System.getProperties()
Properties, getting image	Image.getProperty()
Property, getting database	DriverPropertyInfo
Property, getting and setting	Properties
Push button	Button
Querying a database	Statement.executeQuery()
Radio button	Checkbox

TASK OR SUBJECT	API REFERENCE
Random access, using	RandomAccessFile
Random number, getting	Math.random(), Random
Range, double	Double
Range, float	Float
Range, int	Integer
Range, long	Long
Raw image data, getting	PixelGrabber
Raw image data, using	MemoryImageSource
Reading a column of data	ResultSet
Reading a sequence of files	SequenceInputStream
Reading across the net	Socket.getInputStream()
Reading data across a network	Socket.getInputStream()
Reading double type from a string	Double
Reading file attributes	File
Reading float type from a string	Float
Reading from a file	FileInputStream, *often converted to* DataInputStream
Reading from the keyboard	DataInputStream, System.in
Reading input from a string	StringBufferInputStream
Reading integers from a string	Integer.parseInt()
Reading keyboard input	DataInputStream, System.in
Reading long integers from a string	Long.parseLong()
Reading random-access records	RandomAccessFile
Reading rows of a table	ResultSet
Receiving low-level net data	DatagramPacket
Rectangle, drawing a	Graphics.drawRect()
Red	Color.red
Refreshing the display	Component.repaint()
Region, painting a	Graphics.fillRect()
Remainder, taking the	Math.IEEEremainder()
Removing a component	Container.remove()

TASK OR SUBJECT	API REFERENCE
Removing a menu item	Menu.remove()
Removing a table	Appendix B (DROP TABLE)
Renaming a file	File.renameTo()
Repaint, forcing	Component.repaint()
Repainting the display	Component.repaint()
Replacing string text	String.replace()
Requesting the focus	Component.requestFocus()
Resizing a frame or window	Frame.setResizable, Component.resize()
Resolution, getting screen	Toolkit.getScreenResolution()
Responding to a menu command	MenuItem
Responding to events (generic)	Component.handleEvent()
Responding to focus changing	Component.gotFocus(), Component.lostFocus()
Responding to keystrokes	Component.keyDown()
Responding to mouse events	Component
Result Set, using	ResultSet
RGB, creating color with	Color
Rolling back changes (JDBC)	Connection.rollback()
Rounded rectangle, painting	Graphics.drawRoundRect(), Graphics.fillRoundRect()
Rounding a floating-point	Math.round()
Running another program	Runtime.exec()
Saving pixel data from image	PixelGrabber
Screen metrics, getting	Toolkit
Screen resolution, getting	Toolkit.getScreenResolution()
Screen, writing output to	PrintStream
Searching a directory	File
Searching a string	String.substring()
Searching a table	Appendix B (SELECT, WHERE)
Searching vectors (arrays)	Vector.firstElement()
Security checks, controlling	SecurityManager

TASK OR SUBJECT	API REFERENCE
Seeking to new file position	RandomAccessFile.seek()
Selecting a file	FileDialog
Selecting and replacing text	TextArea, TextField
Selecting list box items	List.select()
Selecting rows from a table	Appendix B (SELECT)
Sending data across a network	Socket.getOutputStream()
Sending low-level data on the net	DatagramPacket
Separator, file	File.separator
Separator, menu	Menu.addSeparator()
Sequence of files, reading from	SequenceInputStream
Series of files, reading from	SequenceInputStream
Server, acting as a	ServerSocket
Server, creating	ServerSocket
Setting a clipping rectangle	Graphics.clipRect()
Setting a dialog box title	Dialog.setTitle()
Setting a frame title	Frame.setTitle()
Setting a frame's icon	Frame.setIcon()
Setting a layout manager	Container.setLayoutManager()
Setting a menu bar	Frame.setMenuBar()
Setting a property	Properties
Setting background color	Component.setBackground()
Setting bold and italic	Font
Setting font in a menu item	MenuComponent.setFont()
Setting font style	Font
Setting foreground color	Component.setColor()
Setting list box selection	List.select()
Setting scroll bar coordinates	Scrollbar
Setting SQL parameters	PreparedStatement
Setting text	TextComponent
Setting the font	Component.setFont(), Graphics.setFont()

TASK OR SUBJECT	API REFERENCE
Setting the paint mode	Graphics.setXORMode()
Setting thread priority	Thread.setPriority()
Shapes, displaying	Graphics
Shift (modifier) keys, codes for	Event
Showing a window or component	Component.show()
Size of an array	array.length; *see* Part II, "Arrays"
Size of file, getting	File.length()
Size, getting component	Component.size()
Size, getting image	Image
Sleeping	Thread.sleep()
Sound, producing	AudioClip, Applet.play()
Special keys, codes for	Event
Specifying an Internet address	InetAddress, URL
SQL stored procedure, calling	CallableStatement
SQL syntax, using	Appendix B
SQL warning, getting	Connection.getWarnings()
Square, drawing a	Graphics.drawRect()
Stack collection class	Stack
Standard input, output, error	System.in, System.out, System.err
Starting a new thread	Thread.start()
Starting another applet	AppletContext.showDocument()
Statement (SQL), getting	Connection.createStatement()
Static text	Label
Status bar, displaying in	Applet.showStatus()
Stopping a thread	Thread.stop()
Stored SQL procedure, calling	CallableStatement
Stream input	DataInputStream
Stream output	DataOutputStream, PrintStream
String methods	String
String representation, getting a	Object.toString(), String.valueOf()

TASK OR SUBJECT	API REFERENCE
Strings, reading from a file	DataInputStream.readLine(), DataInputStream.readUTF()
Strings, reading from the keyboard	DataInputStream,System.in
Strings, writing to a file	DataOutputStream.writeUTF(), PrintStream
Structure of a database, browsing	DatabaseDataMeta
Structure of a table, reading	DatabaseDataMeta.getColumns()
Style, setting font	Font
Superclass, finding object's	Class.getSuperclass()
Suspending a thread	Thread.suspend()
Sync, ensuring graphics are in	Toolkit.sync()
Syntax, using SQL	Appendix B
System properties, getting	System.getProperties()
Tables, getting a list of	DatabaseDataMeta.getTables()
Testing character type	Character
Testing object for equality	Object.equals()
Text components	TextArea, TextField
Text processing	String, StringBuffer
Text string methods	String
Threads, introduction to	Chapter 5, "Animation and Threads"
Time of last file modification	File.lastModified()
Time, getting current	Date
Title, setting a frame (window)	Frame.setTitle()
Title, setting dialog box	Dialog.setTitle()
Tokenizing file contents	StreamTokenizer
Tokenizing string contents	StringTokenizer
Toolkit, getting	Component.getToolkit()
Tracking image loading	MediaTracker
Translating coordinates	Event.translate()
Trig functions, using	Math
Types, using database	Types

TASK OR SUBJECT	API REFERENCE
Union of rectangles	Rectangle.union()
Updates (SQL), executing	Statement.executeUpdate()
Uppercase, converting to	Character.toUpperCase()
URL, getting local	Applet.getCodeBase(), Applet.getDocumentBase()
Using a properties table	Properties
Using i/o streams	InputStream, OutputStream
Virtual files	ByteArrayInputStream, ByteArrayOutputStream
Waiting for a specified time	Thread.sleep()
Waiting for a thread	Thread.join()
Waiting for client request	ServerSocket.accept()
Waiting for image completion	MediaTracker.waitForID()
Warnings, getting SQL	Connection.getWarnings()
Web page, downloading from	URL
White	Color.white
Width of characters	FontMetrics.stringWidth()
Width of screen	Toolkit.getScreenSize()
Width, getting component	Component.size()
Width, getting image	Image.getWidth()
Window, displaying a	Frame
Window, showing	Component.show()
Writing across the net	Socket.getOutputStream(), *often converted to* PrintStream
Writing random-access records	RandomAccessFile
Writing thread code	Runnable
Writing to a file	FileOutputStream, *often converted to* PrintStream *or* DataOutputStream
XOR painting mode	Graphics.setXORMode()
Yellow	Color.yellow

PART IV

CLASS SUMMARIES

THE JAVA.APPLET PACKAGE

The **java.applet** package contains one class (**Applet**) and three interfaces that support the creation of applets. Applet code typically makes frequent use of the **Applet** class. Two related interfaces—**AppletContext** and **AppletStub**—are lower-level and used less often; they must be implemented by applications (such as browsers) that load and run applets.

java.applet.Applet class	Defines applet methods. Extends **java.awt.Panel**.
java.applet.AppletContext interface	Provides an interface to the browser; provides applet support methods, including interapplet communication.
java.applet.AppletStub interface	Along with **AppletContext**, this interface provides an interface to the browser.
java.applet.AudioClip interface	Defines audio play methods.

THE JAVA.AWT PACKAGE

The **java.awt** package implements the Java Abstract Window Toolkit (AWT). It contains all the classes and interfaces for creating a basic user interface. Although classes in other packages can affect the display, **java.awt** is the package most directly concerned with UI issues. This package includes all component and windows classes along with the important **Event**, **Graphics**, and **Image** classes.

java.awt.BorderLayout class	Layout manager that places components along edges.
java.awt.Button class	Push-button component.
java.awt.Canvas class	Blank component: subclass to create custom components.
java.awt.CardLayout class	Layout manager that simulates a card stack.
java.awt.Checkbox class	Check-box component—can be used as a radio button.
java.awt.CheckboxGroup class	Groups check boxes to create radio button groups.
java.awt.CheckboxMenuItem class	Menu item that has checked state.
java.awt.Choice class	Option-menu component.
java.awt.Color class	RGB color value. This class also defines color constants.
java.awt.Component class	Superclass for all component classes. This class defines many methods for showing, moving, and handling events.
java.awt.Container class	Superclass for all components that can contain other components. Extends **Component**.
java.awt.Dialog class	Dialog-box class. Extends **Window**.
java.awt.Dimension class	Class that contains height and width.
java.awt.Event class	Objects of this class contain information on one event. This class defines many useful constants such as key codes and event IDs.
java.awt.FlowLayout class	Layout manager that uses straight left-to-right placement.
java.awt.Font class	Each **Font** object describes a font.

java.awt.FontMetrics class	Provides detailed measurements for characters in a font.
java.awt.Frame class	Window with borders, system bar, and optional menu bar. Extends **Window**.
java.awt.Graphics class	Provides all drawing and painting methods.
java.awt.GridBagConstraints class	Defines set of constraints for one component; used with **GridBagLayout**.
java.awt.GridBagLayout class	Layout manager that accepts constraints for each component; provides maximum flexibility in layout.
java.awt.GridLayout class	Layout manager that uses tabular arrangement.
java.awt.Image class	Encapsulates an image loaded from disk or created as an offscreen buffer.
java.awt.Insets class	Margins around a component.
java.awt.Label class	Static-text component.
java.awt.LayoutManager interface	Declares methods required for all layout managers.
java.awt.List class	List-box component.
java.awt.MediaTracker class	Monitors loading of an image.
java.awt.Menu class	Pull-down menu component. Extends **MenuItem**.
java.awt.MenuBar class	Menu bar attached to a frame. Extends **MenuComponent**.
java.awt.MenuComponent class	Abstract class that declares common methods for menus.
java.awt.MenuContainer class	Declares methods used in **Menu**, interface **MenuBar**, **Frame**.
java.awt.MenuItem class	An item on a menu. Extends **MenuComponent**.

java.awt.Panel class	Container without definite borders. Extends **Container**.
java.awt.Point class	Class that contains x and y coordinates.
java.awt.Polygon class	Set of points that define a polygon.
java.awt.Rectangle class	Measurements defining a rectangular region.
java.awt.Scrollbar class	Scroll-bar component.
java.awt.TextArea class	Multiline edit-text component. Extends **TextComponent**.
java.awt.TextComponent class	Defines common text-handling methods.
java.awt.TextField class	Single-line edit-text component. Extends **TextComponent**.
java.awt.Toolkit class	Provides access to image-file loading (for applications) and to screen display measurements.
java.awt.Window class	Generic window class; usually, you should use **Frame** instead. Extends **Container**.

THE JAVA.AWT.PEER PACKAGE

The **java.awt.peer** package consists of a peer for each type of component in **java.awt**. A *peer* is an interface that defines how a component responds to commands that affect its display. Implementing your own peer classes enables you to replace API components with components you provide. The new components are functionally identical to the standard components (they respond to extend the same Java code) but with possibly a quite different look.

Obviously, peers are useful only if you are doing very low-level programming. For typical Java programming, you can ignore them. Therefore, because of page-length considerations, I do not document them in this book. If interested, you can find **java.peer** documentation on Sun's Java home page.

THE JAVA.AWT.IMAGE PACKAGE

The **java.awt.image** package should not be confused with the **Image** class, which is a part of the **java.awt** package and not **java.awt.image.** The classes and interfaces in this package are concerned with low-level manipulation of images. Typical application programmers will probably not use this package often. You can ignore the existence of image producers and image sources (which are defined in this package) unless you are using an image filter or extracting pixel data from an image.

java.awt.image.**ColorModel** class	Converts to RGB from another color scheme.
java.awt.image.**CropImageFilter** class	Filters an image by cropping a region. Extends **ImageFilter**.
java.awt.image.**DirectColorModel** class	Uses different bit patterns from standard RGB scheme. Extends **ColorModel**.
java.awt.image.**FilteredImageSource** class	Converts an image filter to an an image producer, which you can use to create new **Image** objects.
java.awt.image.**ImageConsumer** interface	Declares methods implemented by image consumers, which are objects that have requested pixel data.
java.awt.image.**ImageFilter** class	Superclass of image filters.
java.awt.image.**ImageObserver** interface	Declares **imageUpdate()** method, which is called during loading of data for an **Image** object.
java.awt.image.**ImageProducer** interface	Declares methods implemented by image producers (or image sources), which are objects that produce pixel data.
java.awt.image.**IndexColorModel** class	Color model that uses simple integers to represent colors. Extends **ColorModel**.

java.awt.image.MemoryImageSource class	Image producer that provides pixel data from a memory location.
java.awt.image.PixelGrabber class	Image consumer that copies pixel data from an image to memory.
java.awt.image.RGBImageFilter class	Filter that changes color values for each pixel. Extends **ImageFilter**.

THE JAVA.IO PACKAGE

The **java.io** package is mainly concerned with file and console input/output. (The **java.awt** package handles GUI i/o by itself, and **java.net** is involved with network i/o.) The **File** class encapsulates file path, name, and attributes for files and directories. To read and write to files, use **FileInputStream** and **FileOutputStream** and then convert the object to a more flexible type such as **DataInputStream**. The **DataInputStream** class can also be used for reading the keyboard (see the example in the topic). The **java.io** package is relatively large, because it supports a number of variations on basic file input/output.

java.io.BufferedInputStream class	Input stream that uses a buffer. Extends **FilterInputStream**.
java.io.BufferedOutputStream class	Output stream that uses a buffer. Extends **FilterInputStream**.
java.io.ByteArrayInputStream class	In-memory input stream. Extends **InputStream**.
java.io.ByteArrayOutputStream class	In-memory output stream. Extends **OutputStream**.
java.io.DataInput interface	Declares methods for reading Java primitive data types.
java.io.DataInputStream class	Input stream that handles all Java primitive data types. Extends **FilterInputStream**.

java.io.DataOutput interface	Declares methods for writing Java primitive data types.
java.io.DataOutputStream class	Output stream that handles all Java primitive data types. Extends **FilterOutputStream**.
java.io.File class	Encapsulates file and directory attributes (but not contents).
java.io.FileDescriptor class	Encapsulates low-level file descriptor.
java.io.FileInputStream class	Opens an input stream from a file. Extends **InputStream**.
java.io.FileOutputStream class	Opens an output stream to a file. Extends **OutputStream**.
java.io.FilenameFilter interface	Declares method for accepting or rejecting a file name. Typically used to filter out file names in a dialog box.
java.io.FilterInputStream class	Superclass for filtered input classes. Extends **InputStream**.
java.io.FilterOutputStream class	Superclass for filtered output classes. Extends **OutputStream**.
java.io.InputStream class	Superclass for all input streams.
java.io.LineNumberInputStream class	Keeps track of line count. Extends **FilterInputStream**.
java.io.OutputStream class	Superclass for all output streams.
java.io.PipedInputStream class	Reads (sinks) a data pipe. Extends **InputStream**.
java.io.PipedOutputStream class	Writes to (sources) a data pipe. Extends **OutputStream**.
java.io.PrintStream class	Writes text representations of data. Extends **FilterOuputStream**.
java.io.PushbackInputStream class	Stream that enables unreading of last character read. Extends **FilterInputStream**.

java.io.RandomAccessFile class	Provides read/write data methods, along with a **seek()** method, for a random-access file.
java.io.SequenceInputStream class	Reads two or more streams as if they were one unbroken stream. Extends **InputStream**.
java.io.StreamTokenizer class	Reads an input stream as a series of tokens.
java.io.StringBufferInputStream	Reads stream input from an in-memory string. Extends **InputStream**.

THE JAVA.LANG PACKAGE

The **java.lang** package provides strings, threads, and wrapper classes for Java primitive types as well as access to system functions. Note that you can always use the classes and interfaces in this package without having to qualify their names or use an **import** statement.

java.lang.Boolean class	Wrapper class for **boolean** type.
java.lang.Character class	Wrapper class for **char** type.
java.lang.Class class	Provides information about the class that a given object belongs to.
java.lang.ClassLoader class	Provides access to Java class loader. This is very low-level, and I do not document it in this book.
java.lang.Cloneable interface	Implementing this class indicates that a class provides a usable definition of the **Object.clone()** method.
java.lang.Compiler class	Provides access to Java compiler. This is very low-level, and I do not document it in this book.
java.lang.Double class	Wrapper class for **double** type.

java.lang.Float class	Wrapper class for **float** type.
java.lang.Integer class	Wrapper class for **int** type.
java.lang.Long class	Wrapper class for **long** (integer) type.
java.lang.Math class	A collection of useful math routines and constants.
java.lang.Number class	Superclass of the four numeric wrapper classes: **Integer**, **Long**, **Float**, and **Double**.
java.lang.Object class	Ancestor class of all Java classes.
java.lang.Process class	Provides control over a process returned by **Runtime.exec()**.
java.lang.Runnable interface	Declares **run()** method, which you implement to define behavior for a thread.
java.lang.Runtime class	Provides access to system and Java interpreter routines.
java.lang.SecurityManager class	Sets permissions for various Java operations.
java.lang.String class	Standard text-string class.
java.lang.StringBuffer class	Special text-string class for more efficient in-memory manipulation of a string.
java.lang.System class	Provides access to system routines and standard i/o streams; overlaps with **Runtime**.
java.lang.Thread class	Encapsulates a thread.
java.lang.ThreadGroup class	Enables operations on a set of threads.
java.lang.Throwable class	Ancestor class for Java exceptions and runtime errors.

The java.net Package

The **java.net** package provides access to network communications through several different levels: connectionless i/o (UDP), which sends data without requiring acknowledgments of a connection; connection-based socket i/o; and URLs, which can be used to download information from a Web page. Several of the classes in this package (**ContentHandler**, **SocketImpl**, **URLStreamHandler**) provide alternative or extended implementations of network i/o; you can generally ignore these classes unless you're dealing with low-level platform issues.

java.net.ContentHandler class	Subclass to provide extended content-reading of objects on the net.
java.net.ContentHandlerFactory interface	Used to generate instances of **ContentHandler**.
java.net.DatagramPacket class	Data packet using a simple protocol (UDP).
java.net.DatagramSocket class	Encapsulates a socket; can send and receive packets.
java.net.InetAddress class	Encapsulates a network address.
java.net.ServerSocket class	Encapsulates connection-based port i/o; can listen and respond to clients.
java.net.Socket class	Encapsulates connection-based port i/o.
java.net.SocketImpl class	Subclass to provide an alternative socket implementation.
java.net.SocketImplFactory interface	Used to generate instances of **SocketImpl**.
java.net.URL class	Encapsulates a Web page as a URL specification.
java.net.URLConnection class	Similar to URL, but provides more methods.

java.net.URLEncoder class	Provides a method for converting URL strings to a standard form.
java.net.URLStreamHandler class	Subclass to provide an alternative implementation for interpreting URL specifications.
java.net.URLStreamHandlerFactory interface	Used to generate instances of **URLStreamHandler**.

THE JAVA.UTIL PACKAGE

The **java.util** package includes a number of support classes that are frequently useful in programming. The **Enumeration** and **Properties** classes, in particular, are used by a number of other Java packages. Other collection classes in this package include **Hashtable**, **Stack**, and **Vector**.

java.util.BitSet class	Provides capabilities similar to C bit fields.
java.util.Date class	Represents a date and time. Constructor gets value of "now."
java.util.Dictionary class	Superclass to **Hashtable** class.
java.util.Enumeration interface	Declares methods for traversing an enumerated list.
java.util.Hashtable class	Provides storage for a set of elements, each identified by a key.
java.util.Observable class	Provides ability to maintain and notify a list of observers.
java.util.Observer interface	Declares methods that enable an object to act as an observer.
java.util.Properties class	A specialized form of **Hashtable** in which both keys and values are strings. Can include default property values.
java.util.Random class	Generates random numbers using a variety of schemes. Note that **Math.random()** is often simpler.

java.util.Stack class	Collection class providing **push()** and **pop()** methods. Extends **Vector**.
java.util.StringTokenizer class	Tokenizes strings. See also **java.io.StreamTokenizer**.
java.util.Vector class	Collection class that encapsulates an expandable array.

THE JAVA.SQL PACKAGE

The **java.sql** package is an extension to the Java core API, so you might need to install it separately. See Chapter 7, "JDBC Quick Start." The **java.sql** package implements JDBC. Reading and writing to a database involves execution of SQL statements, which are encapsulated by the **Statement**, **PreparedStatement**, and **CallableStatement** interfaces. To get a statement object, however, you must first use **DriverManager** to get a connection to a specific database. The **Connection** interface encapsulates database connections and in turn is used to create statements.

java.sql.CallableStatement interface	Enables execution of a SQL stored procedure. Extends **PreparedStatement**.
java.sql.Connection interface	Represents a database connection, which you can use to get **Statement** objects and other objects for executing SQL.
java.sql.Date class	Subset of **java.util.Date**, giving only DATE values.
java.sql.DatabaseMetaData interface	Describes complete structure and capabilities of a database.
java.sql.Driver interface	Represents a JDBC driver.
java.sql.DriverManager class	Manages the drivers main tained on the system and provides database connections. See **Connection** interface.

java.sql.DriverPropertyInfo class	Describes a property you may have to query user about before connecting to a database.
java.sql.Numeric class	Number class that stores decimal fractions precisely.
java.sql.PreparedStatement interface	Enables execution of a preparsed SQL statement. Extends **Statement**.
java.sql.ResultSet interface	Provides access to contents of a SQL result set.
java.sql.ResultSetMetaData interface	Describes complete structure of a result set.
java.sql.Statement interface	Enables you to execute any number of different SQL statements.
java.sql.Time class	Subset of **java.util.Date**, giving only TIME values.
java.sql.Timestamp class	Extends **java.util.Date** to include nanoseconds.
java.sql.Types class	Provides constants representing JDBC data types.

PART V

API QUICK REFERENCE

APPLET CLASS

Full Name	**java.applet.Applet**
Extends	**Panel->Container->Component -> Object**
Description	Public class. You nearly always use this class by subclassing it and then overriding methods such as **init()**, **start()**, **stop()**, and **paint()**—which is inherited from **Component**. No Java code creates an **Applet** object unless it is a browser or appletviewer program (which it is possible to write in Java). Some of the **Applet** methods are used only internally and should never be called or overridden. In your own code, you may find it useful to call **getImage()**, **getAudioClip()**, and **getDocumentBase()**. When you're looking up methods, remember that many useful methods are inherited from the **Container** and **Component** classes.

Constructors

public **Applet**();

Default constructor.

Instance Methods

public void **destroy**();

This method is called just before the applet is terminated. Occasionally, it is useful to override this method to clean up system resources that are not automatically released by Java.

public AppletContext **getAppletContext**();

This method is usually used internally, although it is sometimes useful for interacting with other applets and Web pages. This method returns an object that represents the browser or appletviewer running the applet. See AppletContext interface.

public String **getAppletInfo**();

Returns a string that contains information about the applet, including author and version.

public AudioClip **getAudioClip**(URL url);
public AudioClip **getAudioClip**(URL url, String name);

Returns an object that supports the **AudioClip** interface for playing audio clips. The string argument, if specified, is a file name. See also **play()**.

public URL **getCodeBase();**
public URL **getDocumentBase();**

These methods return a URL object that represents a Web-page address. These addresses are the location of the applet and the location of the document (HTML file), respectively.

public Image **getImage**(URL url);
public Image **getImage**(URL url, String name);

Returns an **Image** object that contains instructions for loading the image. Actual loading is initiated by calling **Graphics.drawImage()**. The string argument, if specified, is a file name.

public String **getParameter**(String name);

Returns the value of the specified parameter. HTML files can pass parameter names and values to the applet by using <PARAM> tags.

public String[ ][ ] **getParameterInfo**();

Returns a two-dimensional string array that describes all the parameters understood by the applet. Each row contains three strings: name, type, and description. For example, if the result of the method is assigned to the variable parms, then the strings parms[0][0], parms[0][1], and parms[0][2] provide information describing the first parameter.

public void **init**();

This method is called when the applet is loaded into memory. Applets frequently override this method, using it to initialize instance variables.

public boolean **isActive**();

Returns **true** if the current applet is active.

public void **play**(URL url);
public void **play**(URL url, String name);

Plays an audio clip if the specified location implements the **AudioClip** interface. The string argument, if specified, is a file name.

public final void **setStub**(AppletStub stub);

Used internally. This method is called by the browser or appletviewer application shortly after creating the applet. The applet responds by storing a reference to the stub. The applet can then call the stub to perform certain services. See Appletstub interface. This is one of those methods that your own applet subclass would have no reason to call.

public void **showStatus**(String msg);

Displays a message in the browser or appletviewer's status bar.

public void **start**();

This method is called when the applet starts running and whenever it resumes operation after being suspended. In contrast to **init()**, the **start()** method may be called more than once. Applets typically override this method to start or resume running of additional threads.

public void **stop**();

This method is called when running of the applet is suspended temporarily or because of applet termination.

public void **resize**(Dimension d);
public void **resize**(int width, int height);

Overrides method definitions in the **Component** class. The appletviewer program responds to this method as you would expect, resizing the window immediately. Behavior of a browser may differ.

AppletContext Interface

Full Name	**java.applet.AppletContext**
Description	Public interface. Browsers and appletviewer programs implement this interface to enable communication between the applet and the browser. The process of applet creation is as follows: browser creates an applet stub; browser calls applet constructor; browser calls the applet's **setAppletStub()** method to tell the applet where the stub is; applet uses the stub to get a reference to the applet context. In general, you don't have to worry about this interface unless you're creating a browser or appletviewer program, although it is occasionally useful for interapplet communication.

public abstract Applet **getApplet**(String name);

Returns the applet with the given name, as defined in the document (HTML file). The <APPLET> tag for an applet can optionally specify a name by using the NAME attribute.

public abstract Enumeration **getApplets**();

Returns an **Enumeration** object that contains references to all other applets in the context (started by the same browser). See **Enumeration** class.

public abstract AudioClip **getAudioClip**(URL url);
public abstract Image **getImage**(URL url);

These methods are called in response to the corresponding **Applet** class methods.

public abstract void **showDocument**(URL url);
public abstract void **showDocument**(URL url, String target);

Requests the browser to start the specified document (HTML file). The second argument, if included, is a file name.

public abstract void **showStatus**(String status);

Called in response to **Applet.showStatus()**.

AppletStub Interface

Full Name	**java.applet.AppletStub**
Description	Public interface. Browsers and appletviewer programs need to implement this interface. Along with the **AppletContext** interface, **AppletStub** provides services of use to an applet. In particular, the **getAppletContext()** method returns a reference to an object that implements **AppletContext**. In general, you don't have to worry about this interface unless you're creating a browser or appletviewer program. Low-level applet code uses this interface to support certain **Applet** class methods.

public abstract void **appletResize**(int width, int height);

Requests that the browser or appletviewer resize the window displaying the applet. This is not guaranteed to be successful with all browsers.

public abstract AppletContext **getAppletContext**();

Returns a reference to the applet context, which represents the browser or appletviewer and provides services of use to the applet.

public abstract URL **getCodeBase**();
public abstract URL **getDocumentBase**();
public abstract String **getParameter**(String name);
public abstract boolean **isActive**();

These methods are called in response to corresponding **Applet** class methods.

AudioClip Interface

Full Name	**java.applet.AudioClip**
Description	Public interface. This interface declares services for playing and stopping audio clips. You can get a reference to an object that implements these services—for a particular audio clip—by calling the **Applet.getAudioClip()** method.

public abstract void **loop**();

Does the same thing as **play()** except that the audio clip plays in a continuous loop until stopped.

public abstract void **play**();

Plays the audio clip from beginning to end. Immediately restarts from beginning if audio clip is currently playing.

public abstract void **stop**();

Interrupts and stops audio clip if it is currently playing.

BitSet Class

Full Name	**java.util.BitSet**
Extends	**Object**
Implements	**Cloneable**
Description	Public class. Creates a compact set of bit flags, not unlike the bit-field mechanism in C and C++: each bit in the set stores one independent Boolean value. This is the most efficient storage mechanism for a set of Boolean values, but it takes slightly more time than the use of the primitive **boolean** type, which is not compact.

The following example declares a **BitSet** object and sets the three least significant bits, which are bits 0, 1, and 2. (Incidentally, this can be done more efficiently by using **and(7)** in place of **set()** calls.)

```
BitSet flags = new BitSet(5);  // Five bits: 0 to 4
flags.set(0);
flags.set(1);
flags.set(2);
```

public **BitSet**();
public **BitSet**(int nbits);

Constructors. The nbits argument, if given, specifies the number of bit flags.

public void **and**(BitSet set);
public void **or**(BitSet set);
public void **xor**(BitSet set);

These methods all perform bitwise logical operations combining the current object with the specified argument. For example, the **and()** method can be used to apply bit masks.

public void **clear**(int bit);
public boolean **get**(int bit);
public void **set**(int bit);

Each of these methods clears, sets, or gets the value of an individual bit. The argument specifies bit position, in which 0 is the least significant bit.

public int **size**();

Returns the number of bits.

public Object **clone**();
public boolean **equals**(Object obj);
public int **hashCode**();
public String public int **hashCode**();

These methods override method definitions in the **Object** class.

Boolean Class

Full Name	**java.lang.Boolean**
Extends	**Object**
Description	Public final class. Wrapper class for the **boolean** primitve data type. Most common use is to pass Boolean values by reference. Several methods read a string containing "true" or "false." In these cases, case does not have to match, and false is assumed when the string does not match "true."

The following example shows two equivalent ways of initializing a wrapper object for Boolean values. In any given example, you could use either statement but not both together.

```
Boolean b = new Boolean(true);

Boolean b = Boolean.TRUE;
```

Constructors

public **Boolean**(boolean value);
public **Boolean**(String s);

Constructors. See class description for interpretation of string argument.

Class Variables

public final static Boolean **FALSE**;
public final static Boolean **TRUE**;

Class constants. Remember that these constants are objects and not primitive data.

Class Methods

public static boolean **getBoolean**(String name);
public static Boolean **valueOf**(String s);

Class methods. These methods read a string and return primitive data and an object, respectively.

Instance Methods

public boolean **booleanValue**();

Returns the primitive-data value (**true** or **false**) of the current object.

Overridden Instance Methods

public boolean **equals**(Object obj);
public int **hashCode**();
public String **toString**();

These methods override method definitions in the **Object** class.

BorderLayout Class

Full Name	**java.awt.BorderLayout**
Extends	**Object**
Implements	**LayoutManager**
Description	Public class. Creates layout manager objects that use the **BorderLayout** scheme described at the end of Chapter 4, "Components and Events."

The following example sets the current container to use an instance of **BorderLayout**:

```
setLayout(new BorderLayout());
```

Constructors

public **BorderLayout**();
public **BorderLayout**(int hgap, int vgap);

Constructors. You can optionally specify horizontal and vertical margins (gaps) around components.

Instance Methods

public void **addLayoutComponent**(String name, Component comp);
public void **layoutContainer**(Container target);
public Dimension **minimumLayoutSize**(Container target);
public Dimension **preferredLayoutSize**(Container target);
public void **removeLayoutComponent**(Component comp);

These five methods implement the **LayoutManager** interface; none of these methods is normally called by applications.

Overridden Instance Methods

public String **toString**();

This method overrides the method definition in the **Object** class.

BufferedInputStream Class

Full Name	**java.io.BufferedInputStream**
Extends	**FilterInputStream->InputStream->Object**
Description	Public class. This class takes an existing input stream and creates buffered input stream around it. Data is read directly from the buffer; when the buffer is exhausted, more data is read from the stream. If the underlying input stream is from a file, the buffering mechanism speeds file i/o, because it cuts down on the amount of disk access.

Constructors

public **BufferedInputStream**(InputStream in);

public **BufferedInputStream**(InputStream in, int size);

Constructors. InputStream is the underlying stream to be buffered, and size is the buffer size to use. The default buffer size is 512.

Overridden Instance Methods

public int **available**() throws IOException;
public void **mark**(int readlimit);
public boolean **markSupported**();
public int **read**() throws IOException;
public int **read**(byte b[], int off, int len) throws IOException;
public void **reset**() throws IOException;
public long **skip**(long n) throws IOException;

These methods override method definitions in the **InputStream** class. **markSupported()** returns true for all instances of this class, indicating that the **mark()** and **reset()** methods are supported.

BUFFEREDOUTPUTSTREAM CLASS

Full Name	**java.io.BufferedOutputStream**
Extends	**FilterOutputStream->OutputStream->Object**
Description	Public class. This class takes an existing output stream and creates buffered output stream around it. Data is written directly to the buffer; when the buffer is full, the entire buffer is written to the stream. If the underlying output stream is to a file, the buffering mechanism speeds file i/o, because it cuts down on the amount of disk access.

Constructors

public **BufferedOutputStream**(OutputStream out);
public **BufferedOutputStream**(OutputStream out, int size);

Constructors. OutputStream is the underlying stream to be buffered, and size is the buffer size to use. The default buffer size is 512.

Overridden Instance Methods

public void **flush**() throws IOException;
public void **write**(byte b[], int off, int len) throws IOException;
public void **write**(int b) throws IOException;

These methods override method definitions in the **OutputStream** class. The **flush()** method forces the current contents of the buffer to be written now. Then buffer is then emptied.

Button Class

Full Name	**java.awt.Button**
Extends	**Component -> Object**
Description	Public class. A **Button** object is a command button or push button. This component generates all standard keyboard and mouse events except for **MOUSE_DOWN** and **MOUSE_UP**. These events translate into **ACTION_EVENT**, resulting in calls to **action()**. The second argument to **action()** is a string that contains the button label.

The following example creates a button and adds it to the current frame or applet:

```
Button btn1 = new Button("Press Me.");
add(btn1);
```

Constructors

public **Button**();
public **Button**(String label);

Constructors. You can optionally specify initial button label text.

Instance Methods

public String **getLabel**();
public void **setLabel**(String label);

These methods get and set the label text.

Overridden Instance Methods

public void **addNotify**();

Overrides the method definition in **Component**. Used internally.

BYTEARRAYINPUTSTREAM CLASS

Full Name	**java.io.ByteArrayInputStream**
Extends	**InputStream->Object**
Description	Public class. Creates an input stream from an array of bytes. The effect is to treat an area of memory as a virtual sequential-access file.

The following example creates an input stream object around an existing array, **dataArray**. The resulting stream can then be used in the same way as any instance of **InputStream**.

```
ByteArrayInputStream bytes_in =
     new ByteArrayInputStream(dataArray);
DataInputStream dis = new DataInputStream(bytes_in);
```

Constructors

public **ByteArrayInputStream**(byte buf[ ]);
public **ByteArrayInputStream**(byte buf[ ], int offset, int length);

Constructors. Optional offset and length give starting point in the array and size. If these are not specified, the entire array is used.

Overridden Instance Methods

public int **available**();
public int **read**();
public int **read**(byte b[ ], int off, int len);
public void **reset**();
public long **skip**(long n);

These methods override method definitions in the **InputStream** class.

ByteArrayOutputStream Class

Full Name	**java.io.ByteArrayOutputStream**
Extends	**OutputStream->Object**
Description	Public class. Creates an output stream from an array of bytes. The effect is to treat an area of memory as a virtual sequential-access file. An object of this class automatically grows as it is written to. For this reason, it does not correspond to a fixed location in memory, as a **ByteArrayInputStream** object does. Instead, if you want to access the data, you need to periodically write it to another object by using the **toByteArray()**, **toString()**, or **writeTo()** method. These methods give snapshots of the current state of the output stream.

The following example creates a stream that can be written to as if it were a file. The result is an array, **dataArray**, containing all the data written.

```
ByteArrayOutputStream bytes_out =
     new ByteArrayOutputStream();
// ... Write to the bytes_out stream.
byte dataArray[] = bytes_out.toByteArray();
```

Constructors

public **ByteArrayOutputStream**();
public **ByteArrayOutputStream**(int size);

Constructors. You can optionally specify an initial buffer size, but in any case this will grow as needed.

Instance Methods

public byte[ ] **toByteArray**();

Writes data from the buffer to a byte array, which is allocated with exactly the size needed.

public String **toString**();
public String **toString**(int hibyte);

These methods fill a string with the contents of the buffer. Each byte is written to a string character. The high order bits of each character are set to 0x00, or to the eight low-order bits of hibyte, if specified.

Overridden Instance Methods

public void **reset**();
public int **size**();
public void **write**(byte b[ ], int off, int len);
public void **write**(int b);

These methods override method definitions in the **OutputStream** class. Note that in this implementation, they affect the buffer maintained by the object. **size()** gives the number of bytes that have been written to.

CallableStatement Interface

Full Name	**java.sql.CallableStatement**
Extends	**PreparedStatement->Statement**
Description	Public JDBC interface, providing access to a SQL *stored procedure*, which is defined in the SQL language but can be accessed from Java. You can use this interface to set parameter values, denoted as "?" in the initial SQL string. (See example.) Many methods are inherited from **PreparedStatement** and **Statement**; the methods in **CallableStatement** add the ability to get *out* parameter values. Note that not all database drivers support this interface. You can get an object that implements this interface by calling the **prepareCall()** method of a **Connection** object.

The following example gets an object that implements **CallableStatement** and uses it to call a stored procedure, **myproc**. The first two parameters are **in** parameters and are integers. The last parameter is an **out** parameter and must be registered before the call.

```
Connection con = DriverManager.getConnection(dbname);
// Use Statement, if needed, to define stored proc.
// myproc
// ...
String s = "{call myproc(?, ?, ?)}";
CallableStatement cstm = con.prepareCall(s);
// Next statement registers parm 3.
cstm.registerOutParameter(3, Types.VARCHAR);
cstm.setInt(1, 10); // Set parm 1 to 10.
cstm.setInt(2, 30); // Set parm 2 to 30.
cstm.executeUpdate();
String resString = cstm.getString(3);  // Get parm 3.
```

Interface Methods

public abstract boolean **getBoolean**(int parameterIndex) throws SQLException;
public abstract byte **getByte**(int parameterIndex) throws SQLException;
public abstract byte[ ] **getBytes**(int parameterIndex) throws SQLException;
public abstract Date **getDate**(int parameterIndex) throws SQLException;
public abstract double **getDouble**(int parameterIndex) throws SQLException;
public abstract float **getFloat**(int parameterIndex) throws SQLException;
public abstract int **getInt**(int parameterIndex) throws SQLException;
public abstract long **getLong**(int parameterIndex) throws SQLException;

All these methods get the value of corresponding parameters using a one-based index.

public abstract Numeric **getNumeric**(int parameterIndex, int scale) throws SQLException;

Gets the value of a **Numeric** parameter using a one-based index. The scale specifies the position of the decimal point. See **Numeric** class for more information about the use of the scale.

public abstract Object **getObject**(int parameterIndex) throws SQLException;
public abstract short **getShort**(int parameterIndex) throws SQLException;
public abstract String **getString**(int parameterIndex) throws SQLException;
public abstract Time **getTime**(int parameterIndex) throws SQLException;
public abstract Timestamp **getTimestamp**(int parameterIndex) throws SQLException;

All these methods get the value of corresponding parameters using a one-based index.

public abstract void **registerOutParameter**(int parameterIndex, int sqlType) throws SQLException;
public abstract void **registerOutParameter**(int parameterIndex, int sqlType, int scale) throws SQLException;

Registers an *out* parameter using a one-based index; must be called for each *out* parameter before the statement is executed. The sqlType argument uses one of the constants defined in the **Types** class, such as **Types.BIT**, **Types.INTEGER**, **Types.VARCHAR** (for strings) and **Types.FLOAT**. The scale argument is used for **Numeric** and **Decimal** parameters.

public abstract boolean **wasNull**() throws SQLException;

Returns **true** if the last value read has the SQL **null** value.

CANVAS CLASS

Full Name	**java.awt.Canvas**
Extends	**Component -> Object**
Description	Public class. Creates components with no built-in redrawing or response to events. You can create custom components by subclassing **Canvas** and adding your own code to paint the component or to handle events. **Canvas** generates all the standard keyboard and mouse events, including **MOUSE_DOWN** and **MOUSE_UP**.

Note that although there are no explicit constructors for **Canvas**, it implicitly supports a default constructor, **Canvas**().

Overridden Instance Methods

public synchronized void **addNotify**();
public void **paint**(Graphics g);

These methods override method definitions in **Component**. **addNotify()** is used internally.

CardLayout Class

Full Name	**java.awt.CardLayout**
Extends	**Object**
Implements	**LayoutManager**
Description	Public class. Creates layout manager objects that use the **CardLayout** scheme described at the end of Chapter 4, "Components and Events." This scheme displays components in a way similar to HyperCard or a cardfile program.

The following example sets the current container to use an instance of **CardLayout**:

```
setLayout(new CardLayout());
```

Constructors

public **CardLayout**();
public **CardLayout**(int hgap, int vgap);

Constructors. You can optionally specify horizontal and vertical margins (gaps) around components.

Instance Methods

public void **first**(Container parent);
public void **last**(Container parent);
public void **next**(Container parent);
public void **previous**(Container parent);
public void **show**(Container parent, String name);

These five methods bring a component to the top of the "stack." The component made visible is the first, last, next, or previous component on the stack, depending on which method you call. The **show()** method uses a name to identify a component—this is the same string specified when the **add**(String, Component) method was used to add the component to the container.

Instance Methods (Supporting Interface)

public void **addLayoutComponent**(String name, Component comp);

public void **layoutContainer**(Container target);

public Dimension **minimumLayoutSize**(Container target);

public Dimension **preferredLayoutSize**(Container target);

public void **removeLayoutComponent**(Component comp);

These five methods implement the **LayoutManager** interface; none of these methods is normally called by applications.

Overridden Instance Methods

public String **toString**();

This method overrides the method definition in the **Object** class.

CHARACTER CLASS

Full Name	**java.lang.Character**
Extends	**Object**
Description	Public final class. Wrapper class for the **char** primitve data type. This class contains many useful operations for testing and converting individual characters. Remember that strings are not arrays of **char**. See **String** class for string operations.

The following example calls a **Character** class method to test a character:

```
char c;
// Read a character, c.
// ...
if (Character.IsDigit(c)) //...
```

Constructors

public **Character**(char value);

Constructor. The value is a Unicode character value.

Class Variables

public final static int **MAX_RADIX**;
public final static char **MAX_VALUE**;
public final static int **MIN_RADIX**;
public final static char **MIN_VALUE**;

Constants. These specify the minimum and maximum value in the **char** data range, and the minimum and maximum radix that can be used in the **digit()** method.

Class Methods

public static int **digit**(char ch, int radix);
public static char **forDigit**(int digit, int radix);

Class methods. These methods convert between a printable digit character and its face value.

public static boolean **isDefined**(char ch);

Returns **true** if the argument has a meaningful value in the Unicode character set.

public static boolean **isDigit**(char ch);
public static boolean **isJavaLetter**(char ch);
public static boolean **isJavaLetterOrDigit**(char ch);
public static boolean **isLetter**(char ch);
public static boolean **isLetterOrDigit**(char ch);
public static boolean **isLowerCase**(char ch);
public static boolean **isSpace**(char ch);
public static boolean **isUpperCase**(char ch);

Class methods. These methods, starting with **isDigit()**, report a particular condition. The **isJavaLetter()** and **isJavaLetterOrDigit()** methods return **true** if the character is accepted as an initial character and a non-initial character, respectively, in a Java identifier.

public static char **toLowerCase**(char ch);
public static char **toUpperCase**(char ch);

Class methods. These return a converted character.

Instance Methods

public char **charValue**();

Returns the char value stored in the current object.

Overridden Instance Methods

public boolean **equals**(Object obj);
public int **hashCode**();
public String **toString**();

These methods override method definitions in the **Object** class. The **toString()** method returns a string of length 1 that contains the character stored in the current object.

Checkbox Class

Full Name	**java.awt.Checkbox**
Extends	**Component -> Object**
Description	Public class. Creates check boxes with a simple on/off state, as well as checkboxes that work as part of a group (in which selecting one automatically deselects the others). These are often called "radio buttons" or "option buttons." To create a group, create a **CheckboxGroup** object and then specify this group when you create a check box. You can also call the **setCheckboxGroup()** method after a check box has been created. A check box generates an **action()** event (ID: **ACTION_EVENT**) when the user clicks it. The second argument to **action()** is a Boolean that is true or false depending on the check box state.

For an example, see **CheckGroup** class.

Constructors

public **Checkbox**();
public **Checkbox**(String label);
public **Checkbox**(String label, CheckboxGroup group, boolean state);

Constructors. The third constructor sets initial conditions as well as specifies a group.

Instance Methods

public CheckboxGroup **getCheckboxGroup**();
public String **getLabel**();
public boolean **getState**();
public void **setCheckboxGroup**(CheckboxGroup g);
public void **setState**(boolean state);
public void **setCheckboxGroup**(CheckboxGroup g);

All these methods get or set an attribute of the component. Some check boxes work as stand-alone components rather than as part of a group: calling **getCheckboxGroup()**, in those cases, returns **null**.

Overridden Instance Methods

public synchronized void **addNotify**();

Overrides the method definition in the **Component** class. Used internally.

CheckboxGroup Class

Full Name	**java.awt.CheckboxGroup**
Extends	**Object**
Description	Public class. A **CheckboxGroup** object can be used to place one or more check boxes in a common group. Boxes in a group are often called "radio buttons" or "option buttons." A check box can be associated

with a group when it is created. It can also be associated by calling its **setCheckboxGroup()** method. The check box group object is not very interesting, although you can use it to get or set the current item.

The following example creates a group of two check boxes:

```
CheckboxGroup fruit = new CheckboxGroup();
Checkbox chkAp = new Checkbox("Applets", fruit, true);
Checkbox chkOr = new Checkbox("Oranges", fruit, false);
add(chkAp);
add(chkOr);
```

Constructors

public **CheckboxGroup**();

Constructor.

Instance Methods

public Checkbox **getCurrent**();

Returns a reference to the current item, if any, in the group. Returns **null** if there is no current item.

public void **setCurrent**(Checkbox box);

Sets the current item—that is, the specified object is selected as a result of this method call.

protected String **toString**();

Overrides the method definition in the **Object** class.

CheckboxMenuItem Class

Full Name	**java.awt.CheckboxMenuItem**
Extends	**MenuItem->MenuComponent->Object**
Description	Public class. Similar to **MenuItem** class except that it creates a menu item that optionally appears with a check mark. The Boolean (true/false) state determines whether the menu item is currently checked. See **MenuItem** for most fields.

The following example adds two menu items to an existing menu, **m**, and checks the first one. See **Menu** and **MenuItem** classes for more examples.

```
CheckboxMenuItem miBold = new CheckboxMenuItem("Bold");
CheckboxMenuItem miItal = new CheckboxMenuItem("Italic");
m.add(miBold);
m.add(miItal);
miBold.setState(true);
```

Constructors

public **CheckboxMenuItem**(String label);

Constructor. The label must be specified at the time the object is created.

Instance Methods

public boolean **getState**();
public void **setState**(boolean t);

These methods get and set the state: **true** means that the menu item is checked.

public void **addNotify**();

Overrides the method definition in **MenuItem**. Used internally.

CHOICE CLASS

Full Name	**java.awt.Choice**
Extends	**Component->Object**
Description	Public class. In Java, a **Choice** object is much like a drop-down list or option menu. A set of choices is displayed when the object gets focus. Use the **addItem()** method to initialize the list. When a new item is selected, the object generates an event of type **ACTION_EVENT**, resulting in calls to the **action()** method. The second argument to **action()** is a string that contains the selected item. Some **Choice** methods use an index: this index is zero-based, so the first item is 0.

The following example creates and initializes a **Choice** component:

```
Choice chooseCountry = new Choice();
chooseCountry.addItem("Oh Canada!");
chooseCountry.addItem("La Belle France");
chooseCountry.AddItem("USA");
add(chooseCountry);
```

Constructors

public **Choice**();

Constructor. Note that list must be initialized with addItem().

Instance Methods

public synchronized void **addItem**(String item) throws NullPointer-Exception;

Adds item in string form. This is the only way to add items.

public int **countItems**();
public String **getItem**(int index);
public int **getSelectedIndex**();
public String **getSelectedItem**();

These four methods return information about the list: number of items, contents of selected item, zero-based index of current item, and current item in string form, respectively.

public synchronized void **select**(int pos) throws IllegalArgument-Exception;
public void **select**(String str);

The **select()** method changes current selection as indicated, if possible. The pos argument is a zero-based index.

Class Class

Full Name	**java.lang.Class**
Extends	**Object**
Description	Public final class. A **Class** object provides information about a Java class. The practical uses of a **Class** object are limited, but you can use it to browse the Java class system. The **newInstance()** method is one of the few ways to create an object other than using **new**. This class has no constructors, but the **Object.getClass()** method returns a **Class** object, as does **Class.forName()**.

The following example registers the class **imaginary.sql.iMsqDriver**, the mSQL driver for JDBC:

```
Class.forName("imaginary.sql.iMsqDriver");
```

Class Methods

public static Class **forName**(String className);

Class method. Registers a class by name and then returns the corresponding Class object.

Instance Methods

public ClassLoader **getClassLoader**();
public Class[ ] **getInterfaces**();
public String **getName**();
public Class **getSuperclass**();
public boolean **isInterface**();

Each of these methods returns some information about the class. **getClassLoader()** returns a class loader object that loads Java classes over the network; most applications would never use this.

public Object **newInstance**() throws InstantiationException, IllegalAccessException;

Returns a new instance of the class. This object needs to be cast to the appropriate type.

Overridden Class Methods

public String **toString**();

Returns a string representation of the class.

CLONEABLE INTERFACE

Full Name	**java.lang.Cloneable**
Description	Public interface. An API class that implements this interface indicates that it supports a usable definition for the **Object.clone()** method. In other words, if a class implements this interface, an object of the class can be cloned. The **Vector** and **Hashtable** classes are examples of cloneable classes.

This interface declares no fields.

Color Class

Full Name	**java.awt.Color**
Extends	**Object**
Description	Public final class. A **Color** object represents a color value. In addition, this class provides a number of useful constants and class methods. (Class constants and methods can be used without being accessed through an object.) Because it is a final class, **Color** cannot be subclassed.

The following example shows three ways to create the same **Color** object. In actual code, you would only use one of these constructors.

```
Color yuckGreen = new Color(212, 255, 0);
Color yuckGreen = new Color(0Xd4ff00);
Color yuckGreen = new Color(0.83, 1.0. 0.0);
setBackground(yuckGreen);
```

Constructors

public **Color**(int r, int g, int b);
public **Color**(int rgb);
public **Color**(float r, float g, float b);

Constructors. In all cases, the color is specified as an RGB (red/green/blue) value. Where integers are used, each color intensity is specified as a number between 0 and 255. Where floating-point is used, each color intensity is specified as a number between 0.0 and 1.0. The second constructor uses a packed value, in which each of the three lowest bytes holds a color value.

Class Variables

public final static Color **black**;
public final static Color **blue**;
public final static Color **cyan**;
public final static Color **darkGray**;
public final static Color **gray**;
public final static Color **lightGray**;
public final static Color **magenta**;
public final static Color **orange**;
public final static Color **pink**;
public final static Color **red**;
public final static Color **white**;
public final static Color **yellow**;

Color constants. You can refer to these constants directly without having to first instantiate your own color object. Each has the correct RGB value for the stated color. Note that it is a standard Java convention to use all-uppercase names for constants; that convention is broken here.

Class Methods

public static int **HSBtoRGB**(float hue, float saturation, float brightness);
public static float[ ] **RGBtoHSB**(int r, int g, int b, float[ ] hsbvals);

Class methods. The **HSB** methods create a color value from values for hue, saturation, and brightness, in which each is a floating-point number ranging from 0.0 to 1.0. In the **RGBtoHSB()** method, if you specify **null** for the array argument, the method allocates an array in which to return the hue, saturation, and brightness values.

public static Color **getColor**(String nm);
public static Color **getColor**(String nm, Color v);
public static Color **getColor**(String nm, int v);

Class methods. **getColor()** takes a string as input, which it looks up as a system property. The second argument, if specified, gives a default value to use if the color name is not found. Returns a **Color** object with the color value found.

public static Color **getHSBColor**(float hue, float saturation, float brightness);
Class method. Takes values for hue, saturation, and brightness (each ranging from 0.0 to 1.0) and returns the equivalent **Color** object.

Instance Methods

public Color **brighter**();
public Color **darker**();

These methods return a **Color** object that is a shade brighter or darker than the current object. These methods are useful for creating a palette of colors differing in degree of brightness.

public int **getBlue**();
public int **getGreen**();
public int **getRed**();
public int **getRGB**();

These four methods get the current setting of one or more of the primary colors associated with the current object. The **getRGB()** method returns an integer containing red, green, and blue intensities, each packed into a byte.

Overridden Instance Methods

public **equals**(Object obj);
public int **hashCode**();
public String **toString**();

These three methods override method definitions in the **Object** class.

ColorModel Class

Full Name	**java.awt.image.ColorModel**
Extends	**Object**
Description	Abstract public class. The API supports the following usable subclasses: DirectColorModel and IndexColorModel. Most applications and applets never have any reason to interact with these

classes. In general, there is never any need to use a ColorModel class unless you're processing image data that does not use the default RGB model.

Constructors

public **ColorModel**(int bits);

Constructor. Specifies number of bits per pixel.

Class Methods

public static ColorModel **getRGBdefault**();

Class method. Returns a color model that uses the RGB default.

Instance Methods

public abstract int **getAlpha**(int pixel);

Translates a pixel from the color model into the default model (RGB plus alpha). The alpha, which is returned by this method, gives a transparency number from 0 to 255, 0 being completely transparent and 255 being solid, or opaque.

public abstract int **getBlue**(int pixel);
public abstract int **getGreen**(int pixel);
public abstract int **getRed**(int pixel);

These methods translate a pixel from the color model into the default model (RGB), returning the particular color intensity (a number from 0 to 255).

public int **getPixelSize**();

Returns the number of bits per pixel.

public int **getRGB**(int pixel);

Translates a pixel from the model into its RGB representation.

COMPONENT CLASS

Full Name	**java.awt.Component**
Extends	**Object**
Implements	**ImageObserver**
Description	Abstract, public class. Cannot be directly instantiated. However, many classes in the AWT inherit directly or indirectly from this class, which declares the sizing, movement, focus, and event-handling methods for all Java components (other than menus) as well as **paint()**, **show()**, and related methods. In Java, a component is any graphical object that can be displayed and receive events. This class cannot be directly subclassed; to create a custom component, use the **Canvas** class.

Instance Methods

public boolean **action**(Event evt, Object what);

Event handler for events having **ACTION_EVENT** as their ID. Such events indicate an active choice on the part of the user, as in "make something happen." The format of the second argument varies with the component, but it typically contains the component's label. Returns true if the event is handled. This method is often overridden in applet and application code.

public void **addNotify**();

Causes the component to create a peer—this is an object that determines the look of the component on the specific platform. Although it is possible to override this method to create components with a different look (but same functionality), it is generally for internal use only.

public Rectangle **bounds**();

Returns the rectangle containing the display area, in terms of its container's coordinates.

public int **checkImage**(Image image, ImageObserver observer);
public int **checkImage**(Image image, int width, int height, Image-Observer observer);

Reports progress of a loading image by returning flags described in the **ImageObserver** class. Does not cause loading. Generally, you should use a **MediaTracker** object to monitor loading.

public Image **createImage**(ImageProducer producer);
public Image **createImage**(int width, int height);

Creates an **Image** object. The first version uses an image producer such as a filter or in-memory pixel data. (See **FilteredImageSource** and **MemoryImageSource** classes.) The second version is used to create an offscreen buffer. To load an image from a file, see Applet and Toolkit classes.

public void **deliverEvent**(Event e);

Used internally. When an event is generated, the Java interpreter calls **locate()** to determine whether the event occurred in a child component (if any) and then calls **deliverEvent()** to pass the event to the child. There is rarely any reason to call this method directly.

public synchronized void **disable**();
public synchronized void **enable**();

These methods disable and enable the component: disabling a component causes it be grayed out and to stop responding to the user.

public Color **getBackground**();
public synchronized ColorModel **getColorModel**();
public Font **getFont**();
public FontMetrics **getFontMetrics**(Font font);
public Color **getForeground**();

These methods return basic information about the component, including foreground and background color. The color model is used internally to translate RGB values, if necessary, to the particular color scheme in use on this platform.

public Graphics **getGraphics**();

Gets a graphic object, which can be used to draw to the component's screen area directly rather than waiting for a repaint.

public Container **getParent**();

Returns the component's container.

public ComponentPeer **getPeer**();

Used internally to return the platform-specific peer for this component. See **addNotify().**

public Toolkit **getToolkit**();

Returns the component's toolkit, which (especially in applications) is useful for loading an image or getting information about the platform's screen display.

public boolean **gotFocus**(Event evt, Object what);

Event handler for the **gotFocus** event. The second argument is **null**. Returns **true** if the event is handled.

public boolean **handleEvent**(Event evt);

The general event-handling dispatcher. By default, this method checks the event ID and calls the appropriate handler, if any. (See Part V for a summary of events for which there is a handler.) If you override, be careful to preserve default behavior for cases you don't handle directly. You implement default behavior by using the statement "return super.handleEvent()." **handleEvent()** returns **true** if an event is handled. Otherwise, event is passed to the object's container.

public synchronized void **hide**();

Makes the component invisible until **show()** is called.

public boolean **imageUpdate**(Image img, int flags, int x, int y, int w, int h);

This method implements the **ImageObserver** interface. This method is called internally as new image data is loaded into memory. Default response is to repaint the display with the new image data. See **ImageObserver** for more information.

public synchronized boolean **inside**(int x, int y);

Returns true if the specified point is located in the component's region.

public void **invalidate**();

Marks the component as having changed. The next call to **validate()** causes the component to be laid out again if it is a container. Note that this method, along with **validate()** and **layout()**, is most relevant to containers and does not affect repainting. See also **repaint()**.

public boolean **isEnabled**();
public boolean **isShowing**();
public boolean **isValid**();

These methods return basic information about the component. The **isValid()** method returns **false** if the component is a container that needs to be layed out. See validate().

public boolean **keyDown**(Event evt, int key);
public boolean **keyUp**(Event evt, int key);

Event handlers for all keystroke events. Both **KEY_PRESS** and **KEY_ACTION** event IDs result in a call to **keyDown()**. See **Event** class for key codes. All event handlers return **true** if event is handled; otherwise the event is passed to the container.

public void **layout**();

By default, this method does nothing. If the component is a container, **layout()** causes the layout manager to reposition components. This method is called by **validate()**. Application code should generally not call this method directly.

public void **list**();
public void **list**(PrintStream out);

public void **list**(PrintStream out, int indent);

Prints a string representation of this component. This can be useful for debugging. Output is sent to a print stream, if specified, and to standard output by default. The optional indent argument specifies number of spaces to indent.

public Component **locate**(int x, int y);

Returns the child component, if any, at the specified coordinates.

public Point **location**();

Returns the current location.

public boolean **lostFocus**(Event evt, Object what);

Event handler called just before the component loses focus. Second argument is **null**.

public Dimension **minimumSize**();

Returns the minimum size that the component takes up on the screen. For example, if the component is a button, its minimum size is the space needed to display the label along with a sufficient margin on each side. Used by layout managers.

public boolean **mouseDown**(Event evt, int x, int y);
public boolean **mouseDrag**(Event evt, int x, int y);
public boolean **mouseEnter**(Event evt, int x, int y);
public boolean **mouseExit**(Event evt, int x, int y);
public boolean **mouseMove**(Event evt, int x, int y);
public boolean **mouseUp**(Event evt, int x, int y);

These six methods are all handlers for mouse events. In each case, the x and y coordinates give the new or most recent mouse position. All event handlers return **true** if the event was handled. Otherwise, event is passed to the container.

public void **move**(int x, int y);

Moves the top-left corner of the component to the indicated location within its container.

public void **nextFocus**();

Moves focus to the next component, in which "next" is defined by the container. Typically, the container uses the order in which components were added. This is an appropriate response to the **Tab** key.

public void **paint**(Graphics g);

Called when the display needs to be updated either because the component is being displayed for the first time, or part of the component is newly visible. This is one of the most commonly overridden methods in application and applet code.

public void **paintAll**(Graphics g);

Paints the component and all subcomponents, if any.

public boolean **postEvent**(Event e);

Used internally, although it can also be used to generate events. Default response is to call component's **handleEvent()** method; event is posted to container if **handleEvent()** returns **false**.

public Dimension **preferredSize**();

Returns the preferred size of the component. This is its "natural" size. This information can be used by some layout managers.

public boolean **prepareImage**(Image image, ImageObserver observer);
public boolean **prepareImage**(Image image, int width, int height, ImageObserver observer);

Used internally to start image loading. In application code, using **Graphics.drawImage()** is much easier. **prepareImage()** returns **true** if all image data is available now.

public void **print**(Graphics g);

Called by a net browser to print the page that shows the component. Default behavior is to call **paint()**. Application code can override this method to do special processing, if any, before calling **paint()**.

public void **printAll**(Graphics g);

Calls **print()** for the component and all child components, if any.

public synchronized void **removeNotify**();

Used internally to request that the component destroy its peer. See **addNotify()**.

public void **repaint**();
public void **repaint**(long tm);

Forces a repaint, resulting in calls to **update()** and **paint()**. The optional tm argument specifies the number of milliseconds before repainting.

public void **requestFocus**();

Requests that the focus move to this component. Focus enables the component to get keyboard events.

public synchronized void **reshape**(int x, int y, int width, int height);
public void **resize**(int width, int height);
public void **resize**(Dimension d);

These methods change the size or position (or both) of the component.

public synchronized void **setBackground**(Color c);
public synchronized void **setFont**(Font f);
public synchronized void **setForeground**(Color c);

These methods set background and foreground color and default font for drawing.

public synchronized void **show**();
public void **show**(boolean cond);

Displays the object, or hides the object if cond is specified and is **false**. Components that have a container are usually displayed automatically, but this method is useful for top-level components such as a frame or dialog box.

public Dimension **size**();

Returns the height and width of the component's area as a **Dimension** object.

public void **update**(Graphics g);

Called to repaint the component's display. The default behavior is as follows: fill region with background color, set graphics object to component's foreground color, and call **paint()**. This method is sometimes overridden to eliminate the background repainting. This is safe only if the program is written so that the background color is not used.

public void **validate**();

Calls the **layout()** method to cause the component to be laid out (assuming it is a container). Then the method marks the component as valid (meaning correctly laid out). See also **invalidate()**.

Overridden Instance Methods

public String **toString**();

Overrides the method definition in the **Object** class.

CONNECTION INTERFACE

Full Name	**java.sql.Connection**
Description	Public JDBC interface. An object that implements this interface manages a connection to a specific database. By calling one of the three SQL statement methods—**createStatement()**, **prepareStatement()**, and **prepareCall()**—you get an object that encapsulates a SQL statement and that you can use to perform queries and other actions. The effects of a statement are automatically committed if the AutoCommit state is on (the default). Otherwise, you must explicitly call **commit()** to realize changes to the database. You can get an object that implements this interface by calling **DriverManager.getConnection( )** .

The following example uses a connection to create **Statement** and **PreparedStatement** objects:

```
Connection con = DriverManager.getConnection(dbname);
Statement stm = con.createStatement();
String s = "INSERT INTO stuff (name, dat) VALUES (?, ?)";
PreparedStatement pstm = con.prepareStatement(s);
```

Interface Constants

public final static int **TRANSACTION_NONE;**
public final static int **TRANSACTION_READ_UNCOMMITTED;**
public final static int **TRANSACTION_READ_COMMITTED;**
public final static int **TRANSACTION_REPEATABLE_READ;**
public final static int **TRANSACTION_SERIALIZABLE;**

These constants are used with **getTransactionIsolation()** and **setTransactionIsolation()**. **TRANSACTION_SERIALIZABLE** is the most flexible, allowing repeated reads on all rows of a transaction. **TRANSACTION_READ_COMMITTED** is less flexible, allowing reads to be repeated only on the current row.

Interface Methods

public abstract void **clearWarnings**() throws SQLException;

Clears the warnings attached to the database so that **getWarnings()** returns **null**.

public abstract void **close**() throws SQLException;

Closes the database and associated resources immediately. A database connection in a Java program is eventually closed automatically, but not necessarily right away.

public abstract void **commit**() throws SQLException;

Commits all changes made since the last commit or rollback operation.

public abstract Statement **createStatement**() throws SQLException;

Creates a **Statement** object that can be used to specify and execute SQL statements. See **Statement** class. As an alternative, you can use **prepareCall()** or **prepareStatement()**, which are more efficient, although not supported by every database.

public abstract boolean **getAutoClose**() throws SQLException;
public abstract boolean **getAutoCommit**() throws SQLException;

Creates a **CallableStatement** or **PreparedStatement** object, respectively. These objects set a SQL command string at the time of declaration and are more efficient than **Statement** objects when you execute the same statement repeatedly. Note, however, that not all JDBC-conforming databases support these interfaces. **CallableStatement** calls a stored procedure written in the SQL language, whereas **PreparedStatement** supports a simple command string. See the respective interface topics for more information.

public abstract String **getCatalog**() throws SQLException;

Returns the catalog name of the database.

public abstract DatabaseMetaData **getMetaData**() throws SQLException;

Gets a **DatabaseMetaData** object, which you can use to query information about the database.

public abstract int **getTransactionIsolation**() throws SQLException;

Gets the current transaction-isolation level. See the interface constants listed earlier.

public abstract SQLWarning **getWarnings**() throws SQLException;

Gets the first warning reported by calls on this connection; this warning can in turn be used to get other warnings.

public abstract boolean **isClosed**() throws SQLException;

Returns **true** if the database connection is currently closed.

public abstract boolean **isReadOnly**() throws SQLException;

Returns **true** if the database connection uses read-only mode.

public abstract String **nativeSQL**(String sql) throws SQLException;

Converts the JDBC SQL statement into the native SQL grammar in use on the database's system. The driver manages this conversion, if any, and normally it is transparent to a Java program.

public abstract CallableStatement **prepareCall**(String sql) throws SQLException;
public abstract PreparedStatement **prepareStatement**(String sql) throws SQLException;

Creates a **CallableStatement** or **PreparedStatement** object, respectively. These objects set a SQL command string at the time of declaration and are more efficient than **Statement** objects when you execute the same statement repeatedly. Note, however, that not all JDBC-conforming databases support these interfaces. **CallableStatement** calls a stored procedure written in the SQL language, whereas **PreparedStatement** supports a simple command string. See the respective interface topics for more information.

public abstract void **rollback**() throws SQLException;

Cancels all changes made since the last commit or rollback operation.

public abstract void **setAutoClose**(boolean autoClose) throws SQLException;
public abstract void **setAutoCommit**(boolean autoCommit) throws SQLException;

These methods set the AutoClose and AutoCommit states, respectively. See **getAutoClose()**.

public abstract void **setCatalog**(String catalog) throws SQLException;
public abstract void **setReadOnly**(boolean readOnly) throws SQLException;

public abstract void **setTransactionIsolation**(int level) throws SQLException;

These methods attempt to set the catalog name, read-only state, and transaction mode. In each case, the change is made only if the database allows it. Note that you cannot change read-only or transaction mode in the middle of a transaction.

CONTAINER CLASS

Full Name	**java.awt.Container**
Extends	**Object**
Description	Abstract, public class. Because this class is abstract, you cannot instantiate it directly, but you can use a number of its subclasses, including **Frame**, **Dialog**, and **Applet**. Objects created from a Container subclass have the ability to physically contain other components. Each such object, or container, has a layout manager assigned to it, which you can change by calling the **setLayout()** method. The importance of containers and layout managers is described in Chapter 4, "Components and Events."

Instance Methods

public Component **add**(Component comp);
public synchronized Component **add**(Component comp, int pos);
public synchronized Component **add**(String name, Component comp);

Adds a child component to the container. Default order of components is the order in which they're added, although you can specify a position. The third version of **add()** is useful in cases in which the layout manager attaches meaning to the string. For example, **BorderLayout** uses the string to identify a zone: "East," "West," "North," "South," and "Center." See end of Chapter 4, "Components and Events," for meaning of these zones.

public int **countComponents**();

Returns the number of child components in the container.

public synchronized Component **getComponent**(int n) throws ArrayIndexOutOfBoundsException;
public synchronized Component[ ] **getComponents**();

These methods return one or more child components. The parameter, n, is a zero-based index into the container's list of components.

public LayoutManager **getLayout**();

Returns the layout manager object currently in use by this container.

public Insets **insets**();

Returns an **Insets** object that specifies margins to use in the container. You can override this method to specify the desired insets (margins) to use.

public void **paintComponents**(Graphics g);

Paints all the components in the container. Internally, this is called automatically as needed.

public void **printComponents**(Graphics g);

Prints all the components in the container. Internally, this is called automatically when the container is printed.

public synchronized void **remove**(Component comp);
public synchronized void **removeAll**();

These methods remove one or more components.

public void **setLayout**(LayoutManager mgr);

Sets a new layout manager.

Overridden Instance Methods

public synchronized void **addNotify**();
public void **deliverEvent**(Event e);
public synchronized void **layout**();
public void **list**(PrintStream out, int indent);

```
public Component locate(int x, int y);
public synchronized Dimension minimumSize();
public synchronized Dimension preferredSize();
public synchronized void removeNotify();
public synchronized void validate();
```

All these methods, starting with **addNotify()**, override method definitions in **Component**. The **locate()** method, although defined in **Component**, is almost always used by containers. Given internal coordinates, it returns the component at that location. **addNotify()**, **deliverEvent()**, and **removeNotify()** are used internally.

ContentHandler Class

Full Name	**java.net.ContentHandler**
Extends	**Object**
Description	Public abstract class. You would only use this class if writing a Web browser that needs to read and understand some new type of content. Most program code will never have any reason to subclass or use this class. A browser program might use this class by subclassing it to create a new type of handler. The program does not instantiate this class directly but instead uses a **ContentHandlerFactory** object.

```
public ContentHandler();
```

```
public abstract Object getContent(URLConnection urlc)
throws IOException;
```

Reads a stream from the specified **URLConnection** and converts this data into an object.

ContentHandlerFactory Interface

Full Name	**java.net.ContentHandlerFactory**
Description	Public interface. Most program code will never have any reason to use this interface in any way. A content handler factory returns a content handler when requested to do so. A URLConnection object sets a content handler factory when a factory object is passed to its **setContentHandlerFactory()** method.

public abstract ContentHandler **createContentHandler**(String mimetype);

Returns a content handler for the named mimetype. This content handler is an instance of a **ContentHandler** subclass.

CropImageFilter Class

Full Name	**java.awt.image.CropImageFilter**
Extends	**ImageFilter**
Description	Public class. Creates an image filter that can be used to produce a new image from an old one, in which the old image is cropped to a specified rectangle. The image filter is connected to an actual image with the help of the **FilteredImageSource** class.

The use of the image filter, producer, and consumer classes and interfaces is not obvious at first. See the description of the **FilteredImageSource** class for an example that takes you through the process of creating a filtered image.

Constructors

public **CropImageFilter**(int x, int y, int w, int h);

Constructor. Arguments determine the region to be cropped from the original image.

Overridden Instance Methods

public void **setDimensions**(int w, int h);
public void **setPixels**(int x, int y, int w, int h, ColorModel model, byte pixels[], int off, int scansize);
public void **setPixels**(int x, int y, int w, int h, ColorModel model, int pixels[], int off, int scansize);
public void **setProperties**(Hashtable props);

These methods override method definitions in the **ImageFilter** class.

DatabaseMetaData Interface

Full Name	**java.sql.DatabaseMetaData**
Description	Public JDBC interface. You can use this interface to get extensive information on a database, including table and column structure and database capabilities. After establishing a connection, you can call the **Connection** object's **getMetaData( )** method to get an object that implements **DatabaseMetaData**.Because this interface is unusually large, I've included only a sample of useful methods. This interface has dozens of methods that report on the availability of a specific capability, such as outer joins. Other methods list items such as extended SQL keywords supported. The methods listed here are especially useful, because they enable you to inspect the structure of a random database. For more documentation, see the Web site at **http://splash.javasoft.com/jdbc/**.

The following example gets a result set describing all tables having type TABLE or VIEW. The percent sign (%) is a wildcard character meaning any series of characters: "%" in the third argument means to get all tables.

```
String myTableTypes[] = {"TABLE", "VIEW"};
Connection con = DriverManager.getConnection(dbname);
DatabaseMetaData meta = con.getMetaData();
ResultSet rs = meta.getTables(null, null, "%",
     myTableTypes);
```

The **getTable( )** method returns a result set, as do a number of other methods. Use the **ResultSe**t and **ResultSetMetaData** interfaces to browse the contents of a result set.

Interface Methods

public abstract ResultSet **getCatalogs( )** throws SQLException;

Returns a result set describing the catalogs in the database. Not all databases support the use of catalogs.

public abstract ResultSet **getColumn**s(String catalog, String schemaPattern, String tableNamePattern, String columnNamePattern) throws SQLException;

Returns a result set describing the specified columns for the specified tables. The ***catalog*** and **schemaPattern** arguments can be passed null if the database doesn't use them. The last three arguments take a string in which wildcards are recognized; see **getTables( )**. See also Table J in Part VI.

public abstract int **getDriverMajorVersion( )** throws SQLException;
public abstract int **getDriverMinorVersion( )** throws SQLException;
public abstract String **getDriverName( )** throws SQLException;
public abstract String **getDriverVersion()** throws SQLException;

These methods provide information on the current database driver. The first two methods return integers for easy numerical comparisons between version numbers.

public abstract int **getMaxConnections( )** throws SQLException;
public abstract int **getMaxStatements( )** throws SQLException;

These methods return the maximum number of connections and statements, respectively, that you can have open at one time.

public abstract ResultSet **getPrimaryKeys**(String catalog, String schema, String table) throws SQLException;

Returns a result set describing primary keys for the specified table. The **catalog** and **schema** arguments can be passed null if the database doesn't use them.

public abstract ResultSet **getProcedures**(String catalog,String schemaPattern, String procedureNamePattern) throws SQLException;

Returns a result set describing the stored procedures specified. The **catalog** and **schemaPattern** arguments can be passed null if the database doesn't use them. The last two arguments take a string in which wildcards are recognized; see **getTables( )**.

public abstract ResultSet **getSchemas( )** throws SQLException;

Returns a result set describing the catalogs in the database. Not all databases support the use of catalogs.

public abstract ResultSet **getTables**(String catalog, String SchemaPattern, String tableNamePattern, String types[]) throws SQLException;

Returns a result set describing specified table or tables.The **catalog** and **schemaPattern** arguments can be passed null if the database doesn't use them. The **schemaPattern** and **tableNamePattern** arguments take a string in which wildcards are recognized: "%" represents any series of characters, and "_" represents any one character. Thus, "stuff" refers only to "stuff," "%" means any name, and "s%" means all names starting with "s." The **types** argument is an array of strings that can include any of the following: "TABLE", "VIEW","SYSTEM TABLE", "GLOBAL TEMPORARY", "LOCAL TEMPORARY", "ALIAS", and "SYNONYM". See the example at the beginning of the topic. See also Table I in Part VI

public abstract ResultSet **getTableTypes( )** throws SQLException;

Returns a result set describing available table types.

public abstract ResultSet **getTypeInfo( )** throws SQLException;

Returns a result set describing available data types. See **Types** class.

public abstract String **getURL( )** throws SQLException;

Returns the URL of the current database.

public abstract String **getUserName( )** throws SQLException;

Returns the current user name recognized by the database.

public abstract boolean **isReadOnly( )** throws SQLException;

Returns **true** if the database is being accessed in read-only mode; this would prevent updates and table creation but not queries.

public abstract boolean **supportsMultipleResultSets( )** throws SQLException;

Returns **true** if multiple result sets are supported; this is relevant to the use of **execute( )**, **getResultSet( )**, and **getMoreResults( )** in the **Statement** interface.

public abstract boolean **supportsStoredProcedures( )** throws SQLException;

Returns **true** if stored procedures are supported, enabling use of the **CallableStatement** interface.

DatagramPacket Class

Full Name	**java.net.DatagramPacket**
Extends	**Object**
Description	Public final class. Creates a packet that can be sent or received over the network. A datagram consists of a simple series of bytes. This form of communication uses the User Datagram Protocol (UDP): there is no guarantee that packets will be received in the same order sent, and the protocol requires no acknowledgment of receipt. This is the most unreliable form of network i/o, but it is also the fastest. After creating a packet, you send it by using a **DataSocket** object. See **Socket** and **URL** classes for more-reliable network i/o.

The following example sends a packet of data to network address **iaddr**:

```
try {
    DatagramSocket sock = new DatagramSocket();
    DatagramPacket pack = new DatagramPacket(
        buffer, n, iaddr, portnum);
    sock.send(pack);
}  catch(Exception e) {System.out.println(e);}
```

Constructors

public **DatagramPacket**(byte ibuf[ ], int ilength);

Constructor: creates a data-packet structure to receive data. After creating the object, call the **DatagramSocket.receive()** method to get the data.

public **DatagramPacket**(byte ibuf[ ], int ilength, InetAddress iaddr, int iport);

Constructor: creates a packet to be sent, along with its destination address and destination port. After creating the object, call the **DatagramSocket.send()** method to send the data.

Instance Methods

public InetAddress **getAddress**();
public byte[ ] **getData**();
public int **getLength**();
public int **getPort**();

These methods return information that was specified in the constructor.

DatagramSocket Class

Full Name	**java.net.DatagramSocket**
Extends	**Object**
Description	Public class. Creates an interface around a communications port, enabling the sending and receiving of datagram packets. These packets are simple arrays of bytes; see **DatagramPacket** for more information. For higher-level, more reliable network i/o, see **Socket** and **URL** classes.

See DatagramPacket class for an example.

Constructors

public **DatagramSocket**() throws SocketException;
public **DatagramSocket**(int port) throws SocketException;

Constructors. Creates a datagram socket around the specified local port. If the port is not specified, then one is assigned.

Instance Methods

public void **close**();

Closes the socket and frees the port.

public int **getLocalPort**();

Returns the socket's port number.

public void **receive**(DatagramPacket p) throws IOException;

Receives a datagram packet. This method assumes that data has been sent.

public void **send**(DatagramPacket p) throws IOException;

Sends a datagram packet. The packet must specify an Internet address and a port number.

DataInput Interface

Full Name	**java.io.DataInput**
Description	Public interface. This interface declares methods implemented by **DataInputStream** and **RandomAccessFile**. For descriptions of the methods, see **DataInputStream**.

public abstract boolean **readBoolean**() throws IOException, EOFException;
public abstract byte **readByte**() throws IOException, EOFException;
public abstract char **readChar**() throws IOException, EOFException;
public abstract double **readDouble**() throws IOException, EOFException;
public abstract float **readFloat**() throws IOException, EOFException;
public abstract void **readFully**(byte b[ ]) throws IOException, EOFException;
public abstract void **readFully**(byte b[ ], int off, int len) throws IOException, EOFException;

public abstract int **readInt**() throws IOException, EOFException;
public abstract String **readLine**() throws IOException;
public abstract long **readLong**() throws IOException, EOFException;
public abstract short **readShort**() throws IOException, EOFException;
public abstract int **readUnsignedByte**() throws IOException, EOFException;
public abstract int **readUnsignedShort**() throws IOException, EOFException;
public abstract String **readUTF**() throws IOException;
public abstract int **skipBytes**(int n) throws IOException, EOFException;

DataInputStream Class

Full Name	**java.io.DataInputStream**
Extends	**FilterInputStream->InputStream->Object**
Implements	**DataInput**
Description	Public class. This class, along with **DataOutputStream**, lets you read and write Java data types and strings in a platform-independent way. You can produce output from any Java program using **DataOutputStream**, and any program using **DataInputStream** is guaranteed to read the same data (provided that they agree on which data types and strings to look for). See **FileInputStream** for information about how to hook the stream to a file.

DataInputStream can be used to read input from the keyboard in a console application. After reading a line of input, you can parse it by using **Integer.parseInt()**, **Long.parseLong()**, and other wrapper classes.

```
DataInputStream dis = new DataInputStream(System.in);
String s = "";
```

```
try {
     s = dis.readLine();
}catch(IOException e){;}
```

Constructors

public **DataInputStream**(InputStream in);

Creates a **DataInputStream** object from the specified input stream.

Class Methods

public final static String **readUTF**(DataInput in) throws IOException;

Class method. Reads a string in UTF-8 format from the specified stream. See **readUTF()** near the end of this topic.

Instance Methods

public final boolean **readBoolean**() throws IOException;
public final byte **readByte**() throws IOException;
public final char **readChar**() throws IOException;
public final double **readDouble**() throws IOException;
public final float **readFloat**() throws IOException;

Each of these methods reads an instance of a primitive data type.

public final void **readFully**(byte b[ ]) throws IOException, EOFException;
public final void **readFully**(byte b[ ], int off, int len) throws IOException, EOFException;

Reads enough bytes to fill the array, or reads len bytes if specified. In either case, this method causes the current thread to wait until all the requested data is read.

public final int **readInt**() throws IOException;

Reads an instance of an **int**.

public final String **readLine**() throws IOException;

Reads a character string up to the first newline, carriage return, newline/carriage-return pair, or end of input stream. The terminating characters, if any, are included in the string returned. This method can be used to read from the keyboard: see example at beginning of this topic. However, for reading strings written by **DataOutputStream**, the use of **readUTF()** is recommended.

public final long **readLong**() throws IOException;
public final short **readShort**() throws IOException;
public final int **readUnsignedByte**() throws IOException;
public final int **readUnsignedShort**() throws IOException;

Each of these methods reads an instance of a primitive data type. Although unsigned byte and unsigned short are not Java data types, Java can read them correctly and return them in an **int** field, which has sufficient range to store the number read.

public final String **readUTF**() throws IOException;

Reads a string in the Unicode transformation format (UTF). This format reads the first two bytes as an unsigned short integer indicating the length of the string. The rest of the data consists of UTF-8 character encoding. The UTF-8 format, which is compatible with ASCII, is described in Table H in Part V. See also **DataOutputStream.writeUTF()**.

public final int **skipBytes**(int n) throws IOException;

Skip over n bytes before the next read.

public final int **read**(byte b[ ]) throws IOException;
public final int **read**(byte b[ ], int off, int len) throws IOException;

These methods override method definitions in the **InputStream** class.

DataOutput Interface

Full Name	**java.io.DataOutput**
Description	Public interface. This interface declares methods implemented by **DataOutputStream** and **RandomAccessFile**. For descriptions of the methods, see **DataOutputStream**.

public abstract void **write**(byte b[ ]) throws IOException;
public abstract void **write**(byte b[ ], int off, int len) throws IOException;
public abstract void **write**(int b) throws IOException;
public abstract void **writeBoolean**(boolean v) throws IOException;
public abstract void **writeByte**(int v) throws IOException;
public abstract void **writeBytes**(String s) throws IOException;
public abstract void **writeChar**(int v) throws IOException;
public abstract void **writeChars**(String s) throws IOException;
public abstract void **writeDouble**(double v) throws IOException;
public abstract void **writeFloat**(float v) throws IOException;
public abstract void **writeInt**(int v) throws IOException;
public abstract void **writeLong**(long v) throws IOException;
public abstract void **writeShort**(int v) throws IOException;
public abstract void **writeUTF**(String str) throws IOException;

DataOutputStream Class

Full Name	**java.io.DataOutputStream**
Extends	**FilterOutputStream->OutputStream->Object**
Implements	DataOutput
Description	Public class. This class, along with **DataInputStream**, lets you read and write Java data types and strings in a platform-independent way. You can produce output from any Java program using **DataOutputStream**, and any program using **DataInputStream** is

guaranteed to read the same data (provided that they agree on which data types and strings to look for). See **FileOutputStream** for information about how to hook the stream to a file.

The following example writes an integer to a file, **STUFF.DAT**. The **try-catch** block is required because the **FileOutputSteam()** constructor may throw an exception.

```
try {
  FileOutputStream out = new
         FileOutputStream("STUFF.DAT");
  DataOutputStream dataOut = new
         DataOutputStream(out);
  dataOut.writeInt(5);
} catch (IOException e) {System.out.println(e);}
```

Constructors

public **DataOutputStream**(OutputStream out);

Creates a **DataOutputStream** object from the specified output stream.

Instance Methods

public final void **writeBoolean**(boolean v) throws IOException;
public final void **writeByte**(int v) throws IOException;

These methods write an instance of a primitive data type.

public final void **writeBytes**(String s) throws IOException;

Writes a string to the output stream, converting each character to a byte by discarding the eight high bits. Note that **DataInput-Stream.readLine()** will not read such a string correctly unless you terminate it with a newline or carriage return. See also **writeUTF()**.

public final void **writeChar**(int v) throws IOException;
public final void **writeChars**(String s) throws IOException;
public final void **writeDouble**(double v) throws IOException;
public final void **writeFloat**(float v) throws IOException;
public final void **writeInt**(int v) throws IOException;
public final void **writeLong**(long v) throws IOException;
public final void **writeShort**(int v) throws IOException;

Each of these methods writes the appropriate primitive data type.

public final void **writeUTF**(String str) throws IOException;

Writes a string in the Unicode transformation format (UTF). This format writes the first two bytes as an unsigned short integer indicating the length of the string. The rest of the data consists of UTF-8 character encoding. The UTF-8 format, which is compatible with ASCII, is described in Table H in Part V. See also **DataInput-Stream.readUTF()**.

Overridden Instance Methods

public void **flush**() throws IOException;
public final int **size**();
public void **write**(byte b[ ], int off, int len) throws IOException;
public void **write**(int b) throws IOException;

These methods override method definitions in the **OutputStream** class.

DATE CLASS

Full Name	**java.util.Date**
Extends	**Object**
Description	Public class. A **Date** object combines complete year, day, and time of day information down to milliseconds. The class has many uses: you can use the **Date** default constructor as a seed value for the **Random** class, you can measure durations between events, and you can get the day of the week for arbitrary dates.

The following example prints the current day of the month. See the **Random** class for another example of how **Date** is used.

```
Date dt = new Date(); // Get current date and time.
System.out.println("Day of the month is " + dt.getDate());
```

Constructors

public **Date**();

Constructor. Returns date object representing now (the moment the object was created).

public **Date**(int year, int month, int date);
public **Date**(int year, int month, int date, int hrs, int min);
public **Date**(int year, int month, int date, int hrs, int min, int sec);

Constructor. Takes input in the following format: year = year minus 1900, month = number between 0 and 11, date = number between 1 and 31, hrs = number between 0 and 23, and minutes and seconds = number between 0 and 59.

public **Date**(long date);

Constructor. Uses an argument that represents the number of milliseconds since beginning of January 1, 1970, Greenwich Mean Time (GMT).

public **Date**(String s);

Constructor. Takes a string argument in the same format as the **parse()** method.

Class Methods

public static long **parse**(String s);

Class method. Returns a time value (number of milliseconds since beginning of January 1, 1970) after parsing a string: most standard syntaxes are accepted. The following format is always accepted: "Wed, 17 July 1995 13:30:00 GMT." American time zone abbreviations (such as PDT) are accepted, but time zone specification as

"GMT+0900" (9 hours west of Greenwich) are recommended.

public static long **UTC**(int year, int month, int date, int hrs, int min, int sec);

Class method. Returns a time value (number of milliseconds since beginning of January 1, 1970) from the inputs. See **Date** constructors for interpretation of the numbers.

Instance Methods

public boolean **after**(Date when);
public boolean **before**(Date when);

These methods return **true** or **false** after comparing the current object to another **Date** object. For example, **after()** returns **true** if the current object is after the **Date** argument specified.

public int **getDate**();
public int **getDay**();
public int **getHours**();
public int **getMinutes**();
public int **getMonth**();
public int **getSeconds**();

All these methods return the specified component of the date, where month ranges between 0 and 11, date ranges between 1 and 31, hours range between 0 and 23, and minutes and seconds range between 0 and 59. **getDay()** returns a number between 0 and 6 representing the day of the week; 0 is Sunday.

public long **getTime**();

Returns the number of milliseconds since beginning of January 1, 1970, GMT.

public int **getTimezoneOffset**();

Returns the time zone offset, in minutes, that must be added to GMT to get the local time. The offset includes correction for daylight savings time.

public int **getYear**();

Returns the current year minus 1900.

public void **setDate**(int date);
public void **setHours**(int hours);
public void **setMinutes**(int minutes);
public void **setMonth**(int month);
public void **setSeconds**(int seconds);
public void **setTime**(long time);
public void **setYear**(int year);

These seven "set" methods all set a component of the date/time value. See the corresponding "get" method for the format.

public String **toGMTString**();

Returns a string representation of the date/time value using Internet GMT conventions. Sample output: "17 July 13:30:00 GMT."

public String **toLocaleString**();

Returns a string representation of the date/time value using local conventions. Exact format of this string is implementation-dependent.

Overridden Instance Methods

public boolean **equals**(Object obj);
public int **hashCode**();
public String **toString**();

These methods override method definitions in the **Object** class. The **toString()** method returns a string representation in the following standard format: "Sat Aug 12 04:30:00 PDT 1995."

DATE CLASS (JAVA.SQL)

Full Name	**java.sql.Date**
Extends	**java.util.Date->Object**
Description	Public JDBC class. Unlike its superclass in the **java.util** package, this class stores only the year, month, and date. For time of day information, see **Time** class. To be compatible with the typical organization of databases, the **java.sql** package provides separate and time

Constructors

public **Date**(int year, int month, int day);

Constructor. Takes input in the following format: year = year minus 1900, month = number between 0 and 11, date = number between 1 and 31.

Class Methods

public static Date **valueOf**(String s);

Converts a formatted string to a **Date** object. The string must use the format yyyy-mm-dd.

Overridden Instance Methods

public String **toString**();

Overrides method definition in the **Object** (and **java.util.Date**) class. The **toString()** method returns a string representation in the format yyyy-mm-dd.

Dialog Class

Full Name	**java.awt.Dialog**
Extends	**Window->Container->Component->Object**
Description	Public class. Creates a dialog box, which may be modal. When a modal dialog box is displayed, the user cannot interact with any other parts of the application until the dialog box is closed. However, the modality of a dialog box does not affect the flow of control; a **Dialog** constructor, for example, returns immediately rather than wait for the dialog box to close. A dialog box may optionally have a title and be resizable. Dialog boxes generate all standard keyboard and mouse events as well as window events. (See Part VI for details.) Call **show()** to display the dialog box.

Constructors

public **Dialog**(Frame parent, boolean modal);
public **Dialog**(Frame parent, String title, boolean modal);

Constructors. The dialog box must have a parent frame. The modal argument, if **true**, specifies that the dialog box is modal.

Instance Methods

public String **getTitle**();
public boolean **isModal**();
public boolean **isResizable**
public void **setResizable**(boolean resizable);
public void **setTitle**(String title);

These five methods get and set the dialog box attributes: title bar string, modality (**true** means that the dialog box is modal), and resizable condition (**true** means that the user can resize the dialog).

Overridden Instance Methods

public synchronized void **addNotify**();

Overrides the method definition in **Component**. Used internally.

DICTIONARY CLASS

Full Name	**java.util.Dictionary**
Extends	**Object**
Description	Abstract public class: only subclasses can be instantiated. The role of this class in the API is that it defines some of the methods in the **Hashtable** class, although you can also inherit from it to create your own hashtable-like classes. See **Hashtable** for a description of methods.

Constructors

public **Dictionary**();

Constructor. You cannot call this constructor, because **Dictionary** is an abstract class.

Instance Methods

abstract Enumeration **elements**();

public abstract Object **get**(Object key);
public abstract boolean **isEmpty**();
public abstract Enumeration **keys**();
public abstract Object **put**(Object key, Object value) throws NullPointerException;
public abstract Object **remove**(Object key);
public abstract int **size**();

For descriptions of these methods, see **Hashtable** class.

Dimension Class

Full Name	**java.awt.Dimension**
Extends	**Object**
Description	Public class. Creates a simple object containing height and width measurements.

A dimension object is used to store simple height and weight measurements. For example:

```
Dimension d;
d.width = 200;
d.height = 200;
```

Constructors

public **Dimension**();
public **Dimension**(Dimension d);
public **Dimension**(int width, int height);

Constructors. The object can optionally be initialized in the constructor.

Instance Variables

public int **height**;
public int **width**;

Public instance variables. See earlier example for use.

Overridden Instance Methods

protected String **toString**();

Overrides method definition in the **Object** class.

DirectColorModel Class

Full Name	**java.awt.image.DirectColorModel**
Extends	**ColorModel->Object**
Description	Public class. Specifies a color model by specifying which bits in the pixel correspond to red, green, and blue values. This is useful for translating from color models that use RGB values but map them to different bit positions than the standard model. In general, there is never any need to use this class unless you're processing image data that does not use the default RGB model.

Constructors

public **DirectColorModel**(int bits, int rmask, int gmask, int bmask);
public **DirectColorModel**(int bits, int rmask, int gmask, int bmask, int amask);

Constructors. The arguments specify number of bits per pixel; a bit mask for each of the colors red, green, and blue; and an optional mask for the alpha value. (See **ColorModel** for information on the alpha value.) Each bit mask indicates which bits in each pixel value correspond to the given color.

Instance Methods

public final int **getAlphaMask**();
public final int **getBlueMask**();
public final int **getGreenMask**();
public final int **getRedMask**();

These methods return the bit masks assigned for the alpha and for each color.

Overridden Instance Methods

public final int **getAlpha**(int pixel);
public final int **getBlue**(int pixel);
public final int **getGreen**(int pixel);
public final int **getRed**(int pixel);
public final int **getRGB**(int pixel);

These methods override method definitions in the **ColorModel** class.

Double Class

Full Name	**java.lang.Double**
Extends	**Number->Object**
Description	Public final class. Serves as the wrapper class for the **double** primitive type. This class provides methods for converting between string, object, and numeric data. It also is useful for passing a **double** value by reference.

The following example converts a digit string to type **double**:

```
double d = (new Double(digitString)).doubleValue();
```

Constructors

public **Double**(double value);
public **Double**(String s) throws NumberFormatException;

Constructors. The last constructor initializes from a digit string.

Class Variables

public final static double **MAX_VALUE**;
public final static double **MIN_VALUE**;
public final static double **NaN**;
public final static double **NEGATIVE_INFINITY**;
public final static double **POSITIVE_INFINITY;**

Constants. See Part VII, "Glossary of Java Terminology" for meaning of the last three terms.

Class Methods

public static long **doubleToLongBits**(double value);
public static boolean **isInfinite**(double v);
public static boolean **isNaN**(double v);
public static double **longBitsToDouble**(long bits);
public static String **toString**(double d);
public static Double **valueOf**(String s);

Class methods. The **doubleToLongBits()** and **longBitsToDouble()** methods convert between a long and a double without changing the actual bit values. See description later for **isNaN()**.

Instance Methods

public boolean **isInfinite**();
public boolean **isNaN**();

These methods return **true** if the current value is, respectively, positive or negative infinity, or "not a number." This is the only reliable way to test for an **NaN** value, because **NaN** will always return **false** when compared to itself.

Overridden Instance Methods

public double **doubleValue**();
public float **floatValue**();
public int **intValue**();
public long **longValue**();

These methods return the **double**, **float**, **int**, or **long** equivalent of the value stored in the current object. The methods round as necessary, for there may be loss of precision.

public boolean **equals**(Object obj);
public int **hashCode**();
public String **toString**();

These methods override method definitions in the **Object** class.

DRIVER INTERFACE

Full Name	**java.sql.Driver**
Description	Public JDBC interface. Technically, this interface provides Java language access to a particular database driver. (See also **DriverManager** class.) You don't need to implement this interface yourself unless you're writing a database driver. Each driver should supply an object that implements this interface. The object must provide a default constructor so that it can be instantiated through **Class.newInstance()**. From the standpoint of application code, this interface is probably most useful for greater control over making a connection to a database. In particular, you can call **getPropertyInfo()** to get information about required property values. You can get a **Driver** object by using the **DriverManager** class.

public abstract boolean **acceptsURL**(String url) throws SQLException;

Returns **true** if the driver determines that the database connection will be successful.

public abstract Connection **connect**(String url, Properties info) throws SQLException;

Attempts to connect to the database specified by the URL string. The second argument is a **Properties** table containing tag/value pairs. These should generally include "user" and "password," although other properties may sometimes be required as indicated by **getPropertiesInfo()**. If the connection attempt is unsuccessful, **null** is returned.

public abstract int **getMajorVersion**();
public abstract int **getMinorVersion**();

These methods return major and minor version numbers, respectively, for the driver.

public abstract DriverPropertyInfo[ ] **getPropertyInfo**(String url, Properties info) throws SQLException;

Returns information on property values that are needed to make a database connection. Each member of the array is a **DriverPropertyInfo** object that describes one such property.

public abstract boolean **jdbcCompliant**();

Returns **true** if the driver is fully JDBC-compliant. Note that some drivers may still work with JDBC even though they do not pass all tests to be fully compliant.

DriverManager Class

Full Name	**java.sql.DriverManager**
Extends	**Object**
Description	Public JDBC class. Provides a set of class methods for interacting with the JDBC driver manager. The most useful is probably **getConnection()**, which is the start ing point for most database operations within Java. This method returns a **Connection** object, which you can in turn use to execute SQL operations.

The following example creates a **Connection** object for a sample database, referred to as myDSN. This is the Data Source Name: when you create an ODBC driver, you assign a Data Source Name to refer to a particular database.

```
Class.forName("jdbc.odbc.JdbcOdbcDriver");
Connection con =
    DriverManager.getConnection("jdbc:odbc:myDSN");
```

Constructors

public **DriverManager**();

Constructor. During initialization, this object reads the properties setting for a list of drivers as described earlier. The driver manager can also use any other drivers that have already been recognized (for example, by an appletviewer that has loaded the current program as an applet).

Instance Methods

public static void **deregisterDriver**(Driver driver) throws SQLException;

Removes the specified driver from the list of drivers supported.

public static synchronized Connection **getConnection**(String url, Properties info) throws SQLException;
public static synchronized Connection **getConnection**(String url, String user, String password) throws SQLException;
public static synchronized Connection **getConnection**(String url) throws SQLException;

Gets a connection to the database specified by the url argument. This string has the form jdbc:*subprotocol*:*subname*. The first version of **getConnection()** passes a properties table providing tag/value pairs; these should generally include entries for "user" and "password." JDBC attempts to find a suitable driver for the connection from among the list of drivers. If the connection attempt is unsuccessful, **null** is returned.

public static Driver **getDriver**(String url) throws SQLException;

Attempts to return, from among the list of drivers, a suitable driver for the specified database.

public static Enumeration **getDrivers**();

Returns an enumeration of all the drivers currently available to the driver manager.

public static int **getLoginTimeout**();

Returns the maximum number of seconds that drivers will wait during a login. This value can be set with setLoginTimeout().

public static PrintStream **getLogStream**();

Returns the **PrintStream** object used by drivers for logging and tracing purposes.

public static synchronized void **println**(String message);

Prints a message to the JDBC log stream.

public static synchronized void **registerDriver**(Driver driver) throws SQLException;

Adds a new driver to the list of drivers available to the driver manager. This method should be called if a new **Driver** object has been downloaded on the system.

public static void **setLoginTimeout**(int seconds);
public static void **setLogStream**(PrintStream out);

Sets the login timeout and **PrintStream** object, respectively. See corresponding "get" methods.

DriverPropertyInfo Class

Full Name	**java.sql.DriverPropertyInfo**
Extends	**Object**
Description	Public JDBC class that contains information on one high-level database property returned by the **getPropertyInfo()** method of the **Driver** class. This is typically a property whose value must be supplied for successful connection to a particular database. The Java program may choose to query the user for property values. The fields of this class provide information (such as a list of possible values) that aids in querying the user, although the program itself must supply the user interface. Once property values are ascertained, the program should specify all properties in a **Properties** table during the next attempt at database connection.

Constructors

public **DriverPropertyInfo**(String name, String value);

Constructor. Typically, you get an array of these objects from **Driver.getPropertyInfo()**, so there is rarely reason to allocate a **DriverPropertyInfo** object directly.

Instance Variables

public String **choices**[ ];

An array that contains the accepted property values. This variable is used only if the accepted values are restricted to such a set; otherwise, **choices** is **null**.

public String **description;**

A brief description, if available, or **null** if none is provided by the database.

public String **name;**

The property name.

public boolean **required;**

If **true**, the property value must be provided for successful connection; otherwise, providing a value for this property is optional.

public String **value;**

The default value of the property, or **null** if there is no default.

ENUMERATION INTERFACE

Full Name	**java.util.Enumeration**
Description	Public interface. An object whose class implements this interface can be used to loop through a simple list of elements. This usually involves a **while** or **for** loop. A number of classes, such as **Vector** and **Hashtable**, return an enumeration as one way of providing access to child elements. Note that you can go through an enumeration only once; you cannot reset. (You can store the results of the enumeration in a vector or other structure as you go through it.)

The following example assumes you've been passed a string enumeration, **strEnum**. The example prints all the strings in the enumeration.

```
while (strEnum.hasMoreElements()) {
     String s = (String) strEnum.nextElement();
     System.out.println(s);
}
```

public abstract boolean **hasMoreElements**();

Returns **true** if there are more elements left in the enumeration.

public abstract Object **nextElement**() throws NoSuchElement-Exception;

Gets the next element and advances one position in the list. The object returned usually needs to be cast to a particular type—such as String in the example.

Event Class

Full Name	**java.awt.Event**
Extends	**Object**
Description	Public class. An **Event** object contains detailed information on an event occurring at run time, usually in response to a user action. When an event is generated, the **Event** object is passed from one component to the next until an event handler handles the event and returns **true**. The **Event** class also defines a number of useful constants that represent event types and key codes.

The following example tests a keystroke by comparing it to an **Event** class constant. The **keyDown()** method is a **Component** class method. Note that in this case, testing **evt.key** is equivalent to testing the **key** argument directly.

```
public boolean keyDown(Event evt, Integer key) {
     if (evt.key == Event.F2 ) {
          // Process F2 key...
     }
     return true;
}
```

Constructors

public **Event**(Object target, long when, int id, int x, int y, int key, int modifiers, Object arg);
public **Event**(Object target, long when, int id, int x, int y, int key, int modifers);
public **Event**(Object target, int id, Object arg);

Constructors. All the arguments correspond to instance variables, described next.

Instance Variables

public Object **arg**;

An argument that contains additional information relevant to the event. This corresponds to the second argument passed to an **action()** event handler.

public int **clickCount**;

Number of consecutive mouse clicks. (0 if event is not a mouse event.)

public Event **evt**;

A reference to the next event in a linked list of events.

public int **id**;

ID indicating type of event. Possible values are listed in the event-type constants. (See "Class Variables" in this topic.)

public int **key**;

The key that was pressed, if applicable. Special keys are represented as keycode constants. Alphanumeric keys are represented as their standard Unicode character values.

public int **modifiers**;

State of the modifier keys: these are the keys with "MASK" in their keycode name. The modifier states are combined, using bitwise OR (|), to produce a single integer field.

public Object **target**;

A reference to the object that generated the event (i.e., where the event originated).

public long **when**;

Timestamp giving the time of the event.

public int **x**;
public int **y**;

These two fields give x, y coordinates of current position. For mouse events, this is the most recent mouse position.

Class Variables

public final static int **ACTION_EVENT**;
public final static int **GOT_FOCUS**, **LOST_FOCUS**;
public final static int **KEY_ACTION**;
public final static int **KEY_ACTION_RELEASE**;
public final static int **KEY_PRESS**, **KEY_RELEASE**;
public final static int **LIST_DESELECT**, **LIST_SELECT**;
public final static int **LOAD_FILE**;
public final static int **MOUSE_DOWN**, **MOUSE_DRAG**;
public final static int **MOUSE_ENTER**, **MOUSE_EXIT**;
public final static int **MOUSE_MOVE**, **MOUSE_UP**;
public final static int **SAVE_FILE**;
public final static int **SCROLL_ABSOLUTE**;
public final static int **SCROLL_LINE_DOWN**, **SCROLL_LINE_UP**;
public final static int **SCROLL_PAGE_DOWN**;
public final static int **SCROLL_PAGE_UP**;
public final static int **WINDOW_DESTROY**;
public final static int **WINDOW_EXPOSE**;
public final static int **WINDOW_ICONIFY**;
public final static int **WINDOW_DEICONIFY**;
public final static int **WINDOW_MOVED**;

These constants specify event IDs. See Tables A and B in Part VI for a description of which event handler, if any, is called in response to each event type. Those events that do not have an event handler can be handled only in **handleEvent()**. Note that **LOAD_FILE** and **SAVE_FILE** are not yet generated in the current version of Java.

public final static int **F1**, **F2**, **F3**, **F4**, **F5**, **F6**, **F7**, **F8**, **F9**, **F10**, **F11**, **F12**;

Constants for function keys.

public final static int **HOME**, **END**;
public final static int **LEFT**, **RIGHT**;
public final static int **PGDN**, **PGUP**;
public final static int **UP**, **DOWN**;

Constants for other special keys.

public final static int **ALT_MASK**, **CTRL_MASK**;
public final static int **SHIFT_MASK**, **META_MASK**;

Modifier key codes. These are combined, using bitwise OR (|), to produce the modifier state. Use binary AND (&) to extract them. For mouse events, **ALT_MASK** indicates middle mouse button down, and **META_MASK** indicates right mouse button down.

Instance Methods

public boolean **controlDown**();
public boolean **metaDown**();
public boolean **shiftDown**();

These methods return the states of some of the modifier keys as simple Boolean conditions.

public void **translate**(int dx, int dy);

Translates the current coordinates of the event by adding dx and dy to x and y, respectively.

Overridden Instance Methods

public String **toString**();

Overrides the method definition in the **Object** class.

FILE CLASS

Full Name	**java.io.File**
Extends	**Object**
Description	Public class. A **File** object represents a node in the file system, either a file or a directory. You can use it to get attributes or children or to perform directory-service operations. To get file contents, create a stream object such as **FileInputStream**. See Chapter 6, "Common Programming Tasks," for examples. Note that all Java file methods assume the use of the Unix file separator ("/") in path names, regardless of platform. This convention may be irksome to non-Unix programmers, but it is necessary for platform independence.

The following example gets the path of the current directory:

```
File f = new File(".");
String thePath = f.getAbsolutePath();
```

Constructors

public **File**(File dir, String name);
public **File**(String path);
public **File**(String path, String name);

Constructors. A file or directory must be specified. In the first constructor, dir is another **File** object that happens to be a directory, and name specifies a file name within that directory. The second constructor takes a complete path/file name.

Class Methods

public final static String **pathSeparator**;
public final static char **pathSeparatorChar**;

public final static String **separator**;
public final static char **separatorChar**;

Class methods. These methods return the separator used within path names and the drive-letter separator, respectively, used on the local system. In DOS and Windows, these separators are "\" and ":".

Instance Methods

public boolean **canRead**();
public boolean **canWrite**();

These methods return read/write permissions as **true** or **false**.

public boolean **delete**();

Attempts to delete the file and returns **true** if successful. If the File object refers to a directory, this method never succeeds.

public boolean **exists**();

Returns **true** if the file or directory specified by this object exists. Note that a **File** object can be valid even if the file name referred to does not yet correspond to a disk file or directory. To create a new file, write to it. To create a new directory, use **mkdir()**.

public String **getAbsolutePath**();
public String **getName**();
public String **getParent**();
public String **getPath**();

These methods return information about the file name. **getAbsolutePath()** returns an absolute path name, even if the file object was constructed from a relative path name. **getName()** returns a name without a path. **getParent()** returns **null** if the file object is the root directory.

public boolean **isAbsolute**();
public boolean **isDirectory**();
public boolean **isFile**();

Returns **true** if the specified condition is met. **isAbsolute()** returns **false** if the file object was constructed from a relative path. Note that the file object may represent either a file or a directory.

public long **lastModified**();

Returns time of modification. See **Date** class for interpreting a **long** as a date.

public long **length**();

Returns length in number of bytes.

public String[ ] **list**();
public String[ ] **list**(FilenameFilter filter);

Returns an array of file names in the directory (assuming that the file object represents a directory). If filter is specified, only names not rejected by the filter are returned.

public boolean **mkdir**();

Creates a new directory using the name contained in this file object. Thus, if the current **File** object contains the name "MyDir," then /MyDir is created as a new directory (under the parent directory specified in the object's path). Returns **true** if directory creation was successful.

public boolean **mkdirs**();

Does the same thing as **mkdir()** except that all intermediate directories that are new are also created. For example, if the full path name is "/my/brandnew/folder," then potentially three new directories may be created. If/my already exists, then as many as two directories may be created.

public boolean **renameTo**(File dest);

Renames the file represented by this object. The new name is the name specified in dest. Returns **true** if successful.

Overridden Instance Methods

public boolean **equals**(Object obj);
public int **hashCode**();
public String **toString**();

These methods override method definitions in the **Object** class.

FileDescriptor Class

Full Name	**java.io.FileDescriptor**
Extends	**Object**
Description	Public final class. Represents an internally used handle for an open file or socket. Java applications and applet code should generally avoid using this class. Instead, use the **File** class to get general file and directory information, and use input and output streams for reading and writing to files. You can get an object of this type by calling **getFD()** through a **FileInputStream** or **FileOutputStream** object.

Constructors

public **FileDescriptor**();

Constructor. Used internally. Java applications and applets should never call this constructor.

Class Variables

public final static FileDescriptor **err**;
public final static FileDescriptor **in**;
public final static FileDescriptor **out**;

Class variables (constants). These constants provide file descriptors for standard error, input, and output devices. As file descriptors, they can be used to create **FileInputStream** and **FileOutputStream** objects. However, it is generally easier to use **System.err**, **System.in**, and **System.out**.

Instance Methods

public boolean **valid**();

Returns **true** if the file descriptor is valid.

FileDialog Class

Full Name	**java.awt.FileDialog**
Extends	**Dialog->Window->Container->Component->Object**
Description	Public class. This class, a subclass of the **Dialog** class, adds the built-in functionality of a file-select dialog box. Generally speaking, a **FileDialog** object does not need any additional components, because its built-in capabilities are sufficient. As always, you display the dialog box by calling its **show()** method. Note that in Java 1.0 for Win95, this class was not fully functional. The dialog box should respond by generating a **SAVE.FILE** or **LOAD_FILE** event when the user selects a file. However, not all versions of Java provide the correct support for these events.

Constructors

public **FileDialog**(Frame parent, String title);
public **FileDialog**(Frame parent, String title, int mode);

Constructors. A parent frame must be specified. The constructor always creates a modal dialog box: the mode in this case is either **LOAD** or **SAVE**, indicating either "Open File" or "Save As" dialog box. The default is **LOAD**.

Class Variables

public final static int **LOAD**;
public final static int **SAVE**;

These constants are the two possible values for the mode argument.

Instance Methods

public String **getDirectory**();
public String **getFile**();
public FilenameFilter **getFilenameFilter**();
public int **getMode**();

These methods get the current file directory path, file name, file-name filter, and mode, respectively. File-name filter is described under **setFilenameFilter()**. The mode is **LOAD** or **SAVE**.

public void **setDirectory**(String dir);
public void **setFile**(String file);

These methods set the file directory path and file name, respectively.

public void **setFilenameFilter**(FilenameFilter filter);

Sets the file-name filter by specifying an object whose class implements the **FilenameFilter** interface. No such classes are provided in the API, but you can write your own. The filter determines which file names are displayed. (By default, all files in the directory path are displayed.) See **FilenameFilter** interface.

Overridden Instance Methods

public void **addNotify**();

Overrides the method definition in the **Component** class. Used internally.

FILEINPUTSTREAM CLASS

Full Name	**java.io.FileInputStream**
Extends	**InputStream->Object**
Description	Public class. Creates a low-level input stream from a file. For easy file reading, construct a **DataInputStream** object from the **FileInputStream** object and then use **DataInputStream** methods. See following example. Creating a **FileInputStream** object, if successful, automatically opens the file for reading.

This example gets a **DataInputStream** object for file **STUFF.DAT.** Note that the **FileInputStream()** constructor may throw an exception—if, for example, the file cannot be found. For this reason, the code must have a **try-catch** block.

```
try {
  FileInputStream fis = new FileInputStream("STUFF.DAT");
  DataInputStream dis = new DataInputStream(fis);
} catch(IOException e) {System.out.println(e);}
```

Constructors

public **FileInputStream**(File file)throws FileNotFoundException, IOException;
public **FileInputStream**(FileDescriptor fdObj);
public **FileInputStream**(String name)throws FileNotFoundException,IOException;

Constructors. The third is probably most commonly used. When specifying a path, remember to use the Unix file separator ("/").

Instance Methods

public final FileDescriptor **getFD**() throws IOException;

Returns the **FileDescriptor** for this file.

Overridden Instance Methods

public int **available**() throws IOException;
public void **close**() throws IOException;
public int **read**() throws IOException;
public int **read**(byte b[]) throws IOException;
public int **read**(byte b[], int off, int len) throws IOException;
public long **skip**(long n) throws IOException;

These methods override method definitions in the **InputStream** class.

protected void **finalize**() throws IOException;

Overrides method definition in the **Object** class. Calls the **close()** method.

FilenameFilter Interface

Full Name	**java.io.FilenameFilter**
Description	Public interface. Any object can implement this interface to serve as a file-name filter: the filter determines which files to include in a display or a list. An example of a possible response is to include only those files with a **.doc** suffix. The API does not currently provide any file-name filters, but you can write them yourself. The **FileDialog** class and the **File.list()** method use this interface.

public abstract boolean **accept**(File dir, String name);

Returns **true** if the named file should be accepted (i.e., displayed or listed). This method is called once for each file or subdirectory. Note that you can use the **File** class to get the attributes of the file before deciding whether to accept it. Remember to use UNIX file name conventions.

FileOutputStream Class

Full Name	**java.io.FileOutputStream**
Extends	**OutputStream->Object**
Description	Public class. Creates a low-level output stream to a file. For easy writing to a file, construct a **DataOutputStream** object from the **FileOutputStream** object and then use **DataOutputStream** methods. See following example. Creating a **FileOutputStream** object, if successful, automatically opens the file for writing.

This example gets a **DataOutputStream** object for a file **STUFF.DAT**:

```
FileOutputStream fos = new FileOutputStream("STUFF.DAT");
DataOutputStream dos = new DataOutputStream(fos);
```

Alternatively, you can convert a **FileOutputStream** object into a **PrintStream** object:

```
PrintStream ps = new PrintStream(new
     FileOutputStream("MY.TXT"));
```

Note that the **FileOutputStream()** constructor can throw an exception, so you must add exception handling. See **FileInputStream** class.

Constructors

public **FileOutputStream**(File file) throws IOException;
public **FileOutputStream**(FileDescriptor fdObj);
public **FileOutputStream**(String name) throws IOException;

Constructors. When specifying a path, remember to use the Unix file separator ("/").

Instance Methods

public final FileDescriptor **getFD**() throws IOException;

Returns the **FileDescriptor** for this file.

Overridden Instance Methods

public void **close**() throws IOException;
public void **write**(byte b[ ]) throws IOException;
public void **write**(byte b[ ], int off, int len) throws IOException;
public void **write**(int b) throws IOException;

These methods override method definitions in the **OutputStream** class.

protected void **finalize**() throws IOException;

Overrides the method definition in the **Object** class. Calls the **close()** method.

FilteredImageSource Class

Full Name	**java.awt.image.FilteredImageSource**
Extends	**Object**
Implements	**ImageProducer**
Description	Public class. Creates a new image source from an existing source by passing it through a filter. You can use the resulting image source (or *image producer*) to create a new **Image** object. A **FilteredImageSource** constructor takes two inputs: an existing source and a filter. The result is a new image source that can used to create images. The **FilteredImageSource** is a connector that takes in pixel data at one end (through the filter, an image consumer) and outputs pixel data at the other end. See the example for clarification.

Figure F.1 illustrates the **FilteredImageSource** mechanism; the completed filter is both an image consumer and an image producer (or source).

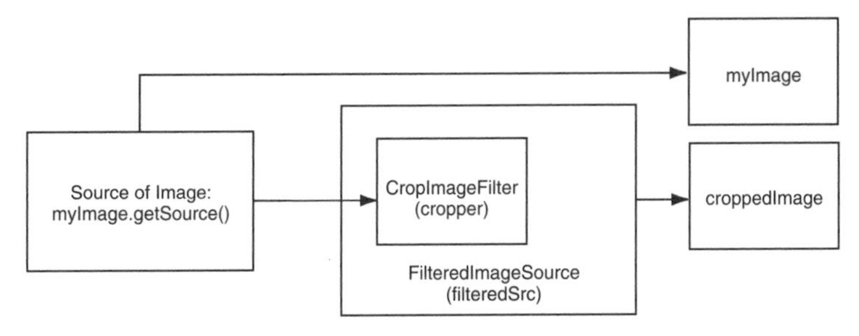

Figure F.1 *Using FilteredImageSource to crop an image*

The following code shows how this example is implemented. The first step is to create the filter itself. All this does is specify how much to crop:

```
CropImageFilter cropper = new CropImageFilter(20, 20, 60,
60);
```

Next, the **FilteredImageSource** class is used to create a new image producer. This object uses the same source that the image, myImage, does, but it passes the data through the filter:

```
FilteredImageSource filteredSrc = new
FilteredImagesource(
     myImage.getSource(),  // Use myImage's producer
     cropper );            // Crop by 20,20,60,60
```

The new variable, filteredSrc, is a bona fide image producer. This means that it can supply data to an image. The last line of code specifies filteredSrc as the new source of data for an image. The result is that croppedImage displays the same picture that myImage does except that it is cropped.

```
Image croppedImage = createImage(filteredSrc);
```

Constructors

public **FilteredImageSource**(ImageProducer orig, ImageFilter imgf);

Constructor. Creates an image producer from another image producer and a filter.

Overridden Instance Methods

public void **addConsumer**(ImageConsumer ic);
public boolean **isConsumer**(ImageConsumer ic);
public void **removeConsumer**(ImageConsumer ic);
public void **requestTopDownLeftRightResend**(ImageConsumer ic);
public void **startProduction**(ImageConsumer ic);

These methods implement the **ImageProducer** methods. See **ImageProducer** interface.

FilterInputStream Class

Full Name	**java.io.FilterInputStream**
Extends	**InputStream->Object**
Description	Public class. This class cannot be instantiated directly but is important as the superclass to all filtered-input classes: **BufferedInputStream**, **DataInputStream**, **LineNumberInputStream**, and **PushbackInputStream**. All these classes maintain an underlying input stream as an instance field and perform a filtering operation on the input. You can also write a filter class by subclassing **FilterInputStream** and overriding one or more methods.

Protected Instance Variables

protected InputStream **in**;

Instance variable referring to the underlying input stream. Because it is protected, it cannot be used outside the package, but it can be referred to in subclasses of **FilterInputStream**.

Overridden Instance Methods

public int **available**() throws IOException;
public void **close**() throws IOException;
public void **mark**(int readlimit);
public boolean **markSupported**();
public int **read**() throws IOException;
public int **read**(byte b[ ]) throws IOException;
public int **read**(byte b[ ], int off, int len) throws IOException;
public void **reset**() throws IOException;
public long **skip**(long n) throws IOException;

These methods override method definitions in the **InputStream** class.

FilterOutputStream Class

Full Name	**java.io.FilterOutputStream**
Extends	**OutputStream->Object**
Description	Public class. This class should not be instantiated directly but is important as the superclass to filtered-output classes: **BufferedOutputStream**, **DataOutputStream**, and **PrintStream**. All these classes maintain an underlying output stream as an instance field and perform a filtering operation before writing the output. You can also write a filter class by subclassing **FilterOutputStream** and overriding one or more methods.

Constructor

public **FilterOutputStream**(OutputStream out);

Constructor. Instead of creating an instance of **FilterOutputStream** directly, you should use a subclass.

Protected Instance Variables

protected OutputStream **out**;

Instance variable referring to the underlying output stream. Because it is protected, it cannot be used outside the package, but it can be referred to in subclasses of **FilterOutputStream**.

Instance Methods

public void **close**() throws IOException;
public void **flush**() throws IOException;
public void **write**(byte b[]) throws IOException;
public void **write**(byte b[], int off, int len) throws IOException;
public void **write**(int b) throws IOException;

These methods override method definitions in the **OutputStream** class.

Float Class

Full Name	**java.lang.Float**
Extends	**Number->Object**
Description	Public final class. Serves as the wrapper class for the **float** primitive type. This class provides methods for converting between string, object, and numeric data. It also is useful for passing a **float** value by reference.

The following example converts a digit string to type **float**:

```
float flt = (new Float(digitString)).floatValue();
```

Constructors

public **Float**(float value);
public **Float**(double value);
public **Float**(String s);

Constructors. The last constructor initializes from a digit string.

Class Variables

public final static double **MAX_VALUE**;
public final static double **MIN_VALUE**;
public final static double **NaN**;
public final static double **NEGATIVE_INFINITY**;
public final static double **POSITIVE_INFINITY**;

Constants. See Part VII, "Glossary of Java Terminology," for meaning of the last three terms.

Class Methods

public static long **floatToIntBits**(float value);
public static double **intBitsToFloat**(int bits);
public static boolean **isInfinite**(float v);
public static boolean **isNaN**(float v);

public static String **toString**(float d);
public static Double **valueOf**(String s);

Class methods. The **floatToIntBits()** and **intBitsToFloat()** methods convert between an **int** and a **float** without changing the actual bit values. See following description for **isNaN()**.

Instance Methods

public boolean **isInfinite**();
public boolean **isNaN**();

These methods return **true** if the current value is, respectively, positive or negative infinity and is "not a number." This is the only reliable way to test for an **NaN** value, because **NaN** will always return **false** when compared to itself.

Overridden Instance Methods

public double **doubleValue**();
public float **floatValue**();
public int **intValue**();
public long **longValue**();

These methods return the **double**, **float**, **int**, or **long** equivalent of the value stored in the current object. The methods round as necessary, for there may be loss of precision.

public boolean **equals**(Object obj);
public int **hashCode**();
public String **toString**();

These methods override method definitions in the **Object** class.

FlowLayout Class

Full Name	**java.awt.FlowLayout**
Extends	**Object**
Implements	**LayoutManager**
Description	Public class. Creates layout manager objects that lay out components from left to right, starting a new row when the right edge is reached. The behavior of these layout managers is described in Chapter 4, "Components and Events."

The following example sets the current container to use an instance of **FlowLayout** with center alignment:

```
setLayout(new FlowLayout(FlowLayout.CENTER));
```

Constructors

public **FlowLayout**();
public **FlowLayout**(int align);
public **FlowLayout**(int align, int hgap, int vgap);

Constructors. Optional arguments specify alignment and margins around components.

Class Variables

public final static int **CENTER**;
public final static int **LEFT**;
public final static int **RIGHT**;

These three constants are the possible values for alignment, which affects placement of components within each row.

Instance Methods

public void **addLayoutComponent**(String name, Component comp);
public void **layoutContainer**(Container target);
public Dimension **minimumLayoutSize**(Container target);
public Dimension **preferredLayoutSize**(Container target);
public void **removeLayoutComponent**(Component comp);

These five methods implement the **LayoutManager** interface; none of these methods is normally called by applications.

Overridden Instance Methods

public String **toString**();

This method overrides the method definition in the **Object** class.

FONT CLASS

Full Name	**java.awt.Font**
Extends	**Object**
Description	Public class. A Font object contains a complete specification for a text font. To get detailed information on height and width, you need to get a **FontMetrics** object by calling the **getFontMetrics()** method of a component or graphics object.

The following example specifies bold Courier font, 12-point size, and then sets it as the default font for the current frame or applet:

```
Font myFont = new Font("Courier", Font.BOLD, 12);
setFont(myFont);
```

Constructors

public **Font**(String name, int style, int size);

Constructor. The second argument specifies one of the three constants listed next (**BOLD**, **ITALIC**, **PLAIN**); the third is a point size.

Class Variables

public final static int **BOLD**;
public final static int **ITALIC**;
public final static int **PLAIN**;

Constants specifying a font style. Bold and italic can be combined in the expression BOLD + ITALIC.

Class Methods

public static Font **getFont**(String nm);
public static Font **getFont**(String nm, Font font);

Class method. Returns a font object looked up in the system properties list database. The format is one of the following: *name-style-pointsize*, *name-style*, *name-pointsize*, and *name*. The defaults are **PLAIN** and 12-point size. The second argument, if specified, is a default font.

Instance Methods

public String **getFamily**();

Returns the platform-specific family name of the font.

public String **getName**();
public int **getSize**();
public int **getStyle**();
public boolean **isBold**();
public boolean **isItalic**();
public boolean **isPlain**();

These six methods, starting with **getName()**, return basic information about a **Font** object.

Overridden Class Methods

public boolean **equals**(Object obj);
public int **hashCode**();
public String **toString**();

These methods override method definitions in the **Object** class.

FontMetrics Class

Full Name	**java.awt.FontMetrics**
Extends	**Object**
Description	Public class. A **FontMetrics** object provides detailed measurements of font characteristics in terms of device units (pixels). Although this class is public, you cannot instantiate it directly; it has no public constructor. You can, however, get a **FontMetrics** object by calling the **getFontMetrics()** method of a **Component** or **Graphics** object.

The following example can be used from within an applet (or component subclass) to get the height of the default font: this is the complete height of a line of type, including leading. See Figure 3.3 (Chapter 3) for a diagram of font metrics.

```
fm = getFontMetrics(getFont());
int height = fm.getHeight();
```

Instance Methods

public int **bytesWidth**(byte data[ ], int off, int len);
public int **charsWidth**(char data[ ], int off, int len);

These methods return the width of a string in this font; the string is specified as an array of bytes or an array of characters. See also **stringWidth()**.

public int **charWidth**(char ch);
public int **charWidth**(int ch);

Returns the width of a single character in this font.

public int **getAscent**();
public int **getDescent**();
public Font **getFont**();
public int **getHeight**();
public int **getLeading**();
public int **getMaxAdvance**();
public int **getMaxAscent**();
public int **getMaxDescent**();

These eight methods, starting with **getAscent()**, return basic information about the font metrics. For a chart showing the significance of each term, see Figure 3.3, "Graphical summary of font metrics," in Part I's Chapter 3. The **getMax** methods return the maximum metric of any character; other methods return an average.

public int[ ] **getWidths**();

Returns an integer array containing the widths of the first 256 characters in this font.

public int **stringWidth**(String str);

Returns the width of a string in this font. This tells you how much horizontal space the string takes up when displayed in the font.

Overridden Instance Methods

public String **toString**();

Overrides method definition in the **Object** class.

Frame Class

Full Name	**java.awt.Frame**
Extends	**Window->Container->Component->Object**
Description	Public class. Creates a window that has borders and a menu bar. (In fact, this class is closer to the commonly accepted idea of "window" than the Java **Window** class is.) The use of frames is introduced in Chapter 4, "Components and Events." Frames generate all the standard keyboard and mouse events, including **MOUSE_DOWN** and **MOUSE_UP**, as well as window events. Note that unlike other components, a frame is not displayed until **show()** is called.

The following example displays a frame after setting title, cursor type, and size. Note that **show()** and **resize()** are inherited from the **Component** class.

```
Frame theFrame = new Frame("You're in the picture.");
theFrame.setCursor(Frame.HAND_CURSOR);
theFrame.resize(150, 250);
theFrame.show();
```

Constructors

public **Frame**();
public **Frame**(String title);

Constructors. Frames have a number of attributes that are not specified in a constructor but can be set by specific methods.

Class Variables

public final static int **CROSSHAIR_CURSOR**;
public final static int **DEFAULT_CURSOR**;

public final static int **E_RESIZE_CURSOR**;
public final static int **HAND_CURSOR**;
public final static int **MOVE_CURSOR**;
public final static int **N_RESIZE_CURSOR**;
public final static int **NE_RESIZE_CURSOR**;
public final static int **NW_RESIZE_CURSOR**;
public final static int **S_RESIZE_CURSOR**;
public final static int **SE_RESIZE_CURSOR**;
public final static int **SW_RESIZE_CURSOR**;
public final static int **TEXT_CURSOR**;
public final static int **W_RESIZE_CURSOR**;
public final static int **WAIT_CURSOR**;

Constants specifying a cursor type. These constants can be given as input to the **setCursor()** method. For a description of these cursor types, see Part VI.

Instance Methods

public int **getCursorType**();
public Image **getIconImage**();
public MenuBar **getMenuBar**();
public String **getTitle**();
public boolean **isResizable**();

These five methods get information about basic frame attributes. Each of these attributes can also be set by a corresponding method.

public void **remove**(MenuComponent m);

Removes a menu component, generally a menu bar.

public void **setCursor**(int cursorType);
public void **setIconImage**(Image image);
public void **setMenuBar**(MenuBar mb);
public void **setResizable**(boolean resizable);
public void **setTitle**(String title);

These five methods set basic attributes of the frame. The **setIconImage()** and **setMenuBar()** methods assume you have created an **Image** or **MenuBar** object, which you can then pass as an argument. The **setCursor()** method takes one of the constants listed earlier.

Overridden Instance Methods

public void **addNotify**();
public void **dispose**();

These methods override method definitions in the **Component** class. **addNotify()** is used internally; **dispose()** closes the frame window and releases all system resources.

Graphics Class

Full Name	**java.awt.Graphics**
Extends	**Object**
Description	Abstract public class. Provides access to all of Java's drawing capabilities. You cannot directly instantiate this class by calling a constructor. However, the **Component** and **Image** classes support a **getGraphics()** method, and certain **Component** methods, such as **paint()**, pass an instance of a **Graphics** subclass.

Instance Methods

public abstract void **clearRect**(int x, int y, int width, int height);

Clears the specified region, filling it with background color.

public abstract void **clipRect**(int x, int y, int width, int height);

Sets a clipping region for this graphics context. Result is the intersection of this rectangle with the current clipping rectangle if any. This method is typically called just before the graphics object is passed to **paint()** or **update()**.

public abstract void **copyArea**(int x, int y, int width, int height, int dx, int dy);

Copies the region at (x, y) to the region whose top left corner is (x + dx, y + dy).

public abstract Graphics **create**();
public Graphics **create**(int x, int y, int width, int height);

Creates a clone of the current graphics object, optionally specifying a subsection.

public abstract void **dispose**();

Immediately releases all system resources associated with the graphics object. This method is useful in programs that grab the display context directly to do quick drawing to the screen. Call **dispose()** at the end of a method such as **paint()** or at the end of a cycle of graphics operations. Keep in mind that once **dispose()** is called, the graphics object becomes invalid.

public void **draw3DRect**(int x, int y, int width int height, boolean raised);

Draws a raised rectangle. If raised is **true**, the rectangle is in the "up" position.

public abstract void **drawArc**(int x, int y, int width, int height, int startAngle, int arcAngle);

Draws an arc along the oval inscribed in a rectangle determined by the first four arguments. **startAngle** sets starting point in degrees, in which 0 is the three o'clock position. Positive numbers move counterclockwise, negative clockwise. **arcAngle** sets number of degrees to draw, again with negative meaning clockwise. Thus, setting **startAngle** and **arcAngle** to 0 and -180 draws a half-circle in the shape of a smile.

public void **drawBytes**(byte data[ ], int offset, int length, int x, int y);
public void **drawChars**(char data[ ], int offset, int length, int x, int y);

Similar to **drawString** except that arrays of bytes or **char** is used for string data.

public abstract boolean **drawImage**(Image img, int x, int y, Color bgcolor, ImageObserver observer);
public abstract boolean **drawImage**(Image img, int x, int y, Image-Observer observer);

public abstract boolean **drawImage**(Image img, int x, int y, int width, int height, Color bgcolor, ImageObserver observer);
public abstract boolean **drawImage**(Image img, int x, int y, int width, int height, ImageObserver observer);

Draws an image at x, y position, optionally specifying background color and size of region to fit the image into. (This is called *scaling*.) Usually, it is adequate to use the "this" keyword for the observer argument. If pixel data referred to by the image is not already loaded, **drawImage()** initiates loading. See also **MediaTracker**. Chapter 3 introduces use of **drawImage()**.

public abstract void **drawLine**(int x1, int y1, int x2, int y2);
public abstract void **drawOval**(int x, int y, int width, int height);
public abstract void **drawPolygon**(int xPoints[ ], int yPoints[ ], int nPoints);
public void **drawPolygon**(Polygon p);
public void **drawRect**(int x, int y, int width, int height);
public abstract void **drawRoundRect**(int x, int y, int width, int height, int arcWidth, int arcHeight);

These methods draw the specified line or graphical shape. **drawRoundRect()** uses degrees to specify the relative size of the rounded corner.

public abstract void **drawString**(String str, int x, int y);

Draws specified string, placing the baseline of the string y units from the top.

public void **fill3DRect**(int x, int y, int width, int height, boolean raised);
public abstract void **fillArc**(int x, int y, int width, int height, int startAngle, int arcAngle);
public abstract void **fillOval**(int x, int y, int width, int height);
public abstract void **fillPolygon**(int xPoints[ ], int yPoints[ ], int nPoints);
public void **fillPolygon**(Polygon p);
public abstract void **fillRect**(int x, int y, int width, int height);

public abstract void **fillRoundRect**(int x, int y, int width, int height, int arcWidth, int arcHeight);

These methods draw a shape and then fill it in with the foreground color. Similar to corresponding draw methods. **fillArc()** and **fillRoundRect()** use degree measurements; see **drawArc()** for other details on **fillArc()** arguments. The effect of fillArc () is to draw a pie section.

public abstract Rectangle **getClipRect**();
public abstract Color **getColor**();
public abstract Font **getFont**();

These methods return the current clipping region, foreground color, and current font, respectively.

public FontMetrics **getFontMetrics**();
public abstract FontMetrics **getFontMetrics**(Font f);

Returns a **FontMetrics** object, using the current font if one is not specified.

public abstract void **setColor**(Color c);
public abstract void **setFont**(Font font);

These methods set the foreground color and current font, respectively.

public abstract void **setPaintMode**();
public abstract void **setXORMode**(Color c);

These methods set the drawing mode to either normal drawing (**setPaintMode**) or **XOR** mode. With **XOR** mode, drawing over the same region twice restores it to its original state. The color, c, is used in an **XOR** bit operation on existing pixels. Results can be unpredictable if more than two colors are in use.

public abstract void **translate**(int x, int y);

Alters the graphics context so that the point currently referred to as (x, y) becomes the new origin, (0, 0).

Overridden Instance Methods

public void **finalize**();
public String **toString**();

These methods override method definitions in the **Object** class. The **finalize()** method calls dispose, so that when a graphics object goes out of scope, it releases its system resources.

GRIDBAGCONSTRAINTS CLASS

Full Name	**java.awt.GridBagConstraints**
Extends	**Object**
Implements	**Cloneable**
Description	Public class. Specifies a set of layout constraints for one component. This class is used in conjunction with the **GridBagLayout** class. The general procedure is as follows: create a set of constraints by using this class (**GridBagConstraints**) and then pass the sets of constraints along with the corresponding component by calling **GridBagLayout.setConstraints()**. Each component must be added to the container in addition to having its constraints specified to the layout manager.

The following example adds a component textA (a **TextArea** component) to a layout managed by **myGridBag**, a layout manager of the **GridBagLayout** class.

```
GridBagConstraints textAConstr = new
     GridBagConstraints();
textAConstr.gridx = 0;      // Place in top left corner.
textAConstr.gridy = 0;
textAConstr.gridwidth = 3;      // Take up 3 x 2 cells.
textAConstr.gridheight = 2;
```

```
textAConstr.fill = GridBagConstraints.BOTH; // Fill up the cell.
// Assign weight 1.0, enabling component to grow.
textAConstr.weightx = textConstr.weighty = 1.0;
// Add the component.
myGridBag.setConstraints(textA, textAConstraints);
myContainer.add(textA);
```

Constructors

public **GridBagConstraints**();

Constructor. The actual constraint values are set by manipulating the instance variables.

Instance Variables

public int **anchor**;

Value specifying the zone (anchor) to place the component inside its cell. Possible values are listed later in the topic and include **CENTER**, **EAST**, **NORTH**, and so on. See Class Variables.

public int **fill**;

One of four values—**NONE**, **BOTH**, **HORIZONTAL**, and **VERTICAL**—that indicate which direction, if any, the component should grow in when the cell's space is larger than the component's minimum size. See Class Variables.

public int **gridheight**;
public int **gridwidth**;

Size of the component's cell, in terms of rows and columns. For example, a cell can take up a 2 by 2 section of the grid. A value of **REMAINDER** (See Class Variables) in either dimension indicates that the cell should get all the space that is left in that dimension.

public int **gridx**;
public int **gridy**;

Position of the component. Using the special value **RELATIVE** (See Class Variables), in either coordinate, means positioning directly to the right (gridx) or just below (gridy) the previous component added.

public Insets **insets**;

An Insets object specifies margins around the component.

public int **ipadx**;
public int **ipady**;

Internal horizontal and vertical padding of the component. These fields create additional margins around the component, increasing the component's minimum size requirement.

public double **weightx**;
public double **weighty**;

Weights controlling how component grows in each direction as the container grows. A weight of 0.0 (the default) means that the component does not get extra space beyond its minimum size. A weight of 1.0 allows the component to grow as the available space does.

Class Variables

public final static int **CENTER**;
public final static int **EAST**;
public final static int **NORTH**;
public final static int **NORTHEAST**;
public final static int **NORTHWEST**;
public final static int **SOUTH**;
public final static int **SOUTHEAST**;
public final static int **SOUTHWEST**;
public final static int **WEST**;

These constants are possible values for the anchor field.

public final static int **BOTH**;

public final static int **HORIZONTAL**;
public final static int **NONE**;
public final static int **VERTICAL**;

These constants are possible values for the fill field.

public final static int **REMAINDER**;

This constant can be used in the **gridWidth** and **gridHeight** fields.

public final static int **RELATIVE**;

This constant can be used in the **gridx** and **gridy** fields.

Overridden Instance Methods

public Object **clone**();

Overrides the method definition in the **Object** class. This class produces objects that are cloneable.

GridBagLayout Class

Full Name	**java.awt.GridBagLayout**
Extends	**Object**
Implements	**LayoutManager**
Description	Public class. Creates layout managers providing the maximum flexibility in sizing and positioning components. When a container uses a **GridBagLayout** manager, each of its components must be assigned constraints. Use the **GridBagConstraints** class to create a set of constraints for each component. Then add the constraints by using the **setConstraints()** method.

See **GridBagConstraints** class for an example.

Constructors

public **GridBagLayout**();

Constructor. All characteristics are set by calling set Constraints ().

Instance Methods

public GridBagConstraints **getConstraints**(Component comp);
public void **setConstraints**(Component comp, GridBagConstraints constraints);

These methods get and set a **GridBagConstraints** object for the specified component. The **setConstraints()** method should be called once for each component to specify a set of constraints.

Instance Methods (Interface Methods)

public void **addLayoutComponent**(String name, Component comp);
public void **layoutContainer**(Container target);
public Dimension **minimumLayoutSize**(Container target);
public Dimension **preferredLayoutSize**(Container target);
public void **removeLayoutComponent**(Component comp);

These five methods implement the **LayoutManager** interface; none of these methods is normally called by applications.

Overridden Instance Methods

public String **toString**();

This method overrides the method definition in the **Object** class.

GridLayout Class

Full Name	**java.awt.GridLayout**
Extends	**Object**
Implements	**LayoutManager**

Description	Public class. Creates layout manager objects that align components into rows and columns not delineated by visible lines, as described in Chapter 4, "Components and Events."

The following example sets the current container to use an instance of **GridLayout** with five rows and three columns:

```
setLayout(new GridLayout(5, 3));
```

Constructors

public **GridLayout**(int rows, int cols);
public **GridLayout**(int rows, int cols, int hgap, int vgap) throws IllegalArgumentException;

Constructor. You must specify number of rows and columns. Each grid cell is a region into which the layout manager attempts to fit a component. The optional **hgap** and **vgap** specify horizontal and vertical gap between grid cells.

Instance Methods

public void **addLayoutComponent**(String name, Component comp);
public void **layoutContainer**(Container target);
public Dimension **minimumLayoutSize**(Container target);
public Dimension **preferredLayoutSize**(Container target);
public void **removeLayoutComponent**(Component comp);

These five methods implement the **LayoutManager** interface; none of these methods is normally called by applications.

Overridden Instance Methods

public String **toString**();

This method overrides the method definition in the **Object** class.

HASHTABLE CLASS

Full Name	**java.util.Hashtable**
Extends	**Dictionary->Object**
Implements	**Cloneable**
Description	Public class. A **Hashtable** object is a collection that stores any number of objects of any type using a key to identify and retrieve each object. The stored objects are called *elements*. Keys may also be of any type, but all keys used in a given table should use the same type. The most useful methods are **put()**, which adds an element to the table, and **get()**, which retrieves it.

The following example stores two Social Security numbers using strings as keys to the table:

```
Hashtable ssnTable = new Hashtable();
ssnTable.put("Joe Bloe", new Long(123004444));
ssnTable.put("Jane Doe", new Long(456227777));
Long ssn = (Long)ssnTable.get("Joe Bloe");
System.out.println("Joe's SSN = " + ssn);
```

Constructors

public **Hashtable**();
public **Hashtable**(int initialCapacity);
public **Hashtable**(int initialCapacity, float loadFactor);

Constructors. You can optionally specify initial capacity and load factor (a number between 0.0 and 1.0), although this is never required. The product of current capacity and load factor determines a temporary limit. As soon as this limit is exceeded, the table is automatically *rehashed*, gaining greater capacity. If you know in advance that a certain minimum capacity is needed, you can prevent some rehashing by specifying it in the constructor. A larger load factor makes more efficient use of memory, but each lookup may require more time.

Instance Methods

public void **clear**();

Removes the entire contents of the table.

public boolean **contains**(Object value);
public boolean **containsKey**(Object key);

These methods return **true** if the specified element or key is found.

public Enumeration **elements**();

Returns an enumeration of all the elements. See also **keys()**.

public Object **get**(Object key);

Returns an element, looking it up by the specified key. Returns **null** if the element is not found. Note that the result must usually be cast to a particular type. (See example.)

public boolean **isEmpty**();

Returns **true** if there are no elements in the table.

public Enumeration **keys**();

Returns an enumeration of all the keys. See also **elements()**.

public Object **put**(Object key, Object value);

Adds an element to the table, assigning it the specified key. Returns the previous element assigned to this same key, or **null** if there was no previous element assigned.

public Object **remove**(Object key);

Remove a key and its corresponding element. This element is returned, and **null** is returned if the key was not mapped to any value.

public int **size**();

Returns number of elements.

Overridden Instance Methods

public Object **clone**();
public String **toString**();

These methods override method definitions in the **Object** class. For this class, the **clone()** method performs a relatively shallow copy; it clones the table but not the keys or the elements.

IMAGE CLASS

Full Name	**java.awt.Image**
Extends	**Object**
Description	Public class. An **Image** object represents a graphics image—an image from a file or an offscreen buffer. Different procedures apply for file images and buffer images. To get an image from a file, call the **getImage()** method of the **Applet** or **Toolkit** class. In this case, the **Image** object returned is not really the same as the data itself. The data must still be loaded even though you have a valid object. Calling **Graphics.drawImage()** initiates actual loading. See also **MediaTracker**. To create an offscreen buffer, call the **createImage()** method of the **Component** class. (As a **Component** method, this method is inherited by many other classes, such as **Applet.**) This call returns a blank image, but, as suggested in the following example, you can draw to this image. When the image is ready, call **Graphics.drawImage()** to display it. See Chapters 3 and 5 for examples of both kinds of **Image** objects.

The following example creates an offscreen buffer the size of the applet's display area. Then it gets a **Graphics** object for drawing to this image. Note that **createImage( )** and **size( )** are applet methods inherited from the **Component** class.

```
int w = size().width;    // Get applet's width.
int h = size().height;   // Get applet's height.
Image buffer = createImage(w, h);  // Image is applet size.
Graphics g = buffer.getGraphics(); // Prepare to draw.
```

Several of the methods take an **ImageObserver** object as an argument. When one of these methods attempts to get data, the method returns immediately even if the requested data is not yet loaded. This circumstance is likely when the image is loading from a file. The **ImageObserver** object is called later, as new data is loaded. All classes derived from the **Component** class serve as image observers, so you can use a reference to a component (the **this** keyword often suffices).

Class Variables

public static Object **UndefinedProperty**;

This object is a special return value used by the **getProperty()** method of this class. Appropriate tests for equality (==) will succeed, because there is only one instance of this object. Note that the object's name is an exception to the Java convention that only class names have initial caps.

Instance Methods

public abstract void **flush**();

Releases system resources being used to render the image. You usually do not need to call this method. It's provided to force correct redrawing of an image that may have changed.

public abstract Graphics **getGraphics**();

Returns a **Graphics** object that can be used to draw into the in-memory image.

public abstract int **getHeight**(ImageObserver observer);

Returns the height of the image, in pixels. If sufficient data is not yet read to determine this, the value –1 is returned, and the **ImageObserver** object is called later.

public abstract Object **getProperty**(String name, ImageObserver observer);

Returns the value of the image property specified by the name argument. (Each image format defines its own set of properties. By convention, the "comment" property is often used to provide general information such as author and description.) If the image is not yet loaded, this method returns **null**, and the **ImageObserver** object is called later. If the specified property is not defined for this image, the method returns the special value **Image.UndefinedProperty**.

public abstract ImageProducer **getSource**();

Returns the image producer, an object that produces the actual pixel data. See FilteredImageSource for an example.

public abstract int **getWidth**(ImageObserver observer);

Returns the width of the image, in pixels. If sufficient data is not yet read to determine this, the value –1 is returned, and the **ImageObserver** object is called later.

IMAGECONSUMER INTERFACE

Full Name	**java.awt.image.ImageConsumer**
Description	Public interface. This is an interface you never need to implement or directly interact with in any way unless you are doing very low-level manipulation of image data. This interface is visible to applications in the following way: image filters, such as **CropImageFilter**, are implicitly image consumers. The **PixelGrabber** class, which collects raw data, is also an image consumer. An image consumer is an object that has requested data from an image producer. When the image producer is ready to send image data, it calls the appropriate methods of the image consumer. (Image consumers should not be confused with image observers, which monitor loading from disk.)

Interface Constants

public final static int **IMAGEABORTED**;
public final static int **IMAGEERROR**;
public final static int **SINGLEFRAMEDONE**;
public final static int **STATICIMAGEDONE**;

These constants are used by the **imageComplete()** method to indicate status. Values are mutually exclusive.

public final static int **COMPLETESCANLINES**;
public final static int **RANDOMPIXELORDER**;
public final static int **SINGLEFRAME**;
public final static int **SINGLEPASS**;
public final static int **TOPDOWNLEFTRIGHT**;

These constants are used by the **setHints()** method. They are flags that are **OR**'ed together.

Interface Methods

public abstract void **imageComplete**(int status);

When the image is complete, the image producer calls this method and passes a status indicator.

public abstract void **setColorModel**(ColorModel model);

Image producer calls this method to set a color model for the image.

public abstract void **setDimensions**(int width, int height);

Image producer calls this method to specify the image dimensions.

public abstract void **setHints**(int hintflags);

Image producer calls this method to set hints as to how it delivers pixel data. See constants.

public abstract void **setPixels**(int x, int y, int w, int h, ColorModel model, byte pixels[ ], int off, int scansize);

public abstract void **setPixels**(int x, int y, int w, int h, ColorModel model, int pixels[ ], int off, int scansize);

Image producer calls this method to copy the actual pixel data. These two versions of the method are the same except for the pixel size (**byte** or **int**).

public abstract void **setProperties**(Hashtable props);

Image producer calls this method to set properties of the image.

ImageFilter Class

Full Name	**java.awt.image.ImageFilter**
Extends	**Object**
Implements	**ImageConsumer**, **Cloneable**

Description	Public class. This class is never used directly but is useful as the superclass to the **CropImageFilter** and **RGBImageFilter** classes. Image filters take data from an image-producing source (an image producer) and translate it some way. Use the **FilterImageSource** class to create a new image producer from a filter.

All the **ImageFilter** methods are used internally. There is rarely any need for application code to call these methods. However, it is possible to subclass **ImageFilter** to create your own filter.

Constructors

public **ImageFilter**();

Constructor. This method performs no initialization.

Instance Variables

protected ImageConsumer **consumer**;

This is the field that contains the consumer, an object that receives the pixel data. Because this field is protected, you can refer to it only if you're subclassing the **ImageFilter** class.

Instance Methods

public ImageFilter **getFilterInstance**(ImageConsumer ic);

Clones the image filter, setting the consumer field to the specified argument.

public void **resendTopDownLeftRight**(ImageProducer ip);

Requests that the image producer resend the pixel data.

Instance Methods (from Interface)

public void **imageComplete**(int status);
public void **setColorModel**(ColorModel model);
public void **setDimensions**(int width, int height);

public void **setHints**(int hints);
public void **setPixels**(int x, int y, int w, int h, ColorModel model, byte pixels[ ], int off, int scansize);
public void **setPixels**(int x, int y, int w, int h, ColorModel model, int pixels[ ], int off, int scansize);
public void **setProperties**(Hashtable props);

These methods implement method declarations in the **ImageConsumer** interface.

Overridden Instance Methods

public Object **clone**();

Overrides method definition in **Object** class.

ImageObserver Interface

Full Name	**java.awt.image.ImageObserver**
Description	Public interface. An object implements this interface to act as an observer during loading of an image; an image observer is notified as new data becomes available. All subclasses of the Java **Component** class implement this interface. Therefore, as a general rule, there usually is little need to implement this interface yourself.

Interface Constants

public final static int **ABORT**;
public final static int **ALLBITS**;
public final static int **ERROR**;
public final static int **FRAMEBITS**;
public final static int **HEIGHT**;
public final static int **PROPERTIES**;
public final static int **SOMEBITS**;
public final static int **WIDTH**;

Constants. These are status flags that indicate how much information of the image is now available; they are passed in the **infoflags** argument of **imageUpdate()**. For example, if the **WIDTH** flag is on, width data is now available. These flags are combined through bitwise **OR** (|).

Interface Methods

public abstract boolean **imageUpdate**(Image img, int infoflags, int x, int y, int width, int height);

This method is called when new data is available during loading. Java API components respond by causing a repaint.

IMAGEPRODUCER INTERFACE

Full Name	**java.awt.image.ImageProducer**
Description	Public interface. An image producer, or *image source*, produces the actual bits to construct an image. You can ignore the existence of image producers except when creating a new image source from data in memory (**MemoryImageSource**) or from a filter (**FilteredImageSource**). Once an image producer is available, you can use it to create a new image by calling the **createImage()** method of the **Component** class. See **FilteredImageSource** for a complete example.

public void **addConsumer**(ImageConsumer ic);

Adds the argument to the list of image consumers serviced by this image producer.

public boolean **isConsumer**(ImageConsumer ic);

Returns **true** if the image consumer is one of the consumers serviced by this image producer.

public void **removeConsumer**(ImageConsumer ic);

Informs the image producer that this image consumer no longer needs to be sent data.

public void **requestTopDownLeftRightResend**(ImageConsumer ic);

Requests resending the image data to this image consumer, in top-down, left-right order.

public void **startProduction**(ImageConsumer ic);

Requests that the image producer send the image data. Data is sent to this image consumer as well as all others on the list of consumers serviced by this image producer.

INDEXCOLORMODEL CLASS

Full Name	**java.awt.image.IndexColorModel**
Extends	**ColorModel->Object**
Description	Public class. Specifies a color model that uses a finite number of colors, in which each number maps to a particular color. A color is translated by using the color number as an index into arrays that give intensity for red, green, and blue. This technique optionally supports one color that represents complete transparency. (Drawing in the transparent color lets the background show through.) In general, there is never any need to use this class unless you're processing image data that does not use the default RGB model.

Instance Methods

public **IndexColorModel**(int bits, int size, byte r[ ], byte g[ ], byte b[ ]);
public **IndexColorModel**(int bits, int size, byte r[ ], byte g[ ], byte b[ ], byte a[]);
public **IndexColorModel**(int bits, int size, byte r[ ], byte g[ ], byte b[ ], int trans);

Constructors. The arguments include the number of bits per pixel in this model, the size of the color component arrays, the arrays themselves (including an optional alpha array), and an optional index indicating the number of the transparency color. If this index is used, all other color values are completely solid, or opaque. See **ColorModel** for explanation of the alpha value.

public **IndexColorModel**(int bits, int size, byte cmap[ ], int start, boolean hasalpha);
public **IndexColorModel**(int bits, int size, byte cmap[ ], int start, boolean hasalpha, int trans);

Constructors. These constructors work in a way similar to the constructors listed previously, except that a single array is used whose elements have packed RGB values. If **hasalpha** is **true**, it indicates that an alpha value is included in the packed RGB value. The **trans** argument is an optional index indicating the number of the transparency color. If this index is used, all other color values are completely solid, or opaque.

public final void **getAlphas**(byte a[ ]);
public final void **getBlues**(byte b[ ]);
public final void **getGreens**(byte g[ ]);
public final void **getReds**(byte r[ ]);

Returns the specified array.

public final int **getMapSize**();

Returns the number of elements in the color index.

Overridden Instance Methods

public final int **getAlpha**(int pixel);
public final int **getBlue**(int pixel);
public final int **getGreen**(int pixel);
public final int **getRed**(int pixel);
public final int **getRGB**(int pixel);
public final int **getTransparentPixel**();

These methods override method definitions in the **ColorModel** class.

InetAddress Class

Full Name	**java.net.InetAddress**
Extends	**Object**

Description	Public final class. Creates an Internet address from a specified machine name or IP address. An **InetAddress** object, in turn, is used by the **DatagramPacket** and **Socket** classes. Although this is a public, non-abstract class, it has no public constructors, so you cannot instantiate it directly. However, several class methods return **InetAddress** objects.

The following example gets an **InetAddress** object for the named computer:

```
InetAddress iaddr =
     InetAddress.getByName("java.sun.com");
```

Class Methods

public static InetAddress[ ] **getAllByName**(String host) throws UnknownHostException;
public static InetAddress **getByName**(String host) throws UnknownHostException;

Class methods. The string argument is a machine name, such as "java.sun.com," or a string representation of an IP address, such as "206.26.48.100." **getAllByName()** returns all the Internet addresses for the specified host.

public static InetAddress **getLocalHost**() throws UnknownHost-Exception;

Class method. Gets the **InetAddress** object for the local machine.

Instance Methods

public byte[ ] **getAddress**();
public String **getHostName**();

These methods return the raw IP address and host name, respectively. Currently, IP addresses are 32 bits (four bytes) but may eventually be 128 bits.

Overridden Instance Methods

public boolean **equals**(Object obj);
public int **hashCode**();
public String **toString**();

These methods override method definitions in the **Object** class.

InputStream Class

Full Name	**java.io.InputStream**
Extends	**Object**
Description	Abstract public class. This class is the superclass for all input streams. Some of the subclasses have more efficient or specialized implementations than the default implementations provided in this class. Of the subclasses, **DataInputStream** is the most generally useful. See also **FileInputStream**.

Instance Methods

public int **available**() throws IOException;

Returns the number of bytes that can be read without waiting.

public void **close**() throws IOException;

Closes the stream and releases all system resources (such as file handles) associated with it.

public void **mark**(int readlimit);

If supported, this method sets a marker at the current file position in the stream. The next call to **reset()** moves back to the marked position. The **readlimit** is the maximum distance that such a reset can move. Not all subclasses necessarily support this method.

public boolean **markSupported**();

Returns **true** if the **mark()** method is supported.

public abstract int **read**() throws IOException;

Returns the next byte in the stream. Returns –1 if at end of the stream.

public int **read**(byte b[ ]) throws IOException;
public int **read**(byte b[ ], int off, int len) throws IOException;

Reads up to **b.length** or **len** bytes, whichever is smaller. Returns the number of bytes read, or –1 if at the end of the stream. The **off** argument gives a starting offset into the array.

public void **reset**() throws IOException;

Resets reading of input to the beginning of the stream, or to the marked position if the **mark()** method is supported.

public long **skip**(long n) throws IOException;

Skips past **n** bytes in the stream before the next read.

Insets Class

Full Name	**java.awt.Insets**
Extends	**Object**
Implements	**Cloneable**
Description	Public class. An **Insets** object contains four values specifying margins, in pixels. See the **insets()** method of the **Container** class and the insets field of the **GridBagConstraints** class.

Constructors

public **Insets**(int top, int left, int bottom, int right);

Constructor. Sets all four instance variables.

Instance Variables

public int **bottom**;
public int **left**;

public int **right**;
public int **top**;

Instance variables, directly accessible to other classes. Each specifies a margin.

Instance Methods

public Object **clone**();
public String **toString**();

These methods override method definitions in the **Object** class.

INTEGER CLASS

Full Name	**java.lang.Integer**
Extends	**Number->Object**
Description	Public final class. Serves as the wrapper class for the **int** primitive type. This class provides methods for converting between string, object, and numeric data. It also is useful for passing an **int** value by reference.

The following example converts a digit string to type **int**:

```
int i = Integer.parseInt(digitString);
```

Constructors

public **Integer**(int value);
public **Integer**(String s);

Constructors. The second constructor initializes from a digit string.

Class Variables

public final static int **MAX_VALUE**;
public final static int **MIN_VALUE**;

Constants. Maximum and minimum values in the **int** range.

Class Methods

public static Integer **getInteger**(String nprop);
public static Integer **getInteger**(String nprop, int val);
public static Integer **getInteger**(String nprop, Integer val);

Class method. Returns the value of the named system property. The second argument, if specified, is returned if the property name is not found in the system properties table.

public static int **parseInt**(String s);
public static int **parseInt**(String s, int radix);

Class method. Returns the face value of a string of digits as an **int**.

public static String **toBinaryString**(int i);
public static String **toHexString**(int i);
public static String **toOctalString**(int i);
public static String **toString**(int i);
public static String **toString**(int i, int radix);

Class methods. These methods return a string representation of the specified **int** value.

public static Integer **valueOf**(String s);
public static Integer **valueOf**(String s, int radix);

Class method. Returns an **Integer** object, initializing it from the digits in the string argument.

Instance Methods (from Number Class)

public double **doubleValue**();
public float **floatValue**();
public int **intValue**();
public long **longValue**();

These methods return the **double**, **float**, **int**, or **long** equivalent of the value stored in the current object.

Instance Methods (from Object Class)

public boolean **equals**(Object obj);
public int **hashCode**();
public String **toString**();

These methods override method definitions in the **Object** class.

Label Class

Full Name	**java.awt.Label**
Extends	**Component->Object**
Description	Public class. Creates a simple component that displays a single line of read-only text. **Label** objects generate no events and cannot get focus. They are useful for labeling other components that do not have their own built-in label or caption.

The following example adds a label to the current frame or applet:

```
Label lab1 = new Label("OK");
add(lab1);
```

Constructors

public **Label**();
public **Label**(String label);
public **Label**(String label, int alignment);

Constructors. Specifying label text and alignment is optional.

Class Variables

public final static int **CENTER**;
public final static int **LEFT**;
public final static int **RIGHT**;

These three constants are the possible values for text alignment.

Instance Methods

public int **getAlignment**();
public String **getText**();
public void **setAlignment**(int alignment);
public void **setText**(String label);

These methods get and set basic attributes of the label.

Overridden Instance Methods

public synchronized void **addNotify**();

Overrides method definition in the **Component** class.

LayoutManager Interface

Full Name	**java.awt.LayoutManager**
Description	Public Interface. This interface defines a set of services that a class must implement to be a layout manager. Note that only code within container classes calls these methods. Java applets and applications do not call these methods directly.

public abstract void **addLayoutComponent**(String name, Component comp);

This method is called when a component is added to a container using the **add(String, Component)** method. Interpretation of the string is up to the layout manager.

public abstract void **layoutContainer**(Container target);

This is the method where most of the work is done. It is called when the container needs to be laid out. The layout manager should respond by resizing and moving each component in the container as appropriate.

public abstract Dimension **minimumLayoutSize**(Container target);

This method returns the minimum layout size for the container after calculating the size required by all its components.

public abstract Dimension **preferredLayoutSize**(Container target);

This method returns the preferred layout size for the container after calculating the size that would best fit the preferred size for all the components.

public abstract void **removeLayoutComponent**(Component comp);

This method is called to inform the layout manager that the specified component is being removed from its container.

LineNumberInputStream Class

Full Name	**java.io.LineNumberInputStream**
Extends	**FilterInputStream->InputStream->Object**
Description	Public class. Creates an input stream that tracks the number of lines read. The current line count advances when any of the following is read: a newline, a carriage return, or a newline/carriage-return pair. The class does not embed line numbers into the stream; they are only used within the class.

Constructors

public **LineNumberInputStream**(InputStream in);

Constructor. Creates a line-numbered stream from another input stream.

Instance Methods

public int **getLineNumber**();

Returns the number of the current line being read.

public void **setLineNumber**(int lineNumber);

Resets the current line number. For example, if you set the current number to 10, the next line read would be numbered 11, the one after that 12, and so on.

Overridden Instance Methods

public int **available**() throws IOException;
public void **mark**(int readlimit);
public int **read**() throws IOException;
public int **read**(byte b[], int off, int len) throws IOException;
public void **reset**() throws IOException;
public long **skip**(long n) throws IOException;

These methods override method definitions in the **InputStream** class.

List Class

Full Name	**java.awt.List**
Extends	**Component->Object**
Description	Public class. A **List** object is a component featuring a scrollable list of items from which the user can select one or more items by clicking on them. Objects of this type generate standard keyboard and mouse events, except for **MOUSE_DOWN** and **MOUSE_UP**. List objects also generate events of type **LIST_SELECT** and **LIST_DESELECT**. When the user double-clicks an item, an **ACTION_EVENT** is generated, resulting in a call to the **action()** method. The second argument to **action()** is a string that contains the list item.

The following example creates and initializes a **List** component, finally adding it to the current frame or applet. The list has three visible rows and permits multiple selection.

```
List countryList = new List(3, true);
countryList.addItem("Oh Canada!");
countryList.addItem("La Belle France");
countryList.addItem("USA");
add(Countrylist);
```

Several methods use an index into the list to specify a position. This index is zero-based; the first item in a list is in position zero, the second is in position 1, and so on.

Constructors

public **List**();
public **List**(int rows, boolean multipleSelections);

Constructors. The **rows** argument specifies the number of visible rows. Specifying 0 lets the layout manager determine the row size. (This produces good results with **BorderLayout** but poor results with **FlowLayout**.) The **multipleSelections** argument, if **true**, specifies that the user can select any numer of items at the same time.

Instance Methods

public void **addItem**(String item);
public void **addItem**(String item, int index);

Adds an item, optionally specifying position with a zero-based index. All list items are simple strings.

public boolean **allowsMultipleSelections**();

Returns **true** if multiple selections are allowed.

public void **clear**();

Clears the list of all items.

public int **countItems**();

Returns the number of items in the list.

public void **delItem**(int position);
public void **delItems**(int start, int end);

These methods delete one or more items. In the case of **delItems()**, all items from start to end positions, inclusive, are deleted. All arguments are zero-based indexes.

public void **deselect**(int index);

Removes selection from the specified item if currently selected. The argument is a zero-based index.

public String **getItem**(int index);

Returns the item specified by a zero-based index.

public int **getRows**();

Returns the number of visible rows. This is not necessarily the same as the number of items.

public int **getSelectedIndex**();
public int[ ] **getSelectedIndexes**();

Returns the zero-based index of the currently selected item or items. **getSelectedIndex()** returns –1 if no item is selected or if there are multiple selections.

public String **getSelectedItem**();
public String[ ] **getSelectedItems**();

Returns the selected item or items. **getSelectedItem()** returns **null** if there is no selection or if there are multiple selections.

public int **getVisibleIndex**();

Returns the zero-based index of the last item made visible by a call to **makeVisible()**.

public boolean **isSelected**(int index);

Returns **true** if the specified item is selected. Index is zero-based.

public void **makeVisible**(int index);

Scrolls the list, if necessary, so that the specified item is visible to the user. The index is zero-based.

public Dimension **minimumSize**(int rows);
public Dimension **preferredSize**(int rows);

These methods return the minimum and preferred size, respectively, assuming that the list had the specified number of visible rows.

public void **replaceItem**(String newValue, int index);

Assigns a new string value to the specified item. Index is zero-based.

public void **select**(int index);

Causes the specified item to be selected. Index is zero-based. The value –1 deselects all items.

public void **setMultipleSelections**(boolean v);

Turns the multiple-selection capability on or off, depending on the argument **v**.

Overridden Instance Methods

public void **addNotify**();
public Dimension **minimumSize**();
public Dimension **preferredSize**();
public void **removeNotify**();

These methods override method definitions in the **Component** class.

LONG CLASS

Full Name	**java.lang.Long**
Extends	**Number->Object**
Description	Public final class. Serves as the wrapper class for the **long** primitive type. This class provides methods for converting between string, object, and numeric data. It also is useful for passing a **long** value by reference.

The following example converts a digit string to type **long**:

```
long lng = Long.parseLong(digitString);
```

Constructors

public **Long**(long value);
public **Long**(String s);

Constructors. The second constructor initializes from a digit string.

Class Variables

public final static long **MAX_VALUE**;
public final static long **MIN_VALUE**;

Constants. Maximum and minimum values in the **long** range.

Class Methods

public static Long **getLong**(String nm);
public static Long **getLong**(String nm, long val);
public static Long **getLong**(String nm, Long val);

Class method. Returns the value of the system property named. The second argument, if specified, is returned if the property name is not found in the system properties table.

public static long **parseLong**(String s);
public static long **parseLong**(String s, long radix);

Class method. Returns the face value of a string of digits as a **long**.

public static String **toString**(long i);
public static String **toString**(long i, long radix);

Class method. Returns a string representation of the **long** value.

public static Long **valueOf**(String s);
public static Long **valueOf**(String s, long radix);

Class method. Returns a **Long** object, initializing it from the digits in the string argument.

Instance Methods (from Number Class)

public double **doubleValue**();
public float **floatValue**();
public int **intValue**();
public long **longValue**();

These methods return the **double**, **float**, **int**, or **long** equivalent of the value stored in the current object.

Instance Methods (from Object Class)

public boolean **equals**(Object obj);
public long **hashCode**();
public String **toString**();

These methods override method definitions in the **Object** class.

MATH CLASS

Full Name	**java.lang.Math**
Extends	**Object**
Description	Public final class. All fields of this class are class fields—they have no connection to individual data objects of type **Math**. Instead, the **Math** class provides a collection of static methods and two useful constants: **E** and **PI**. The **Math** class is like a minilibrary made up of mathematical functions. This class has no constructor, and there is no reason to instantiate it.

The following example produces a random number from 1 to n. The first step is to execute **random()**, which produces a number in the range 0.0 to 1.0. Note that the **floor()** method could be applied to get a number in the range 0 to n-1.

```
int r = Math.ceil(Math.random() * n);
```

Class Variables

public final static double **E** = 2.7182818284590452354;
public final static double **PI** = 3.14159265358979323846;

Constants. Given the limits of **double** precision, these amounts are the closest approximations of the irrational numbers *e* and *pi*.

Class Methods

public static double **abs**(double a);
public static float **abs**(float a);
public static int **abs**(int a);
public static long **abs**(long a);

Returns the absolute value of the amount specified.

public static double **acos**(double a);
public static double **asin**(double a);
public static double **atan**(double a);

Returns the result of an inverse trig function.

public static double **atan2**(double a, double b);

Returns the angle component of the polar coordinates for point (a, b), where a and b use the Cartesian coordinate system.

public static double **ceil**(double a);

Returns the lowest integer amount that is equal to or greater than the argument.

public static double **cos**(double a);

Returns the cosine of the argument.

public static double **exp**(double a);

Returns e to the power of a (in which e is the natural logarithm base).

public static double **floor**(double a);

Returns the highest integer amount that is equal to or less than the argument.

public static double **IEEEremainder**(double f1, double f2);

Returns the remainder as defined by IEEE, when f1 is divided by f2. The remainder is the amount left over after an integer quotient is found.

public static double **log**(double a);

Returns the natural logarithm of a.

public static double **max**(double a, double b);
public static float **max**(float a, float b);
public static int **max**(int a, int b);
public static long **max**(long a, long b);

Returns the maximum of two numbers, where both have the same type.

public static double **min**(double a, double b);
public static float **min**(float a, float b);
public static int **min**(int a, int b);
public static long **min**(long a, long b);

Returns the minimum of two numbers, where both have the same type.

public static double **pow**(double a, double b);

Returns a to the power of b.

public static double **random**();

Returns a psuedo-random number between 0.0 and 1.0. For more sophisticated random-number generation (such as Gaussian distribution), use the **Random** class. However, **Math.random()** is adequate for most code that uses a random number.

public static double **rint**(double a);
public static long **round**(double a);
public static int **round**(float a);

All these methods return the nearest integer value. The difference is that **rint()** returns a **double** rather than an **integer** type and favors even numbers in rounding: 2.5 rounds to 2.0, although 2.51 rounds up to 3.0.

public static double **sin**(double a);
public static double **sqrt**(double a);
public static double **tan**(double a);

These methods return a **sine**, **square root**, and **tangent**, respectively.

MediaTracker Class

Full Name	**java.awt.MediaTracker**
Extends	**Object**
Description	Public class. A **MediaTracker** object monitors the progress of loading an image from disk or a remote site. After creating the tracker, you assign an image to it by calling **addImage()**. A single tracker can monitor any number of images as long as they are being loaded for the same component. The most important methods are **checkID()** and **waitForID()**, which check progress and wait for completion, respectively.

The following example creates a **MediaTracker** object that monitors loading for an **Image** object, **imgFromFile**. **checkID( )** returns **true** if the image is completely loaded. For **MediaTracker** used in context, see the example near the end of Chapter 3.

```
MediaTracker tracker = new MediaTracker(this);
tracker.addImage(imgFromFile, 1);
// ...
boolean b = tracker.checkID(1);  // Image loaded?
```

Constructors

public **MediaTracker**(Component comp);

Constructor. A media tracker always monitors a component, which must be specified.

Class Variables

public final static int **ABORTED**;
public final static int **COMPLETE**;
public final static int **ERRORED**;
public final static int **LOADING**;

These constants are status codes returned by the **statusAll()** and **statusID()** methods.

Instance Methods

public void **addImage**(Image image, int id);
public void **addImage**(Image image, int id, int w, int h);

Registers an image to be tracked, assigning that image an ID number of your choice. The purpose of the ID is to identify the image so that it can be referred to in other **MediaTracker** methods. The **w** and **h** arguments should be specified when you're doing scaling.

public boolean **checkAll**();
public boolean **checkAll**(boolean load);
public boolean **checkID**(int id);
public boolean **checkID**(int id, boolean load);

These four methods check loading status, returning **true** if the specified image has finished loading (**checkID**) or if all images tracked have finished loading (**checkAll**). If the **load** argument is included and is true, then the method initiates loading if not already started.

public Object[ ] **getErrorsAny**();
public Object[ ] **getErrorsID**(int id);
public boolean **isErrorAny**();
public boolean **isErrorID**(int id);

These four methods return information about errors encountered during loading. You can check on all images being tracked or on a single image identified by its ID.

public int **statusAll**(boolean load);
public int **statusID**(int id, boolean load);

Returns status using one of the four status codes defined in the class.

public void **waitForAll**();
public boolean **waitForAll**(long ms) throws InterruptedException;
public void **waitForID**(int id);
public boolean **waitForID**(int id, long ms) throws Interrupted-Exception;

These methods wait for the specified image or images and do not return until the image has finished loading, an error is encountered, or **ms** milliseconds (if specified) have elapsed. Note that calling one of these methods from within the main thread may be a risk, especially if you're loading data from a remote site. The UI is inoperable while the main thread is in a waiting state.

MemoryImageSource Class

Full Name	**java.awt.image.MemoryImageSource**
Extends	**Object**
Implements	**ImageProducer**
Description	Public class. Creates an image source that produces an image from raw pixel data in memory. The resulting image producer can be used to create a new image by calling the **createImage()** method of the **Component** class. This class is the converse of the **PixelGrabber** class, which gets raw pixel data from the image.

The following example loads a 300 x 200 image from **buffer**, an integer array containing pixel data:

```
MemoryImageSource mem = new MemoryImageSource(300,
200, buffer, 0, 300);
Image myImage = createImage(mem);
```

Constructors

public **MemoryImageSource**(int w, int h, ColorModel cm, byte pix[ ], int off, int scan);
public **MemoryImageSource**(int w, int h, ColorModel cm, byte pix[ ], int off, int scan, Hashtable props);

public **MemoryImageSource**(int w, int h, ColorModel cm, int pix[ ], int off, int scan);
public **MemoryImageSource**(int w, int h, ColorModel cm, int pix[ ], int off, int scan, Hashtable props);
public **MemoryImageSource**(int w, int h, int pix[ ], int off, int scan);
public **MemoryImageSource**(int w, int h, int pix[ ], int off, int scan, Hashtable props);

Constructors. The arguments specify size, integer or byte pixel array source, offset into the array, and scansize (typically the same as width). You can optionally specify a color model and a properties table. If a color model is not specified, the default RGB model is used.

Instance Methods

public void **addConsumer**(ImageConsumer ic);
public boolean **isConsumer**(ImageConsumer ic);
public void **removeConsumer**(ImageConsumer ic);
public void **requestTopDownLeftRightResend**(ImageConsumer ic);
public void **startProduction**(ImageConsumer ic);

These methods implement method declarations in the **Image-Producer** interface.

MENU CLASS

Full Name	**java.awt.Menu**
Extends	**MenuItem->MenuComponent->Object**
Implements	**MenuContainer**
Description	Public class. Creates a pull-down menu that can be added to a menu bar by calling **MenuBar.add()**. A menu bar, in turn, can be added to a frame by calling **Frame.setMenuBar()**. Menus may optionally be "tear off" menus if it is supported by the platform. The default is a standard menu. See also **MenuItem**.

Assume that **MyFrameClass** is a subclass of **Frame**. The following **MyFrameClass( )** constructor sets a menu bar with one menu (Commands), under which are two items (Do and Exit). See **MenuItem** class for event-handling code.

```
MyFrameClass() {
// Assume miDo, miExit declared as instance vars.
     miDo = new MenuItem("Do");
     miExit = new MenuItem("Exit");

     Menu m = new Menu("Commands");    // Create menu.
     m.add(miDo);                      // -> Add items.
     m.add(miExit);

     MenuBar mb = new MenuBar();    // Create menu bar.
     mb.add(m);                     // -> Add menu.
     setMenuBar(mb);  // Call Frame.setMenuBar().
}
```

Constructors

public **Menu**(String label);
public **Menu**(String label, boolean tearOff);

Constructors. You can optionally specify a **tearOff** argument, which, if **true**, causes the menu to be created as a "tear off" menu.

Instance Methods

public MenuItem **add**(MenuItem mi);
public void **add**(String label);

Adds the specified item as a string or **MenuItem** object. In either case, the resulting item is stored as a **MenuItem** object. Note that nested menus are possible, because the **Menu** class is a subclass of **MenuItem** and therefore a **Menu** object can be given as an argument to **add()**.

public void **addSeparator**();

Adds a separator bar in the next menu position.

public int **countItems**();
public MenuItem **getItem**(int index);
public boolean **isTearOff**();

These methods return information about the menu. **getItem()** returns the specified menu as a MenuItem object. Index is zero-based.

public void **remove**(int index);
public void **remove**(MenuComponent item);

Removes the menu item specified by zero-based index or by reference to the object.

Overridden Instance Methods

public void **addNotify**();
public void **removeNotify**();

These methods override method definitions in the **MenuComponent** and **MenuItem** classes. These methods are both used internally.

MenuBar Class

Full Name	**java.awt.MenuBar**
Extends	**MenuComponent->Object**
Implements	**MenuContainer**
Description	Public class. Creates a menu bar that may be added to a frame by calling **Frame.setMenuBar()**. A menu bar must be added to a frame to be displayed. A menu bar is a series of menu names; clicking on one pulls down the selected menu.

See **Menu** class for an example.

Constructors

public **MenuBar**();

Constructor. Use the **add()** method to create menu bar content.

Instance Methods

public synchronized Menu **add**(Menu m);

Adds a menu to the bar.

public int **countMenus**();

Returns the current number of menus on the bar.

public Menu **getHelpMenu**();
public Menu **getMenu**(int i);

These methods return the requested **Menu** object. Index is zero-based.

public synchronized void **remove**(int index);
public synchronized void **remove**(MenuComponent m);

Removes the specified menu from the bar. Index is zero-based.

public synchronized void **setHelpMenu**(MenuComponent item);

Causes the menu to be specified as a help menu, which is placed in a reserved location on the menu bar.

Overridden Instance Methods

public synchronized void **addNotify**();
public synchronized void **removeNotify**();

These methods override method definitions in the **MenuComponent** and **MenuItem** classes. These methods are both used internally.

MenuComponent Class

Full Name	**java.awt.MenuComponent**
Extends	**Object**
Description	Abstract public class. Because this class is abstract, you cannot use it to directly create an object. However, this class is the superclass of three menu-related classes—**MenuBar**, **Menu**, and **MenuItem**—and it includes methods useful in all these subclasses.

Constructors

public **MenuComponent**();

Constructor. Because the class is abstract, you cannot call this method to create an object.

Instance Methods

public Font **getFont**();
public MenuContainer **getParent**();

These methods return font and container much as **Component** methods do.

public MenuComponentPeer **getPeer**();
public boolean **postEvent**(Event evt);
public void **removeNotify**();

These three methods are mainly used internally.

public void **setFont**(Font f);

Sets a font used to display menu or menu bar text.

Overridden Instance Methods

public String **toString**();

Overrides method definition in the **Object** class.

MenuContainer Interface

Full Name	**java.awt.MenuContainer**
Description	Public interface. This interface defines a set of methods that a class must implement in order to be a container of other menu structures. Menu-container classes include **Frame**, **Menu**, and **MenuBar**. It is unlikely you'll ever need to implement this interface yourself.

public abstract Font **getFont**();

Returns the current font.

public abstract boolean **postEvent**(Event evt);

Used internally, to pass along events not handled to a container.

public abstract void **remove**(MenuComponent m);

Removes the specified object, which belongs to a class derived from **MenuComponent**: these classes include **Menu** and **MenuItem**.

MenuItem Class

Full Name	**java.awt.MenuItem**
Extends	**MenuComponent->Object**
Description	Public class. Creates an item on a pull-down menu, which can be added to a **Menu** object by calling **Menu.add()**. When a **MenuItem** object is selected, it generates an event of type **ACTION_EVENT**. Menu items do not have event handlers, but the event propogates up to the frame owning the menu bar (**MenuBar** object). This results in a call to the frame's **action()** method; the second argument is a string that contains the menu label.

The following example subclasses **Frame** and responds to selection of **miDo** or **miExit**, two menu items.

```
class MyFrameClass extends Frame {
     MenuItem miDo, miExit;
// Insert MyFrameClass() constructor.
     // from "Menu Class" topic.
   public boolean action(Event e, Object arg) {
          if (e.target == miDo)
              System.out.println("Do activated!");
          else if (e.target == miExit) {
              System.out.println("Exit activated!");
              dispose();
          }
          return true;
     }
}
```

Constructors

public **MenuItem**(String label);

Constructor. Menu item must be identified by a label.

Instance Methods

public synchronized void **addNotify**();

Used internally.

public void **disable**();
public void **enable**();
public void **enable**(boolean cond);

These methods disable or enable the menu item. A disabled item is grayed out and cannot be selected. **enable()** with an argument can be used to enable (**true**) or disable (**false**).

public String **getLabel**();
public boolean **isEnabled**();

These methods return the label and enabled state of the menu item.

public void **setLabel**(String label);

Specifies a new label.

NUMBER CLASS

Full Name	**java.lang.Number**
Extends	**Object**
Description	Public abstract class. Although this class cannot be used directly, it declares several methods that are useful in the wrapper classes **Integer**, **Long**, **Float**, and **Double**. The **Number** class is the immediate superclass of these other classes.

Instance Methods

public abstract double **doubleValue**();
public abstract float **floatValue**();
public abstract int **intValue**();
public abstract long **longValue**();

These methods return the **double**, **float**, **int**, or **long** equivalent of the value stored in the current object. The methods round as necessary, for there may be loss of precision.

NUMERIC CLASS

Full Name	**java.sql.Numeric**
Extends	**Number->Object**
Description	Public final JDBC class. A **Numeric** object stores a number in a *fixed-point* format, as opposed to floating-point. Fixed-point format holds fractional quantities precisely, avoiding rounding errors due to conversion between binary and decimal fractions. For exam

ple, a value of 7.47 is stored as the numeric value 747, with a scale of two. The details of storage are mostly invisible except when you specify scale (the number of digits to the right of the decimal point). The **Numeric** type is often useful in database opera tions, especially for storing things like money, where rounding errors are not suffered gladly.

A **Numeric** object has four basic attributes: *precision*, the total number of digits; *scale*, the number of digits maintained to the right of the decimal point; *sign*, which is the positive or negative sign (unlike integers, a Numeric object stores this separately from the amount); and *value*, which is a vector whose size is determined by precision. These values are determined during construction of the **Numeric** object.

Constructors

public **Numeric**(String s);
public **Numeric**(String s, int scale);
public **Numeric**(int x, int scale);
public **Numeric**(double x, int scale);
public **Numeric**(Numeric x);
public **Numeric**(Numeric x, int scale);

Constructors. The **scale** argument is used, if specified. The constructor attempts to create an amount equal to the face value of the **s** or **x** argument. In some cases, the scale may require rounding. For example, **Numeric("3333.201", 1)** would round down to 3333.2.

Class Methods

public static Numeric **createFromScaled**(long scaled, int s);

Returns a **Numeric** object created by assigning value and scale independently. For example, **createFromScaled(5678, 3)** returns a **Numeric** object with the value 5.678.

public static int **getRoundingValue**();
public static void **setRoundingValue**(int val);

These methods get and set the class rounding value, which by default is four. Where a digit must be rounded, it is rounded down if the next digit is less than or equal to the rounding value. A digit is rounded up if the next digit is equal or greater than the rounding value plus 1.

Instance Methods

public Numeric **add**(Numeric n);

Returns the result of adding the argument **n** to the current object. The result uses the current object's scale.

public void **debug**();
public Numeric **divide**(Numeric x);

Returns the result of dividing the argument **x** into the current object. The result uses the current object's scale.

public int **getScale**();

Returns the current object's scale (digits to the right of the decimal point).

public long **getScaled**();

Returns the value attribute, with the effect of the scale ignored. In theory, this has the same effect as taking the value of the current object and multiplying it by 10 to the power of the scale.

public boolean **greaterThan**(Numeric x);
public boolean **greaterThanOrEquals**(Numeric x);
public boolean **lessThan**(Numeric x);
public boolean **lessThanOrEquals**(Numeric x);

Returns the result of a comparison of the current object to the argument **x**. For example, **greaterThan()** returns **true** if the current object is greater than **x**. All comparisons use the true amounts stored in the objects (factoring in scale). For example, 20.0 is greater than 19.9995.

public Numeric **multiply**(Numeric x);

Returns the result of multiplying the argument **x** by the current object. The result uses the current object's scale.

public Numeric **setScale**(int scale);

Returns an object that preserves the current amount (as much as possible) but uses a new scale.

public Numeric **subtract**(Numeric n);

Returns the result of subtracting the argument **n** from the current object. The result uses the current object's scale.

Overridden Instance Methods (from Number)

public int **intValue**();
public long **longValue**();
public float **floatValue**();
public double **doubleValue**();
Returns the amount stored in the current object—or the closest approximation possible—by converting it to the indicated format.

Overridden Methods (from Object)

public boolean **equals**(Object obj);
public int **hashCode**();
public String **toString**();

These methods override method definitions in the **Object** class. **toString()** returns a string representation that includes the sign only for negative amounts.

OBJECT CLASS

Full Name	**java.lang.Object**
Extends	This class is the only Java class that has no superclass.
Description	Public class. As the ancestor class to all other classes in Java (whether API or not), the **Object** class defines universal methods inherited by all classes. Several of these methods—**clone()**, **equals()**, **finalize()**, and **toString()**—generally need to be overridden by a subclass to be useful. Note that **notify()** and **wait()** are intended mainly for internal use.

Constructors

public **Object**();

Constructor. Subclasses, of course, may support multiple constructors.

Instance Methods

public boolean **equals**(Object obj);

Compares contents of the specified object, **obj**, to those of the current object. Subclasses of **Object** may override this method to perform meaningful comparisons: for example, in the **String** class, this method returns **true** if string contents are equal. Note that the test-for-equality operator (==) returns **true** only if two object variables refer to the same object in memory. This condition is much more restrictive than testing contents for equality.

public final Class **getClass**();

Returns a **Class** object, which provides information on the current object's class.

public int **hashCode**();

Used internally. Some classes override this method to make it easier to work with hash tables. (See **Hashtable** class.) Classes that override this method tend to be those often used as hashtable keys.

public final void **notify**();
public final void **notifyAll**();

Used internally. The **Thread** class calls these methods to wake up a thread that has been waiting for ownership of the current object. This approach is related to use of the **synchronize** keyword.

public String **toString**();

Returns a string representation of the current object. Many API classes override **toString()** to provide meaningful string representations for the particular data they contain.

public final void **wait**();
public final void **wait**(long timeout);
public final void **wait**(long timeout, int nanos);

Used internally. The **Thread** class calls these methods to request ownership of the current object. This is related to use of the **synchronize** keyword.

protected Object **clone**() throws CloneNotSupportedException, OutOfMemoryError;

Returns a complete copy of the object's contents. A subclass may override **clone()** and make it public. In the API, only classes that implement **Cloneable** provide usable implementations of **clone()**. API classes that do not implement **Cloneable** throw an exception if this method is called. Note that with objects, cloning is not the same as assignment (=), which merely causes one object variable to refer to the same memory location as another variable.

protected void **finalize**() throws Throwable;

This method is called just before the object is destroyed by the garbage collector. This is the closest thing to a destructor in Java. In contrast to a destructor, there is no guarantee as to when this method is called.

OBSERVABLE CLASS

Full Name	**java.util.Observable**
Extends	**Object**
Description	Public class. An **Observable** object has the ability to maintain a list of observers, which can include any object whose class implements the **Observer** interface. When a method of an **Observable** object knows of a change to its state, it should call the **notifyObservers()** method, which in turn notifies all the observers in the list. Although the **Observable** class by itself is not useful, it is useful as a superclass to other classes.

Constructors

public **Observable**();

Constructor.

Instance Methods

public void **addObserver**(Observer o);

Adds an observer to the list.

public int **countObservers**();

Returns the number of observers.

public void **deleteObserver**(Observer o);
public void **deleteObservers**();

Removes observers: either a specified observer or all observers in the list.

public boolean **hasChanged**();

Returns **true** if the current object has changed since the last notification. Instead of notifying observers of every minute change, an observable object can instead choose to call the **clearChanged()** and **setChanged()** methods to adjust an internal flag. Observers can call **hasChanged()** to get the state of this flag. **clearChanged()** and **setChanged()** are described at the end of this topic.

public void **notifyObservers**();
public void **notifyObservers**(Object arg);

Notifies observers of a change. The method can optionally specify an argument. Interpreting this argument is application-defined.

Protected Instance Methods

protected void **clearChanged**();
protected void **setChanged**();

These are protected methods, meaning that they can only be called from within the package or a class derived from

Observable. These two methods turn the internal "has changed" flag on and off, respectively. See **hasChanged()** for more information.

OBSERVER INTERFACE

Full Name	**java.util.Observer**
Description	Public interface. Declares a method—**update()**—required for an object to act as an observer. The object that is watched is an instance of an **Observable** subclass. You register an observer by calling the **Observable** object's **addObserver()** method. When the **Observable** object changes, it notifies all its observers. The terminology may be confusing, because the two names are so close. But remember, an **Observable** object is watched, and it *sends out* notification. An object that implements **Observer** is a watcher, and it *receives* the notification, responding in any way appropriate.

public abstract void **update**(Observable o, Object arg);

This method is called when the target object (the one whose class is derived from **Observable**) broadcasts a notification by calling its **notifyObservers()** method. The first argument specifies the exact source of the notification. The second argument is a supplemental argument whose use is application-defined; its use is up to you.

OUTPUTSTREAM CLASS

Full Name	**java.io.OutputStream**
Extends	**Object**

Description	Abstract public class. This class is the superclass for all output streams. Some of the subclasses have more-efficient or specialized implementations than the default implementations provided in this class. Of the subclasses, **DataOutputStream** and **PrintStream** (text output) are the most widely used. See also **FileOutputStream**.

Instance Methods

public void **close**() throws IOException;

Closes the stream and releases all system resources associated with it (such as file handles).

public void **flush**() throws IOException;

Forces the internal buffer, if any, to be immediately written to the stream. The buffer is then emptied.

public void **write**(byte b[]) throws IOException;
public void **write**(byte b[], int off, int len) throws IOException;

Writes a series of bytes to the stream. The number of bytes is **len**, if specified, or all the bytes in the array **b**, if **len** is not specified. The **off** argument gives a starting offset in the array.

public abstract void **write**(int b) throws IOException;

Writes one byte to the stream using the eight low-order bits of b.

Panel Class

Full Name	**java.awt.Panel**
Extends	**Container->Component->Object**
Description	Public class. A panel is a container that has no window of its own. There are no visible borders around a panel. This class is useful for grouping components or for subdividing a window. Panels are used to group components in Chapter 4, "Components and Events."

Constructors

public **Panel**();

Constructor.

Instance Methods

public synchronized void **addNotify**();

Overrides method definition in **Component**. Used internally.

PipedInputStream Class

Full Name	**java.io.PipedInputStream**
Extends	**InputStream->Object**
Description	Public class. Creates a stream that reads from a data pipe. A data pipe is a channel of information between two threads. One thread (the source) sends data through the pipe while the other thread (the sink) reads the data put there. If the sink attempts a read after having read all the data in the pipe, it is blocked until more data is sent. You create a data pipe by setting up a pair of threads, one using a **PipedInputStream** object and the other using a **PipedOutputStream** object. Each of the streams must connect to the other stream. You can use the constructors or the **connect()** method of each object to set up these connections.

Constructors

public **PipedInputStream**();
public **PipedInputStream**(PipedOutputStream src) throws IOException;

Constructor. If **src** is not specified here, you must specify it with **connect()**. The output stream must also connect to this input stream.

Instance Methods

public void **connect**(PipedOutputStream src) throws IOException;

Connects to an output stream (**src**). The output stream must also connect to this input stream.

Overridden Instance Methods

public void **close**() throws IOException;
public int **read**(byte b[ ], int off, int len) throws IOException;
public int **read**() throws IOException;

These methods override method definitions in the **InputStream** class.

PIPEDOUTPUTSTREAM CLASS

Full Name	**java.io.PipedOutputStream**
Extends	**OutputStream->Object**
Description	Public class. Creates a stream that writes to a data pipe. A data pipe is a channel of information between two threads. One thread (the source) sends data through the pipe while the other thread (the sink) reads the data put there. When the source writes data to the pipe, it remains there until both streams are closed. You create a data pipe by setting up a pair of threads, one using a **PipedInputStream** object and the other using a **PipedOutputStream** object. Each of the streams must connect to the other stream. You can use the constructors or the **connect()** method of each object to set up these connections.

Constructors

public **PipedOutputStream**();
public **PipedOutputStream**(PipedInputStream snk) throws IOException;

Constructor. If **snk** is not specified here, you must specify it with **connect()**. The input stream must also connect to this output stream.

Instance Methods

public void **connect**(PipedInputStream snk) throws IOException;

Connects to an input stream (**snk**). The input stream must also connect to this output stream.

Overridden Instance Methods

public void **close**() throws IOException;
public void **write**(byte b[ ], int off, int len) throws IOException;
public void **write**(int b) throws IOException;

These methods override method definitions in the **InputStream** class.

PixelGrabber Class

Full Name	**java.awt.image.PixelGrabber**
Extends	**Object**
Implements	**ImageConsumer**
Description	Public class. Gets raw pixel data from an image, which you can store in memory and analyze. Pixels are returned using the default RGB model. This class is of use to programs that need to store pixel data in memory for some reason. Note that the **MemoryImageSource** class performs a converse operation.

The following example uses the **PixelGrabber** class to extract raw pixel data from an existing image, myImage:

```
int w = myImage.getWidth(this);

int h = myImage.getHeight(this);

int buffer[] = new int[w * h];

PixelGrabber grabber = new PixelGrabber(myImage, 0, 0,

     w, h, buffer, 0, w);

grabber.grabPixels();
```

Constructors

public **PixelGrabber**(Image img, int x, int y, int w, int h, int pix[ ], int off, int scansize);
public **PixelGrabber**(ImageProducer ip, int x, int y int w, int h, int pix[ ], int off, int scansize);

Constructors. Arguments specify the image source, the shape and size of the region, a destination array, an offset to the position in the array to receive the first pixel, and the scan size of each row (which is typically the same as the width argument, **w**).

Instance Methods

public boolean **grabPixels**();
public boolean **grabPixels**(long ms);

Starts copying pixels from the image. The method does not return until it's finished getting pixels or until the specified number of milliseconds (ms) has elapsed, whichever comes first.

public int **status**();

Returns the same status codes as used in the ImageObserver interface.

Instance Methods (from Interface)

public void **imageComplete**(int status);
public void **setColorModel**(ColorModel model);

public void **setDimensions**(int width, int height);
public void **setHints**(int hints);
public void **setPixels**(int srcX, int srcY, int srcW, int srcH, ColorModel model, byte pixels[ ], int srcOff, int srcScan);
public void **setPixels**(int srcX, int srcY, int srcW, int srcH, ColorModel model, int pixels[ ], int srcOff, int srcScan);
public void **setProperties**(Hashtable props);

These methods implement methods declared in the **ImageConsumer** interface.

Point Class

Full Name	**java.awt.Point**
Extends	**Object**
Description	Public class. Creates a two-dimensional point containing an x and a y integer value.

Constructors

public **Point**(int x, int y);

Constructor. You must specify an x and a y value to create a point.

Instance Variables

public int **x**;
public int **y**;

These instance variables contain the x and y values stored in the object.

Instance Methods

public void **move**(int x, int y);

Sets x and y to the values specified.

public void **translate**(int x, int y);

Adds the specified values to the current values of x and y.

Overridden Instance Methods

public synchronized void **equals**();
public int **hashCode**();
public String **toString**();

These methods override methods in the **Object** class.

POLYGON CLASS

Full Name	**java.awt.Polygon**
Extends	**Object**
Description	Public class. Creates an n-sided figure that can be passed to the **drawPolygon()** and **fillPolygon()** methods of the **Graphics** class. Java creates the polygon by "connecting the dots," using a series of points. With **drawPolygon()**, the last point of the polygon should usually be the same as the first point so that the figure connects back to where it started.

The following example creates a triangle connecting the points (10, 10), (10, 100), and (200, 100):

```
Polygon poly = new Polygon();
poly.addPoint(10, 10);
poly.addPoint(10, 100);
poly.addPoint(200, 100);

poly.addPoint(10, 10);
```

Constructors

public **Polygon**();
public **Polygon**(int[ ] xpoints, int[ ] ypoints, int npoints);

Constructors. The second version initializes the first n points, although they can always be added.

Instance Variables

public int **npoints**;
public int[ ] **xpoints**;
public int[ ] **ypoints**;

These instance variables store the number of vertices (points), the set of x coordinates, and the set of y coordinates. Points are stored as x and y coordinates in matching positions. For example, the first point is (xpoints[0], ypoints[0]).

Instance Methods

public void **addPoint**(int x, int y);

Adds a vertex (a point) to the polygon.

public Rectangle **getBoundingBox**();

Returns the smallest rectangular area that includes the entire polygon.

public boolean **Inside**(int x, int y);

Returns **true** if the specified point is located in the interior of the polygon.

PREPAREDSTATEMENT INTERFACE

Full Name	**java.sql.PreparedStatement**
Extends	**Statement**
Description	Public JDBC interface, providing services for executing a SQL statement. This interface provides the same capabilities as the **Statement** interface but is potentially more efficient, because SQL need parse the statement only once. Parameters, denoted as "?," can be fed different values each time the state ment is executed. (See example.) Note that not all database drivers support this interface.

You can get an object that implements this interface by calling the **prepareStatement()** method of a **Connection** object.

The following example uses a **PreparedStatement** object to add two rows of data to the stuff table:

```
Connection con = DriverManager.getConnection(dbname);
String s = "INSERT INTO stuff (name, dat) VALUES (?,
?)";
PreparedStatement pstm = con.prepareStatement(s);
pstm.setString(1, "os");      // Set parm 1.
pstm.setString(2, "unix");    // Set parm 2.
pstm.executeUpdate();
pstm.setString(1, "user");     // Set parm 1.
pstm.setString(2, "Freddy");   // Set parm 2.
pstm.executeUpdate();
```

public boolean **execute**() throws SQLException;

Executes the statement contained in the **PreparedStatement** object: this can be a query that produces multiple result sets. To get these result sets, use the **getResultSet()** and **getMoreResults()** methods inherited from the **Statement** interface.

public ResultSet **executeQuery**() throws SQLException;
public int **executeUpdate**() throws SQLException;

These methods execute the statement contained in the **PreparedStatement** object. Use **executeQuery()** for statements that return a result set.

public void **clearParameters**() throws SQLException;

Clears all parameter values set through interface methods.

public void **setAsciiStream**(int parameterIndex, InputStream x, int length) throws SQLException;
public void **setBinaryStream**(int parameterIndex, InputStream x, int length) throws SQLException;

These methods set the value of a parameter using a one-based index. The value to be assigned is read from an input stream. The **length** argument specifies the number of bytes.

public void **setBoolean**(int parameterIndex, boolean x) throws SQLException;
public void **setByte**(int parameterIndex, byte x) throws SQLException;
public void **setBytes**(int parameterIndex, byte x[]) throws SQLException;
public void **setDate**(int parameterIndex, Date x) throws SQLException;
public void **setDouble**(int parameterIndex, double x) throws SQLException;
public void **setFloat**(int parameterIndex, float x) throws SQLException;
public void **setInt**(int parameterIndex, int x) throws SQLException;
public void **setLong**(int parameterIndex, long x) throws SQLException;
public void **setNull**(int parameterIndex, int sqlType) throws SQLException;
public void **setNumeric**(int parameterIndex, Numeric x) throws SQLException;

These methods set the value of a parameter using a one-based index to the SQL parameter list.

public void **setObject**(int parameterIndex, Object x, int targetSqlType, int scale) throws SQLException;
public void **setObject**(int parameterIndex, Object x, int targetSqlType) throws SQLException;
public void **setObject**(int parameterIndex, Object x) throws SQLException;

These methods set the value of a parameter using a one-based index to the SQL parameter list. A SQL type is used, if specified (see "**Types** Class"). Otherwise, JDBC maps objects according to class, using a standard mapping. Specifying type explicitly gives you more control.

public void **setShort**(int parameterIndex, short x) throws SQLException;
public void **setString**(int parameterIndex, String x) throws SQLException;
public void **setTime**(int parameterIndex, Time x) throws SQLException;
public void **setTimestamp**(int parameterIndex, Timestamp x) throws SQLException;

These methods set the value of a parameter using a one-based index to the SQL parameter list.

public void **setUnicodeStream**(int parameterIndex, InputStream x, int length) throws SQLException;

Sets the value of a parameter using a one-based index. The value to be assigned is read from an input stream. The **length** argument specifies the number of characters.

PrintStream Class

Full Name	**java.io.PrintStream**
Extends	**FilterOutputStream->OutputStream->Object**
Description	Public class. Prints text representations of Java data. Common uses of this class include console output (**System.out**), output to a text file, and output to a socket stream. (See **FileOutputStream** and **Socket**.) There is no exact converse to **PrintStream** on the input side, but you can use **DataInputStream** to read lines of text, which you then parse. All the print methods discard the high-order eight bits of Unicode characters.

The following example uses the **System.out** object, an instance of **PrintStream**, to print a prompt string. The **flush( )** method—unnecessary with **println( )**—forces immediate printing of the string. See Chapter 6, "Common Programming Tasks," for a code in context of an example.

```
System.out.print("Enter a number: ");

System.out.flush();
```

Constructors

public **PrintStream**(OutputStream out);
public **PrintStream**(OutputStream out, boolean autoflush);

Constructors. The **out** argument is another output stream. This argument is often a **FileInputStream** object, which can be constructed from a file name. If **autoflush** is specified and is **true**, output is automatically flushed at the end of each line of text (the default behavior).

Instance Methods

public boolean **checkError**();

Flushes the output stream and returns **true** if an error has been encountered.

public void **print**(boolean b);
public void **print**(char c);
public void **print**(char s[]);
public void **print**(double d);
public void **print**(float f);
public void **print**(int i);
public void **print**(long l);
public void **print**(Object obj);
public void **print**(String s);

All the **print()** methods output a text representation of the argument by calling the object's **toString()** method. The stream must be flushed if you want to force immediate printing.

public void **println**();
public void **println**(boolean b);
public void **println**(char c);
public void **println**(char s[]);
public void **println**(double d);
public void **println**(float f);
public void **println**(int i);
public void **println**(long l);
public void **println**(Object obj);
public void **println**(String s);

All the **println()** methods perform the same action as their **print()** counterparts except that they add a newline character at the end and flush the stream.

Overridden Instance Methods

public void **close**();
public void **flush**();
public void **write**(byte b[], int off, int len) throws IOException;
public void **write**(int b) throws IOException;

These methods override method definitions in the **OutputStream** class.

Process Class

Full Name	**java.lang.Process**
Extends	**Object**
Description	Abstract public class. The **Runtime.exe()** method returns an instance of this class when you execute a file. (Actually, it returns an instance of a subclass, but the effect is the same.) Processes are vaguely similar to threads, but a process originates in a separate executable file and not in the current program. Processes have their own i/o streams. Applets that are run from browsers can start threads but not processes.

Instance Methods

public abstract void **destroy**();

Kills the process.

public abstract int **exitValue**() throws IllegalThreadStateException;

Returns the exit value; call this only after the process is killed or else an exception will be thrown.

public abstract InputStream **getErrorStream**();
public abstract InputStream **getInputStream**();
public abstract OutputStream **getOutputStream**();

Gets the requested error, input, or output stream associated with the process.

public abstract int **waitFor**();

The current thread waits for the process to complete, returning immediately if the process has already terminated.

PROPERTIES CLASS

Full Name	**java.util.Properties**
Extends	**Hashtable->Dictionary->Object**
Description	Public class. Creates a properties table; this is a special kind of hash table (see **Hashtable** class) in which keys and elements are always strings. Property tables have built-in support for reading and writing to streams. They also have a built-in mechanism for providing default property values. **Properties** tables are used by a number of other classes in Java, such as the **System** class. To set property values, use the **put()** method inherited from **Hashtable**.

The following example gets the value of the **os.name** property in the system properties table. For a list of all these properties, see Table L in Part VI.

```
Properties sysProp = System.getProperties();
String sysName = sysProp.getProperty("os.name");
```

Constructors

public **Properties**();
public **Properties**(Properties defaults);

ConstructorS. You can optionally specify a table that contains default values for the new table.

Instance Variables

protected Properties **defaults**;

Protected instance variable. (Because it is protected, it cannot be accessed except by subclasses.) This variable contains a reference to another **Properties** table that contains default values. When a property name is looked up and the name is not found, its value is then looked up in the default table. The **defaults** field is **null** if there is no default property table.

Instance Methods

public String **getProperty**(String key);
public String **getProperty**(String key, String defaultValue);

Returns the property value for the specified name (key). If the search for the name fails, the default property table, if any, is searched.

public void **list**(PrintStream out);

Outputs the table to a print stream. This is useful for debugging purposes.

public void **load**(InputStream in);

Loads the property table from the specified input stream.

public Enumeration **propertyNames**();

Returns an enumeration of all the property names along with names in the default table, if any. See **Enumeration** interface.

public void **save**(OutputStream out, String header);

Saves the property table to the specified output stream.

PUSHBACKINPUTSTREAM CLASS

Full Name	**java.io.PushbackInputStream**
Extends	**FilterInputStream->InputStream->Object**
Description	Public class. This class contains an extra one-character buffer, which can be used to "unread" the last character read. This is often useful for syntax parsers.

Constructors

public **PushbackInputStream**(InputStream in);

The constructor creates a **PushbackInputStream** around the specified input stream.

Instance Variables

protected int **pushBack**;

Protected instance variable that stores a pushed-back character after a call to **unread()**. Because this variable is protected, it cannot be accessed from outside the package, except by a derived class. A value of -1 indicates that there is currently no pushed-back character.

Instance Methods

public void **unread**(int ch) throws IOException;

Pushes back a character. The next time **read()** is called, this character is read first. Calling **unread()** twice before a **read()** operation throws an exception.

Overridden Instance Methods

public int **available**() throws IOException;
public boolean **markSupported**();
public int **read**() throws IOException;
public int **read**(byte bytes[ ], int offset, int length) throws IOException;

These methods override method definitions in the **InputStream** class. The **available()** method adds 1 to the total of available data if there is a pushed-back character stored. The **markSupported()** method always returns **false** for this class. Also note that **read()** empties the one-character buffer.

Random Class

Full Name	**java.util.Random**
Extends	**Object**
Description	Public class. Creates objects that can be used to generate a series of psuedo-random numbers. Note that the **Math.random()** method is often simpler to use.

Constructors

public **Random**( );
public **Random**(long seed);

Constructors. Using the time as a seed is recommended, as in "Random((new Date( )).getTime( ))." See also **setSeed()**.

Instance Methods

public double **nextDouble**();
public float **nextFloat**();

These methods return the next random number as a floating-point value between 0.0 and 1.0.

public double **nextGaussian**();

Returns the next random number from a Gaussian (normal) distribution, with mean value of 0.0 and standard deviation of 1.0.

public int **nextInt**();
public long **nextLong**();

These methods return the next random number as an integer ranging over the data type's range.

public void **setSeed**(long seed);

Resets the pseudo-random series. Using the current time is recommended.

RandomAccessFile Class

Full Name	**java.io.RandomAccessFile**
Extends	**Object**
Implements	**DataInput**, **DataOutput**
Description	Public class. Creates an object that can be used for random access. The unique features of such a stream are that it can be used to read or write at the same time, and you can call the **seek()** method to move directly to any file position. Otherwise, almost all the methods here are found in **DataInputStream** or **DataOutputStream**. Note that typical random-access algorithms assume equal-length records, which may in turn require the use of equal-length string data. One solution is to equalize string lengths with calls to **StringBuffer.setLength()**.

The following example opens a file **RAN.DAT** with read/write permission, moves to record position 30, and writes an integer **n**. Assume that **recsize** and **n** are declared and initialized elsewhere.

```
try {
  RandomAccessFile rf = new
```

```
        RandomAccessFile("RAN.DAT", "rw");
  rf.seek(recsize * 30);
  rf.writeInt(n);
} catch (IOException e) {System.out.prinln(e);}
```

Constructors

public **RandomAccessFile**(File file, String mode) throws IOException;
public **RandomAccessFile**(String name, String mode) throws IOException;

Constructors. The mode is either “r” or “rw,” for read or read/write mode. Successfully creating the object automatically opens the file for random-access i/o.

Instance Methods

public void **close**() throws IOException;

Closes the stream and releases all system resources associated with it (such as file handles).

public final FileDescriptor **getFD**() throws IOException;

Returns the **FileDescriptor** for this file.

public long **getFilePointer**() throws IOException;

Returns the current value of the file pointer. This is an offset from the beginning of the file.

public long **length**() throws IOException;

Returns the current length of the file.

public abstract int **read**() throws IOException;

Returns the next byte in the stream. Returns –1 if at end of the stream.

public int **read**(byte b[ ]) throws IOException;
public int **read**(byte b[ ], int off, int len) throws IOException;

Reads up to b.length or **len** bytes, whichever is smaller. Returns the number of bytes read, or –1 if at the end of the stream. The **off** argument gives a starting offset into the array.

public final boolean **readBoolean**() throws IOException;
public final byte **readByte**() throws IOException;
public final char **readChar**() throws IOException;
public final double **readDouble**() throws IOException;
public final float **readFloat**() throws IOException;

Each of these methods reads an instance of a primitive data type.

public final void **readFully**(byte b[ ]) throws IOException, EOFException;
public final void **readFully**(byte b[ ], int off, int len) throws IOException, EOFException;

Reads enough bytes to fill the array or reads **len** bytes if specified. In either case, this method causes the current thread to wait until all the data requested is read.

public final int **readInt**() throws IOException;

Reads an instance of an **int**.

public final String **readLine**() throws IOException;

Reads a character string up to the first newline, carriage return, newline/carriage-return pair, or end of input stream.

public final long **readLong**() throws IOException;
public final short **readShort**() throws IOException;
public final int **readUnsignedByte**() throws IOException;
public final int **readUnsignedShort**() throws IOException;

Each of these methods reads an instance of a primitive data type. Although unsigned byte and unsigned short are not Java data types, Java can read them correctly and return them in an **int** field, which has sufficient range to store the number read.

public final String **readUTF**() throws IOException;

Reads a string in the Unicode transformation format (UTF). This format reads the first two bytes as an unsigned short integer indicating the length of the string. The rest of the data consists of UTF-8 character encoding. The UTF-8 format, which is compatible with ASCII, is described in Table H in Part VI. See also **writeUTF()**.

public void **seek**(long pos) throws IOException;

Sets the file pointer to a new position.

public int **skipBytes**(int n) throws IOException;

Advances the file pointer n bytes before the next file i/o operation.

public void **write**(byte b[]) throws IOException;
public void **write**(byte b[], int off, int len) throws IOException;

Writes a series of bytes to the stream. The number of bytes is **len**, if specified, or all the bytes in the array b if **len** is not specified. The **off** argument gives a starting offset in the array.

public abstract void **write**(int b) throws IOException;

Writes one byte to the stream using the eight low-order bits of b.

public final void **writeBoolean**(boolean v) throws IOException;
public final void **writeByte**(int v) throws IOException;

Writes an instance of a primitive data type, **boolean** or **int**.

public final void **writeBytes**(String s) throws IOException;

Writes a string to the output stream, converting each character to a byte by discarding the eight high bits. Note that **readLine()** will not read such a string correctly unless you terminate it with a newline or carriage return. See also **writeUTF()**, which is more reliable.

public final void **writeChar**(int v) throws IOException;
public final void **writeChars**(String s) throws IOException;
public final void **writeDouble**(double v) throws IOException;
public final void **writeFloat**(float v) throws IOException;
public final void **writeInt**(int v) throws IOException;
public final void **writeLong**(long v) throws IOException;
public final void **writeShort**(int v) throws IOException;

Each of these methods writes the appropriate primitive data type.

public final void **writeUTF**(String str) throws IOException;

Writes a string in the Unicode transformation format (UTF). This format writes the first two bytes as an unsigned short integer indicating the length of the string. The rest of the data consists of UTF-8 character encoding. The UTF-8 format, which is compatible with ASCII, is described in Table H in Part V. See also **readUTF()**.

Rectangle Class

Full Name	**java.awt.Rectangle**
Extends	**Object**
Description	Public class. Creates a rectangle represented as a point (top left corner), width, and height. The **Rectangle** class is frequently useful in specifying clipping regions for repainting. Note that to draw rectangles, you need to use the **Graphics** class. As with Polygons, rectangles are not automatically displayed.

The following example creates a rectangle from the union of two other rectangles. The new rectangle has x and y of (10, 10), width 290, and height 290.

```
Rectangle rect1 = new Rectangle(10, 10, 150, 200);
Rectangle rect2 = new Rectangle(50, 50, 250, 250);
Rectangle rectNew = rect1.union(rect2);
```

Constructors

public **Rectangle**();
public **Rectangle**(Dimension d);
public **Rectangle**(int width, int height);
public **Rectangle**(int x, int y, int width, int height);
public **Rectangle**(Point p);
public **Rectangle**(Point p, Dimension d);

Constructors. If a value is not specified, a default value of 0 is assumed.

Instance Variables

public int **height**;
public int **width**;
public int **x**;
public int **y**;

Public instance variables. You can manipulate these directly.

Instance Methods

public void **add**(int newx, int newy);
public void **add**(Point pt);
public void **add**(Rectangle r);

All these methods expand the rectangle object so that it contains the specified point or rectangle.

public void **grow**(int h, int v);

Increments the width (h, for horizontal) and height (v, for vertical).

public boolean **inside**(int x, int y);

Returns true if the given point is contained in the rectangle.

public Rectangle **intersection**(Rectangle r);

Returns the rectangle that results from the intersection of the current object and rectangle r.

public boolean **intersects**(Rectangle r);
public boolean **isEmpty**();

These methods return **true** or **false** for the specified condition.

public void **move**(int x, int y);
public void **reshape**(int x, int y, int width, int height);
public void **resize**(int width, int height);

These methods directly specify new values for the rectangle's instance variables.

public void **translate**(int dx, int dy);

Increments the rectangle's x and y values.

public Rectangle **union**(Rectangle r);

Returns the rectangle that results from the union of the current object and rectangle r.

Overridden Instance Methods

public boolean **equals**(Object obj);
public int **hashCode**();
public String **toString**();

All these methods override method definitions in the **Object** class.

ResultSet Interface

Full Name	**java.sql.ResultSet**
Description	Public interface. Several JDBC interfaces—**Statement**, **PreparedStatement**, and **CallableStatement**—can return one or more *result sets* in response to execution of SQL query statements. An object implementing the **ResultSet** interface encapsulates this data. A result set is somewhat similar to the structure of a table, with data organized into rows and columns. Almost all the methods in this interface read the current row. The **next()** method gets a row, returning *false* when rows are exhausted. (See example.)

The following example reads and prints the contents of the stuff table; **name** and **dat** are columns in the table. If there are other columns, these contents are not read.

```
Connection con = DriverManager.getConnection(dbname);
Statement stm = con.createStatement();
String s = "SELECT name, dat FROM stuff";
ResultSet rs = stm.executeQuery(s);
while(rs.next()) {
```

```
        System.out.print(rs.getString(1) + " ");
        System.out.println(rs.getString(2));
}
```

public void **clearWarnings**() throws SQLException;

Clears the warnings so that the next call to **getWarnings** returns **null**.

public void **close**() throws SQLException;

Immediately closes the result set and releases its resources. Note that the garbage collector eventually closes the result set automatically.

public int **findColumn**(String columnName) throws SQLException;

Returns the one-based index of the column that has the matching name.

public InputStream **getAsciiStream**(int columnIndex) throws SQLException;
public InputStream **getAsciiStream**(String columnName) throws SQLException;
public InputStream **getBinaryStream**(int columnIndex) throws SQLException;
public InputStream **getBinaryStream**(String columnName) throws SQLException;
public boolean **getBoolean**(int columnIndex) throws SQLException;
public boolean **getBoolean**(String columnName) throws SQLException;
public byte **getByte**(int columnIndex) throws SQLException;
public byte **getByte**(String columnName) throws SQLException;
public byte[ ] **getBytes**(String columnName) throws SQLException;
public byte[ ] **getBytes**(int columnIndex) throws SQLException;

All these methods return data stored in the column specified by the one-based index or name.

public String **getCursorName**() throws SQLException;

Returns the name of the SQL cursor (this, in effect, is the "current row" indicator).

public Date **getDate**(int columnIndex) throws SQLException;
public Date **getDate**(String columnName) throws SQLException;
public double **getDouble**(int columnIndex) throws SQLException;
public double **getDouble**(String columnName) throws SQLException;
public float **getFloat**(int columnIndex) throws SQLException;
public float **getFloat**(String columnName) throws SQLException;
public int **getInt**(int columnIndex) throws SQLException;
public int **getInt**(String columnName) throws SQLException;
public long **getLong**(int columnIndex) throws SQLException;
public long **getLong**(String columnName) throws SQLException;

All these methods return data stored in the column specified by the one-based index or name.

public ResultSetMetaData **getMetaData**() throws SQLException;

Returns the corresponding **ResultSetMetaData** object, which you can use to get information about the result set's structure.

public Numeric **getNumeric**(int columnIndex, int scale) throws SQLException;
public Numeric **getNumeric**(String columnName, int scale) throws SQLException;
public Object **getObject**(int columnIndex) throws SQLException;
public Object **getObject**(String columnName) throws SQLException;
public short **getShort**(int columnIndex) throws SQLException;
public short **getShort**(String columnName) throws SQLException;
public String **getString**(int columnIndex) throws SQLException;
public String **getString**(String columnName) throws SQLException;
public Time **getTime**(int columnIndex) throws SQLException;
public Time **getTime**(String columnName) throws SQLException;
public Timestamp **getTimestamp**(int columnIndex) throws SQLException;
public Timestamp **getTimestamp**(String columnName) throws

SQLException;
public InputStream **getUnicodeStream**(int columnIndex) throws SQLException;
public InputStream **getUnicodeStream**(String columnName) throws SQLException;

All these methods return data stored in the column specified by the one-based index or name.

public SQLWarning **getWarnings**() throws SQLException;

Gets the next **SQLWarning** object. You can use this object to get the other warnings.

public boolean **next**() throws SQLException;

Advances reading of the result-set data to the next row. This is probably the single most important method in the interface, because you have to call it before reading a row of data.

public boolean **wasNull**() throws SQLException;

Returns **true** if the result set is **null** (no entries).

ResultSetMetaData Interface

Full Name	**java.sql.ResultSetMetaData**
Description	Public interface. Provides information about the structure of a particular result set. The **getMetaData()** method of the **ResultSet** interface returns an object that implements this interface. You can use this object, in turn, to query for the number of columns, the data type of each column, and so on.

Interface Constants

public final static int **columnNoNulls**;
public final static int **columnNullable**;
public final static int **columnNullableUnknown**;

These constants are returned by the **isNullable()** method to indicate whether a specified column can or cannot contain the value **null**.

Interface Methods

public String **getCatalogName**(int column) throws SQLException;

Returns the database catalog name.

public int **getColumnCount**() throws SQLException;

Returns the total number of columns in this result set.

public int **getColumnDisplaySize**(int column) throws SQLException;
public String **getColumnLabel**(int column) throws SQLException;
public String **getColumnName**(int column) throws SQLException;
public int **getColumnType**(int column) throws SQLException;
public String **getColumnTypeName**(int column) throws SQLException;
public int **getPrecision**(int column) throws SQLException;
public int **getScale**(int column) throws SQLException;
public String **getSchemaName**(int column) throws SQLException;
public String **getTableName**(int column) throws SQLException;

Each of these methods returns the requested information about one of the columns in the result set. The argument is a one-based index into the columns. **getColumnType()** returns a SQL type (see **Types** class). **getPrecision()** and **getScale()** return information relevant to columns that have the **Numeric** type. See **Numeric** class for more information.

public boolean **isAutoIncrement**(int column) throws SQLException;
public boolean **isCaseSensitive**(int column) throws SQLException;
public boolean **isCurrency**(int column) throws SQLException;
public boolean **isDefinitelyWritable**(int column) throws SQLException;

Returns the corresponding condition. The argument is a one-based index. The **isDefinitelyWritable()** condition ensures that a write to the column *must* succeed (therefore, no values of the appropriate type are out of range). See also **isWritable()**.

public int **isNullable**(int column) throws SQLException;

Returns one of the constants **ColumnNoNulls**, **ColumnNullable**, or

ColumnNullabeUnknown, depending on which condition is true: the column cannot contain a null, the column can contain a null, or the condition is unknown. The argument is a one-based index.

public boolean **isSearchable**(int column) throws SQLException;
public boolean **isSigned**(int column) throws SQLException;
public boolean **isReadOnly**(int column) throws SQLException;
public boolean **isWritable**(int column) throws SQLException;

Returns the corresponding condition. The argument is a one-based index. The **isWritable()** condition implies that a write operation *may* succeed. This does not preclude the possibility that some values may be out of range. See also **isDefinitelyWritable()**.

RGBImageFilter Class

Full Name	**java.awt.image.RGBImageFilter**
Extends	**ImageFilter**
Description	Abstract public class. Creates a color filter for images. The use of this class is somewhat similar to using the **CropImageFilter** class, but with the following difference: instead of instantiating this class directly, you create a color filter by subclassing this class. In the majority of cases, the one method you need to override is **filterRGB();** you use this method to determine how to translate each pixel.

Protected Instance Methods

protected boolean **canFilterIndexColorModel**;
protected ColorModel **newmodel**;
protected ColorModel **origmodel**;

Protected instance variables. (Because they are protected, they cannot be accessed from outside, but subclass code can refer to them.) You can choose to set **canFilterIndexColorModel** to **true** and then use an **IndexColorModel** object rather than filter pixels individually.

Instance Methods

public IndexColorModel **filterIndexColorModel**(IndexColor-Model icm);

If **canFilterIndexColorModel** is **true**, this method returns the **IndexColorModel** object to be used. Otherwise, the returned value is ignored.

public abstract int **filterRGB**(int x, int y, int rgb);

Converts a pixel by taking the position and current RGB value and outputting a new RGB value. When subclassing, you should override this method unless you are going to use an **IndexColor-Model** object. This is usually the only method you should be interested in overriding.

public void **filterRGBPixels**(int x, int y, int w, int h, int pixels[ ], int off, int scansize);

Processes pixels in a buffer by sending them, one by one, through the **filterRGB()** method. You should never override this method.

public void **substituteColorModel**(ColorModel oldcm, ColorModel newcm);

Replaces use of the old color model with the new color model.

Overridden Instance Methods

public void **setColorModel**(ColorModel model);
public void **setPixels**(int x, int y, int w, int h, ColorModel model, byte pixels[ ], int off, int scansize);
public void **setPixels**(int x, int y, int w, int h, ColorModel model, int pixels[ ], int off, int scansize);

These methods override method definitions in the **ImageFilter** class.

Runnable Interface

Full Name	**java.lang.Runnable**
Description	Public interface. Any class that implements this interface can define the behavior of a thread. After writing the class, you hook it up to a thread in the following way: create an instance of your class; specify this instance as an argument to a **Thread** constructor. This constructor, of course, creates a thread. When this thread is started, it calls the **run()** method defined in your class.

public **run**();

This method is called in response to a thread's **start()** method. A thread is hooked to a particular **Runnable** class.

Runtime Class

Full Name	**java.lang.Runtime**
Extends	**Object**
Description	Public class. This class provides a connection to the capabilities of the local computer as well as interaction with the Java interpreter (Sometimes called the Java Virtual Machine). Some of these capabilities—such as **exec()**—can be used by applications but (for security reasons) are not allowed in browser-run applets. See also **System** class, which supports related capabilities.

Class Methods

public static Runtime **getRuntime**();

Class method. Returns the system's **Runtime** object.

Instance Methods

public Process **exec**(String command);
public Process **exec**(String command, String envp[ ]);
public Process **exec**(String cmdarray[ ]);
public Process **exec**(String cmdarray[ ], String envp[ ]);

Executes a new process on the local machine: this process may be an executable that runs outside the Java interpreter. The **cmdarray** argument, if specified, is an array of strings in which the first string is the command name. The **envp** argument, if specified, is an array of strings: each **envp** string has the form "name=value."

public void **exit**(int status);

Causes the Java program to exit, passing the specified exit code to the system.

public long **freeMemory**();

Returns the amount of unused memory; this is always less than the amount returned by **totalMemory()**. Calling **gc()** may result in some objects being destroyed, thus increasing free memory.

public void **gc**();

Requests that the garbage collector (which normally runs as a low-priority background process) be invoked right away to start destroying objects no longer used.

public InputStream **getLocalizedInputStream**(InputStream in);
public OutputStream **getLocalizedOutputStream**(Output-Stream out);

These methods get localized input and output streams: such streams convert between the local character code and Unicode. This is not normally necessary for ASCII characters.

public void **load**(String filename) throws UnsatisfiedLinkError;
public void **loadLibrary**(String libname) throws Unsatisfied-LinkError;

Mainly used internally. These methods load native-code implementations. **load()** specifies a complete path name, whereas **loadLibrary()** relies on the system to search in the library directories.

public void **runFinalization**();

Requests that the Java interpreter call the **finalize()** method for all objects that have been destroyed. Normally, an object's **finalize()** method may not necessarily be run right away.

public long **totalMemory**();

Returns the total amount of memory available to the Java interpreter, including memory currently used by objects and variables. See **freeMemory()**.

public void **traceInstructions**(boolean on);
public void **traceMethodCalls**(boolean on);
Causes Java to print a statement or method trace if the interpreter supports this feature. Calling these methods with **on** set to **false** turns off the tracing.

SCROLLBAR CLASS

Full Name	**java.awt.Scrollbar**
Extends	**Component->Object**
Description	Public class. A **Scrollbar** object encapsulates the standard scroll-bar control found in GUI environments. In Java, scroll bars are best positioned in a container by using a **BorderLayout** manager and assigning the scroll bar to an edge of the container. Scroll bars generate all standard keyboard and mouse events except **MOUSE_DOWN** and **MOUSE_UP**. Scroll bars also generate a number of special **SCROLLBAR_*** events, as summarized in Tables A and B in Part VI.

The following example adds a horizontal scroll bar to the current frame or applet. Values corresponding to scroll bar position run from 0 to 100, and the initial position is halfway (50).

```
Scrollbar sb = new Scrollbar(Scrollbar.HORIZONTAL, 50,
     25, 0, 100);
add(sb);
```

Constructors

public **Scrollbar**();
public **Scrollbar**(int orientation);
public **Scrollbar**(int orientation, int value, int visible, int minimum, int maximum);

Constructors. Optionally set scroll-bar attributes. The minimum and maximum attributes specify integers corresponding to the end points. The **value** attribute corresponds to the current position of the scroll-bar indicator, which changes in response to user actions. Thus, if minimum and maximum are 100 and 200, a value of 150 indicates the scroll-bar midpoint. A value of 190 is close to the right (or bottom) end point. The **visible** attribute means "size of a visible page," and its effect is to determine the page increment (the amount of movement when the user clicks the bar on either side of the indicator).

Class Variables

public final static int **HORIZONTAL**;
public final static int **VERTICAL**;

Possible values for the orientation attribute.

Instance Methods

public int **getLineIncrement**();
public int **getMaximum**();
public int **getMinimum**();
public int **getOrientation**();
public int **getPageIncrement**();
public int **getValue**();
public int **getVisible**();

All these "get" methods all set various attributes of the scroll bar. (See the **Scrollbar** constructor for descriptions). The **visible** and **page increment** attributes are closely related although not necessarily equal to each other. Calling **getValue()** reports the current position of the scroll-bar indicator.

public void **setLineIncrement**(int l);
public void **setPageIncrement**(int l);
public void **setValue**(int value);
public void **setValues**(int value, int visible, int minimum, int maximum);

These "set" methods set the various scroll-bar attributes. (See the **Scrollbar** constructor for information.) Calling **setValue()** moves the scroll-bar indicator.

Overridden Instance Methods

public void **addNotify**();

Overrides the method definition in the **Component** class.

SecurityManager Class

Full Name	**java.lang.SecurityManager**
Extends	**Object**
Description	Abstract public class. Applications that browse the net, view applets, or download classes across the network can install a security manager by subclassing this class and writing and overriding methods. The security manager is installed by calling **System.setSecurityManager()**. A new security manager cannot be installed if there is already one in place; applets, therefore, cannot install one. Before a potentially sensitive operation is performed, the appropriate "check" method of the security manager (if any) is called. The method responds by doing nothing or by throwing a **SecurityException**, thus preventing the operation. The default behavior for each method is to throw an exception. Note that

applications do not have a security manager unless the program installs one. The Netscape browser and appletviewer install different security managers; this is why appletviewer is able to be more lenient.

Instance Methods

public void **checkAccept**(String host, int port) throws Security-Exception;

Checks whether a port may be accessed.

public void **checkAccess**(Thread g) throws SecurityException;

Checks whether the thread may be modified.

public void **checkAccess**(ThreadGroup g) throws SecurityException;

Checks whether the thread group may be modified.

public void **checkConnect**(String host, int port) throws SecurityException;

public void **checkConnect**(String host, int port, Object context) throws SecurityException;

Checks whether the specified port may be connected to. See also **getSecurityContext()**.

public void **checkCreateClassLoader**() throws SecurityException;

Checks whether the program may create a new class loader.

public void **checkDelete**(String file) throws SecurityException;

Checks whether the file may be deleted.

public void **checkExec**(String cmd) throws SecurityException;

Checks whether the file may be executed.

public void **checkExit**(int status) throws SecurityException;

Checks whether the program may call **exit()** with the specified status code.

public void **checkLink**(String lib) throws SecurityException;

Checks whether the program may dynamically load a library.

public void **checkListen**(int port) throws SecurityException;

Checks whether the program may wait for a connection request.

public void **checkPackageAccess**(String pkg) throws SecurityException;
public void **checkPackageDefinition**(String pkg) throws SecurityException;

Checks whether the program may load and define classes in the package, respectively.

public void **checkPropertiesAccess**() throws SecurityException;
public void **checkPropertyAccess**(String key) throws SecurityException;

Checks whether the program may use the systems properties table and access the specified property, respectively.

public void **checkRead**(FileDescriptor fd) throws SecurityException;
public void **checkRead**(String file) throws SecurityException;
public void **checkRead**(String file, Object context) throws SecurityException;

Checks whether the program may read the file. See also **getSecurityContext()**.

public void **checkSetFactory**() throws SecurityException;

Checks whether the program may set a socket factory or stream handler factory.

public boolean **checkTopLevelWindow**(Object window);

Returns **true** if the program is trusted to make the specified window visible.

public void **checkWrite**(FileDescriptor fd) throws SecurityException;

public void **checkWrite**(String file) throws SecurityException;

Checks whether the program may write to the file.

public boolean **getInCheck**();

Returns **true** if a security check is in progress.

public Object **getSecurityContext**();

Returns an object that encapsulates a security context. This object can be given as an argument to **checkConnect()** and **checkRead()**. If a trusted method is asked to open a socket or read a file on behalf of another method, that other method's security context is passed: the security manager needs to know whether that other method would be allowed to read or connect on its own.

SequenceInputStream Class

Full Name	**java.io.SequenceInputStream**
Extends	**InputStream->Object**
Description	Public class. Creates a single input stream from two or more separate input streams. As soon as the end of one stream is read, the next byte is read from the next stream in the sequence. This happens seamlessly so that the sequence is read as a single, unbroken stream.

Constructors

public **SequenceInputStream**(Enumeration e);
public **SequenceInputStream**(InputStream s1, InputStream s2);

Constructors. If an enumeration is specified, each object returned by the enumeration must be an **InputStream** object. (You can implement your own enumerations: see **Enumeration** interface.)

Overridden Instance Methods

public void **close**() throws IOException;
public int **read**() throws IOException;
public int **read**(byte buf[ ], int pos, int len) throws IOException;

These methods override method definitions in the **InputStream** class.

ServerSocket Class

Full Name	**java.net.ServerSocket**
Extends	**Object**
Description	Public final class. Creates an object that listens for a connection request from another machine. (The machine making the connection request is called a *client.*) To initiate listening, you call the **accept()** method. As soon as a connection is made, it returns a **Socket** object that you can use to communicate with the client.

The following example waits for a client computer to contact this computer (the server). Then the program establishes input and output streams to talk to the client. Port number 8189 is used, because it is not used by system devices.

```
try {
     ServerSocket server = new ServerSocket(8189);
     Socket client = server.accept();
     InputStream fromClient = client.getInputStream();
     OutputStream toClient = client.getOutputStream();
     // ...
     client.close();
} catch (IOException e) System.out.println(e);
```

In communicating with the client, usually it is easiest to use **DataInputStream** and **DataOutputStream** (or **PrintStream**) objects:

```
DataInputStream dis = new DataInputStream(fromClient);
PrintStream psToClient = new PrintStream(toClient);
psToClient.println("Greetings, client.");
```

Constructors

public **ServerSocket**(int port) throws IOException;
public **ServerSocket**(int port, int count) throws IOException;

Constructors. These constructors create a server socket around the specified local port (specifying 0 asks for the first free port). The optional **count** argument specifies a maximum number of client connection requests to store in a queue.

Class Methods

public static void **setSocketFactory**(SocketImplFactory fac) throws IOException, SocketException;

Specifies a new **SocketImplFactory** to use. Application code typically never calls this method. It is used by code that needs to modify the socket implementation for a particular platform.

Instance Methods

public Socket **accept**() throws IOException;

Initiates listening for a client connection request. The method does not return until a request is received. Returns a **Socket** object that can be used to send or receive data to the client.

public void **close**() throws IOException;

Closes the socket and frees the port.

public InetAddress **getInetAddress**();
public int **getLocalPort**();

These methods return the Internet address and the server's local port number, respectively.

Overridden Instance Methods

public String **toString()**;

Overrides method definition in the **Object** class.

SOCKET CLASS

Full Name	**java.net.Socket**
Extends	**Object**
Description	Public final class. Creates a socket, which is an object, built around a local port, that provides the ability to communicate with another machine. To perform i/o, you call **Socket** methods to get input and output streams. You read or write to these streams just as you would read or write to file streams. You can create a socket directly and use it as a client socket: this presumes that the other machine is a server that can listen to and respond to a request for a connection. You can also get a socket from the **ServerSocket** class: in this latter case, you use the socket to read and write data as a server.

The following example reads data from port 13 (the time indicator) of the server named **java.sun.com**.

```
try {
     Socket sock = new Socket("java.sun.com", 13);
     printInstream(sock.getInputStream());
} catch (IOException e) {System.out.println(e);}
```

This example assumes that **printInstream( )** is a method in your program that prints the contents of an input stream. Here is one way of writing such a method:

```
static void printInstream(InputStream in) throws
IOException {
     DataInputStream dis = new DataInputStream(in);
```

```
        String s = "";
        do {
            System.out.println(s);
            s = dis.readLine();
        } while (s != null);
}
```

Constructors

public **Socket**(InetAddress address, int port) throws IOException;
public **Socket**(InetAddress address, int port, boolean stream) throws IOException;
public **Socket**(String host, int port) throws IOException;
public **Socket**(String host, int port, boolean stream) throws IOException;

Constructors. You specify destination address and destination port (the local port is assigned for you). For specification of host, see **InetAddress** class. If the optional **stream** argument is **true**, then a connection-based protocol (TCP) that supports stream i/o is used. This is the default. If the argument is **false**, then the connectionless User Datagram Protocol is used.

Class Methods

public static void **setSocketImplFactory**(SocketImplFactory fac) throws IOException, SocketException;

Specifies a new **SocketImplFactory** to use. Application code typically never calls this method. It is used by code that needs to modify the socket implementation for a particular platform.

Instance Methods

public void **close**() throws IOException;

Closes the socket and frees the port.

public InetAddress **getInetAddress**();

Gets the **InetAddress** object that encapsulates the other machine's address.

public InputStream **getInputStream**() throws IOException;

Returns an input stream. You can use this stream to read data as you would any other input stream. Incoming data is read from the port.

public int **getLocalPort**();

Returns the local port being used by this socket.

public OutputStream **getOutputStream**() throws IOException;

Returns an output stream. You can use this stream to write data as you would any other input stream. Data written is sent to the machine on the other end of the network connection.

public int **getPort**();

Returns the port number in use by the other machine.

Overridden Instance Methods

public String **toString**();

Overrides method definition in the **Object** class.

SocketImpl Class

Full Name	**java.net.SocketImpl**
Extends	**Object**
Description	Abstract public class. Used internally. Application code rarely has any reason to use or subclass this class. **SocketImpl** implements a number of low-level native methods that support **Socket** objects. Once a **SocketImpl** subclass has been declared, it can be set by using the **SocketImplFactory** class. Generally, you would subclass only **SocketImpl** to deal with special low-level issues of a platform (such as firewalls).

SocketImpl declares a number of protected methods not listed here. See API documentation on the Java home page for a listing.

SocketImplFactory Interface

Full Name	**java.net.SocketImplFactory**
Description	Public interface. Most program code will never have a reason to use this interface. A **SocketImpl** factory returns a **SocketImpl** object when requested to do so by a socket. A **Socket** object sets a new **SocketImpl** factory when a factory object is passed to its **setSocketImplFactory()** method. In general, you should write a new socket implementation (**SocketImpl**) only if you need to adapt the implementation of sockets to deal with certain low-level platform issues (such as firewalls).

public abstract SocketImpl **createSocketImpl**();

Creates a new instance of a **SocketImpl** subclass and returns it.

Stack Class

Full Name	**java.util.Stack**
Extends	**Vector->Object**
Description	Public class. Creates a stack mechanism onto which you can push and pop any type of objects. A stack is a collection in which the main access is a last-in-first-out (LIFO) mechanism. Popping the stack returns the last item pushed onto the stack.

The following example creates a stack, pushes two strings, and pops the last one off. Note that the **pop( )** return value needs to be cast from **Object** to whatever type you're using (in this case, **String**).

```
Stack mystack = new Stack();
mystack.push("First item.");
mystack.push("Second item.");
String topOfStack = (String) mystack.pop();
```

Constructors

public **Stack**();.

Instance Methods

public boolean **empty**();

Returns **true** if the stack contains no objects.

public Object **peek**();
public Object **pop**();
public Object **push**(Object item);

These methods perform the peek, pop, and push operations. **peek()** returns the top object without removing it, whereas **pop()** both returns this object and removes it from the stack. **push()** places a new item on the top of the stack and returns that item. Remember to cast the return value of **push ( )**, as shown in the example.

public int **search**(Object o);

Returns 0-based position of the object from top of the stack, or –1 if the object is not found.

Statement Interface

Full Name	**java.sql.Statement**
Description	Public JDBC interface, providing the ability to execute any SQL statement supported by JDBC, including those that get result sets. The **PreparedStatement** and **CallableStatement** interfaces have some advantages but should be used with care, because they are not universally supported. As shown in the example,

you get a **Statement** object from a **Connection** object. You can then use the **Statement** object to execute any number of different SQL statements.

The following example uses a **Statement** object to add a row of data to the stuff table, which has two columns: **name** and **dat.** The **INSERT INTO** command string is broken up for convenience here.

```
Connection con = DriverManager.getConnection(dbname);
Statement stm = con.createStatement();
stm.executeUpdate("INSERT INTO stuff (name, dat) " +
    "VALUES ('os', 'win95')");
```

public void **cancel**() throws SQLException;

Interrupts execution of the current statement. This method can be called only from a thread that is separate from the one performing the execution.

public void **clearWarnings**() throws SQLException;

Clears the list of warnings so that the next call to **getWarnings()** returns **null**.

public void **close**() throws SQLException;

Closes the statement immediately, releasing all associated JDBC resources. Note that the Java garbage collector eventually closes the statement in any case.

public boolean **execute**(String sql) throws SQLException;
public ResultSet **executeQuery**(String sql) throws SQLException;
public int **executeUpdate**(String sql) throws SQLException;

All these statements execute the SQL statement contained by the specified string. The **execute()** method can execute a query that returns multiple result sets. In this case, use **getResultSet()** and **getMoreResults()** to navigate through the result sets.

public int **getMaxFieldSize**() throws SQLException;
public int **getMaxRows**() throws SQLException;

These methods get the maximum field size and number of rows, respectively. **getMaxFieldSize()** applies only to columns of type BINARY, VARBINARY, LONGVARBINARY, CHAR, VARCHAR, and LONGVARCHAR. 0 means unlimited field size.

public boolean **getMoreResults**() throws SQLException;

Advances through the list of result sets (see **execute()**), returning **true** if there is another result set. Call **getResultSet()** to get the result set itself.

public int **getQueryTimeout**() throws SQLException;

Gets the timeout value, in seconds. This is the maximum time allowed for the statement to execute.

public ResultSet **getResultSet**() throws SQLException;

Gets the next result set after a call to **execute()**. A **null** value indicates that the result is an integer and should be read by calling **getUpdateCount()**.

public int **getUpdateCount**() throws SQLException;

Returns the result of a query if it is an integer rather than a result set.

public SQLWarning **getWarnings**() throws SQLException;

Gets first warning. You can use the returned **SQLWarning** object to get additional warnings.

public void **setCursorName**(String name) throws SQLException;

Sets the name of the cursor; this determines the result-set cursor name.

public void **setEscapeProcessing**(boolean enable) throws SQLException;

If **true**, escape characters are processed before the SQL string is sent to the database.

public void **setMaxFieldSize**(int max) throws SQLException;
public void **setMaxRows**(int max) throws SQLException;

These methods set maximum field size and number of rows, respectively. See **getMaxFieldSize()**.

public void **setQueryTimeout**(int seconds) throws SQLException;

Sets the maximum number of seconds that the database driver will wait for a statement to execute. A value of 0 means no time limit.

StreamTokenizer Class

Full Name	**java.io.StreamTokenizer**
Extends	**Object**
Description	Public class. Creates an input stream with built-in support for tokenizing input. *Tokenizing* is the process of breaking text into words and symbols. This class is somewhat similar to **java.util.StringTokenizer** but is more sophisticated. Among other things, this class can interpret comments, quoted strings, and numbers. Generally, this class is most useful to people writing compilers, interpreters, and other programs that analyze complex input.

Instance Methods

public **StreamTokenizer**(InputStream I);

Constructor. Builds a **StreamTokenizer** object around the specified input stream.

Class Variables

public final static int **TT_EOF**;
public final static int **TT_EOL**;
public final static int **TT_NUMBER**;
public final static int **TT_WORD**;

Constants indicating type of input just read. **TT_EOF** and **TT_EOL** indicate end of file and end of line, respectively. **TT_NUMBER** indicates a number was read, and **TT_WORD** indicates a word.

public double **nval**;
public String **sval**;
public int **ttype;**

Instance variables that store temporary information used during tokenization. **nval** and **sval** store last number and string (word) just read, respectively. **ttype** is equal to one of the four **TT_*** constants or the value of an *ordinary character* (typically an operator or other nonword symbol).

Instance Methods

public void **commentChar**(int ch);

Recognizes specified character as end-of-line comment symbol in the stream. A forward slash (/) is a comment symbol by default.

public void **eolIsSignificant**(boolean flag);

If true, EOL is recognized as a token. If false, EOL is treated as a whitespace (the default).

public int **lineno**();

Returns number of current line read.

public void **lowerCaseMode**(boolean fl);

If true, tokens are converted to all-lowercase.

public int **nextToken**();

Returns the type of the next token. After a call to **nextToken()**, this value is available in the **ttype** field. Depending on ttype, the token's contents may be stored in **nval** or **sval**.

public void **ordinaryChar**(int ch);
public void **ordinaryChars**(int low, int hi);

The specified character (or all characters in the range) loses any special meaning and is treated as an ordinary character. When the character is read, it is treated as a one-character token, and **ttype** is set to the value of this character. Operators, for example, are usually ordinary characters. See also **wordChars()**.

public void **parseNumbers**();

Specifies that numbers are to be handled separately from words. Numeric data is stored in **nval**, and token type is **TT_NUMBER** instead of **TT_WORD**. This is the default condition.

public void **pushBack**();

Causes the next call to **nextToken()** to return the current value of the **ttype** field.

public void **quoteChar**(int ch);

Specifies a quotation mark symbol. When any quotation mark is encountered, all input up to the next occurrence of the same symbol is read into a string; **ttype** is set to **ch**, and the string is stored in **sval**. (See Class Variables.) By default, both single and double quotation marks are quote characters.

public void **resetSyntax**();

Resets the syntax table so that all characters are treated as ordinary characters. See **ordinaryChar()**.

public void **slashSlashComments**(boolean flag);
public void **slashStarComments**(boolean flag);

When **flag** is **true**, each of these methods enables recognition of C++ and C comment symbols, respectively. These symbols are not recognized by default.

public void **whitespaceChars**(int low, int hi);

Specifies that characters in the range **low** to **hi**, inclusive, are whitespace characters. By default, this includes standard whitespace characters such as space and tab.

public void **wordChars**(int low, int hi);

Specifies that the characters in the range **low** to **hi**, inclusive, are treated as word characters. A word consists of one of these characters followed by any combination of word characters and digits. By default, all letters are word characters.

Overridden Instance Methods

public String **toString**();

Overrides the method definition in the **Object** class.

STRING CLASS

Full Name	**java.lang.String**
Extends	**Object**
Description	Public final class. Represents a character string. Although there are other ways to represent a string, Java uses the **String** class as the standard format. String literals are translated into **String** objects by the Java compiler. A **String** object, once created, cannot change. This fact is usually not noticeable, for **String** operations constantly create new strings. But if you're going to do large amounts of string manipulation, consider using the **StringBuffer** class or an array of **char**. The final results can be translated back into **String** form. In addition to the many methods listed here, you can use the concatenation operator (**+**). The **String** class is unique in supporting its own operator.

The following example creates two strings—s1 and s2—containing the values "the end" and "THE END." The **equalsIgnoreCase( )** method returns the value **true** in this case.

```
String s1 = "the" + " " + "end";
String s2 = s1.toUpperCase();
System.out.println("Length of s1 is: " + s1.length());
if (s1.equalsIgnoreCase(s2))
    // ...
```

Constructors

public **String**();
public **String**(byte ascii[ ], int hibyte);
public **String**(byte ascii[ ], int hibyte, int offset, int count) throws StringIndexOutOfBoundsException;
public **String**(char value[ ]);
public **String**(char value[ ], int offset, int count) throws StringIndexOutOfBoundsException;
public **String**(String value);
public **String**(StringBuffer buffer);

Constructors. The string can be initialized from another string, from an ASCII array, from an array of **char** (Unicode), or from a **StringBuffer** object.

Class Methods

public static String **copyValueOf**(char data[ ]);
public static String **copyValueOf**(char data[ ], int offset, int count);

Class method. Returns the value of the **char** data as an equivalent **String** object.

public static String **valueOf**(boolean b);
public static String **valueOf**(char c);
public static String **valueOf**(char data[ ]);
public static String **valueOf**(char data[ ], int offset, int count);
public static String **valueOf**(double d);
public static String **valueOf**(float f);
public static String **valueOf**(int i);
public static String **valueOf**(long l);
public static String **valueOf**(Object obj);

Class methods. All these methods allocate new strings, initializing them from the argument data. Where the argument is numeric, **valueOf()** translates it into a string representation of the digits.

Instance Methods

public char **charAt**(int index) throws StringIndexOutOfBounds-Exception;

Returns the character at the zero-based index.

public int **compareTo**(String anotherString);

Returns 1, 0, or –1, depending on whether the current object is greater, equal to, or less than, respectively, the string argument. "Less than" means listed earlier in an alphabetical arrangement.

public String **concat**(String str);

Returns a new string that is the concatenation of the string argument onto the current string.

public boolean **endsWith**(String suffix);

Returns **true** if the last characters in the current string match the suffix.

public boolean **equalsIgnoreCase**(String anotherString);

Performs a comparison in which case is ignored: "true" equals "TRUE."

public void **getBytes**(int srcBegin, int srcEnd, byte dst[ ], int dstBegin);

public void **getChars**(int srcBegin, int srcEnd, char dst[ ], int dstBegin);

Copies characters from the current string to the destination location. **getBytes()** uses the eight low-order bits of the character.

public int **indexOf**(int ch);
public int **indexOf**(int ch, int fromIndex);
public int **indexOf**(String str);
public int **indexOf**(String str, int fromIndex);

Searches for first occurance of specified character or string. You can optionally specify where to begin the search. See also **lastIndexOf()** and **substring()**. Returns -1 if search target is not found.

public String **intern**();

Returns an identical string that is from a set of unique strings. No strings are repeated in this set. This means that if string1 and string2 have identical contents, then **string1.intern()** and **string2.intern()** refer to the same object in memory.

public int **lastIndexOf**(int ch);
public int **lastIndexOf**(int ch, int fromIndex);
public int **lastIndexOf**(String str);
public int **lastIndexOf**(String str, int fromIndex);

This method is the same as **indexOf()** except that the search starts at the back of the string and moves toward the front.

public int **length**();

Returns the number of characters in the string.

public boolean **regionMatches**(boolean ignoreCase, int toffset, String other, int ooffset, int len);
public boolean **regionMatches**(int toffset, String other, int ooffset, int len);

Compares a subset of the current string to a subset of **other**, the string argument. **toffset** is a zero-based index into this string, and **ooffset** is an index into **other**.

public String **replace**(char oldChar, char newChar);

Returns a new string created by replacing every occurrence of **oldChar** with **newChar**.

public boolean **startsWith**(String prefix);
public boolean **startsWith**(String prefix, int toffset);

Returns **true** if the first characters in the current string match **prefix**. You can optionally look for **prefix** starting at **toffset**, a zero-based index.

public String **substring**(int beginIndex);
public String **substring**(int beginIndex, int endIndex) throws StringIndexOutOfBoundsException;

Returns the substring at the specified zero-based index. If **endIndex** is not specified, **substring()** returns all the characters from **beginIndex** onward.

public char[ ] **toCharArray**();

Returns the **char** array equivalent to the current string.

public String **toLowerCase**();
public String **toUpperCase**();

Returns a new string made by converting the current string to all uppercase or all lowercase.

public String **trim**();

Returns a string created by removing all whitespace from the current string.

Overridden Instance Methods

public boolean **equals**(Object anObject);
public int **hashCode**();
public String **toString**();

These methods override method definitions in the **Object** class. **equals()** is especially useful for determining equality of contents. **toString()** returns a reference to the string; it does not clone a new string

StringBuffer Class

Full Name	**java.lang.String**
Extends	**Object**
Description	Public final class. This class is similar to the **String** class. The main difference is that **StringBuffer** objects can be internally modified. For example, **append()** adds characters to the end of the buffer and returns a reference to the current object—unlike **String.concat()**, which creates a completely new object. As with **Vector** objects, **StringBuffer** objects automatically grow as needed. When you are finished manipulating string data, you can efficiently convert back to string form by calling **StringBuffer.toString()** or a **String** constructor.

The following example uses a **StringBuffer** object to insert a word. The results are then converted back to **String** format.

```
StringBuffer strBuf = new StringBuffer("the end");
strBuf.insert(4, "living ");
String s = new String(strBuf);
```

Constructors

public **StringBuffer**();
public **StringBuffer**(int length);
public **StringBuffer**(String str);

Constructors. If a **length** argument is specified, it sets the initial capacity. (The buffer can grow beyond this capacity, but each capacity adjustment takes processor time.)

Instance Methods

public StringBuffer **append**(boolean b);
public StringBuffer **append**(char c);
public StringBuffer **append**(char str[ ]);
public StringBuffer **append**(double d);
public StringBuffer **append**(float f);
public StringBuffer **append**(int i);
public StringBuffer **append**(long l);
public StringBuffer **append**(Object obj);
public StringBuffer **append**(String str);

Appends a string, or string representation of the argument, onto the end of the current string. Returns a reference to the current object.

public int **capacity**();

Returns the current capacity of the string buffer.

public char **charAt**(int index);

Returns the character at the zero-based index. See also **setCharAt()**.

public void **ensureCapacity**(int minimumCapacity);

Ensures that the string buffer can store at least this many items.

public void **getChars**(int srcBegin, int srcEnd char dst[ ], int dstBegin);

Copies indicated characters from the string buffer (from **srcBegin** to **srcEnd**) into destination **char** array.

public StringBuffer **insert**(int offset, boolean b);
public StringBuffer **insert**(int offset, char c);
public StringBuffer **insert**(int offset, char str[ ]);
public StringBuffer **insert**(int offset, double d);
public StringBuffer **insert**(int offset, float f);
public StringBuffer **insert**(int offset, int i);
public StringBuffer **insert**(int offset, long l);
public StringBuffer **insert**(int offset, Object obj);
public StringBuffer **insert**(int offset, String str);

Inserts a substring into the middle of the string buffer using a string or a string representation of the specified argument. The offset is a zero-based index. Returns a reference to the current object.

public int **length**();

Returns the current length. This is not necessarily the same as capacity.

public StringBuffer **reverse**();

Reverses the order of all characters in the string. Returns a reference to the current object.

public void **setCharAt**(int index, char ch);

Changes the value of the character at the zero-based index.

public void **setLength**(int newLength);

Sets a new length. If this is greater than current length, the method pads the end of the string with **nulls**. If this is less than the current length, the method deletes characters at the end.

public String **toString**();

Overrides method definition in the **Object** class. This creates a **String** equivalent of the string buffer.

STRINGTOKENIZER CLASS

Full Name	**java.util.StringTokenizer**
Extends	**Object**
Implements	**Enumeration**
Description	Public class. Creates an object that breaks up contents of a string, returning one item at a time. Each item (called a *token*) is a series of characters surrounded by delimiters: in other words, a word, symbol, or number. For example, the string "Big Ugly Fish" contains three tokens. Delimiters include white space characters by default, but you can optionally specify a string that contains delimiter characters, See the constructors. Also, for a more powerful tokenizing class, see **StreamTokenizer** class.

The following example gets the contents of a text field, **Text1**, and then prints all the items in that text field, each on a separate line:

```
StringTokenizer st = new
     StringTokenizer(Text1.getText());
while(st.hasMoreTokens())
     System.out.println(st.nextToken());
```

Constructors

public **StringTokenizer**(String str);
public **StringTokenizer**(String str, String delim);
public **StringTokenizer**(String str, String delim, boolean returnTokens);

Constructors. The **returnTokens** argument, if **true**, causes the delimiters to be returned as tokens in addition to the items in between.

Instance Methods

public int **countTokens**();

Returns the number of tokens found.

public String **nextToken**() throws NoSuchElementException;
public String **nextToken**(String delim);

Gets the next token. You can optionally specify new delimiters, which affect tokenization of the remainder of the string.

public boolean **hasMoreTokens**();

Returns **true** if there are any remaining tokens in the string.

Overridden Instance Methods

public Object **nextElement**() throws NoSuchElementException;
public boolean **hasMoreElements**();

These methods implement methods in the **Enumeration** interface.

SYSTEM CLASS

Full Name	**java.lang.System**
Extends	**Object**
Description	Public final class. This class, along with **Runtime**, provides access to a number of useful system functions. Some methods appear in both classes: **exit()**, **gc()**, **load()**, and **loadLibrary()** respond by calling methods of the same name in **Runtime**. Especially useful are the class variables **err**, **in**, and **out**, which provide access to basic console i/o. The **System** class consists entirely of class fields, which are accessed as **System**.*variable* and **System**.*method*(). This class cannot be instantiated.

Class Variables

public static PrintStream **err**;
public static InputStream **in**;
public static PrintStream **out**;

Class objects. Each of these is a unique object available to the entire program. These objects provide access to system input, output, and error output.

Class Methods

public static void **arraycopy**(Object src, int src_position, Object dst, int dst_position, int length);

This is a general-purpose fast-copy routine. The **src** and **dst** arguments must be arrays of primitive data. Data areas may be part of the same array and may overlap.

public static long **currentTimeMillis**();

Returns the number of milliseconds since beginning of January 1, 1970, Greenwich Mean Time. Equivalent to (new Date()).getTime().

public static void **exit**(int status);

Causes the Java program to exit, passing the specified status code to the system.

public static void **gc**();

Requests that the garbage collector (which normally runs as a low-priority background process) be invoked right away to start destroying objects no longer used.

public static Properties **getProperties**();

Returns the system properties table.

public static String **getProperty**(String key);
public static String **getProperty**(String key, String def);

Looks up a property in the system properties table. If the property name is not found and if the **def** argument is specified in **getProperty()**, then **def** is returned.

public static SecurityManager **getSecurityManager**() throws SecurityException;

Returns a reference to the currently assigned security manager.

public static void **load**(String filename);
public static void **loadLibrary**(String libname);

Mainly used internally. These methods load native-code implementations. **load()** specifies a complete path name, whereas **loadLibrary()** relies on the system to search in the library directories.

public static void **runFinalization**();

Requests that the Java interpreter call the **finalize()** method for all objects that have been destroyed. Normally, an object's **finalize()** method may not necessarily be run right away.

public static void **setProperties**(Properties props);

Replaces the systems property table with the properties table specified in the argument. Note that this throws an exception if the security manager does not allow it.

public static void **setSecurityManager**(SecurityManager s);

Sets a security manager, throwing a **SecurityException** if a security manager is already assigned.

TextArea Class

Full Name	**java.awt.TextArea**
Extends	**TextComponent->Component->Object**
Description	Public class. Creates a multiline edit box. Remember that this class inherits all the methods of **TextComponent**, including the **setText()** and **getText()** methods. Consult **TextComponent** class if you can't find a method here. **TextArea** objects generate all standard keyboard and mouse events except **MOUSE_DOWN** and **MOUSE_UP**. A TextArea object may create an internal scroll bar, but it is not under programmer control.

The following example creates a text area with 10 rows, 50 columns, and initial text. Later, the contents are retrieved into a string variable, **multiLine**.

```
TextArea myTextBox = new TextArea("Some text", 10, 50);
add(myTextBox);    // Add to current applet or frame.
// ...
String multiLine = myTextBox.getText();
```

Constructors

public **TextArea**();
public **TextArea**(int rows, int cols);
public **TextArea**(String text);
public **TextArea**(String text, int rows, int cols);

Constructors. If rows and columns are not specified, the default is 0. This produces good results when the **TextArea** object is at the **Center** zone with a **BorderLayout** manager, because it results in the text area using all the space in the container. The default of 0 for rows and columns does not produce good results with **FlowLayout** manager.

Instance Methods

public void **appendText**(String str);

Appends the indicated string onto the end of the existing text.

public int **getColumns**();
public int **getRows**();

These methods get the number of visible columns and rows.

public void **insertText**(String str, int pos);

Inserts a text string into existing text at the zero-based position indicated. For example, pos of 0 means beginning of the string.

public Dimension **minimumSize**(int rows, int cols);
public Dimension **preferredSize**(int rows, int cols);

These methods return minimum and preferred size, given the number of visible rows and columns specified.

public void **replaceText**(String str, int start, int end);

Replaces the text between the two positions with the indicated string. The positions are zero-based indexes: see the **select()** method of the **TextComponent** class.

Overridden Instance Methods

public Dimension **minimumSize**();
public Dimension **preferredSize**();
public void **addNotify**();

Overrides method definition in the **Component** class.

TextComponent Class

Full Name	**java.awt.TextComponent**
Extends	**Component->Object**
Description	Public class that has no constructors and cannot be instantiated directly. This class contains common methods for the **TextField** and **TextArea** classes.

Instance Methods

public String **getSelectedText**();

Returns selected text, if any. This is the text that the user has highlighted.

public int **getSelectionEnd**();
public int **getSelectionStart**();

These methods get the ending and starting positions of the selected (highlighted) text. **getSelectionEnd()** returns the position of the last character inside the selection, so the methods return the same value—equal to current position—when no text is highlighted. If text is highlighted, the difference between the two values yields the number of characters selected. See **select( )**.

public String **getText**();

Returns the entire text contents of the object as a single string.

public boolean **isEditable**();

Returns **true** if the object is in the editable state. See **setEditable()**.

public void **select**(int selStart, int selEnd);
public void **selectAll**();

These methods set the selection highlight to the indicated positions and to the entire contents, respectively. The first version uses indexes. If the cursor sits in front (to the left) of the first character, the index of that position is zero. The index of the position in front of the second character is 1, and so on. Thus, select (0,1) selects the first character of the string; select (0,2) selects the first two.

public void **setEditable**(boolean t);

Sets the object to the editable state (**true**) or noneditable state (**false**). If it is editable (the default setting), the user can enter and delete text.

public void **setText**(String t);

Sets the entire text contents of the object to the specified string.

Overridden Instance Methods

public void **removeNotify**();

Overrides method definition in the **Component** class. Used internally.

TEXTFIELD CLASS

Full Name	**java.awt.TextField**
Extends	**TextComponent->Component->Object**
Description	Public class. Creates a single-line text-entry component. This class supports an optional echo-character feature for password protection. Remember that this class inherits all the **TextComponent** methods, which includes **setText()** and **getText()**. Consult **TextComponent** class if you can't find a method here. **TextField** objects generate the standard keyboard and mouse events except **MOUSE_DOWN** and **MOUSE_UP**. When the user presses **Return**, an **ACTION_EVENT** is generated, resulting in a call to the **action()** method. The second argument to **action()** is a string that contains the text contents.

The following example creates a text field with 50 columns and some initial text. Later, the contents are retrieved into a string variable, **theText**.

```
TextField myTextField = new TextField("Some text", 50);
add(myTextField);    // Add to current applet or frame.
// ...
String theText = myTextField.getText();
```

Constructors

public **TextField**();
public **TextField**(int cols);
public **TextField**(String text);
public **TextField**(String text, int cols);

Constructors. You can optionally specify starting text and width in columns. If you don't specify a width, the size is determined by the container's layout manager.

Instance Methods

public boolean **echoCharIsSet**();

Returns **true** if character echoing is in use. This condition is set by **setEchoCharacter()**, and it results in the same character being echoed no matter what is typed.

public int **getColumns**();

Returns the number of columns: this tells you how many characters can be visible at one time.

public char **getEchoChar**();

Returns the current echo character, if any. See **setEchoCharacter()**.

public Dimension **minimumSize**(int cols);
public Dimension **preferredSize**(int cols);

Returns minimum and preferred size of the text field object, given the specified number of columns.

public void **setEchoCharacter**(char c);

Sets an echo character, which causes the same character to be echoed as the user types. For example, if "*" is the echo character, then "*" appears in response to each keystroke rather than the character typed. The typical use of this feature is for password entry.

Overridden Instance Methods

public void **addNotify**();
public Dimension **minimumSize**();
public Dimension **preferredSize**();

These methods override method definitions in the **Component** class. **addNotify()** is used internally.

THREAD CLASS

Full Name	**java.lang.Thread**
Extends	**Object**

Implements	**Runnable**
Description	Public class. Creates independent threads of execution: these are tasks that run concurrently with the program's main thread. One of the most important methods is **start()**, which causes the thread to start executing the **run()** method of the target object. This object is specified in the **Thread** constructor. Other methods include **stop()**, **suspend()**, **resume()**, **sleep()**, and **join()**, which waits for another thread to terminate. See Chapter 5, "Animation and Threads," for an introduction to threads.

The following example starts a background thread (**bkgrnd**) and puts the current thread to sleep:

```
// When bkgrnd starts, it will use run() from THIS class.
Thread bkgrnd = new Thread(this);
//...
bkgrnd.start();
try {Thread.sleep(500);}  // Sleep for .5 secs.
catch (InterruptedException e){;}
```

Constructors

public **Thread**();
public **Thread**(Runnable target);
public **Thread**(Runnable target, String name);
public **Thread**(String name);
public **Thread**(ThreadGroup group, Runnable target);
public **Thread**(ThreadGroup group, Runnable target, String name);
public **Thread**(ThreadGroup group, String name);

Constructors. The target is an object whose class implements the **Runnable** interface. When the thread starts, the **run()** method of target's class is called. If no target is specified, then the **run()** method of the thread itself is used. Although **Thread.run()** does nothing, you can subclass **Thread** and override the **run()** method. You can optionally give a name to the thread.

Class Variables

public final static int **MAX_PRIORITY** = 10;
public final static int **MIN_PRIORITY** = 1;
public final static int **NORM_PRIORITY** = 5;

Constants. These constants indicate the maximum, minimum, and average priority level. You can set priority level for a thread by calling its **setPriority()** method.

Class Methods

public static int **activeCount**();
public static Thread **currentThread**();
public static void **dumpStack**();
public static int **enumerate**(Thread tarray[]);

Class methods, all applying to the currently executing thread. **activeCount()** returns the number of active threads in the thread group, **currentThread()** returns a reference to the thread, **dumpStack()** prints a stack trace, and **enumerate()** gets all the threads in the thread group.

public static void **sleep**(long millis) throws InterruptedException;
public static void **sleep**(long millis, int nanos) throws InterruptedException;

Class method. Causes current thread to wait for the specified time.

public static void **yield**();

Class method. Temporarily pauses and lets other threads execute.

Instance Methods

public void **checkAccess**() throws SecurityException;

Throws an exception if the security manager does not allow access to this thread.

public int **countStackFrames**() throws IllegalThreadStateException;

Returns the number of stack frames in this thread (useful for debugging purposes). The thread must be suspended, or else an exception is thrown.

public final String **getName**();
public final int **getPriority**();
public final ThreadGroup **getThreadGroup**();

These methods return basic information about the attributes of the thread.

public final boolean **isAlive**();

Returns **true** if the thread is alive. A live thread is one that has been started and has not died.

public final boolean **isDaemon**();

Returns **true** if the thread is a daemon. Daemon threads exist only to support other threads. The Java interpreter stops executing when the only live threads are daemons. See also **setDaemon()**.

public final void **join**() throws InterruptedException;
public final void **join**(long millis) throws InterruptedException;
public final void **join**(long millis, int nanos) throws InterruptedException;

The thread that calls this method waits until this thread (the thread through which **join** was called) dies: for example, "thread1.join()" means pause until thread1 dies. A maximum waiting time may be specified.

public final void **resume**();

If the thread is in a suspended state, it now resumes running.

public void **run**();

This method implements the **Runnable** interface. Does nothing, but subclasses may override it.

public final void **setDaemon**(boolean on) throws IllegalThread-StateException;
public final void **setName**(String name);
public final void **setPriority**(int newPriority) throws Illegal-ArgumentException;

These methods set the daemon condition, name, and thread priority. See also is**Daemon()**.

public void **start**() throws IllegalThreadStateException;

Starts thread execution. Response is to spin off the thread by executing the **run()** method implemented by the target object. (See **Thread** constructors.)

public final void **stop**();
public final void **stop**(Throwable obj);

Abruptly terminates execution of the thread. The argument, if specified, is an exception that the thread throws. If no argument is specified, **stop()** generates a **ThreadDeath** exception. Note that threads may also terminate normally because their **run()** method completes execution. **stop()** interrupts the thread in the middle of whatever it is doing.

public final void **suspend**();

Temporarily suspends thread execution. Thread resumes execution when **resume()** is called.

public String **toString**();

Overrides method definition in the **Object** class.

ThreadGroup Class

Full Name	**java.lang.ThreadGroup**
Extends	**Object**
Description	Public class. A **ThreadGroup** object is useful for operating on a set of related threads. Several of the **ThreadGroup** methods return a **SecurityException**; this exception is generated when the security manager does not permit the currently executing thread to make the requested change. Note that thread groups may be nested inside each other.

Constructors

public **ThreadGroup**(String name);
public **ThreadGroup**(ThreadGroup parent, String name) throws NullPointerException;

Constructors. The thread group may be made the child of another thread group.

Instance Methods

public int **activeCount**();
public int **activeGroupCount**();

Returns the number of active threads in the group (plus all child groups) and the number of active child thread groups (plus all their descendants), respectively.

public final void **checkAccess**() throws SecurityException;

Throws an exception if the security manager does not allow access to this thread group.

public final void **destroy**() throws IllegalThreadStateException;

Destroys the contents of the thread group and all child groups (nested to any level). An exception is thrown if there is an active thread in the group.

public int **enumerate**(Thread list[ ]);
public int **enumerate**(Thread list[ ], boolean recurse);
public int **enumerate**(ThreadGroup list[ ]);
public int **enumerate**(ThreadGroup list[ ], boolean recurse);

Copies all active threads, or all active thread groups, into an array. Use **activeCount()** or **activeGroupCount()** to determine how big the array needs to be.

public final int **getMaxPriority**();

Gets the maximum priority permitted in this group. See also **setMaxPriority()**.

public final String **getName**();
public final ThreadGroup **getParent**();
public final boolean **isDaemon**();

These methods return basic information about the thread group. A daemon thread group is automatically destroyed when its last thread has stopped. See also **setDaemon()**.

public void **list**();

Prints information useful for debugging purposes.

public final boolean **parentOf**(ThreadGroup g);

Returns **true** if this thread group is the parent of the specified group, g.

public final void **resume**() throws SecurityException;

Causes all threads in the group that have stopped to resume operation.

public final void **setDaemon**(boolean daemon) throws SecurityException;

Sets the daemon condition on or off: A daemon thread group is automatically destroyed when its last thread has stopped.

public final void **setMaxPriority**(int pri) throws SecurityException;

Sets the maximum priority for threads in the group. Does not affect threads that already have a higher priority.

public final void **stop**() throws SecurityException;

Stops all threads in the group.

public final void **suspend**()throws SecurityException;

Suspends all threads in the group.

public void **uncaughtException**(Thread t, Throwable e);

Responds to an uncaught exception that stops one of the threads in the group. The default response is to do nothing if the exception is **ThreadDeath** but otherwise to call **e.printStackTrace()**. You can override this method to specify different behavior.

Overridden Instance Methods

public String **toString**();

Overrides the method definition in the **Object** class.

Throwable Class

Full Name	**java.lang.Throwable**
Extends	**Object**
Description	Public class. This is the ancestor class for all exception classes. The methods defined in this class (which are all inherited by every exception class) are useful for debugging purposes.

Constructors

public **Throwable**();
public **Throwable**(String message);

These constructors are rarely used, because **Throwable** is not often instantiated directly.

Instance Methods

public Throwable **fillInStackTrace**();

Fills in the stack trace and returns the exception, which is convenient if you rethrow it. "Fills in" means that if and when a stack trace is printed (see **printStackTrace()**), previous exceptions are not reported, and a new exception is reported at the line of code that calls **fillInStackTrace()**.

public String **getMessage**();

Gets the error-message text associated with the exception.

public void **printStackTrace**();
public void **printStackTrace**(PrintStream s);

Prints a stack trace, optionally sending the output to a specified print stream. A stack trace lists each program location that threw or passed along an exception.

public String **toString**();

Overrides the method definition in the **Object** class. The string representation generally identifies the particular exception class.

Time Class

Full Name	**java.sql.Time**
Extends	**java.util.Date->Object**
Description	Public JDBC class. This class inherits from the Java core Date class but uses only those fields (hours, minutes, seconds) needed to represent the SQL type TIME. See also Timestamp class, which measures time to the nanosecond.

Constructors

public **Time**(int hour, int minute, int second);

Constructs a **Time** object using values in the ranges 0 to 23 (hour) and 0 to 59 (minutes and seconds).

Class Methods

public static Time **valueOf**(String s);

Returns a **Time** object from a string in the format "hh:mm:ss."

Instance Methods

public String **toString**();

Returns a string that contains the time value formatted as "hh:mm:ss."

Timestamp Class

Full Name	**java.sql.Timestamp**
Extends	**java.util.Date->Object**

Description	Public JDBC class. Extends the Java core **Date** class to include nanoseconds. This enables the class to be used for timestamps of extremely high precision required in database operations. Depending on the platform, the database may or may not support precision to the nanosecond; if it doesn't, values are rounded as appropriate.

Constructors

public **Timestamp**(int year, int month, int date, int hour, int minute, int second, int nano);

Constructs a **Timestamp** object using the following arguments: **year** is **year** – 1900; **month** ranges from 0 to 11; **date** ranges from 0 to 31; **hour** ranges from 0 to 23; **minute** and **second** range from 0 to 59; and **nano** (nanoseconds) ranges from 0 to 999,999,999.

Class Methods

public static Timestamp **valueOf**(String s);

Creates a **Timestamp** object from a string in the format "yyyy-mm-dd hh:mm:ss.f." Here, "f" represents a fraction: 0.1 seconds results in a setting of 100,000,000 for nanoseconds.

Instance Methods

public boolean **equals**(Timestamp ts);

Returns **true** if the two objects have equal contents; all fields must match.

public int **getNanos**();
public void **setNanos**(int n);

These methods get and set the value for the nanoseconds field.

public String **toString**();

Returns a string representation in the format "yyyy-mm-dd hh:mm:ss.f." See **valueOf()**.

TOOLKIT CLASS

Full Name	**java.awt.Toolkit**
Extends	**Object**
Description	Abstract public class. A Toolkit object provides a link to platform-dependent graphics. The getImage() method, like its counterpart in the Applet class, is useful for loading image files. The Toolkit class also has methods that return information on fonts and screen-display characteristics. Because this class is abstract, you cannot instantiate it directly; however, you can call Component.getToolkit().

The following example uses the **Toolkit** class to supply a **getImage( )** method for applications. It is similar to the **Applet.getImage( )** method that loads image files.

```
Toolkit tk = Toolkit.getDefaultToolkit();
// ...
Image getImage(String filename) {
     return tk.getImage(filename)
}
Image getImage(URL url) {
     return tk.getImage(url)
}
```

Class Methods

public static Toolkit **getDefaultToolkit**();

Because this method is a class method, you can always call it directly (but remember the class prefix). Returns a reference to the current toolkit in use.

Instance Methods

public abstract int **checkImage**(Image image, int width, int height, ImageObserver observer);

Returns the status of image loading using the same return flags that the **ImageObserver** class uses. This method is mostly for internal use. Applications and applets should usually use a **MediaTracker** object instead.

public abstract Image **createImage**(ImageProducer producer);

Used internally. To get an **Image** object, you should use **getImage()** or **Component.createImage()** instead. The latter is used for off-screen buffering.

public abstract ColorModel **getColorModel**();
public abstract String[ ] **getFontList**();

These methods return the color model and list of fonts supported on the current platform. The color model is mainly for internal use. It is used to translate RGB colors into the system's own color scheme if necessary.

public abstract FontMetrics **getFontMetrics**(Font font);

Returns a **FontMetrics** object for the specified font.

public abstract Image **getImage**(String filename);
public abstract Image **getImage**(URL url);

Returns an **Image** object that contains instructions for loading an image file from disk or a network site. Actual loading is initiated by calling **Graphics.drawImage()**.

public abstract int **getScreenResolution**();
public abstract Dimension **getScreenSize**();

These methods return information about the current platform. The screen resolution is returned in number of dots per inch.

public abstract boolean **prepareImage**(Image image, int width, int height, ImageObserver observer);

Used internally, by **Component.prepareImage()**. You probably never need to call this method yourself.

public abstract void **sync()**;

Ensures that the screen image is completely up-to-date. This is sometimes useful because some graphics methods may use buffering of screen data.

Types Class

Full Name	**java.sql.Types**
Extends	**Object**
Description	Public class. This class consists strictly of a set of constants: each constant is an ordinal number specifying a type recognized by JDBC. Several classes, such as ResultSetMetaData, use these constants to indicate what type of data is stored in a particular column. Note that there is no reason to instantiate this class, because it consists only of class variables (which are all constants). See Table K in Part VI for more information on JDBC data types.

Class Variables

public final static int **BIGINT**;
public final static int **BINARY**;
public final static int **BIT**;
public final static int **CHAR**;
public final static int **DATE**;
public final static int **DECIMAL**;
public final static int **DOUBLE**;
public final static int **FLOAT**;
public final static int **INTEGER**;
public final static int **LONGVARBINARY**;
public final static int **LONGVARCHAR**;
public final static int **NUMERIC**;

public final static int **NULL**;
public final static int **OTHER**;
public final static int **REAL**;
public final static int **SMALLINT**;
public final static int **TIME**;
public final static int **TIMESTAMP**;
public final static int **TINYINT**;
public final static int **VARCHAR**;
public final static int **VARBINARY**;

URL CLASS

Full Name	**java.net.URL**
Extends	**Object**
Description	Public final class. A URL object represents a uniform resource locator (URL) and can be used to download data from the Web page that the URL identifies. The **URL** class is a relatively simple mechanism for downloading information. For more complete control over the communication channel, you can use a **URLConnection** object, which you can get by calling **openConnection()**. Some of the most common URL methods are **getContent()** and **openStream()**, which perform downloading.

The easiest way to specify a URL is to use a single string. For example:

```
URL u = new
URL("http://java.sun.com/products/apiOverview.html");
```

This string combines the following substrings: protocol ("http"), host ("java.sun.com"), and file ("products/apiOverview.html"). These elements could have been specified separately. The protocol "http" means Hypertext Transport Protocol.

Instance Methods

public **URL**(String spec) throws MalformedURLException;
Constructor specifying the URL location as a single string.

public **URL**(String protocol, String host, int port, String file) throws MalformedURLException;
public **URL**(String protocol, String host, String file) throws MalformedURLException;

Constructors specifying the protocol, host, and file separately: these make up parts of the URL specification string, as explained earlier. If no destination port is specified, the http default (80) is assumed.

public **URL**(URL context, String spec) throws MalformedURL-Exception;

Constructor specifying a relative spec. The missing information is supplied by the **context** argument. For example, **spec** might specify only the file portion of the URL.

Class Methods

public static void **setURLStreamHandlerFactory**(URLStream-HandlerFactory fac) throws Error;

Class method. Sets the stream handler factory. Normal program code rarely calls this method.

Instance Methods

public final Object **getContent**() throws IOException;

Downloads the URL contents as a Java object.

public String **getFile**();
public String **getHost**();
public int **getPort**();
public String **getProtocol**();

These methods get information specified in the constructor.

public String **getRef**();

Returns the reference (or anchor) of this URL. This suffix is used in some URL specifications and is preceded by a pound sign (#). The reference acts as a tag that identifies a particular part of the file.

public URLConnection **openConnection**() throws IOException;

Returns a **URLConnection** object for this URL.

public final InputStream **openStream**() throws IOException;

Returns an input stream that can be used to read the location. This presumes the location is a file.

public boolean **sameFile**(URL other);

Returns **true** if the URL argument refers to the same host, port, and file as this URL.

public String **toExternalForm**();

Returns a string representation of this URL.

Overridden Instance Methods

public boolean **equals**(Object obj);
public int **hashCode**();
public String **toString**();

These methods override method definitions in the **Object** class.

URLCONNECTION CLASS

Full Name	**java.net.URLConnection**
Extends	**Object**
Description	Abstract public class. You cannot directly instantiate this class, but you can get an instance by calling the **openConnection()** method of the URL class. This class can be used to download information from an Internet location, and it supports a much larger set of methods than **URL**. Some of these methods are

of interest to only a few programmers, although **getInputStream()** and **getOutputStream()** are often useful, as are the date/time methods **getLastModified()** and **setIfModifiedSince()**.

Class Methods

public static boolean **getDefaultAllowUserInteraction**();
public static void **setDefaultAllowUserInteraction**(boolean defaultallowuserinteraction);

Class methods. These methods get and set the default value of the **AllowUserInteraction** setting. See **getAllowUserInteraction()**.

public static String **getDefaultRequestProperty**(String key);
public static void **setDefaultRequestProperty**(String key, String value);

Class methods. These methods get and set default values for properties downloaded from the URL.

public static void **setContentHandlerFactory**(ContentHandler-Factory fac) throws Error;

Class method. Sets the content handler factory. Normal program code rarely calls this method.

Instance Methods

public abstract void **connect**();

Opens a communications link for the URL. No effect if connection has already been made.

public boolean **getAllowUserInteraction**();

If **true**, the context allows user interaction such as responding to a dialog box.

public Object **getContent**() throws IOException, UnknownServiceException;

Downloads the URL contents as a Java object.

public String **getContentEncoding**();

Returns the content-encoding string for the URL, or **null** if it is not known.

public int **getContentLength**();

Returns the length of the URL resource, or –1 if it is not known.

public String **getContentType**();

Returns a string describing the content type, or **null** if it is not known.

public long **getDate**();

Returns the sending date of the URL resource as the number of milliseconds since the beginning of January 1, 1970, GMT.

public boolean **getDefaultUseCaches**();

If **true**, the protocol uses caches as often as possible.

public boolean **getDoInput**();
public boolean **getDoOutput**();

These methods return **true** if the respective i/o operation is allowed. The default is to enable input but not output.

public long **getExpiration**();

Returns the expiration date as the number of milliseconds since beginning of January 1, 1970, GMT.

public String **getHeaderField**(int n);
public String **getHeaderField**(String name);

Returns the value of the specified header field.

public long **getHeaderFieldDate**(String name, long Default);
public int **getHeaderFieldInt**(String name, int Default);

Returns the numeric value of the specified header field, returning **Default** if the field is missing.

public String **getHeaderFieldKey**(int n);

Returns the key for the nth header field.

public long **getIfModifiedSince**();

Returns the value of the **ifModifiedSince** field. If this is nonzero, it indicates a timestamp: data is fetched only if it has a timestamp later than this date. Time is measured in milliseconds since beginning of January 1, 1970, GMT.

public InputStream **getInputStream**() throws IOException, UnknownServiceException;

Returns an input stream for reading data from the URL location. Data is read as if from a file.

public long **getLastModified**();

Returns a timestamp giving the time of last modification of the URL resource.

public OutputStream **getOutputStream**() throws IOException, UnknownServiceException;

Returns an output stream for writing data to the URL location. Data is written as if to a file.

public String **getRequestProperty**(String key);

Gets the value of the requested property.

public URL **getURL**();

Returns the associated URL object for this connection.

public boolean **getUseCaches**();

If true, Java is enabled to use caches for reading and writing to the URL connection. If false, Java is required to reload after each read or write. You can set this condition with setUseCaches().

public void **setAllowUserInteraction**(boolean allowuserinteraction);
public void **setDefaultUseCaches**(boolean defaultusecaches);
public void **setDoInput**(boolean doinput);
public void **setDoOutput**(boolean dooutput);
public void **setIfModifiedSince**(long ifmodifiedsince);
public void **setRequestProperty**(String key, String value);
public void **setUseCaches**(boolean usecaches);

These methods set the value of various properties. See the corresponding "get" methods.

public String **toString**();

Overrides method definition in the **Object** class.

URLENCODER CLASS

Full Name	**java.net.URLEncoder**
Extends	**Object**
Description	Public class. A **URLEncoder** object supports a method that translates URL strings into a standard, internationally accepted form. Note that you cannot instantiate this class, but you don't need to, because its one method is a class method.

Class Methods

public static String **encode**(String s);

Returns a string that has the same content as the argument but is translated into URL canonical form. This form restricts characters to an internationally accepted (and hence portable) subset of ASCII. The method converts each space to a plus sign (+) and converts each non-alphanumeric character (other than the underscore) into the form %XX, where XX is two hexadecimal digits.

URLStreamHandler Class

Full Name	**java.net.URLStreamHandler**
Extends	**Object**
Description	Abstract public class. Mainly used internally. You would use this class (by subclassing it) only if writing a Web browser that used a different scheme for interpreting a URL and setting up a connection. Most program code will never have reason to subclass or use this class in any way. This class is used with **URLStreamHandlerFactory**.

Instance Methods

protected abstract URLConnection **openConnection**(URL u) throws IOException;
protected void **parseURL**(URL u, String spec, int start, int limit);
protected void **setURL**(URL u, String protocol, String host, int port, String file, String ref);
protected String **toExternalForm**(URL u);

URLStreamHandlerFactory Interface

Full Name	**java.net.URLStreamHandlerFactory**
Description	Public interface. Most program code will never have any reason to use this interface in any way. A stream handler factory returns a stream handler when requested to do so by a **URL**. A **URL** object sets a stream handler factory when a factory object is passed to its **setStreamHandlerFactory()** method.

public abstract URLStreamHandler **URLStreamHandler**(String protocol);

Returns a stream handler for the named protocol. This stream handler is an instance of a **StreamHandler** subclass.

VECTOR CLASS

Full Name	**java.util.Vector**
Extends	**Object**
Implements	**Cloneable**
Description	Public class. A vector object is similar to an array but is more flexible: a vector automatically grows as new members are needed. You can also call **trimToSize()** to trim a vector when desired, so that it gets rid of excess capacity. Vectors have a wealth of other useful functions for adding, removing, and deleting elements.Vectors have one major limitation in comparison to arrays: elements must be objects and not primitive data. Consequently, types such as **int** must first be converted to a wrapper-class equivalent (in this case, **Integer**). Strings, however, are objects and can be added directly.

The following example creates a vector, adds three elements, and then returns the first element. Note that the return value of **elementAt( )** needs to be cast from **Object** to whatever type you're using (in this case, **String**).

```
Vector vec = new Vector();
vec.addElement("Here is a string.");
vec.addElement("'Nuther string.");
vec.addElement("Third string.");
String firstElem = (String) vec.elementAt(0);
```

Constructors

public **Vector**();
public **Vector**(int initialCapacity);
public **Vector**(int initialCapacity, int capacityIncrement);

Constructors. You can optionally specify the initial capacity and the amount by which capacity grows each time it is exceeded.

Instance Methods

public final void **addElement**(Object obj);

Adds the specified element to the vector.

public final int **capacity**();

Returns the current capacity. Remember, this is increased whenever the number of elements exceeds it.

public final boolean **contains**(Object elem);

Returns **true** if the specified object is currently an element of the vector.

public final void **copyInto**(Object anArray[]);

Copies the contents of the vector into an array.

public final Object **elementAt**(int index) throws ArrayIndexOutOfBoundsException;

Returns the element at the specified zero-based index. The return value must usually be cast to a particular type.

public final Enumeration **elements**();

Returns the contents of the vector into an enumeration. See **Enumeration** interface.

public final void **ensureCapacity**(int minCapacity);

Ensures that the vector can store at least this number of items.

public final Object **firstElement**() throws NoSuchElementException;

Returns the first element in the vector. See also **elementAt()** and **lastElement()**.

public final int **indexOf**(Object elem);
public final int **indexOf**(Object elem, int index);

Searches the vector for the specified element and returns its zero-based index, optionally starting at a specified index. Returns –1 if the item is not found.

public final void **insertElementAt**(Object obj, int index) throws ArrayIndexOutOfBoundsException;

Inserts a new element at the specified position (a zero-based index), bumping the elements that follow it up by one index. See also **setElementAt()**.

public final boolean **isEmpty**();

Returns **true** if the vector contains no elements.

public final Object **lastElement**() throws NoSuchElementException;

Returns the last element. See also **firstElement()** and **elementAt()**.

public final int **lastIndexOf**(Object elem);
public final int **lastIndexOf**(Object elem, int index);

Similar to **indexOf()** except that the search starts at the back and moves toward the front.

public final void **removeAllElements**();
public final boolean **removeElement**(Object obj);
public final void **removeElementAt**(int index) throws ArrayIndex-OutOfBoundsException;

These methods remove the specified element or elements. If an individual element is removed, indexes of elements that follow it are shifted down by one.

public final void **setElementAt**(Object obj, int index) throws ArrayIndexOutOfBoundsException;

Replaces the specified item with a new value. Indexes are zero-based.

public final void **setSize**(int newSize);

Sets a new size. If this is greater than the current size, the method pads the end of the vector with **null** items. If this is less than the current size, the method deletes items at the end.

public final int **size**();

Returns the number of elements.

public final void **trimToSize**();

Reduces the capacity of the vector to that of the number of elements. This maximizes storage efficiency.

Overridden Instance Methods

public Object **clone**();
public final String **toString**();

These methods override method definitions in the **Object** class.

WINDOW CLASS

Full Name	**java.awt.Window**
Extends	**Container->Component->Object**
Description	Public class. Although the class can be used directly, its child classes—**Frame** and **Dialog**—are much more commonly used. The **Frame** class adds visible borders and a menu bar and is actually closer to the common notion of "window."

Constructors

public **Window**(Frame parent);

Constructor. Creates a window that has a default **BorderLayout** manager.

Instance Methods

public synchronized void **dispose**();

Closes the window and releases all its resources. Note that unlike most Java resources, windows are not automatically destroyed by the garbage collector; this is because windows are maintained by the native window manager. You must explicitly call **dispose( )** to remove a window.

public final String **getWarningString( )**;

Returns the warning string that is displayed when there is a **SecurityManager** object and it determines that the current window is insecure.

public synchronized void **pack( )**;

Lays out child components in their preferred size.

public void **toBack( )**;
public void **toFront( )**;

These methods move the window to the front or back of the layers of visible windows.

Overridden Instance Methods

public synchronized void **addNotify( )**;
public Toolkit **getToolkit( )**;
public synchronized void **show( )**;

These methods override method definitions in **Component**. The **show( )** method is particularly useful for windows: it displays the window and moves it to the front of other windows.

PART VI

USEFUL TABLES

This part of the book is divided into four sections: event tables, graphics tables, text-handling tables, and miscellaneous tables.

Event Tables

Interpretation of an **Event** object and event-handling arguments can be complex, because the precise meaning of an event or an argument differs from one context to the next. The tables in this section help clarify the meaning of events and event arguments.

Table A describes the meaning of each possible event type, according to the event ID. The third column shows the method that **handleEvent()** calls, if any. If none is shown, it means that to respond to the event, you must override **handleEvent()** itself. Take extra care when overriding this method, as mentioned in Chapter 4, "Components and Events."

Table A *Events by ID and object type*

Event ID	Type of Object That May Generate Event	Description of Event and Method Called by handleEvent, If Any
ACTION_EVENT	Button	User clicked the button. `action(evt, label);`
ACTION_EVENT	Checkbox	User clicked the checkbox. `action(evt, boolean_state);`
ACTION_EVENT	Choice	User selected an item. `action(evt, label);`
ACTION_EVENT	List	User double-clicked an item. `action(evt, label);`

continued

Table A Events by ID and object type, continued

Event ID	Type of Object That May Generate Event	Description of Event and Method Called by handleEvent, If Any
ACTION_EVENT	MenuItem	User clicked a menu item. `action(evt, label);`
ACTION_EVENT	TextField	User pressed **Return**. `action(evt, text_contents);`
GOT_FOCUS	All components	Component has just received focus. `gotFocus(evt, null);`
KEY_ACTION	All components	User pressed a function key. Second argument is an Event class keycode. `keyDown(evt, key);`
KEY_ACTION_RELEASE	All components	User released the function key. `keyUp(evt, key);`
KEY_PRESS	All components	User pressed a nonfunction key. Second argument is a Unicode character value. `keyDown(evt, key);`
KEY_RELEASE	All components	User released a non-function key. `keyUp(evt, key);`
LIST_DESELECT	List	User removed selection from a list item: Event's **arg** field contains the zero-based index of item.
LIST_SELECT	List	User selected a list item: Event's **arg** field contains the zero-based index of item. This is not the same action as double-clicking

continued

Table A Events by ID and object type, continued

EVENT ID	TYPE OF OBJECT THAT MAY GENERATE EVENT	DESCRIPTION OF EVENT AND METHOD CALLED BY HANDLEEVENT, IF ANY
LOST_FOCUS	All components	Component is just about to lose focus. `gotFocus(evt, null);`
MOUSE_DOWN	Panels, windows, Canvas	User pressed a mouse button `mouseDown(evt, x, y);`
MOUSE_DRAG	All components	User dragged the mouse. `mouseDrag(evt, x, y);`
MOUSE_ENTER	All components	User just moved mouse into component's area. `mouseDown(evt, x, y);`
MOUSE_EXIT	All components	User just moved mouse out of component's area: x and y are last coordinates before leaving. `mouseDrag(evt, x, y);`
MOUSE_MOVE	All components	During a mouse move, this event is generated at small but nonzero time intervals. `mouseDown(evt, x, y);`
MOUSE_UP	Panels, windows, Canvas	User released a mouse button. `mouseDrag(evt, x, y);`
SCROLL_ABSOLUTE	Scrollbar	User moved scroll-bar indicator directly. Event's **arg** field gives value of new position.
SCROLL_LINE_DOWN	Scrollbar	User scrolled down one line. Event's **arg** field gives value of new position.
SCROLL_LINE_UP	Scrollbar	User scrolled up one line. Event's **arg** field gives value of new position.
SCROLL_PAGE_DOWN	Scrollbar	User clicked on the bar below the indicator. Event's **arg** field gives value of new position.

continued

Table A Events by ID and object type, continued

Event ID	Type of Object That May Generate Event	Description of Event and Method Called by handleEvent, If Any
SCROLL_PAGE_UP	Scrollbar	User clicked on the bar above the indicator. Event's **arg** field gives value of new position.
WINDOW_DESTROY	All windows	User is requesting the window be closed (for example, by clicking the window-close button on the system bar).
WINDOW_EXPOSE	All windows	Window is now visible.
WINDOW_DEICONIFY	All windows	User restored window from an icon state. (Not typically supported on Mac platforms.)
WINDOW_ICONIFY	All windows	User iconized the window. (Not typically supported on Mac platforms.)
WINDOW_MOVED	All windows	User has moved the window.

Note that in this table, as well as Table B, "windows" includes all components derived from the **Window** class; this includes components of the **Frame** and **Dialog** classes.

Table B summarizes the events that each type of component can get. Note that **MOUSE_UP** and **MOUSE_DOWN** events are swallowed by most types of components: these events are either translated as **ACTION_EVENT** or are used only for user manipulation of the component. Panels, **Canvas** class components, and windows generate all mouse events.

Table B Events summarized by component type

Type of Component	Events	Handler (If Any)
Generic (all components)	GOT_FOCUS	gotFocus()
	KEY_ACTION	keyDown()
	KEY_ACTION_RELEASE	keyUp()
	KEY_PRESS	keyDown()
	KEY_RELEASE	keyUp()
	LOST_FOCUS	lostFocus()
	MOUSE_ENTER	mouseEnter()
	MOUSE_EXIT	mouseExit()
	MOUSE_MOVE	mouseMove()
	MOUSE_DRAG	mouseDrag()
Panels, windows, Canvas	MOUSE_DOWN	mouseDown()
	MOUSE_UP	mouseUp()
Button	ACTION_EVENT	action()
Checkbox	ACTION_EVENT	action()
Choice	ACTION_EVENT	action()
List	ACTION_EVENT	action()
	LIST_SELECT	—
	LIST_DESELECT	—
MenuItem	ACTION_EVENT	action()
Scrollbar	SCROLL_ABSOLUTE	—
	SCROLL_LINE_UP	—
	SCROLL_LINE_DOWN	—
	SCROLL_PAGE_UP	—
	SCROLL_PAGE_DOWN	—
TextField	ACTION_EVENT	action()
		—
Windows	WINDOW_DESTROY	—
	WINDOW_DEICONIFY	—
	WINDOW_ICONIFY	—
	WINDOW_MOVED	—

Table C summarizes how an **Event** object indicates which mouse button is down. The **META_MASK** and **ALT_MASK** flags are used; in keystroke events, these flags have a completely different meaning.

Table C *Mouse buttons and the modifiers field*

MOUSE BUTTON DOWN	CORRESPONDING FLAG IN THE MODIFIERS FIELD OF THE EVENT OBJECT
Left button	(sets no modifiers)
Middle button	Event.ALT_MASK
Right button	Event.META_MASK

GRAPHICS TABLES

This section summarizes the meaning of several types of constants that are useful in graphics and text operations: fonts, colors, and cursor types. Table D lists Java fonts and their Windows equivalents. Java font names can be passed to constructors in the **Font** class.

Table D *Java fonts*

FONT IN JAVA	FONT ON A WINDOWS SYSTEM
Java default font (no font specified)	Arial
Courier	Courier New
Dialog	MS Sans Serif
DialogInput	MS Sans Serif
Helvetica	Arial
TimesRoman	Times New Roman
ZapfDingbats	WingDings

Table E lists the color constants provided in the **Color** class. These same constants are listed in Part V, “API Quick Reference.”

Table E Color class constants

Color.black	Color.magenta
Color.blue	Color.orange
Color.cyan	Color.pink
Color.darkGray	Color.red
Color.gray	Color.white
Color.green	Color.yellow
Color.lightGray	

Table F summarizes cursor types, which can be set in the **setCursor()** method of the **Frame** class.

Table F Java cursor settings

CURSOR	DESCRIPTION
Frame.CROSSHAIR_CURSOR	Cursor using a simple crosshair.
Frame.DEFAULT_CURSOR	Default cursor used if you don't specify a cursor. Appears as an arrow.
Frame.E_RESIZE_CURSOR	Resizing cursor for right edge.
Frame.HAND_CURSOR	Hand pointing at the current position.
Frame.MOVE_CURSOR	Move-window cursor.
Frame.NE_RESIZE_CURSOR	Resizing cursor for the top right corner.
Frame.NW_RESIZE_CURSOR	Resizing cursor for the top left corner.
Frame.N_RESIZE_CURSOR	Resizing cursor for the top edge.
Frame.SE_RESIZE_CURSOR	Resizing cursor for the bottom right corner.
Frame.SW_RESIZE_CURSOR	Resizing cursor for the bottom left corner.
Frame.S_RESIZE_CURSOR	cursor for the bottom edge.

continued

Table F Java cursor settings, continued

Cursor	Description
Frame.TEXT_CURSOR	Cursor used in editable text fields. Usually appears as a large I-shaped divider.
Frame.WAIT_CURSOR	Usually an hourglass or watch picture of some kind, indicating that the user should wait while an operation is being carried out.
Frame.W_RESIZE_CUSOR	Resizing cursor for the left edge.

Text-Handling Tables

Most text handling in Java is straightforward. There are at least a couple of situations, however, in which you need to handle text characters in a special way: when you want to embed special characters into strings, and when you read and write to text files. As mentioned throughout this book, the Unicode character set can represent many characters beyond those in the English alphabet. However, a complete guide to Unicode is beyond the scope of this book.

Table G summarizes escape sequences recognized in Java strings. You can use these sequences to embed some of the more standard special characters. Remember that each character is actually stored in two bytes.

Table G Java escape sequences

Escape Sequence	Description
\b	Backspace
\t	Tab
\n	Newline
\f	Form feed
\"	Double quotation mark
\'	Single quotation mark

continued

ESCAPE SEQUENCE	DESCRIPTION
\\	Backslash
\r	Carriage return
\xxx	Character with octal value xxx in the Unicode system, in which xxx is between \000 and \377. This corresponds to the decimal range 0 to 255; you can use octal only to represent values that require no more than one byte.
\uxxxx	Chrachter with hexadecimal value xxxx in the Unicode system. This encoding enables you to represent the entire possible Unicode range; you can represent any unsigned two-byte integer value.

The next table is relevant to file input and output operatiolns. When you read and write text strings to data files, you can use the UTF-8 encoding scheme. In fact, this is recommended for best results, although you must use it consistently. (See **DataInputStream** and **DataOutputStream** for more information.)

Table H shows how the UTF-8 encoding scheme handles various characters in the Unicode range. Methods such as **DataOutputStream.writeUTF()** perform the encoding for you. Notably, all ASCII characters are translated into strings with exactly one character per byte, a compact arrangement that makes them easy to read if you scan the file. This works because the lowest 128 Unicode characters correspond to ASCII characters with the same value.

Table H *UTF-8 encodings*

START OF RANGE	END OF RANGE	REQUIRED BITS	BINARY SEQUENCE (x = 1 OR 0)
\u0000	\u007F	7	0xxxxxxx
\u0080	\u07FF	11	110xxxxx 10xxxxxx
\u0800	\uFFFF	16	1110xxxx 10xxxxxx 10xxxxxx

JDBC TABLES

Table I shows the structure of the result set returned by the **getTables()** method of **DatabaseMetaData**. Each row in the result set describes a table found by **getTables()**. There are five columns in the result set itself.

Table I *Result set for DatabaseMetaData.getTables()*

POSITION/NAME	TYPE	DESCRIPTION
1. TABLE_CAT	String	Table catalog (may be null).
2. TABLE_SCHEM	String	Table schema (may be null).
3. TABLE_NAME	String	Name of table.
4. TABLE_TYPE	String	Type of table.
5. REMARKS	String	Description.

The possible values for the TABLE_NAME column are "TABLE", "VIEW", "SYSTEM TABLE", "GLOBAL TEMPORARY", "LOCAL TEMPORARY", "ALIAS", and "SYNONYM".

Table J shows the structure of the result set returned by the **getColumns()** method of **DatabaseMetaData**. Each row in the result set describes a column found by **getColumns()**. There are 18 columns in the result set itself.

Table J *Result set for DatabaseMetaData.getColumns()*

POSITION/NAME	TYPE	DESCRIPTION
1. TABLE_CAT	String	Catalog name (may be null).
2. TABLE_SCHEM	String	Schema name (may be null).
3. TABLE_NAME	String	Table name.
4. COLUMN_NAME	String	Column name.
5. DATA_TYPE	short	Data type from **java.sql.Types**.
6. TYPE_NAME	String	Source-specific type name.

continued

POSITION/NAME	TYPE	DESCRIPTION
7. COLUMN_SIZE	int	Maximum number of characters or precision.
8. BUFFER_LENGTH	NA	Unused.
9. DECIMAL_DIGITS	int	Digits to right of decimal point.
10. NUM_PREC_RADIX	int	Radix (if numeric).
11. NULLABLE	int	Is NULL accepted?
12. REMARKS	String	Description (may be null).
13. COLUMN_DEF	String	Default value (may be null).
14. SQL_DATA_TYPE	NA	Unused.
15. SQL_DATETIME_SUB	NA	Unused.
16. CHAR_OCTET_LENGTH	int	Maximum number of bytes (for **CHAR** types).
17. ORDINAL_POSITION	int	One-based index of column.
18. IS_NULLABLE	String	Nullable indicator.

The **IS_NULLABLE** field indicates or not whether the column accepts NULL as a value. The possible values are "YES", "NO", and "NULL", which indicates that the status is unknown.

Table K summarizes the data types that can be found in a JDBC-compliant table along with the Java equivalents:

Table K *Database types and Java equivalents*

TYPE (FROM JAVA.SQL.TYPES)	JAVA TYPE/DESCRIPTION
BIGINT	**long**
BINARY	**byte[]** (fixed length)
BIT	**boolean**
CHAR	**String** (fixed length)
DATE	**java.sql.Date**

continued

Table K *Database types and Java equivalents, continued*

TYPE (FROM JAVA.SQL.TYPES)	JAVA TYPE/DESCRIPTION
DECIMAL	**java.sql.Numeric** (variable scale)
DOUBLE	**double**
FLOAT	**double**
INTEGER	**int**
LONGVARBINARY	**byte[]** (variable length)
LONGVARCHAR	**String** (variable length; may be used to store large binary objects)
NUMERIC	**java.sql.Numeric**
NULL	Special: represents absence of a value.
OTHER	Special: see note.
REAL	**float**
SMALLINT	**short**
TIME	**java.sql.Time**
TIMESTAMP	**java.sql.Timestamp**
TINYINT	**byte**
VARBINARY	**byte[]** (variable length)
VARCHAR	**String** (variable length)

Note: If the type is OTHER, the data type is specific to the database and requires additional method calls to access properly. Use the **getObject()** and **setObject()** methods of the following interfaces: **PreparedStatement**, **CallableStatement**, and **ResultSet.**

MISCELLANEOUS TABLES

This final section includes two tables of importance, especially for applications: the default systems properties table and a summary of class and field modifiers.

Table L lists the default systems properties. These properties are contained in the table that you get by calling **System.getProperties()**. You can also look up individual properties in this table by calling **System.getProperty()**. Browsers do not grant applets the right to read all these properties—any information that would reveal private information about the user is denied to applets.

Table L *Default systems properties*

PROPERTY NAME	DESCRIPTION	CAN APPLET READ?
java.version	Version number of Java interpreter running on system.	yes
java.vendor	String identifying vendor of Java interpreter.	yes
java.vendor.url	Java vendor's URL.	yes
java.home	Home directory on local machine where Java is installed.	no
java.class.version	Version number of the Java API in use.	yes
os.name	Name of the operating system running.	yes
os.version	Version number of the operating system.	yes
file.separator	File separator used in path names (Windows, UNIX, and Mac use \, /, and :, respectively).	yes
path.separator	Directory-name separator used in paths (: or ;).	yes
line.separator	Line separator used in text files and elsewhere (\n or \r\n). As with other separators, this is platform-specific.	yes

continued

Table L Default systems properties, continued

PROPERTY NAME	DESCRIPTION	CAN APPLET READ?
user.name	The username recognized in the local environment.	no
user.home	The home directory of the current user.	no
user.dir	The current working directory.	no

In addition, the API uses several other properties whose value you can change to customize behavior. These properties include **awt.toolkit** (specifies the name of the class that implements the **Toolkit** class), **awt.appletWarning** (specifies the warning string that appears in applet windows), and **awt.font.***fontname*, which specifies the font corresponding to *fontname*. You could, for example, specify a different font for **awt.font.***fontname*, thus creating an alias or altering the interpreter's standard set of fonts.

Table M summarizes the relationship of Java modifiers to classes and fields. Unlike those in C++, Java classes have a smaller set of modifiers available than methods or variables.

Table M *Class and field modifiers in Java*

MODIFIER	CLASSES?	VARIABLES?	METHODS?	DESCRIPTION
abstract	yes	no	yes	Classes: cannot be instantiated. Methods: the method definition is not provided in this class. Class must also be abstract.
(default access)	yes	yes	yes	Class or field is visible everywhere within the package but not outside the package

continued

Table M Class and field modifiers in Java, continued

MODIFIER	CLASSES?	VARIABLES?	METHODS?	DESCRIPTION
final	yes	yes	yes	Classes: cannot be subclassed. Variables: cannot be modified. Methods: cannot be overridden.
native	no	no	yes	Code is provided by a dynamic link library rather than Java code. The method is implemented in another language, such as C or C++.
private	no	yes	yes	Field is not visible outside the class.
private protected	no	yes	yes	Field is not visible outside the class except in subclasses.
protected	no	yes	yes	Field is not visible outside the package except in subclasses.
public	yes	yes	yes	Classes: class is visible outside package. Fields: field is visible outside the package, but only if class is also public (otherwise, field has default access).
static	no	yes	yes	Field is a class field (can be accessed as class.field as well as obj.field).
synchronized	no	no	yes	Only one thread may execute the method at a time.

continued

Table M Class and field modifiers in Java, continued

MODIFIER	CLASSES?	VARIABLES?	METHODS?	DESCRIPTION
volatile	no	yes	no	Value is subject to change without warning; Java is instructed to never store in a register or temporary location. This attribute cannot be used with **final**.

Interfaces follow the same rules that classes follow except in the following ways: interfaces are automatically **abstract** whether declared so or not. Interface methods are automatically **abstract** and do not need to be explicitly declared so (doing so is always optional). Interface methods can take only **abstract** and **public** as modifiers. Interfaces can have variables, but the variables must be declared **final static**. Interfaces cannot be declared **final**.

PART VII

Glossary of Java Terminology and Concepts

abstract class

A class with one or more abstract methods. An abstract class cannot be used directly to create objects. However, an abstract class can be a useful place to declare a set of methods common to a number of subclasses. A good example in the Java API is the **Number** class in the **java.lang** package. The subclasses of **Number** include **Integer**, **Long**, **Float**, and **Double**. Abstract classes are similar to interfaces, because both of these constructs include abstract methods. However, Java recognizes abstract classes and interfaces as two separate parts of the language and imposes different rules on them. See the topic "abstract Keyword" in Part II for more information.

abstract method

A method that has no implementation—that is, no function-definition code. The implementation must be filled in by a subclass. Abstract methods appear only in abstract classes and interfaces. When you declare a class that inherits from an abstract class, you must provide implementations for all the methods (unless you're declaring another abstract class). Similarly, when a class implements an interface, it must provide implementations for all the abstract methods. An abstract method is therefore like a stand-in or prototype for an actual method definition to be provided elsewhere. The concept of pure virtual functions in C++ is the same as abstract methods in Java. See the topic "abstract Keyword" in Part II for more information.

abstraction

The process of making something simpler by hiding the details. There are many reasons that hiding the details can be desirable, especially in a multiplatform language like Java. For example, the Java **Socket** class is an abstraction of the idea of a network connection. Different platforms can have widely varying ways of connecting to a network, complete with their own procedures and protocols. Even if you master all the protocols for all the possible platforms, having to deal with them all means maintaining many different versions of the code. But when you work with **Socket**, which is the Java network abstraction, you don't have to concern yourself with the details of any particular platforms. Similarly, many classes may be thought of as being abstractions for something potentially complex or nonstandardized (the **Thread** class, for example). One of the virtues of object-oriented programming is that it encourages data abstraction in the form of classes. Be aware, however, that abstraction is more a philosophy or a general quality than something measurable or precise.

access level

The visibility of a field relative to other classes. Java supports five access levels and not just three as in C++. In addition to **public**, **private**, and **protected**, Java provides the default access level. Unlike access levels in C++, Java's default access level is not the same as **private**. The default visibility of a field is to be accessible to all classes in the same package. You must specifically declare a field **private** to restrict its access by other classes.

API

Application programming interface. In general, an API is a set of any combination of classes, functions, variables, and methods that provides a general model for creating applications. In simple terms, this means working with certain standard functions and classes rather than programming close to the hardware. The Java API is particularly helpful to programmers, because it generalizes universal features of modern computers, such as displays, threads, network connections, and mouse and keyboard input, and is guaranteed to work consistently on all Java-compatible platforms. In addition, the Java API uses a programming model that is conceptually simpler than most other widely used GUI systems. All items in the Java API are contained in packages, interfaces, and classes, as required by the structure of the Java language.

applet

A program that runs inside a Web page. This is currently the most popular use for Java programming, although Java can be used in other ways. (See "application.") Java programs that are structured as applets must subclass the general class **Java.applet.Applet**.

appletviewer

A utility for viewing applets that is provided in the Java Development Kit. End users typically run a Java applet by using a Java-compatible Web browser and accessing the appropriate Web page on the Internet. However, the appletviewer utility is convenient for developers who want to run an applet on their local computer. When you run appletviewer, you specify an HTML file that has a link to the appropriate applet. See Chapter One, "Applets andOranges," for more information.

application

A stand-alone Java program that can be run directly on a local computer without the need to access it across the Web. Although Java's most glamorous use is probably the creation of applets, Java applications are also potentially very useful. A Java application can do anything that most other high-level languages can do. Moreover, the Java API provides an easy-to-use mechanism for writing applications that communicate across the network. Another advantage is that Java applications can run without change on any Java-compatible platform, just as applets can.

array

An organized collection of data in which each element has the same base type. As with most other programming languages, an element of a Java array can be accessed through a numeric index. As in C and C++, indexes are always zero-based. If the name of an array is A, the first element is A [0], the second is A[1], and so on. Java arrays are objects allocated with the **new** operator. Multidimensional arrays are treated as true arrays of arrays. As a consequence, you can, if you choose, allocate each row of a multidimensional array separately and each give each row a different size. For more information, see the topic "Arrays" in Part II.

ASCII

American Standard Code for Information Interchange (pronounced "ask-key"): the standard format for mapping printable characters to bytes of data. ASCII is used in virtually all personal computers in the United States and other English-speaking countries. The ASCII character set is not large enough to represent the character sets of all human languages, so Java uses the Unicode system, which maps each character to two bytes of data rather than one. The first 128 Unicode characters correspond to ASCII characters.

AWT

Abstract Windowing Toolkit. An important part of the Java API (see "API"), the AWT provides windows, buttons, check boxes, scroll bars, events, and other components of interest to GUI programmers. These features can be used in both applets and applications. The AWT consists of classes and interfaces provided in the **java.awt** package. For an in-depth introduction, see Chapter 4, "Components and Events."

The AWT also contains layout managers, each of which uses a general strategy for sizing and positioning components inside a container. If the user resizes a window, for example, the container's layout manager repositions the components.

bitmap (.bmp file)

A binary representation of a rectangular screen image using pixel data. Each dot, or pixel, in the image maps to an element of data in the bitmap. The pixel in the top left corner maps to the first element, the adjacent pixel on the right maps to the second element, and so on. Bitmaps can have any rectangular area: a subsection of the screen, the entire screen, or even a larger area. In GUI systems, one of the principal ways to display an image is to copy a bitmap to the screen. Although there are other ways to display graphics (such as drawing lines), a bitmap has the advantage of containing the complete snapshot of an area. Note that .bmp is Microsoft's bitmap format; there are others, such as .xbm (Xbitmap format).

Boolean expression

An expression that has one of only two possible values: **true** or **false**. Control structures such as **if** and **while** require the use of Boolean expressions. In C, C++, Microsoft Visual Basic, and some other programming languages, Boolean values are treated as just another way to use integers. So, for example, a numeric expression that evaluates to 0 is considered false, and all other values are considered true. Java, using an approach similar to Pascal's, treats Boolean values as distinct from integers and provides a separate data type, **boolean**. Java's approach is straightfoward, because the results of all comparisons (such as Sum > 0) are Boolean, as you would expect. However, some programming tricks picked up from C and C++—such as using while(n) instead of while(n!=0)—do not work. See the topics "Boolean expression," "true Keyword," and "false Keyword" in Part II for more information.

byte codes

Binary data representing a Java program. Byte codes are the intermediate language between Java and ordinary machine language. When you run the Java compiler, it translates your program into a series of **.class** files, each containing byte codes for a particular class. These codes are read by a Java interpreter when you execute the program. Byte codes consist of binary, not human-readable data, containing instructions to a hypothetical Java computer (the Java Virtual Machine). The interpreter simulates this machine.

The use of byte codes is one of the things that make Java platform-independent. No matter which computer compiles a Java program, any other Java-enabled computer can run it. As explained in Chapter 1, "Applets and Oranges," each platform has its own Java interpreter. This arrangement differs from most software development, in which a compiler produces machine instructions aimed at a particular processor and operating system.

C

A popular computer language created by Brian Kernighan. Originally created as a tool for writing the UNIX operating system, C has eclipsed nearly all other traditional programming languages in popularity, with the exception of Basic. Much of C's success lies in its combining high-level control and data structures with useful and powerful operators, such as shift and bit operations. Java inherits much of C's syntax, although Java has some major differences and is more nearly akin to C++.

C++

The standard object-oriented version of C, created by Bjarne Stroustrup. At least superficially, C++ is the language closest to Java. But as a general rule, C++ and Java are too different from each other to make it particularly easy to port code from one to the other. One of the most important differences is that C and C++ rely heavily on the use of pointers, whereas Java eliminates pointers. Because they were creating a language for Internet applications, Java's designers omitted pointers because of the security problems they present. Moreover, Java is a leaner, smaller language and does not support some of the more obscure features of C++. On the other hand, C++ programmers will find that Java's use of such concepts as classes, references, and the **new** operator make Java familiar and easy to learn.

cast

An operator that changes the type of an expression. The result is a new, temporary value that has the same value as its operand but a different type. Sometimes the compiler casts data for you. For example, in the declaration **double d = 1;** the integer 1 is implicitly cast to **double** and then assigned to d. Explicit casts are needed when an assignment results in loss of precision-for example, when you assign a floating-point constant (stored by default as type **double**) to a variable of type **float**. You also need a cast is you assign an expression to a variable of subclass type. For example, the **vector.elementAt()** method returns an **Object** type. Any variable you assign the result to belongs to a subclass of **Object** (because every class is, directly or indirectly, a subclass of **Object**). Therefore, the result needs to be cast. You can go in the other direction—assigning to a variable of superclass type—without an explicit cast. See the topic "casts" in Part II for example code.

character string

See "string."

character, Unicode

A 16-bit value used to represent a printable character on the display. Although an eight-bit (ASCII) value is sufficient to represent all characters in the English alphabet, it is too small to represent all characters from certain other natural languages. See "Unicode."

class

The most basic unit, or division, in a Java program. A class is a collection of variable declarations or function code (called *methods*) or both. Once a class is declared, you can use it to create any number of objects. The class's variable declarations determine each object's data fields, and methods determine object behavior. Another way to think of a class is to consider it a user-defined type and to consider objects as instances of such a type. The concept of a Java class is similar to a C++ class, C structure, Pascal record, or Visual Basic module. Java does not support the C++ **structure** and **union** keywords; instead, the **class** keyword must be used to declare all user-defined types.

Classes have other uses. Sometimes they are simply convenient program divisions. A class can include static fields, which are like global variables and functions except in their scope. In Java, a class might be the starting point of a program or a general pattern for other classes (an *abstract class*). However, the most common use of a class is as a type used to generate objects.

class method

A method that applies to an entire class and not to individual objects. Class methods are declared **static**. The principal feature of class methods is that you can call such a method through its class (as *class.method*()) rather than having to create an object and then call the method through the object (as *object.method*()).

For example, one of the class methods of the **Integer** class is **parseInt()**. The following is a valid method call even if no **Integer** objects have been created:

```
int n = Integer.parseInt(inputstring);
```

Class methods have an important restriction: they can refer to other fields only if they are class fields (static). Another restriction is that class methods cannot use the **this** keyword. See also "instance method."

class variable

A variable that is shared by an entire class rather than stored in individual objects. Class variables are declared **static**. The principal feature of a class variable is that you can refer to it through its class (as *class.variable*) rather than having to create an object and then refer to the variable through the object (as *object.variable*).

For example, you can refer to the **BOLD** and **ITALIC** variables of the **Font** class even if no **Font** objects have been created:

```
Font.BOLD
Font.ITALIC
```

In the API, many class variables are constants, so they are not variables in the traditional sense. However, the syntax is the same. See also "instance variable."

CLASSPATH

An environment variable, or setting, maintained by the local operating system: if **CLASSPATH** is defined, the Java interpreter searches the **CLASSPATH** directories when it looks for a class; otherwise, it searches only the current directory. Note that when you set **CLASSPATH**, you should include the current-directory symbol ("." in DOS and UNIX) to preserve the default behavior.

client

The user of a service provided by another computer, database, or object. In network operations, a client computer initiates a network connection with another computer, called a *server*, and then makes requests through function calls. A client may request the server to send information, store data, or execute some other task. The terms *client* and *server* are used most often in network operations, but sometimes used in database operations and in some object-oriented programming. See also "server".

compiler, Java

A program, called **javac.exe** on Intel platforms, that translates Java source code into byte codes. The byte codes, in turn, can be run on any Java-compatible platform through the use of a Java interpreter. Traditionally, compilers translate source code into machine instructions so that it can be executed directly on a computer. The Java compiler does roughly the same thing but translates the program into byte-code format, which consists of instructions to a virtual (*imaginary*) machine. See also "interpreter, Java."

component (Component class)

An independent graphical object capable of receiving and responding to events. Components are often called *controls* in other programming systems. In the Java API, all standard components are defined in the **java.awt** package. Examples include applets, windows, buttons, frames, choice boxes, and labels. In the Java API, the **java.awt.Component** class is a high-level abstract class that includes attributes and methods common to all components. Specific classes that inherit from the **Component** class include **Applet, Button**, **Frame**, **Choice**, **Label**, and many others.

constant

A value that does not change throughout the course of a program. Java variables declared **final** are constants; the compiler does not permit changes to these variables. For more information, see "final Keyword" in Part II. Constants also include literal values, such as quoted strings and digits.

constructor

A method that is automatically called when an object is created. Constructors, though optional, are useful for performing initialization of objects. As in C++, a constructor has no return type and has the same name as the class for which it is written. See the topic "Constructors" in Part II.

container (Container class)

A component that can physically contain other components. The standard containers defined in the Java API include windows, frames, and dialog boxes. These containers are defined in classes in the **java.awt** package, and all of them inherit from the **Container** class. The **Applet** class is also a container class, although it is located in the **java.applet** package.

copy constructor

A constructor that tells how to create an object from another object of the same class. The signature of a copy constructor is *class*(*class*). Copy constructors do not have quite the same importance in Java that they do in C++, because Java does not pass objects by value. However, they are still useful.

critical section

See "synchronized methods and threads."

double buffering

A technique for smoothing out the effects of animation in graphics programs. In double buffering, a program manipulates an internal graphics display that is not seen by the user but is stored in memory. When a series of graphics changes have been completed, the in-memory display is copied to the display through a single operation that copies pixel info to the screen. Double buffering requires more memory but is often the only technique for achieving smooth animation effects that do not flicker.

encapsulation

Protecting part of an object from the outside world; it amounts to declaring a method or variable **private**. It is a good policy to make the contents of a class (and thus an object) private except for the parts that must interact with other classes. These points of interaction should, ideally, be as few as possible. The advantage of encapsulating some or most of the class is that the internals of the class can be freely rewritten without breaking the code that uses the class. Another advantage is that it's frequently useful to hide the details. These are fundamental principles of object-oriented design, although they are helpful in traditional programming as well.

Encapsulation is often used in a slightly more general sense, meaning roughly "an abstraction for." For example, the **String** class can be considered to encapsulate the contents and attributes of character strings. (See "string.") The capabilities you associate with an array of characters are represented by an object of type **String** in Java. This object can do all the same things that a character string can do, but it hides most of the details of how the data is stored, ultimately making the **String** class easier to work with.

escape sequence

A two-character sequence that represents a single special character, such as a tab (**\t**) or newline (**\n**). As in C and C++, Java escape sequences begin with the backslash. See the topic "Strings" in Part II for a list of escape sequences.

exception

An unusual occurrence during program execution that requires immediate handling. Most exceptions are run-time errors of some kind, although some exceptions (such as reaching the end of a file) do not necessarily indicate catastrophe. Java's exception-handling syntax, which is close to that in ANSI C++, enables you to centralize exception-handling code so it is easier to maintain. When an exception is reported (or *thrown*), execution is automatically transferred to the closest exception handler no matter what method was executing when the exception was thrown. See the topic "Exception Handling" in Part II for more information.

event

An action, normally a user action such as a keystroke or a mouse event, that your program can respond to at run time through specific methods. For example, the **mouseDown()** method is called when the user presses a mouse button at run time. Only certain kinds of graphical objects, called *components*, receive events. You write event-handling code by subclassing the component's class (for example, **Button**) and overriding the event-handling methods by writing your own method definitions.See Chapter Four, "Components and Events."

field

An item in a class declaration. Fields determine the attributes of each object in the class, (except for fields declared **static**). A field may be either a variable or a method. Fields are called *members* in C structures and C++ classes. Java's designers had a passion for borrowing from C++ but changing the terminology, perhaps to keep C++ programmers from becoming complacent. Note that in Java terminology, a variable (data member in C++) may actually be a constant.

finalizer method

A method that all classes inherit from the **Object** class but don't necessarily implement. The **finalizer()** method is the closest thing in Java to a C++ destructor: it includes code executed when an object is about to be removed from memory. The purpose of this method is to clean up resources that were being used by the object. However, because almost all such cleanup is automatic in Java, writing a **finalizer()** method is usually unnecessary.

firewall

A security layer that protects parts of a network from outsiders. For example, it may be desirable to connect a proprietary network, such as a LAN, to the Internet, while making only parts of the network available to the outside world. Other parts are protected through a firewall. Creation and maintenance of a firewall are generally low-level systems issues.

fixed point

An alternative format for representing fractional values, used in the JDBC **Numeric** class. A fixed-point variable is an integer with a built-in scale. For example, a scale of two means that instead of storing the number of dollars, you store the number of cents: a value stored as 179 would be displayed as 1.79. If the scale were three, the value would be displayed as 0.179. In contrast, the floating-point format cannot store 1.79 or 0.179 precisely. Although values are displayed in decimal radix, they are stored in binary. This conversion of fractional data from one radix to another involves loss of data, and the floating-point format accumulates errors in dollars-and-cents calculations. Understandably, the fixed-point format is more popular with accountants.

floating point

A data type that can represent fractions; floating point can also represent very large quantities. Floating-point number formats use scientific notation, which includes sign, mantissa, and exponent. (Don't worry if you don't recognize these terms, because there's almost never any practical reason for dissecting a floating-point number.) The important thing to know is that Java uses the same floating-point formats for all platforms: you can rely on the value of a **float** or **double** variable. Other programming languages do not always enforce a binary standard, so transfer of data between platforms is unreliable. The other thing to know about floating-point data is that there is a trade-off: integers can be processed faster, whereas floating-point numbers take longer to process but can hold much bigger and smaller quantities. Yet the gap between integer and floating-point efficiency is narrowing as more and more hardware platforms contain powerful built-in floating-point coprocessors. Even so, you should avoid using floating point, when an integer variable would suffice.

FTP

File Transfer Protocol: the standard protocol used in network communications for downloading files. The World Wide Web supports this protocol in a transparent way; a Web user automatically logs into the target server by clicking the appropriate link. File-downloading locations on the Web are identified by the **ftp:** prefix.

garbage collector

A lazy programmer's dream come true: a background thread, run by the Java interpreter, that releases memory used by objects that are no longer around. Because of the garbage collector, you generally don't need to explicitly destroy objects or release memory even though you must explicitly create them using the **new** operator. Unused objects are simply cleaned up when you're not looking, so to speak. Typically, the garbage collection process takes over when all the variables referring to a particular object in memory have gone out of scope (although the Java interpreter could be optimized to start garbage collection even sooner). The garbage collector runs as a low-priority thread, minimizing its impact on program efficiency. It gets priority whenever memory is scarce.

GIF (.gif file)

Graphics Interchange Format: a popular format for storing graphics images that is used widely in Web pages and Java applications. If you examine the JDK, you'll find a number of examples of .gif files that you can readily load into a Java **Image** object. Unlike bitmap (.bmp) files, the GIF format uses space-compression techniques to store an image (See also "JPEG.")

GUI

Graphical user interface. GUI systems are famous for being easy to use and notoriously difficult to program. When you write applets, the Java API provides a strong offering of GUI features—windows, buttons, scroll bars, graphics, mouse events, and so on—in a form that is relatively easy to program. A particularly strong advantage of Java is that you can use it to create GUI programs that run, without change, on different kinds of computers.

host

A synonym for *server*. You can think of a client as "visiting" a server and being treated to guest services. Note that the client must be a good guest, behaving itself and using the correct procedures (protocol) to make requests.

HotJava

A Web browser developed by Sun Microsystems to support Java applets. Netscape and other vendors soon followed suit by adding Java support to their browsers. HotJava is itself an application written entirely in Java, thus demonstrating the power of the language.

HTML

Hypertext Markup Language: the standard programming language for encoding a Web page. An HTML file consists mainly of a series of tags: commands, enclosed in angle brackets (<>), that cause a browser to display text and graphics. In addition, a Java-compatible browser recognizes the <APPLET> tag, which specifies a subclass of the Java **Applet** class to load and run.

HTTP

Hypertext Transport Protocol: the protocol used by World Wide Web servers for providing hypertext documents, or Web pages. *Hypertext* enables a document to contain text, images, and sound as well as links (or jumps) to other documents. The reason that Web URLs start with **http:** is that they use the HTTP protocol. See "FTP" for an example of another protocol.

implement

In Java, this term has a specific technical meanings in addition to its more general meaning: to implement a method is to provide a method definition (the statements between the braces: {}); to implement an interface is to provide definitions for all the methods in the interface. In Java, as in other object-oriented systems, different classes may provide different definitions for the same method. Each definition is a different implementation.

In general usage, to implement means to fulfill or complete something. The Java usage is consistent with this general idea. A method declaration implies the idea of a certain task or activity; an implementation defines one way to perform that task. Similarly, an interface declares a list of services; an implementation for an interface defines a way to perform those ervices. Java also supports an **implements** keyword (see Part II), and a version of Java on a particular platform is sometimes called an implementation of Java.

infinity

See "POSITIVE_INFINITY" and "NEGATIVE_INFINITY."

inheritance

Defining a new class or interface in terms of an existing class or interface. Inheritance, which conjures up visions of family trees and biological classification schemes, is one of the most highly touted features of object-oriented programming. But inheritance is probably best viewed as a convenient way of repeating all the fields of one class inside another class without having to retype the declarations. For example, when class A inherits from class B, A automatically has all the same fields that B does, including method declarations and definitions, if any. (But note that private fields of B are not visible in A.) B is then the *superclass* of A. Any explicit declarations in A create additional or overridden fields. A can reuse, adapt, and amend the code already created for B.

Java limits inheritance to single inheritance, meaning that any given class inherits directly from only one superclass. Yet a class may inherit *indirectly* from other classes, because B may have its own superclass, and that superclass may have another superclass, and so on. This arrangement creates an inheritance hierarchy, at the root of which is the **Object** class defined in the Java API. Thus, all classes inherit from **Object**, although there may be intervening generations. For more information, see the topic "extends Keyword" in Part II.

Although Java restricts inheritance to single inheritance, it lets a class implement any number of interfaces. Implementing an interface is a variation on inheritance: in C++, it is the same as inheriting from a purely abstract class. But interfaces have special restrictions that classes do not have. Limiting multiple inheritance to interfaces reduces the possible complexity that the Java compiler must deal with. For more information, see "interface."

instance

Simply put, an object. The fact that object-oriented terminology uses both *object* and *instance* to mean the same thing may seem like a plot to confuse the novice. However, the term *instance* emphasizes an object's relationship to its class and is sometimes useful for this reason. For example, suppose there is a Car class used to create the objects herbie, hotrod, and chittybang. All of these objects have their fields defined in the Car declaration. It's convenient to speak of herbie, hotrod, and chittybang as "instances of Car."

instance method

A method that operates on individual objects (instances). All methods not declared **static** are instance methods. Unlike class methods, instance methods have unlimited access to all other fields (variables and methods) in the same class, even those that are nonstatic or **private**. Generally, an instance method's main purpose is to manipulate an object or communicate with it in some way. Unlike a class method, an instance method can be called only through an object. For example, you can call the **setLabel()** method of the **Button** class only after creating a **Button** object:

```
Button b = new Button();
b.setLabel("My button.");
```

If **setLabel()** were a class method rather than an instance method, the expression "Button.setLabel("My button")" would be legal—which it is not. See also "class method."

instance variable

A variable that represents a field of an object (i.e., an instance). All variables are instance variables unless declared **static**. You must create an object before referring to an instance variable. Then you refer to the variable through the object and not through its class. For example, the variable **width** is an instance variable of the **Dimension** class. The variable, **width**, takes up storage inside the instance, d:

```
Dimension d = new Dimension();
int w = d.width;
```

If **width** were a class variable rather than an instance variable, then "Dimension.width" would be a legal expression—which it is not. See also "class variable."

instantiation

A multisyllabic word that means creating an object of a particular class. A class that has at least one object is said to be instantiated. Some classes (abstract classes in particular) cannot be instantiated, meaning that you cannot use them to create objects directly. The term is almost unnecessary, but object-oriented devotees seem to like it.

integer

The common way that numbers are stored in computers: as simple whole-number quantities that do not have a fractional part. Although some kinds of calculations require fractions (see "floating point"), a program typically has many calculations that do not involve fractions at all. For example, one of the most common types of variables is a loop variable, which counts iterations through a loop. For such situations, it is more efficient to use an integer than a floating-point number. Java integer types include **byte**, **short**, **int**, and **long**. In Java, all integer types store negative as well as positive numbers. (See "two's complement" for more information on negative numbers).

interface

Simply put, a list of services. An interface consists of abstract methods—and, optionally, constants—but you can think of it as a contract between the class that implements it and the class's users. By implementing an interface, you agree to provide definitions for each method declared in the interface (a method being a "service"). Implementing an interface is similar to subclassing an abstract class.

Beyond that, interfaces are sometimes used in the API almost as if they were classes. For example, certain API methods have the return type **Enumeration**. This means that you get back an object whose class implements the **Enumeration** interface. In this case, you don't know what the object's actual class is. However, you don't care; the only thing that matters is that you can call any **Enumeration** method through this object. In effect, you can treat **Enumeration** as if it were the object's class.

The Java concept of interface is close to that of abstract class. In C++, an abstract class is exactly what you would use in place of an interface. The main difference is that abstract classes are not bound to all the restrictions that interfaces are bound to. Java limits multiple inheritance to interfaces, which in turn have greater restrictions. Consequently, the Java compiler is leaner, because some of the messier problems of multiple inheritance never arise.

On a final note, don't confuse Java's use of "interface" with the rather general use of the term I made in *C++ in Plain English*. In Java, "interface" has a much narrower and more technical meaning.

interpreter, Java

A program that reads Java byte codes (stored in **.class** files) and responds by performing actions. The program **java.exe** is an interpreter, as is the appletviewer program and any Java-compatible Web browser. You can think of byte codes as instructions for a virtual, or imaginary, processor. A Java interpreter decodes these instructions by executing them on its platform. Because each platform has its own Java interpreter, a Java program and compiler can target just one virtual machine, in effect making Java a universal language. It is theoretically possible that a computer could be developed that would process Java byte codes directly; until then, interpreters suffice. See also "compiler, Java."

Java

A computer programming language that is highly object-oriented, smaller than C++, and targeted for new environments such as the Internet. Much more so than other languages, Java is a unified language: Java has a built-in API and a precise binary standard for all its data types. Unlike C and C++, Java has tighter security features that make it safer for distribution across a network; for example, you cannot use Java to read and write random memory addresses. The ever-increasing adoption of the Java format and widespread availability of Java interpreters make it an ideal language for writing programs to be distributed throughout the microcomputer and minicomputer world as well as for use in specialized computerized devices of the future. (See "compiler, Java" and "interpeter, Java.")

JavaScript

A programming language based on Java and C, that can be embedded directly into HTML files. JavaScript has some similarities to Java, but it is a separate language; it is not a macro language for generating Java code nor a tool for creating Java applications. People with little programming experience may prefer to learn JavaScript, because it is a smaller language. However, it is less much flexible and lacks many of Java's object-oriented features, such as inheritance. JavaScript was designed to integrate tightly into HTML browsers, with direct access to browser objects. This makes it better at interacting directly with elements of Web pages. Althought generally slower than Java, JavaScript usually loads faster because it's embedded in the Web page.

Java Beans

Java's answer to Microsoft's ActiveX controls: a technology for creating custom Java components that can be dragged and dropped into a visual development environment. The predecessor to ActiveX and Java Beans was Visual Basic custom controls, which established the success of a component-based model of developing software. Java Beans and ActiveX are not necessarily mutually exclusive. An important difference is that Java Beans is an extension to the Java API (in Java 1.1, regrettably not covered here because of size constraints).

Java compiler (javac)

See "compiler, Java."

Java interpreter (java)

See "interpreter, Java."

Java Virtual Machine

A term that means almost the same thing as the Java interpreter. When the Java compiler translates a program, it produces machine instructions for a hypothetical system called the Java Virtual Machine. (The instructions are called *byte codes.*) . On any given computer, the Java interpreter executes these instructions, thus simulating Virtual Machine behavior. But the Java Virtual Machine is more than just a way to interpret individual instructions; it is the entire run-time environment supporting Java programs. Thus the Java Virtual Machine provides features such as background threads and garbage collection.

JDBC

Java database connectivity: the Java 1.1 extension for interacting with database systems. The **java.sql** package contains the set of classes and interfaces that support all the JDBC capabilities, using SQL statements to execute commands. For more information, see Chapter 7, "JDBC Quick Start."

JDK

Java Development Kit. You can download the JDK free from the Internet by going to the JavaSoft home page (http://javasoft.com). It is also available on CD-ROM. The JDK includes a Java compiler, an interpreter, demos, and appletviewer as well as other useful utilities such as a debugger.

JPEG (.jpg file)

Joint Photographic Experts Group: a graphics-image format that, like GIF, uses compression techniques to store an image in a smaller space than required by a standard bitmap (.bmp) file. The JPEG format produces the best compression for a single photographic image by eliminating redundant picture information. (For example, a field of solid blue sky is reduced to a few bytes indicating the pattern.) Contrast this compression technique with MPEG.

keyword

A word that has a predefined meaning in a language. Common Java keywords include **if**, **else**, **while**, and **do**, all inherited from C/C++, as well as **extends**, **implements**, **package**, and **interface**, which are new in Java. The main thing to know about keywords is that you cannot choose them as names for your own variables. Yet it probably isn't worth your time to memorize lists of keywords. Picking meaningful, highly specific names will usually avoid conflicts. Beyond that, the Java compiler will tell you when there is a problem. For a table of keywords, see the topic "Keywords" in Part II.

local variable

A variable declared inside a method, a compound statement, or (in Java only) a **for** statement. Memory occupied by a local variable is returned as soon as it goes out of scope. See the topic "for Statement" in Part II for information about Java's unique use of local variables inside a **for** loop.

Local variables have a purpose limited to a specific section of code, such as a loop or calculation. In contrast, variables declared at the class level (called *class variables* and *instance variables*) have longer life spans and can share information between methods. One of the principles of good programming is to always use local variables except when a larger scope is needed. Unlike C and C++, Java has no true global variables, although class variables have global life span and storage. See also "scope." and "stack."

lock

See "synchronized methods and threads."

MAX_VALUE

A constant, defined in the number classes **Integer**, **Long**, **Float**, and **Double**, equal to the highest positive value the type in question can hold. Note that these wrapper classes give ranges and other information for the primitive data types **int**, **long**, **float**, and **double**, but wrapper classes are not identical to primitive data types.

members

See "field."

method

A function or subroutine declared inside a class. In Java, methods are the only functions or subroutines allowed. In other words, you must place all function code inside class declarations. As with C functions, a Java method may or may not return a value, depending on its return type. (A **void** method returns no value.) By default, methods in Java are late bound and polymorphic. For information on how to declare methods, see the topic "Methods" in Part II.

All methods are either instance methods or class methods. A method declared **static** is a *class* method and works very much like a global function in the way that it is used. For example, the class method **Math.random()** has nothing to do with individual objects and, except for the **Math** prefix, is like a C function. A method not declared **static** is an instance method. Generally, the purpose of such a method is to program behavior into individual objects. For example, the method might manipulate the state of a particular object through which it is called.

MIDI

Musical Instrumental Digital Interface: a format for storing audio data. MIDI can store musical information in a compact format and is especially useful for communication of data between computers, synthesizers, and muscial instruments.

MIN_VALUE

A constant, defined in the number classes **Integer**, **Long**, **Float**, and **Double**, equal to the lowest value the type in question can hold. This is the negative number of greatest magnitude (farthest from zero). Note that these wrapper classes give ranges and other information for the primitive data types **int**, **long**, **float**, and **double**, but wrapper classes are not identical to primitive data types.

MPEG

Motion Picture Experts Group: a format for storing video (and, optionally, audio) information. Unlike JPEG, which is a single-image format, MPEG reduces redundant picture information within groups of frames. Specifically, MPEG eliminates most individual frames in favor of data that summarizes changes between them. MPEG produces the highest compression for video, but JPEG is still preferred for some purposes. MPEG is designed only for distribution, and not for editing, because of its elimination of individual frames.

multithreaded program

A program that uses more than one thread, or sequence of execution. In a sense, each thread operates as an independent program except that all threads share common program code and resources. All Java programs have at least one thread. (In addition, running in the background are threads you don't see such as the Java garbage collector.) By running more than one thread, a program gains the ability to do more than one activity at a time. See "thread."

NaN

Not a Number, a special floating-point value that indicates an undefined result. Certain mathematical operations produce this value—most notably, division by zero in a floating-point expression. Unlike integer division, floating-point division produces this result rather than throw an exception. The constants **Float.NaN** and **Double.NaN** represent the NaN value for the **float** and **double** types, respectively. When NaN is tested for equality to itself, it returns **false**, so use **Float.isNaN()** or **Double.isNaN()** to test for this value.

native code

The machine language of the local processor. In reality, a computer never executes any code except native code. All other types of programming code must somehow be translated. This translation is performed by other programs, called compilers and interpreters, which themselves are directly or indirectly running native code.

For the most part, the existence of native code and translators is not an issue in Java programming unless you want to step outside the Java language and plug in external code modules. These modules may be written in C, C++, or assembly language before being compiled into machine language. Java provides the **native** keyword for implementing a method with non-Java code. This technique is strictly prohibited in applets, because native code, once executed, circumvents all security checks.

NEGATIVE_INFINITY

A special floating-point value that indicates an overflow involving a negative number. Unlike integer arithmetic, floating-point operations produce this result rather than throw an exception. The constants **Float.NEGATIVE_INFINITY** and **Double.NEGATIVE_INFINITY** represent this value for the **float** and **double** types, respectively. In any comparison, negative infinity is always lower than any other value represented by the type, although it is equal to itself.

null

A special value indicating "no object assigned." In Java, object variables are references, which means that they can be associated with different objects in memory at different times. A null value means that the variable is currently not associated with any object. In Java, the **null** keyword is a predefined value that can be assigned to an object variable or tested for equality with the variable.

object

A packet of data with both state and behavior. An object is an instance of a data structure that knows how to respond to a set of messages. In Java, messages are actually method calls, which are like function calls except that they involve a reference to a particular object. For example, a method call such as **myobject.clearAllFields()** might tell **myobject** to zero out all its data fields. A Java object is therefore like a C structure or Pascal record with the added feature of responsiveness, or intelligence. (Note, however, that it is also valid for an object to consist only of data fields.)

One of the major confusions in object-oriented programming, when people first approach the subject, is the distinction between objects and classes. An object responds to method calls at run time, but all methods are declared and defined in an object's class, which provides complete type information. Objects of the same class therefore tend to have similar behavior, although differences in state (the particular values stored in the data fields) can affect what happens during execution of a method.

object orientation

An approach to program design and coding that is one of the essential features of Java. Although object orientation has many things in common with traditional, structured programming, there is one fundamental difference: the major division is not between code and data but between individual objects, which are self-contained units having both state (data) and behavior (code). The general model of object orientation is that of a network of objects, each able to respond intelligently to messages from other objects. Object orientation has proved to be increasingly appropriate for modern programming systems, because graphical, event-driven systems act very much like collections of independent objects. In Java, object structure and behavior are programmed by writing a *class*.

One of the major goals of object orientation is to facilitate and encourage reusable code. Object-oriented languages, including Java, support inheritance, which is a useful technique for reusing and adapting code.

one-based indexing

An indexing scheme in which the first position is 1, the second position is 2, the third position is 3, and so on. This approach may seem the obvious way to do things, but most of Java uses zero-based indexing instead. JDBC classes (**java.sql**) use one-based indexing to indicate column position.

overloading

Reusing a method name so that you define different versions for different argument types. For example, suppose you want to write a function, **square_it()**, that works with both **int** and **double**. The Java solution is to write two versions of the function: **square_it(int)** and **square_it(double)**. Each has a different signature and method definition.

Overloading is resolved at compile time: the Java compiler knows how to evaluate a method call such as **square_it(5)**. Java knows that **int** is the type of the argument, 5, and so calls **square_it(int)**. Overloading is basically a convenience—it eliminates the need to generate different method names for each argument type, such as **square_it_int()** and **square_it_double()**. Contrast this with polymorphism (see "polymorphism"), which is a run-time, not a compile-time, operation.

Another type of overloading is *operator overloading*, which Java does not currently let you extend to your own classes. In operator overloading, the meaning of an operator (such as + or *) is determined by the types of its operands. In Java, the only class that overloads an operator is **String**, which defines its own operation for the plus sign (+).

overriding

The process of inheriting a method from a superclass but substituting a new method definition. Because Java classes can override any method definition (except those declared **final**), there can be multiple definitions of the same method. Java methods are polymophic; this means that the appropriate method definition for an object is always called at run time, regardless of how that object is accessed.

package

A collection of related classes placed in the same subdirectory. The most commonly used packages are in the API, which uses packages to help organize API classes into meaningful groups. Another use for packages is to set aside a group of classes as a separate subproject in a large software project. Packages create a layer of software insulation over and above classes. When you refer to a class inside another package, the class referred to must be declared **public**. Also, you must prefix the name of the class with the name of its package or else use the **import** keyword. (But note that the API class **java.lang** is an exception; access to that class is automatic.)

The intricacies of packages, directories, and searching for **.class** files may at first be counterintuitive to C and C++ programmers, because there is nothing exactly like them in these other languages. For more information, consult Chapter 2, "Java Building Blocks."

pixel

Picture element: a single dot on the display screen. A pixel is the smallest unit of distance on the screen as well as being the smallest unit in an off-screen buffer. Many graphics formats use pixels as units, although some formats use compression techniques to save space. Pixel data includes all information needed to display a single dot, including color and intensity.

platform

A combination of processor, computer architecture, and operating system. The platform is simply the underlying type of system on which you are running. For example, an Intel processor running Windows 95 is one platform; a Macintosh is another platform, and UNIX is yet another. Until Java, there was no widely available technique for writing a program that could run, without change, on multiple platforms.

pointer

A variable that stores an address in memory. Support for pointer operations makes C, C++, and assembly language very powerful, but it also makes them dangerous. A C programmer can use pointer operations to overwrite large sections of memory (often unintentionally). Certain highly specialized kinds of software will always require pointers; for example, you generally need C, C++, or assembly language to write a new operating system. Java, however, is a sophisticated application-writing language in which security issues are important. Despite its similarity to C++, therefore, Java eliminates pointers in favor of other techniques. See the topic "Pointers" in Part II.

polymorphism

The capability of responding to the same message in infinitely many ways (from the Greek for "many forms"). Polymorphism may sound esoteric, but it is what enables you to define custom responses to standard API methods, such as **paint()** and **mouseDown()**. Polymorphism enables you to subclass an existing class C, override methods, and have other software treat an instance of your subclass as though it were an instance of C. Other software need have no foreknowledge of your subclasses. So, for example, the AWT thinks that it is calling **Button.action()**, when actually it is calling your implementation of the **action()** method. In effect, polymorphism lets you plug your own code into an existing structure.

The mechanism that makes this possible is late binding, which means that the address of the actual implementation to be called is not determined until run time. The object's exact type is known at run time, so calls are correctly resolved. Consequently, the knowledge of how to respond to method calls is built into an individual object. Program control is decentralized. Polymorphism is realized through the use of virtual functions in C++ and through callback functions in C. By default, all methods are polymorphic in Java unless declared **final**.

POSITIVE_INFINITY

A special floating-point value that indicates an overflow involving a positive number. Unlike integer arithmetic, floating-point operations produce this result rather than throw an exception. The constants **Float.POSITIVE_INFINITY** and **Double.POSITIVE_INFINITY** represent this value for the **float** and **double** types, respectively. In any comparison, positive infinity is always greater any other value represented by the type, although it is equal to itself.

primitive data type

One of the data types predefined in the Java language, most of which are numeric: **boolean**, **char**, **byte**, **short**, **int**, **long**, **float**, and **double**. Java variables having a primitive data type work very much as they do in other programming languages. Unlike objects, primitive data is allocated directly in memory by simply declaring variables. The **new** keyword is not used unless you are creating arrays. For a table describing primitive data sizes and ranges, see the topic "Data Types" in Part II.

private access

An access level for fields: a method or variable declared **private** can be accessed only within the method definitions of its own class. This corresponds closely to the C++ use of **private**. The **private** keyword cannot be applied to class declarations. However, a class that is not public is accessible only within its own package, making it private as far as code outside the package is concerned. For more information, see "private Keyword" in Part II or Table J in Part V.

property

A string value stored in a simple table. To access a value, you use another string called a *key*. For example, in the Java system properties table, the key "file.separator" returns a string containing the file separator character. (This is "\" for Windows systems and "/" for UNIX systems.) Property tables are relatively simple structures that do not require JDBC. You can create property tables for your own purposes, and Java provides a system property table that contains information of general use. For more information, see the **Properties** and **System** classes in Part IV, and Table L, "Default system properties" in Part VII.

protected access

An access level for fields: a method or variable can be declared **protected**. This is the intermediate access level between public and private. A field declared **protected** cannot be accessed outside its package, except in subclasses; and a field declared **private protected** cannot be accessed outside its class at all, except in subclasses. For more information, see "protected Keyword" in Part II or Table M in Part VII.

protocol

An agreed-on procedure, or set of rules, for communication, especially across a network. Without a common protocol, two computers could send each other random streams of data, and the result would be chaos. A protocol enables computers to talk to each other in a meaningful way: a computer follows a protocol to initiate a conversation; inform the other if data is to be sent and how much; and indicate what, if any, response is expected.

public access

An access level for fields as well as a modifier for class declarations. A class declared **public** is accessible everywhere, even outside its package. But note that only one class can be declared **public** in each source file, and it must have the same name as the source file. A field declared **public** has the same visibility as its class; this means that **public** has no effect on fields unless the class is also **public**. For more information, see "public Keyword" in Part II or Table M in Part VI.

raising an exception

See "throwing an exception."

reference

A variable, argument, or return value that refers to an object. In Java, all object variables are references. Java references look exactly like ordinary variables (there is no reference operator, as in C++), but there are a couple of critical differences. First, a reference variable cannot be used until associated with an actual object. The object is usually created with the **new** operator and is then associated with a variable through assignment (=). Second, assigning one reference to another does not create a copy of the object but rather causes both references to refer to the same thing. For example, if A and B are references, A = B causes A to be associated with the same object that B is. But there is still only one copy of the data.

Consequently, a reference is like a handle or a pointer, although it looks like an ordinary variable. The most important point is that there are only a few ways to create new objects in memory. Passing a reference, whether through assignment, return value, or argument value, simply passes a handle to an existing object. If you need to create a new copy—for example, so that you can modify the new copy while retaining the original data—use **clone()**, if available, or use a copy constructor. If you've programmed extensively in C++, you've already seen references. But remember that in Java, all object variables and return types are automatically references, so there is no need for a reference operator (&). If you've programmed in C, you can think of references as pointers without the pointer syntax. For more information, see the topic "References" in Part II.

reserved word

A word that cannot be used for variable names. Most reserved words are keywords. A few are reserved for possible use by future versions of Java. See "keyword."

result set

A result from a database query structured in tabular format. Although some simple queries return integers, most of them involve result sets. The JDBC package, **java.sql**, provides the **ResultSet** interface for reading the contents of a result set and **ResultSetMetaData** for inspecting the structure of a given result set.

scope

The visibility of a variable or method within a program. Despite its apparent similarity to C and C++, Java has different scope rules. The rules for declaring and using local variables are roughly the same as in C++. Java has no global variables, so all variables, except local variables, are declared at the class level. Here, the visibility of a variable is determined by its access level and the visibility of its class. For the complete rules applying to access levels, see the topics "public Keyword," "private Keyword," and "protected Keyword" in Part II.

security features, Java

Features of Java intended to make for safe surf on the Internet. Java security is an issue with two sides: how to create applications that prevent invading code—viruses or Trojan horses—from being loaded and placing restrictions on applets so that they cannot invade other systems. Java places few restrictions, other than bounds checking, type checking, and elimination of pointer operations, on applications. Generally, you are writing applications for use on your own computer, so applications are assumed to be fairly safe. Applications can optionally use the Java API to download information from the network. The **java.lang.SecurityManager** class can be used by applications to filter out certain types of code during downloading. It is up to you to subclass **SecurityManager** to impose restrictions for downloading code.

Java-enabled browsers (for example, the appletviewer and Netscape Navigator 3.0 browser) are designed to restrict anyone from writing applets that could violate the integrity of any user's system. The restrictions imposed by these interpreters prevent applets from doing any of the following: reading, writing, or trashing files on the local computer; opening a new network connection (a socket); executing a program on the local machine; or using **native** methods. (**native** methods automatically evade all security checks.) The potential effects of these actions in the hands of an evil programmer could be catastrophic. For example, permitting an applet to execute local programs would give an applet writer the ability to execute an MS-DOS command such as **DEL *.*** or **FORMAT C:** on the local computer.

server

The provider of a service. In network operations, a server is a computer that waits to be contacted by another computer (called a *client*) and then responds to requests. To be useful, a server must keep running continually, or at least during a window of time known to the client. The term *server* also is used in other contexts, including database operations and object-oriented programming.

signature

A method declaration giving complete type information. For example:

```
int Class1.max(int, int)
```

A signature uniquely identifies a specific method as understood by the compiler; this does not include argument names, which are arbitrary and can differ each time a method is used. Because of method overloading (see "overloading"), the compiler differentiates methods not by name but by signature.

signed data

Integer data that can represent both positive and negative numbers. In Java, all numeric types are signed. See "two's complement" for details of how negative numbers are represented.

socket

A network connection in a Java program. You open a network connection by creating an object of the **Socket** class. When creating the object, you specify a string containing the host or an Internet address as well as a port number. The Java API throws an exception if it cannot successfully connect. Once the connection is made, you can then use the socket to get objects of the **InputStream** and **OutputStream** classes: these are the same classes used for stream-based file input and output. For more information, see "Socket Class" and "ServerSocket Class" in the API Quick Reference.

SQL

Structured Query Language: a widely recognized standard language for querying, sorting, and modifying a database. SQL is relatively independent of database architecture. For this reason, it is used by JDBC to interact with a potentially wide variety of databases. JDBC methods enable you to build and execute SQL statements and execute them.

stack

A last-in-first-out (LIFO) storage mechanism. Stacks are highly useful in computer programming. The essence of a stack is that you can push as many items as you want on top of the stack. Then, when you start popping items off the stack, they are removed in reverse order, beginning with the last item to be pushed onto the stack. At any time, you can push new items on top of the stack.

Stacks have two uses. First, almost all modern processors use an internal stack to keep track of subroutine calls, arguments, and values of local variables. This stack usage is automatic, and you generally have no direct access to it unless you are writing assembly language. A stack can also be used as a storage mechanism in your own programs. The API provides the **Stack** class for handling groups of objects for which you want LIFO access.

static initializer

An initializer for an entire class, consisting of code in braces ({}) followed by the **static** keyword. Static initializers are useful for initializing static variables and other operations that should be performed once for the entire class. For more information, see "static Keyword" in Part II.

string

A sequential group of characters, typically forming a word, phrase, or sentence in a natural language such as English. Technically, strings should be called *character strings* or *text strings*, although they are almost always called *strings* for short. Strings are used often in computer programming, because there is often a need to display readable text.

In Java, a string is represented as an object of type **String**. A *string literal* is a quoted string, and it automatically has type **String**. String data is not null-terminated, and you should not treat strings as arrays of type **char**, although you can convert any **String** object to an array of **char** by calling the **toCharArray( )** method of the **String** class. Doing so, in fact, might be useful if you needed to dissect a string character by character. However, the Java **String** class has a large number of useful methods, generally making character-by-character operations (the kind you would write in C) unnecessary. See "String Class" in the API Quick Reference for more information. For some examples of simple string-handling code, see the topic "Strings" in Part II.

Individual objects of type **String** cannot be modified. Nevertheless, string operations are easy to do with the **String** objects; for example, when you apply the concatenation operator (+) on two strings, Java creates a new **String** object so that neither of the operands is modified. However, for efficient, complex string operations, you should convert a string to an object of type **StringBuffer**. Such objects can be modified without causing additional objects to be created.

subclass

A class that inherits from another class. Subclasses are also called *child classes* or *derived classes*. A class may have any number of subclasses, though it may have only one direct superclass. See "Inheritance."

superclass

A class that provides the base declarations for another class. (See "inheritance.") Superclasses are also called *parent classes* or *base classes*. In Java, a class may only have one superclass, although a class may have many indirect superclasses. (For example, C inherits from B, which inherits from A. A is an indirect superclass of C.) If no superclass is specified, the superclass is automatically the **Object** class in the **java.lang** package of the API. For more information, see the topic "extends Keyword" in Part II.

synchronized methods and threads

A technique for avoiding simultaneous execution of certain sections of code, often called *critical sections*, by more than one thread. Before a thread executes such code, it may need a way to temporarily lock out other threads, because if two threads operate on the same resource simultaneously, they may interfere with each other to disastrous effect. (Consider two threads attempting to write over the same file record or sort the same array at the same time.) The solution is for one thread to wait until another finishes and relinquishes its lock. Java provides an easy way to implement locks through the use of the **synchronized** keyword. Although you don't manipulate locks directly, locks are used as appropriate for the given platform. The **synchronized** keyword provides a high level of abstraction that works effectively on many different systems. For more information, see "synchronized Keyword" in Part II.

system property

See "property." For a list of system properties, see Table L, "Default system properties" in Part VII.

thread

An independent sequence of execution, much like a separate process. (But note that some operating systems make a distinction between threads and processes.) Every program has at least one thread; when a program starts a second or third thread, it gains the ability to do more than one thing at a time. For example, a program might have one thread that responds to user input, another thread to animate a bouncing ball, and a third thread that prints a document in the background. Although in actuality a single processor can do only one thing at a time, almost all CPUs being made today have the ability to achieve the practical effect of simultaneous running of threads. Multithreaded code should easily be able to take advantage of parallel-processor platforms, with threads truly running concurrently, when they become available.

Java encapsulates the capabilities of threads on all platforms by providing the **Thread** class in the API. Starting a second, third, or other thread is as easy as declaring a **Thread** object and calling its **start()** method. When you create a thread, you specify an object that implements the **Runnable** interface. Implementing **Runnable** guarantees that the object's class has a **run()** method. When the thread is started, Java calls this method.

One way to use threads is to implement **Runnable** in the class that uses the thread. Another way is to use **Thread** subclasses for which you override **run()** with your own thread behavior. For examples, see Chapter 5, "Animation and Threads."

throwing an exception

The act of generating an exception, which has the effect of transferring control to the nearest exception handler of the appropriate type. As described in the Glossary entry "exception," an exception is an unusual occurrence that requires immediate handling. In many but not all cases, an exception indicates an error of some kind. Another typical case that generates an exception is an attempt to read past the end of a file. The API raises exceptions as appropriate. In addition, you can raise exceptions yourself by using the **throw** keyword. For more information, see the topic "Exception Handling" in Part II.

two's complement

A popular format for representing signed integers (numbers that can be negative). A negative number is represented by taking the corresponding positive number, inverting all the digits through bitwise negation, and adding 1. For example, to get –1 for the **byte** integer type, we take 00000001, invert it to get 11111110, and finally add 1: 11111111. One of the consequences of two's complement arithmetic is that any number with a 1 in its leftmost digit is negative. The great majority of microprocessors being made today include efficient built-in support for two's complement arithmetic. For this reason, Java uses two's complement as its binary standard for integer data. Keep in mind that two's complement arithmetic is performed under the covers and generally does not affect you unless you analyze bit patterns.

Unicode

A scheme for representing individual characters in terms of numeric values. Unicode is similar to the ASCII system, but a Unicode character occupies 16 bits (two bytes) rather than eight. All implementations of Java use Unicode characters, because Unicode's 16-bit character size enables it to represent character sets for natural languages other than English. However, the lowest 128 Unicode values are equal to their ASCII counterparts. Java is a language designed to produce applications that run without change in many environments. Unicode is therefore a logical choice for the character set, because it does not pose the same limitations that ASCII does. The importance of making software available for an international audience is a sign of our times—and of the international acceptance of computers.

unsigned data

An integer data type that does not represent any negative numbers. In a language such as C, unsigned types are occasionally useful, because, given a particular size, an unsigned integer can represent twice as many positive numbers as a signed integer can represent. Java does not support any unsigned data. In Java, the lack of unsigned types is made palatable by the fact that **int** and **long** have relatively large ranges, making unsigned types almost unnecessary.

URL

Uniform resource locator, which is a string of characters containing the address of an Internet location (although a URL can also refer to the local computer). URLs can be relative, but a complete URL contains at least three major parts in the form *protocol://server/file*. For example, in the URL **http://stay.com/now/please**, the protocol is **http:** (see "HTTP"), the server name is **stay.com**, and the file on that server is **/now/please**. (Note that a network server is also called a *host*.) The Java **URL** class supports the specification and use of URLs.

variable

A named location for holding data. Generally speaking, a variable is a value that may change during the course of the program; a variable has a name—such as i, n, count, amount, temperature, and so on—so that you can refer to it in the source code. In Java, variables come in three major varieties: local variables, declared inside methods or even smaller code blocks; instance variables, declared at the class level; and class variables, declared at the class level but also declared **static**. Unlike most languages, Java has no facility for declaring global variables. For more information, see "class variable," "instance variable," and "local variable."

Variables work in roughly the same way in Java as they do in other languages. There is one peculiarity, though, in addition to the lack of global variables: variables of a user-defined type (a class) do not actually contain data, because they are references. This means that they must be associated with an existing object before they can be used. Most often, the object itself is allocated by using **new**. Variables that have a primitive data type (such as **int**, **long**, or **float**) are not references and work just as they do in other languages.

variable, class

See "class variable."

variable, instance

See "instance variable."

variable, local

See "local variable."

Visual J++

Microsoft's integrated development environment for Java programs. Visual J++ provides an environment similar to Visual C++, which automates some of the tasks of designing and writing a program. The code generated by Visual J++ is Java code, and the standard rules apply.

WAV (.wav file)

A format for storing audio data, used on Windows systems. WAV files are sometimes embedded in Web pages and used in Java applications.

wrapper class

An API class that stores a simple numeric value. A primitive-data value such as an **int** is not part of the class hierarchy, does not inherit from **Object**, and therefore cannot be stored in a collection-class object such as **Vector** or **Stack**. However, an **int** can be converted to its wrapper class, **Integer**, and then stored in a **Vector** or **Stack** object. A wrapper class creates an object around a single bit of primitive data. Wrapper classes also provide useful methods for dealing with primitive data, such as **Integer.parseInt().** The API's wrapper classes are **Integer**, **Long**, **Float**, **Double**, **Character**, and **Boolean**.

zero-based indexing

An indexing scheme in which the first position is 0, the second position is 1, the third position is 2, and so on. For consistency with C and C++, the Java language and core API use zero-based indexing in every situation involving an index. Thus, for example, myArray[9] refers to the tenth (and not the ninth) element of myArray. The exception is JDBC (**java.sql**), which uses one-based indexing to indicate column positions.

APPENDIX A

Java Exceptions and Errors

Java exceptions and unrecoverable errors are implemented as classes, all of them derived from the **Throwable** class. These classes fall into three broad categories:

- Optional exceptions, derived from *RuntimeException*
- Mandatory exceptions.
- Unrecoverable errors.

Exception Classes Generally

Nearly all exception classes have two constructors: a default constructor and one that takes a **String** argument. Other methods are inherited from the **Throwable** class; these methods include methods for getting an exception message text and for printing a stack trace. See "Throwable Class" in Part V, "API Quick Reference." The general pattern for exception-class constructors is that of the **Exception** class itself:

Exception();

Exception(String msg);

Optional Exceptions (RuntimeException)

All the exceptions in this group are derived, directly or indirectly, from the **RuntimeException** class, which itself is a subclass of **Exception** (see Table A.1). Handling these exceptions is always optional.

Table A.1 Optional Exceptions (derived from RuntimeException)

Exception Class	Package (If Not java.lang)	Superclass (If Not RuntimeException)
ArithmeticException		
ArrayIndexOutOfBoundsException		IndexOutOfBounds-Exception
ArrayStoreException		
ClassCastException		
EmptyStackException	java.util	
IllegalArgumentException		
IllegalMonitorStateException		
IllegalThreadStateException		IllegalArgument-Exception
IndexOutOfBoundsException		
NegativeArraySizeException		
NoSuchElementException	java.util	
NullPointerException		
NumberFormatException		IllegalArgument-Exception
SecurityException		
StringIndexOutOfBoundsException		IndexOutOfBounds-Exception

Remember that catching a superclass exception (such as **IllegalArgumentException**) implicitly catches all its subclasses as well.

Mandatory Exceptions

The exceptions in this group are not derived from the **RuntimeException** class. Whenever you call a method that throws one of these exceptions, you must respond by catching the exception or by placing a **throws** clause in the caller's method declaration (see Table A.2).

Table A.2 Mandatory Exceptions

Exception Class	Package (If Not java.lang)	Superclass (If Not Exception)
AWTException	java.awt	
ClassNotFoundException		
CloneNotSupportedException		
DataTruncation	java.sql	SQLWarning
EOFException	java.io	IOException
FileNotFoundException	java.io	IOException
IllegalAccessException		
InstantiationException		
InterruptedException		
InterruptedIOException	java.io	IOException
IOException	java.io	
MalformedURLException	java.net	IOException
NoSuchMethodException		
NullData	java.sql	SQLWarning
ProtocolException	java.net	IOException
SocketException	java.net	IOException
SQLException	java.sql	
SQLWarning (*see next section for additional information*)	java.sql	SQLException
UnknownHostException	java.net	IOException
UnknownServiceException	java.net	IOException
UTFDataFormatException	java.io	IOException

Remember that catching a superclass exception (such as **IO-Exception**) implicitly catches all its subclasses as well.

THE SQLWARNING CLASS

The **SQLWarning** class adds a couple of methods to those normally supported for exception classes:

public SQLWarning **getNextWarning**();

gets next warning in the chain (the linked list of warnings).

public void **setNextWarning**(SQLWarning w);

sets a warning exception to the end of the chain (the linked list).

ERRORS

The **Error** class is another class that extends the **Throwable** class. Classes derived from **Error** represent unrecoverable errors such as running out of memory. These errors should not be caught. When they occur, the interpreter prints an error message and terminates. The only class derived from **Error** that is not fatal is **ThreadDeath**, which does not affect other threads and does not cause the program to terminate.

Appendix B

Common SQL Statements

SQL deserves an entire book to itself, and a growing number of books are available on the topic. But in case one isn't handy, I've summarized the common SQL statements in this appendix. Keep in mind that this is not an exhaustive reference. It's intended to help you through basic Java database programming:

- Creating a table (**CREATE TABLE**)
- Adding rows (**INSERT INTO**)
- Selecting rows (**SELECT**)
- Using a condition (**WHERE** clause)
- Advanced use of **SELECT**
- Deleting selected rows (**DELETE FROM**)
- Removing a table (**DROP TABLE**)

Throughout this appendix, you'll see that sometimes a SQL statement is placed on a single line and other times it's broken into two or more lines. SQL ignores line breaks, and you should, too. In this appendix and in Chapter 7, line breaks are simply a matter of convenience.

Creating a Table (CREATE TABLE)

The **CREATE TABLE** statement adds a new table to the database, throwing an exception if the table already exists.

CREATE TABLE *tablename* **(***column_descriptions***)**

In this syntax, *column_descriptions* is a comma-separated list of descriptions. Each description has the following format:

name data_type [**DEFAULT** *expression*]

Here, the brackets indicate an optional item. The *expression*, if specified, gives a default value for the column. The following examples show two table-creation statements, the second one using a default value:

```
CREATE TABLE List (name char(20), addr char(30), rank int)

CREATE TABLE Collection
     (collect_cardname char(20),
      collect_cardtype char(20),
      collect_number   int  DEFAULT 1)
```

Adding Rows (INSERT INTO)

The **INSERT INTO** statement adds rows to a table.

INSERT INTO *tablename* **(***column_names***)**
  VALUES (*expressions***)**

Here, *column_names* and *expressions* are comma-separated lists. For example:

```
INSERT INTO List (name, addr, rank)
     VALUES ('Bill C.', '1600 Pen. Ave.', 1)
```

Instead of a **VALUES** clause, you can insert a result set by specifying a query specification (generally a **SELECT** statement):

INSERT INTO *tablename* **(***column_names***)** *select_statement*

For example, the following statement selects all the columns found in another table named **List2** and adds them to the table named **List**:

```
INSERT INTO List (name, addr, rank)
     SELECT * FROM List2
```

Selecting Rows (SELECT)

The **SELECT** statement specifies a query, which is typically executed by being passed to the **executeQuery()** method. The simple version of **SELECT** is:

SELECT *selection_list* **FROM** *tablename*
  [**WHERE** *conditional_expression*]

Here, as elsewhere, the brackets indicate optional items. In this syntax, the *selection_list* is either a *column_list* (a list of column names, separated by commas if there are more than one) or an asterisk (*), which selects all columns. See also "Advanced Use of SELECT" later in this appendix.

The first statement in the following example selects all the columns in the **Employees** table. The second statement selects only the column values **emp_name** and **emp_salary**. Both examples select from every row in the table.

```
SELECT * FROM Employees
SELECT emp_name, emp_salary FROM Employees
```

The syntax for the **SELECT** statement can be much more complex. The next section explains the use of the **WHERE** clause, which is used in **SELECT** statements.

Selecting on a Condition (WHERE Clause)

Use of the **WHERE** clause enables you to get a subset of a table. The argument to the **WHERE** clause is a conditional expression, which can be any of the following:

expression comparison_op expression
expression **LIKE** *pattern*
column_name **IS NULL**
column_name **IS NOT NULL**

For example, the following is a valid conditional expression:

```
rank < 10
```

It can therefore be used as the argument to **WHERE**. The following statement selects all rows from the **List** table in which the value in the **rank** column is less than 10.

```
SELECT * from List WHERE rank < 10
```

The conditional operators are <, >, =, <>, >=, and <=. Note that the test-for-equality operator (=) is different from the Java test-for-equality operator (==). You can apply test-for-equality (=) to strings.

Combining Conditionals

You can use **AND**, **OR**, and **NOT** to combine conditional expressions. For example, the following statement selects any row (or rows) whose **emp_age** value is greater than its **emp_rank** value and whose **emp_job** value is engineer.

```
SELECT * FROM Employees
     WHERE emp_age > emp_rank AND emp_job = 'engineer'
```

The LIKE Conditional

The **LIKE** operator compares a string expression to a string pattern: the pattern can include percent (%), which matches zero or more characters, and the underscore (_), which matches any one character. For example, the following statement selects all rows whose name value starts with **D**:

```
SELECT * FROM List WHERE name LIKE 'D%'
```

Advanced Use of SELECT

The **SELECT** statement can get considerably more complex. Here's a more comprehensive syntax:

SELECT [**ANY** | **DISTINCT**] *selection_list* **FROM** *table_list*
[**WHERE** *conditional_expression*]
[**GROUP BY** *column_list*]
[**ORDER BY** *column_asc/desc_list*]

In this syntax, the brackets indicate optional items. The *table_list* consists of one or more table names, which are separated by columns if there are more than one. Sometimes it is useful to select for values that appear in more than one table.

For example, the following statement performs a join of two tables: it compares each row in **Orders** to each row in **Vendors**. When the vendor numbers match, it selects **ord_ordernum** from **Orders** and **ven_desc** from **Vendors** to create a row in the result set.

```
SELECT ord_ordernum, ven_desc FROM Orders, Vendors
    WHERE ord_vendornum = ven_vendornum
```

Figure **BB.1** illustrates how this join works. Notice how the vendor number links the two tables.

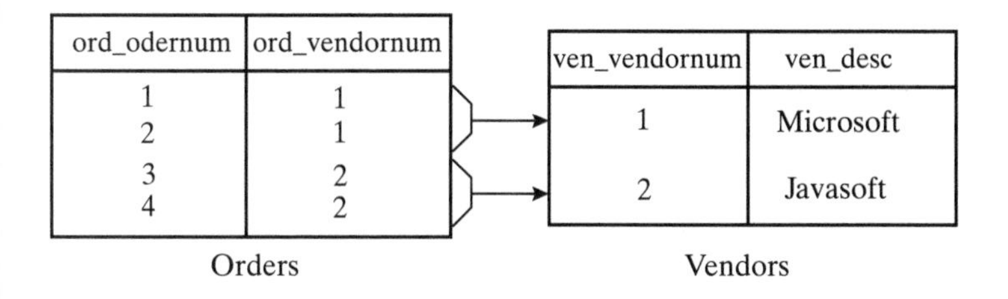

Figure BB.1 *Join on vendor numbers*

Figure BB.2 shows the contents of the result set.

ord_odernum	ven_desc
1	Microsoft
2	Microsoft
3	Javasoft
4	Javasoft

Figure BB.2 *Result set for Order/Vendor join*

In other parts of the syntax, the optional keywords **ALL** and **DISTINCT** control how duplicates are handled. For example, the following statement selects all the vendor numbers for which there are orders—but each vendor number will appear only once in the result set:

```
SELECT DISTINCT ord_vendornum FROM Orders
```

The ORDER BY Clause

The **ORDER BY** clause controls the order of rows in the result set. The syntax is **ORDER BY** followed by one or more column names, with a comma separating them if there is more than one.

ORDER BY *column_names*

Each column name can optionally be followed by the **ASC** or **DESC** keyword (but not both):

column_name [**ASC** | **DESC**]

Ascending order **(ASC)** is the default. For example, the following query lists results in ascending order of the vendor description value:

```
SELECT ord_ordernum, ven_desc FROM Orders, Vendors
    WHERE ord_vendornum = ven_vendornum
    ORDER BY ven_desc
```

The GROUP BY Clause

The **GROUP BY** clause causes only one record to be selected for each unique value of the of the grouping column(s). The syntax is **GROUP BY** followed by one or more column names, with a comma separating them if there is more than one.

GROUP BY *column_names*

For example, the following query performs a join similar to the previous, but the result set will have only one record for each vendor.

```
SELECT ven_desc, COUNT(ord_ordernum) FROM Orders, Vendors
    WHERE ord_vendornum = ven_vendornum
    GROUP BY ven_desc
```

The **COUNT( )** function is an aggregate function used with **GROUP BY**; here it returns the number of orders in a group. (Therefore, the query determines the number of orders per vendor.) Other aggregate functions are **AVG( )**, **SUM( )**, **MIN( )**, and **MAX( )**, each of which take a column-name argument. For example, **MAX(ord_ordernum)** returns the highest order number in a group. The other functions work in a similar manner.

DELETING SELECTED ROWS (DELETE FROM)

The **DELETE FROM** statement removes all rows of a table (if no **WHERE** clause is specified) or all rows that match the specified condition.

DELETE FROM *tablename* [**WHERE** *conditional_expression*]

For example, the following statement removes all rows from the **List** table in which the value of **rank** is greater than 50:

```
DELETE FROM List WHERE rank > 50
```

REMOVING A TABLE (DROP TABLE)

The **DROP TABLE** statement terminates a table with extreme prejudice. For obvious reasons, you should use this statement with caution.

DROP TABLE *table_name*

For example:

```
DROP TABLE silly
```

INDEX